Denis Bingham

A Selection from the Letters and Despatches of the First Napoleon

With explanatory notes. Vol. 3

Denis Bingham

A Selection from the Letters and Despatches of the First Napoleon
With explanatory notes. Vol. 3

ISBN/EAN: 9783337350505

Printed in Europe, USA, Canada, Australia, Japan

Cover: Foto ©ninafisch / pixelio.de

More available books at **www.hansebooks.com**

A SELECTION FROM

THE LETTERS AND DESPATCHES

OF THE

FIRST NAPOLEON.

VOL. III.

A SELECTION FROM

THE LETTERS AND DESPATCHES

OF THE

FIRST NAPOLEON.

With Explanatory Notes.

BY

CAPTAIN THE HON. D. A. BINGHAM,
AUTHOR OF "MARRIAGES OF THE BONAPARTES."

IN THREE VOLUMES.
VOL. III.

LONDON: CHAPMAN AND HALL,
LIMITED.

1884.

CONTENTS.

CHAPTER I.
PAGE
THE YEAR 1810 1

CHAPTER II.
THE YEAR 1811 77

CHAPTER III.
THE YEAR 1812 134

CHAPTER IV.
THE YEAR 1813 201

CHAPTER V.
THE YEAR 1814 290

CHAPTER VI.
THE YEAR 1815 357

INDEX 433

A SELECTION FROM

THE LETTERS AND DESPATCHES

OF THE

FIRST NAPOLEON.

THE CORRESPONDENCE OF NAPOLEON.

CHAPTER I.

THE YEAR 1810.

THE principal event of 1810 was undoubtedly the marriage of Napoleon with the Archduchess Marie Louise, and it is a curious fact that nearly all the documents connected with this brilliant matrimonial alliance have disappeared from the national archives. While reading the few letters bearing upon this remarkable event it will be well to bear in mind the following facts. Napoleon had long contemplated putting Josephine away: she had borne him no children, and he wished to found a dynasty. He would have been contented to leave the throne to the eldest son of Louis, but the "little Napoleon" died while the Emperor was campaigning in Poland. Shortly afterwards, at Erfurth, Napoleon sounded the Czar with regard to his sister the Grand Duchess Catherine. Alexander, while showing himself favourable to an alliance, said that his father Paul had left the Empress Mother absolute control in such matters, and that in all probability it would be difficult to vanquish her resistance. The Czar expressed himself highly flattered, and hoped that one day it might be possible to arrange this union. As for the Empress, she declared that she would sooner see her daughter at the bottom of the Neva than the wife of Napoleon; and for fear the French Emperor might again press his suit she lost no time in wedding the Grand Duchess to the Duke of Oldenburg.

It was not until after the battle of Wagram that the question of a matrimonial alliance with Russia was again mooted. On the 28th December, 1809, Caulaincourt broached the subject of a marriage between the Grand Duchess Anne, the sister of the Grand Duchess Catherine, and Napoleon. Alexander was much surprised at this demand: his mind was entirely filled at that moment with apprehensions concerning the re-establishment of Poland and the execution of the Treaty of Tilsit. The draft of a convention had just been drawn up between France and Russia upon the following bases:—1st. Reciprocal engagement never to permit the re-establishment of Poland; 2nd. The suppression of the words "Poland" and "Poles" in all public acts, &c. When the matrimonial demand was made Alexander perceived the price which he was expected to pay for the convention. The Czar was highly irritated, but still he disguised his wrath and promised to use his influence with his mother to obtain her consent, well knowing, after what had occurred, that that consent would never be given. On the 4th January, 1810, Alexander having expressed his ability to remove the opposition of his mother, Caulaincourt at once signed the convention, being convinced that this important concession would decide matters. On his side the Czar dragged on negotiations with the Empress in hopes that Napoleon would ratify the convention before receiving a definite reply. On the 10th January Caulaincourt received orders to demand a positive reply within ten days. The effect of this ultimatum may be easily imagined. It took couriers from fifteen to twenty days to accomplish the distance between St. Petersburg and Paris. It was on the 28th December only that the first demand had been made, and Napoleon had not had time to receive a despatch from Caulaincourt on the subject. Then why this ultimatum, which was equivalent to a rupture? The fact is that the perspective of another alliance more flattering in a dynastic point of view had presented itself, and that the Emperor had received assurances from several quarters that a demand addressed to Vienna would meet with a favourable reply. His vanity was intensely gratified, and he at once determined to break off negotiations with St. Petersburg.

On the 21st January, that is to say, a fortnight before the time had expired for receiving a reply from Russia, Napoleon assembled a privy council at the Tuileries to deliberate on the choice of an alliance. Five privy councillors voted in favour of an Austrian, two in favour of a Russian, and two in favour of a Saxon princess. Talleyrand was for an Archduchess, and Cambacérès for a Grand Duchess; because, as he said afterwards—"The Emperor is sure to make war against the Power to which he is not allied, and I dread a march to St. Petersburg more than a march to Vienna."

On the 6th February despatches from Caulaincourt arrived announcing that the Court of St. Petersburg had not come to a decision. The fact is that the Empress had declared that a Russian princess was not to be wooed and won in a week, and that her daughter, who was only sixteen, was too young to be married before three years. She had lost two daughters by marrying them at too early an age, and she would not sacrifice a third. Then, according to the Greek rite, the Grand Duchess could not marry a man who had divorced his first wife. The Czar did not absolutely reject the alliance, but he insisted that, in the event of a marriage, his sister should be allowed the free exercise of her religion. On the reception of this despatch Napoleon at once wrote to Caulaincourt saying that he considered himself disengaged. The very same day he had his marriage contract with Marie Louise drawn out on the model of that between Louis XVI. and Marie

Antoinette, and this contract was immediately signed by the Austrian ambassador, Prince Schwartzenberg, who a few months before had been sent to St. Petersburg to demand the hand of a Russian Grand Duchess for an Austrian Archduke. The rapidity with which this contract was concluded naturally proved that negotiations had been going on with Austria and with Russia at the same time, although Napoleon afterwards denied this. Prince Metternich says in his *Memoirs* that he was puzzled in which negotiations to put faith; in those openly carried on with Russia, or in those secretly carried on with Austria. With any one else but Napoleon he would not have hesitated about believing in the secret negotiation.

The diplomatists who were opposed to the Austrian marriage urged that no alliance with the Court of Austria could be sincere. That Austria had suffered too much at the hands of France for the wounds to be healed by a matrimonial arrangement; that she would never be able to forget and forgive the loss of Lombardy, Venice, the Tyrol, Suabia, Dalmatia, Illyria, Galicia, and Belgium, and the Imperial Crown of Germany, while Tuscany had been taken from one of the Archdukes and finally handed over to Napoleon's sister Eliza. However, the Court of Vienna accepted the proffered alliance without hesitation. The fact is that it had learned with terror that negotiations had been opened with St. Petersburg, whereas its policy, before and after Wagram, had been to sow dissension between the two Powers which threatened the existence of Austria. It was for this reason that she had offered Galicia to Napoleon, foreseeing the irritation which Russia would feel upon finding France at her frontier and a co-partner of Poland. She caught eagerly at the suggestion of a matrimonial alliance, which would save her from the perils with which she was menaced; and the overtures once commenced ran smoothly, especially as Austria nobly declared that this marriage was not to form the subject of any bargaining. The alliance was accepted unconditionally, but at the same time it was hoped that it would give Austria time to recover from her reverses, and that it would prevent a schism in the Church by healing the breach between the Emperor and the Pope. It was to further the latter object that Josephine exerted her influence in favour of the Austrian alliance.

On the day that Napoleon received Caulaincourt's despatch (6th February) he refused to ratify the convention with regard to Poland. As soon as the marriage with Marie Louise was arranged the Emperor set to work to procure the dissolution of the religious tie which either bound him, or was supposed to bind him, to Josephine. There had been no difficulty in having the civil marriage annulled. Mutual consent was sufficient for that. But before wedding the daughter of his most apostolical majesty of Austria it was necessary for his most Christian majesty the eldest son of the Church to procure a divorce.

Strange to say, it is still a matter of doubt whether Napoleon and Josephine were ever married at the altar. There is not a scrap of documentary evidence to prove it. The official account relates that on the eve of the coronation the Pope refused to officiate unless the Emperor made Josephine his wife, the Church not recognising the civil marriage. To avoid a scandal Napoleon consented, and the religious ceremony was secretly performed at the Tuileries by Cardinal Fesch, with the consent of the Pope, and in presence of Duroc, Berthier, and Talleyrand, on the night of the 1st December, 1804. M. Thiers, in his *History*, says that no one heard a word about this religious ceremony until the divorce was applied for. Is it possible that so important a matter could have been kept secret for more than five years? M. Thiers says that the Pope and Cardinal Consalvi were bound to secrecy by the seal of confession. But this was not the case with Cardinal Fesch, nor with the witnesses, nor with Madame de Rémusat, who says that Josephine told all about the wedding the day after it was performed; nor with Prince Eugene, to whom

Josephine said that she sent the marriage certificate lest Napoleon should take it from her and destroy it — a certificate which has never been brought into court.

Prince Metternich, in his *Memoirs*, says that Consalvi, shortly after he left the ministry, confided this tale to him:—"The Pope made up his mind not to appear at the coronation unless first satisfied of the validity of the marriage between Napoleon and Josephine. Upon this, two or three bishops whom Cardinal Consalvi named to me, paid the Holy Father a visit, removed his doubts, and gave him full details of the sacramental tie which united the Emperor and the Empress. The Holy Father deceived, crowned them the next morning, and it was not until several days after the coronation that he learned he had been imposed upon." The Pope was tempted at first to make a scandal, but for various reasons he changed his mind. "This circumstance," continues Prince Metternich, "was known to only three cardinals, who were horror-struck at the perfidy of the bishops, but they also taxed the Pope with too much credulity on this occasion."

In considering the above statement it is right to remember that Prince Metternich was interested in showing that no sacred tie united Napoleon and Josephine. The court of Vienna always declared that the existence of such a tie would stand in the way of an alliance with Austria.

The only way out of this dilemma was to prove that the secret marriage had not been performed in accordance with canon law, and that the Church could therefore declare that it had never taken place, that it was null and void. It had always been the custom for popes to decide upon such matters when they affected crowned heads; but how could Napoleon appeal to Pius VII., whom he held a close prisoner at Savona, and who had so obstinately refused a divorce in the case of Prince Jerome? Cambacérès helped his Majesty out of this difficulty by telling him that the intervention of the Pope would be necessary to dissolve a regular marriage, but that it was not required in the case of a marriage in which no rules had been observed, and that the matter concerned only the officiality of Paris, an ecclesiastical tribunal of three degrees — the diocesan, the metropolitan, and the primatial officialities.

It was to this court that the case was referred. It was argued on the part of the Emperor that the secret marriage was null for three reasons—1st, because the parish priest was not present, as required by canon law; 2nd, owing to the absence of proper witnesses; 3rd, owing to want of consent! As regards the first plea, the permission which Cardinal Fesch obtained from the Pope to celebrate the marriage did away with the necessity of the presence of the parish priest. As regards plea two, the Council of Trent lays down that there should be two witnesses, and there were three. With respect to the last plea, no wonder that a member of the court found it absurd, as he said, "on the part of a man before whom we all trembled, this plea never being invoked except in the case of a minor, the victim of surprise or of violence."

The diocesan officiality declared the marriage null because it had been contracted in the absence of the parish priest and of proper witnesses. Their majesties were therefore declared free to form other alliances, were forbidden to hold any further communion with each other, and were condemned to pay a certain sum to the poor of Paris for having sinned against the Church by indulging in a false marriage.

From the diocesan the case was taken up to the metropolitan officiality, which also pronounced the marriage null, but based its decision on the non-consent of the Emperor, who pleaded that he had been forced into it. The upper court, too, struck out the fine, which it considered degrading.

The position of Cardinal Fesch was curious enough in this affair; the secret marriage which he declared to have been regular was condemned as irregular, but this did not prevent him from consenting to officiate at the marriage of Marie Louise. Now Abbé Lyonnet, in his life of the Cardinal, says that at this very period he was asked to obtain a divorce for a lady. The Cardinal replied:—"The Catholic religion forbids divorce, and the ecclesiastical authorities have no right to dissolve a tie the nature of which is divine."

Thus wrote the prelate who declared that the secret marriage with Josephine was valid, and who nevertheless consented to join together Napoleon and Marie Louise in holy wedlock. It was also curious to find the Pontiff in 1804 declaring that he would not crown a woman who was living, in the eye of the Church, in a state of concubinage; and the court of Vienna, so punctilious in matters of religion, declaring that had Josephine been anything else but a concubine it would have rejected the proffered alliance. The Pope asked for proof that a state of sin had ceased to exist, and Austria demanded proofs to the contrary. The court of Vienna objected to a prince who had been previously married, and yet gave the hand of the Archduchess Marie Louise to a prince who was labouring under a sentence of excommunication, and had constituted himself the jailer of the vicar of Christ upon earth.

A good many letters touching upon the strained relations between Church and State in 1810 are published in *The Correspondence*, but a good many also have been omitted, as we shall see. The irritation displayed by Napoleon at this period was intensified by the opposition of some of the prelates to his wishes. Twenty-seven cardinals had been summoned from Rome to form an ecclesiastical committee intended to act as a council and to supersede the Pope, who obstinately refused to consecrate the bishops appointed by Napoleon or to acquiesce in the loss of his temporal power. Out of these twenty-seven cardinals thirteen, headed by Consalvi, the papal legate, refused to attend the second marriage, in spite of the threats of Fouché, considering that none but the Pope could annul the first marriage.

Marie Louise was first married by proxy at Vienna, then the civil marriage was performed at St. Cloud, and finally the religious marriage at the Tuileries. It was from this last ceremony that Consalvi and his brother cardinals absented themselves, to the great wrath of Napoleon, who felt that a slur was thus cast on the legitimacy of his second marriage. The cardinals paid dearly for their boldness. Consalvi says that the Emperor gave orders for Cardinals di Pietro, Oppizoni, and himself to be shot, but that they were saved by the intervention of Fouché. They were all, however, stripped of their external attributes, were deprived of the scarlet, and were afterwards known as the "black cardinals"; they were deprived even of the means of existence, had to subsist on charity, and were exiled to various towns in France, and remained under the supervision of the police until the concordat of Fontainebleau was signed. It was certainly trying to Napoleon's temper to find, after having wittingly indulged in two false marriages, the validity of one in which he was deeply concerned indirectly denounced by thirteen cardinals.

During the year 1810 the Pope remained inflexible; he refused to listen to the offers made by Comte Salmatoris on the part of Napoleon, to the entreaties of Cardinals Fesch, Maury, Caprera, Spina, and Caselli, or to the political reasons advanced by the Austrian diplomatist Lebzeltern. He had been accustomed to the austerities of a monastic life, and he could support the severity of his captivity at Savona.

In 1809 Napoleon wished to exchange the Hanse towns with Louis for Brabant. In 1810 his Majesty, having driven Louis from his throne by his vexatious policy, in regard to the continental blockade, annexed both the Hanse towns and Holland, not to speak of Valais, the Duchy of Oldenburg, a portion of Hanover, and the whole coast from the Ems to the Elbe. With Russia Napoleon was already on bad terms, and he appeared determined to goad Sweden to desperation.

In 1810 King Charles XIII., finding himself without a successor, consulted Napoleon on the advisability of choosing the brother of the Duke of Augustenburg as his heir. The Emperor gave it to be understood that he would prefer another candidate, and secretly urged the King of Denmark to come forward. The king took the advice of Napoleon, and wrote to Charles XIII. on the subject. Now the King of Denmark was so unpopular in Sweden that the very announcement of his candidature caused a popular rising. The Emperor left his ambassador without instructions, and Charles XIII., embarrassed at having to choose between a candidate hateful to the nation and one disagreeable to Napoleon, adopted a third course, and offered the succession to Bernadotte, who had made himself exceedingly popular with all classes when in command of a French force in Pomerania. This choice was highly approved of by the chambers and by the people. Bernadotte was elected Prince Royal of Sweden under the idea that a marshal allied to the imperial family would be grateful to the Emperor, and that all the difficulties with France would be removed. When Napoleon heard of this election he overwhelmed the Swedish ambassador with invectives, accused Sweden of not observing the continental blockade, and told poor Lagerbielke to choose between the cannon-balls of the English and war with France.

Prince Metternich says that the dilatoriness of Napoleon in this affair arose from the fact of his desire to place a member of his own family on the throne, and that when Josephine heard that Bernadotte had been elected she exclaimed—" The wretch! to desert his God for a throne; none of mine would do that." And in fact Napoleon appears to have offered the Swedish succession to Prince Eugene, whose eldest daughter, by the way, afterwards became Queen of Sweden, having married in 1823 Bernadotte's eldest son, who reigned as Oscar I. Two matters somewhat consoled Napoleon for this little accident. He argued that if Sweden elected a French marshal it was with the idea of recovering Finland, and that she would therefore aid him in a war with Russia. Again he considered that placing a French marshal on the throne of Gustavus Adolphus was playing England a nice trick. He did not foresee the triple alliance between Russia, England, and Sweden, when France shortly afterwards declared war against Alexander.

Another important event which occurred in 1810 was the sudden fall of the ex-oratorian and ex-Jacobin minister of police, Fouché, who was driven from office for indulging in a little private diplomacy. No greater compliment could have been paid to Fouché than the universal terror which reigned in Paris when it was known that he had been succeeded by Savary.

In Spain we shall find Massena, after losing Busaco, afterwards obliged to beat a retreat from before the lines of Torres Vedras. There were to be no more laurels for the Duke of Rivoli, Prince of Essling, the "darling child of victory."

On the 3rd January Napoleon addressed a letter to General Clarke in which he said: "Since the English have had the kindness to leave the fortifications of Flushing intact no time must be lost in repairing them. . . . This will save us several millions."

To M. FOUCHÉ, Duc d'Otrante.

"Paris, 5*th January*, 1810.

"A man called Bruguières has written a bad work entitled *Napoléon en Prusse*, which people believe to be acknowledged by the Government. All the sovereigns have sent him presents. Have this work criticised as it deserves, for I have only thrown my eye over it.

"Napoleon."

To M. DE CHAMPAGNY, Duc DE CADORE.

"PARIS, 6*th January*, 1810.

"My affairs are not progressing. That of Holland has not advanced a step; present a note to the Minister of Foreign Affairs in conformity with my letter to the King. Tell him that I cannot allow that nation to be the auxiliary of England; attack the evil advisers of the king, and insist upon the necessity of my employing all the power which God has given me to damage England and to ruin her commerce. . . .

"NAPOLEON."

On the 8th January his Majesty wrote a letter to his Minister for Foreign Affairs in reply to a communication from his brother Jerome. He said: "I cannot give the sovereignty of Hanover to the King of Westphalia because I do not possess that sovereignty, but I can cede him Hanover and all my rights to that province; that is all I can do."

From this extraordinary letter one gathers that the revenue of the domains in Hanover produced a revenue of 5,200,000 francs, and that Napoleon had disposed of domains to the value of 4,559,000 francs. King Jerome was at liberty to keep what remained.

To COMTE BIGOT, *Minister of Worship.*

"PARIS, 10*th January*, 1810.

"Order General Miollis to pack up the archives of the Holy See and to send them to France in charge of a good escort.

"NAPOLEON."

The next day his Majesty submitted the following questions to a committee of bishops:—

FIRST SERIES.

" 1st. Is the government of the Church arbitrary ?

" 2nd. Can the Pope, owing to temporal affairs, refuse to interfere in spiritual affairs ? "

The bishops were then asked if it would not be suitable to convoke a council composed of prelates of all nations.

SECOND SERIES.

" 1st. Has the Emperor or have his ministers infringed the Concordat ?

" 2nd. Has the condition of the clergy been improved since the Concordat came into operation ?

" 3rd. If the French Government has not violated the Concordat can the Pope refuse to install archbishops and bishops ? . . . "

THIRD SERIES.

" 1st. His Majesty, who has a right to consider himself the most powerful Christian in the lofty rank to which Providence has elevated him, would be troubled in conscience were he to pay no attention to the complaints of the German churches forsaken by the Pope for the last ten years. . . ."

As the heir of Charlemagne, as the real Emperor of the the west, as the eldest son of the Church, Napoleon wished to know what he should do if the Pope remained obstinate.

" 3rd. The bull of excommunication of the 10th June, 1809, being contrary to Christian charity as well as to the independence and the honour of the throne, what must be done to prevent popes in time of trouble and calamity from resorting to such excesses ? "

The replies of the committee, presided over by Cardinal Fesch, were for the most part ambiguous, but the bull of excommunication was pronounced to be an excess of power not likely to be indulged in again.

Having obtained a report on the replies of the bishops, Napoleon wrote to Champagny to make out that—" The Pope declared war against me ; *that he refused to close his ports to the English,* and to enter into the league for the defence of Italy ; that he recalled Cardinal Caprera from Paris, and broke off relations ; that the result of this conduct was war ; the result of war the conquest of his states ; and the result of this conquest is that I am at liberty to change the government. . . ."

To KING JOSEPH, AT MADRID.

"PARIS, 14*th January*, 1810.

"I thank you for your compliments on the occasion of the new year. The Duc de Dalmatie should have the title of chief of the staff of the army of Spain. This I think was the title of Marshal Jourdan when I was in Spain.

"NAPOLEON."

Jourdan, who was a great favourite of King Joseph, had been replaced by Soult, who was not destined to manage affairs much better than his predecessor.

To COMTE BIGOT.

"PARIS, 14*th January*, 1810.

" Write to Rome for the fisherman's ring,[1] the seals of the pontiff, the ornaments of the tiara, and everything

---

[1] PRINCE BORGHESE TO NAPOLEON.

"PARIS, 14*th March*, 1811.

" At the time of the seizure of the papers of the Pope and those of his household a packet of golden pieces was found in the portfolio of the prelate Doria, which was returned to him without its being remarked that the seal of the Pope, called the 'Fisherman's ring,' was among the pieces. Having been informed of this I gave orders

used by the Pope in ceremonies. Every time a person announces himself as holding powers from the Pope to manage his spiritual affairs, he must be sent to Paris.

"NAPOLEON."

To the EMPRESS, at the MALMAISON.

"TRIANON, 17*th January*, 1810.

"MY FRIEND,—D'Audenarde, whom I sent to you this morning, tells me that you have no courage since you went to the Malmaison. That place, however, must bring back feelings which cannot and never ought to change, at least on my side. I long to see you, but I must know that you are strong and not weak: I am a little so, and this afflicts me terribly.

"Adieu, Josephine! good night. Should you doubt me you will be very ungrateful. "NAPOLEON."

In a postscript to a letter written to Champagny on the 19th the Emperor said:—

"Inform the King of Holland that he cannot leave; that that would interfere with the course of affairs; that people would suppose the crisis past; that if he leaves I shall annex the country. . . ."

To HORTENSE, Queen of Holland.

"PARIS, 22*nd January*, 1810.

"MY DAUGHTER,—I have directed St. Leu to be handed over to you. Order your man of business to take possession of it in your name, and to repair it. . . . You require a country seat, and you cannot have a more agreeable one.

"NAPOLEON."

for the seal to be procured, without, however, any violence being employed if it were in the hands of the Pope. A long time having elapsed without finding it, the captain of Gendarmery Lagorse, a few days ago, decided upon asking the Pope for the ring, who handed it to him in a very bad temper, after having broken it. It is therefore in this condition that I have the honour to send it to your Majesty."

To M. DE CHAMPAGNY.

"PARIS, 27*th January*, 1810.

"Write to M. Laforest at Madrid, telling him to present notes on the impossibility of meeting the enormous expenses of Spain ; that I have already sent 300,000,000 francs there ; that the despatch of such considerable sums of money exhausts France. . . . M. Laforest must add that the war with Austria cost me a great deal of money. . . . There is a great deal of money in the provinces. If the soldiers are not paid they will plunder, and then I shall not know what to do.[1]

"NAPOLEON."

And the same day the War Minister was ordered to write to Marmont, who was operating in Illyria, not to expect any supplies from France, and that the country must nourish his army.

On the 29th January was commenced a correspondence with the Court of St. Petersburg on the subject of Poland, the Czar wishing to extort from the French Emperor a declaration that "Poland shall never be re-established," whereas Napoleon was not inclined to go further than to promise not to favour any attempt to re-establish Poland. A long and angry controversy ensued, which ended in Napoleon saying — "What does Russia mean by such language ? Does she wish for war ? Why these continual complaints ? Why this insulting suspicion ? If I had wished to re-establish Poland I should not have withdrawn my troops from Germany. . . ."

Napoleon, who was fond of declaring that this and that house had ceased to reign, refused, as he said, to render

---

[1] In consequence of this state of affairs Spain was divided into separate military governments formed in each province, in Biscay, Navarre, Aragon, Catalonia, Old Castille, and Leon, whose duty it was to collect customs and to see that the army was provided for. This system soon exhausted the country and destroyed trade. As for King Joseph, he found himself reduced to the greatest straits.

himself ridiculous by employing the language of the Divinity, and to sully his memory by affixing his seal to an act of Machiavelic policy; for to declare that Poland should never be re-established would be doing more than to acknowledge the partition of that country. He added— "If ever I were to sign that *the kingdom of Poland shall never be re-established*, it would be because I had the intention of re-establishing it. It would be a trap set for Russia, and the infamy of such a declaration would be effaced by the fact which denied it." After this explosion of virtuous indignation the subject in question was dropped by mutual consent for a season.

Napoleon, on the 31st January, wrote to the Minister of the Interior to know if it were true, as Senator Monbadon declared, that no more wine was exported from Bordeaux, as the English would not receive it! The Minister was also informed that on the same day that a statue was to be set up to Desaix, the foundation stones of four new slaughter-houses were to be laid.

Napoleon then addressed a series of military instructions to King Joseph, which he concluded by stating that "there is nothing dangerous in Spain but the English; the rest cannot keep the field."

The Emperor, once more intent upon speedily settling affairs with Rome, addressed a long letter to the captive Pope, in which he said :—

"MOST HOLY FATHER,—I send you the Bishops of —— to inform you of my desire to see concord re-established between your Holiness and myself. I do not wish your Holiness to entertain any doubt with regard to my principles or my intentions. Your Holiness forgot the principles of justice and charity when you fulminated your bull of excommunication; it was to bless and strengthen thrones that Jesus Christ laid down His life. But this excommunication must have been obtained from your Holiness by surprise and by wicked men. I appeal to the Church and to your Holiness, who is now better informed. I despise this excommunication, and only consider it as the work of evil-doers and the enemies of religion. It is based, too, upon false assertions. Not only have I not neglected to execute the Concordat, but, far from that, I have ameliorated more and more the situation of the Catholic religion, and every day I bless the God of our fathers for having selected me to restore His worship and His altars, and to cause Him to be honoured in France, Italy, Germany and Poland. Your Holiness also bases your excommunication on temporal reasons; and here I must acquaint you with all I think on this subject. In re-establishing worship in France I desired to restore to my people true religion and the salutary influence of its spiritual chief, and not to re-establish the intolerable pretensions of Gregory VII. I intended to give my people a chief pastor, and not to subject them to a foreign sovereign. My throne is from God, and I am accountable only to Him. I recognise the spiritual power of your Holiness, but I will not, and cannot, recognise any temporal influence. The triple tiara is a monstrous production of pride and ambition, entirely contrary to the humility of the Vicar of Christ. The irascible passions of the persons who surround your Holiness would have done great harm if God had not granted me calmness and the true knowledge of the sublime principles of our religion. Neither France nor Italy will ever recognise the influence of a foreign sovereign, but they will always recognise the salutary authority of the Vicar of Jesus Christ, the chief pastor, having charge of souls, like St. Peter and the first Pontiffs. I execrate the principles of Julius, of Boniface, and Gregory, which caused half the Christian world to separate itself from the Catholic religion, and they are now rendering account to God for all the souls which were damned in consequence of their mad ambition. It is for your Holiness to choose; France and I have chosen. We desire the religion of St. Peter, of St. Paul, and of St. Bernard, founded on the principles of the Gallican Church. We recognise the principles and utility of the unity and influence of the Chair of St. Peter, the rock upon which Jesus Christ permitted His Church to be built, but we are determined not to submit to a sovereign who governs territory, men, and temporal matters. If your Holiness desires to preserve this temporal influence and to meddle with the affairs of the world; if you consider yourself the king of kings, we shall oppose you with the Scriptures, and shall look upon you as the enemy of religion; we shall appeal to a general council. If, on the contrary, your Holiness desires only the inheritance of Jesus Christ and of St. Peter; if you are satisfied with the care of souls; if you are animated with the true spirit of the Gospel; if you preach union and the principles of morality and charity, we are ready to be reconciled to you. If, like Jesus Christ, your Holiness considers that your kingdom is not of this world; if you have no other thoughts but those concerning another life, we shall recognise your spiritual authority, and support it with all the force of our sceptre, for we shall look upon it as the firmest support of our throne and of the prosperity of our people.

"We do not address your Holiness in dubious or insidious language. Religion is clear; Jesus Christ and His apostles preached it on the house-tops so that it might be known to all. Do you desire to be Pope, the Vicar of Jesus Christ, the successor of St. Peter? We shall receive you in triumph, and fold you in our arms. But if you are dominated by the pride and ostentation of the world, think you our throne ought to serve you as a footstool, and that we shall place our crown under the dust of your feet? We shall consider you only as the work of the demon; as spoiled by pride and worldly interest, and as the enemy of religion, of our throne, and of our people. Your influence is powerful and your empire is great, when you remain within the limits traced by Jesus Christ; but your power becomes ridiculous and despicable when you wish to march with the potentates of the earth, surrounded by pride, menaces, and force. You are nothing when your empire is of this world; you are everything when your empire is not of this world. But now Rome irrevocably forms part of my Empire. You have enough to do when confining yourself to spiritual affairs and the care of souls. My mission is to govern the west; do not meddle with me; and if your Holiness had been occupied with nothing else but the salvation of souls, the Church of Germany would not be in its present state of disorganisation. For a long time the Roman Pontiffs have meddled with matters which do not concern them, neglecting the true interests of the Church. I recognise you for my spiritual chief, but I am your Emperor."

"The principal aim of the negotiation is to decide the Pope to consent to reside in France. I alone have the power and the wealth necessary to meet the wants of the Church. It is my intention, in case he can be persuaded to come to France, to establish him at Rheims."

We now come to the matrimonial alliance. The first letter upon this subject, published in the *Correspondence*, runs thus:—

To M. DE CHAMPAGNY.

"PARIS, *6th February*, 1810.

"Send a courier this evening to Caulaincourt, to inform him that a council was held a few days ago, and that opinion was divided between a Russian and an Austrian princess; that opinion is divided also in France, especially owing to religion, and that people who attach the least importance to religion cannot accustom themselves to the idea of not seeing the Empress observe the ceremonies of the Church alongside of the Emperor; that the presence of a Pope [1] presents a greater inconvenience still. You must add that these lines were written when the courier of

[1] Of the Greek church.

the 21st arrived, and that you interrupted your letter in order to decipher the despatches he brought; that the Emperor remarks that the Princess Anne is not yet formed, and that sometimes girls remain for two years between the first signs of nubility and maturity; that to remain three years without the hope of children would not answer the intentions of his Majesty; that, on the other hand, the delay of ten days expired on the 16th, and that there was no reply on the 21st; that the Emperor cannot conceive how, when the Empress mother has given her consent, when the opinion of the Princess Anne is favourable, no positive answer is returned; that these delays contrast with the devotion and readiness of Austria; that his Majesty intends holding a council to-morrow to settle this uncertainty, having no time to lose; that at Erfurth there was a question of the Princess Catherine, but that his Majesty considers himself sufficiently free, not from any engagement, for there never was one, but from any tacit obligation imposed by honesty, and his friendship for the Emperor Alexander, owing to the delay of a month which he has taken to reply to a simple question.

"NAPOLEON."

In a second letter of the same date, Napoleon wrote thus to his Minister of Foreign Affairs:—

"Send off the courier to Russia before you go to bed. Do not mention the 'sitting' for this evening. To-morrow evening, after having signed with Schwartzenberg, you can despatch another courier, stating that I have decided in favour of the Austrian. Being me the marriage contract of Louis XVI. . . .

"NAPOLEON."

In a third letter of the same date to Champagny, his Majesty said:—" The engagements of kings are sacred, and the Prussian debt is the same as if it had been paid into the French treasury. Since the opening of the war with Austria nothing has been paid, and it is evident that by setting aside half her revenue Prussia might have paid 60,000,000 francs. The 22,000,000 francs in letters of change were protested as soon as Prussia knew that France was engaged in a war with Austria...." And the French Minister at Berlin was to declare that if Prussia did not pay 160,000*l.* a month, the Emperor would march 60,000 men against Magdeburg. Prussia, however, might indemnify France by handing over to her Glogau and a portion of Silesia.

The next day came another letter to Champagny, on the subject of the marriage, in which the Emperor said:—

"The Prince of Neuchâtel (Berthier) having been appointed extraordinary ambassador, in order to demand the princess in marriage, will arrive at Vienna on the 29th, and will make his demand the next day. M. Otto will have arranged all the ceremonial. This marriage can take place on the 2nd March. The princess can finish the carnival at Vienna, and start on Ash Wednesday. Matters can be arranged so that she may arrive in Paris about the 26th. The handing over of the princess will take place at Braunau, where she will find her household.... M. Otto must let it be well understood that the princess must bring no one with her; if, however, she has a lady's maid to whom she is attached, she can bring her to remain with her for a month. You must inform M. Otto that the dowry fixed for the Empress appears to me ridiculous; but in that it was wished to follow what was done at the marriage of Louis XVI. The dowry of French empresses is fixed at 160,000*l.*...."

To COMTE DE RÉMUSAT.

"PARIS, 8*th February*, 1810.

"You furnish me with no report respecting the administration of the theatres, and you have new pieces rehearsed without informing me. I learn that the *Mort d'Abel* and a ballet are being rehearsed. You should not have any new piece rehearsed without my consent. Let me have a report on this.

"NAPOLEON."

On the same day Berthier was ordered to write to the King of Spain to say that his Majesty could no longer meet the enormous expenses of his army of Spain, and that henceforth he could send only 80,000*l.* a month for the pay of the troops round Madrid. All the resources of *the conquered country* were to be applied to the army.

To M. DE CHAMPAGNY.

" PARIS, 12th February, 1810.

"I beg that you will send for the Dutch Minister. You will tell him that the Minister of Police has had several interviews with the King of Holland, who desires to conciliate the independence of his country with my views, and he consequently proposes—1st. To cede to France the left bank of the Rhine. 2nd. To put a stop to all communication with England. . . .

"NAPOLEON."

Writing to General Clarke, on the 18th February, Napoleon said:—"I am of opinion that two or three castles, like Ham, which serve as state prisons, should be handed over to the police. . . . In having Sedan demolished I directed that the citadel should be preserved, but I do not wish to spend any money on it." These two places, Ham and Sedan, were destined, the first to be the prison of Napoleon's successor, the second to witness his downfall.

The first almoner, an archbishop of the great de Rohan family, having written a most fulsome letter congratulating his Majesty on his approaching marriage—

DECISION.

"PARIS, 15*th February*, 1810.

"The Duc de Frioul (Duroc) will pay 12,000 francs to the first almoner *out of the theatrical fund.*

"NAPOLEON."

Ferdinand Comte de Rohan certainly gave the Emperor something for his money. After saying that he could now repeat, with joyful heart, the words of Simeon, *Nunc dimittis.* . . . he added—"Yes, sire, my existence is dear to me only in order that I may sacrifice it to the great Napoleon; he is my tutelary deity, and it would cause me the most lively grief should your Majesty doubt it; but no, my probity is well known, and at my age one does not change. As long as I breathe the breath of life, it shall be devoted to you. Besides, favours are bonds, motives of indissoluble attachment, and I await them with respect. The greatest of Emperors will not forget one of his oldest servants—the only one of his name who from the first moment adhered to him."

On the 17th February his Majesty addressed some remarks to the Senate on the Senatus-Consultum by which the Papal States were united to France, and which he said was one of the greatest political events of the period. He added—

"It unites the Papal States to France.

"It draws a deep line between political interests and those of religion.

"It insures the temporal, honourable, and independent existence of the head of the Church."

Napoleon then gave a long list of the crimes of the Papal Court which had welcomed hostile fleets:—"An English minister, the disgrace of his country, found an asylum at Rome; there he hatched plots, hired brigands, concocted perfidies, paid assassins, and Rome protected the traitor and his agents; and Rome allowed its cabinet to be poisoned with his corrupting breath ; and Rome became the theatre of defamation, the workshop of libels, the asylum of brigands. . . . The time of justice arrived. The imperial eagles took possession once more of their ancient territory ; the domain of Charlemagne returned to his most worthy heir. Rome belongs to the Emperor, who will reign over the Tiber as over the Seine."

Among other things, it was decided that the heir to be born to the French crown should be called the King of Rome ; that future French emperors, after being crowned at Notre Dame, should be crowned at St. Peter's ; that the Popes on their election should swear never to do anything against the four propositions of the Gallican Church ; that the Pope was to have palaces in different parts of the empire, and a revenue of 80,000*l*., &c.

The English minister above referred to was no doubt Acton, who was in the service of the Court of Naples.

To JULIE NAPOLEON, QUEEN OF SPAIN.

"RAMBOUILLET, 22*nd February*, 1810.

"Affairs in Spain are quieting down. I therefore think that it will be suitable for you to start for Madrid with your children, in order to rejoin the King.

"NAPOLEON."

King Joseph's wife received several orders to this effect, but they were always countermanded, and her Majesty never saw Madrid.

To MADAME MÈRE.

"PARIS, 23*rd February*, 1810.

"I hasten to inform you that the marriage contract between myself and the Archduchess Marie Louise, daughter of the Emperor of Austria, was ratified on the 16th at Vienna. "NAPOLEON."

Similar letters were addressed to all the members of the imperial family.

To the EMPEROR OF AUSTRIA.

"RAMBOUILLET, 23rd *February*, 1810.

"SIR, MY BROTHER,—My cousin the vice-constable, Prince of Neuchâtel, will leave to-morrow in order to demand from your Majesty the Archduchess Marie, your daughter, in marriage. The high qualities which so eminently distinguish that princess, and the precious advantage she enjoys of belonging to you, make me greatly desire this union. I am allowed to hope that your Majesty will give your consent. I therefore do not delay a moment, and send Comte Lauriston, my aide-de-camp, who is known to your Majesty, to bear you this letter. I have charged him to inform you of the price I attach to this alliance; I expect from it, for myself and for my people, great happiness.

"NAPOLEON."

To the ARCHDUCHESS MARIE LOUISE.

"RAMBOUILLET, 23rd *February*, 1810.

"MY COUSIN,—The brilliant qualities which distinguish your person have inspired us with the desire to serve and to honour you. In addressing the Emperor, your father, begging him to confide to us the happiness of your imperial highness, may we hope that you will take a favourable view of the feelings which lead us to take this step? Can we flatter ourself that you will not be solely determined by duty and obedience to your parents? To whatever extent the feelings of your imperial highness may be partial to us, we shall cultivate them with such care, and we shall so constantly endeavour to please you in all things, that we flatter ourself that we shall one day succeed in making ourself agreeable; this is the object which we desire to attain, and for which we beg your Highness to be favourable to us.

"NAPOLEON."

There was considerable difference between this imperial wooing and the passionate ardour with which the young general stormed and won the heart of Josephine de Beauharnais.

The following letter was addressed to Josephine's son, the Viceroy of Italy:—". . . Having determined to celebrate my marriage with the Archduchess Marie Louise of Austria on the 29th March, at Paris, I desire that you will convoke the grand officers, officers, and ladies of my household of Italy, retaining only those who are necessary for your service and that of your wife."

On the 1st March Napoleon announced to the Senate that having separated temporal from spiritual affairs he had cancelled the nomination of Cardinal Fesch as successor to the Primate of the Confederation. The ex-army contractor was spoken of as a prelate distinguished alike for his piety and his virtues, who had made known the repugnance he would feel at being called away from the administration of his diocese!

To M. DE CHAMPAGNY.

"PARIS, 2nd March, 1810.

"I send you the draft of a treaty with Holland. You must try and finish with this affair. Let the minister negotiate with you and not send me any more notes.

"NAPOLEON."

By the treaty above referred to, Holland was to cede South Brabant to France, was to bind herself to furnish a fleet of nine ships of the line and six frigates, and was to observe the obligations of the continental blockade.

To COMTE DE RÉMUSAT.

"PARIS, 2nd March, 1810.

"*La Mort d'Abel* should be performed on the 20th March; the ballet of *Persée et Andromède* on Easter

Monday; *Les Bayadères*, a fortnight afterwards; *Sophocle* and *Armède* during the summer; *Les Danaïdes* in the autumn; *Les Sabines* at the end of May. As a general rule I wish to have as many new pieces as possible in the *month* of Easter, as there are a great many foreigners in Paris for the fêtes.

"NAPOLEON."

To the ARCHDUCHESS MARIE LOUISE.

"MADAM, MY SISTER,—The success of the demand which I addressed to your father to unite myself to you in marriage is a precious mark of esteem and consideration which he accords to me. I am extremely flattered by the consent that you yourself have given to a union which overwhelms me with real joy, and which is calculated to embellish my life. I await with impatience the moment which is to accelerate its conclusion. I appreciate above everything else in this alliance the care which I shall take to render you happy. My wishes in this respect are all the more sincere because my own happiness will be essentially linked with yours. I have charged the Prince of Neuchâtel to hand you my portrait. I beg of you to receive it as a pledge of those sentiments which are engraved upon my heart and which will be unchangeable.

"NAPOLEON."

To GENERAL CLARKE.

"PARIS, 15*th March*, 1810.

"I attach great importance to the Congreve rockets. As soon as the success of this fabrication has been established, and that some can be sent to Spain to serve against Cadiz, Ciudad-Rodrigo, and Badajoz, forward them to the commanders of the 7th and 3rd Army Corps in Catalonia and Arragon. Give notice that as soon as the artillery officer is sure to succeed that I shall be present at the trials of these rockets.

"NAPOLEON."

To M. DE CHAMPAGNY.

"PARIS, 16th March, 1810.

"Prepare a despatch for St. Petersburg in which you must inform Caulaincourt that I find the complaints made by Russia ridiculous. He must reply in a firm tone to the Czar and to Romanzof, and say that the Czar is mistaken if he thinks that there was a double negotiation; that I know nothing of eventual treaties; that I am too powerful for that; that they four times asked for ten days to give a reply; that it was only when it became clear that the Czar was not master in his family, and that he did not keep to his promises of Erfurth that negotiations were opened with Austria—negotiations which were begun and terminated in twenty-four hours, because Austria had taken all necessary precautions, and had sent the necessary authorisations to her minister; that as for religion, it was not religion itself which caused alarm, but the obligation of having a pope at the Tuileries; that as far as the convention is concerned [convention relative to Poland], I was unable to ratify that act. . . .

"NAPOLEON."

The ratification depended in fact upon the matrimonial affair; had that succeeded Poland would have been sacrificed.

TO THE EMPEROR OF AUSTRIA.

"PARIS, 17th March, 1810.

"SIR, MY BROTHER AND FATHER-IN-LAW,—The Count of Schœnbrünn has handed me the letter of your Imperial Majesty of the 6th March. I am extremely flattered by the feelings which it expresses. Your Majesty will have only to praise yourself for having confided to me your daughter. She will be a source of happiness to myself and to France. If her own happiness depends on the sincerity of my affection no one will be more happy than Marie Louise. She will everywhere perceive, while passing through France, the necessity which my people experience to love her and to tell her so.

"NAPOLEON."

To THE QUEEN LOUISE DE BOURBON OF SPAIN.

"PARIS, 17*th March*, 1810.

"I have received your Majesty's letter of the 10th. I thank you for all the amiable things which it contains, and the good wishes which your Majesty has addressed to me on the occasion of my marriage. . . .

"NAPOLEON."

A similar letter was addressed to Charles IV., but no notice seems to have been taken of Ferdinand.

To M. DE CHAMPAGNY.

"COMPIÈGNE, 22*nd March*, 1810.

"I have read with interest the details of the ceremonies which took place at Vienna. I desire you to appoint a committee to examine if the ceremonial was in conformity with that followed on previous occasions, and to make sure that nothing was done contrary to the rights of my extraordinary ambassador, especially as concerns his relations with the archdukes.[1]

"NAPOLEON."

---

[1] Berthier's own account of the affair runs thus :—

"On reaching the hall where the Emperor was waiting, the grand master of the ceremonies stepped forward and announced me. His Majesty was standing at the extreme end of the hall, under a daïs. At my second reverence all the ministers of the Emperor and the ladies and gentlemen of the court stopped short in the middle of the hall, and I advanced alone over the long space which separated me from his Majesty. When I reached the end of the carpet which covered the estrade I put on my hat. On delivering my credentials I addressed a few words to the Emperor, taking care to remove my hat, and to put it on every time that I pronounced the name of your Majesty or that of the Emperor of Austria. I uncovered at the

To the Emperor of Austria.

"Compiègne, 29*th March*, 1810.

"Sir, my Brother and Father-in-Law,—Your Majesty's daughter arrived here two days ago. She fulfils all my hopes, and, for two days I have not ceased to give her and to receive proofs of the tender feeling which unites us. We agree together perfectly. I shall make her happy, and I shall owe your Majesty my happiness. Allow me to thank you for the splendid present which you have made me, and let your paternal heart rejoice in the assurances of the happiness of your darling child.

"We leave to-morrow for St. Cloud, and on the 2nd April our marriage ceremony will be celebrated at the Tuileries. . . .

"Napoleon."

On the 31st March Napoleon sent several decorations of the Legion of Honour to his father-in-law, and wrote as follows to his old adversary the Archduke Charles:—

"My Cousin,—I owe your Imperial Highness many thanks for having been so good as to represent me at my marriage with the Archduchess Marie Louise. She has been here for the last two days, and I have renewed, from the bottom of my heart, the promises which you made in my name.

"Your highness knows that the esteem which I bear you is of old date, and founded upon your great qualities and

moment I handed him my letters. The Emperor having begun to speak, I covered myself. When he had ceased speaking I uncovered once more. His Majesty then assumed a conversational tone, and I presented my secretary, my aide-de-camp, and the gentlemen of the embassy to him. I then retired with the same ceremony as on entering, and paid a visit to the Empress."

As no more was heard of any slight or irregularity, it is probable that none occurred.

actions. I am very desirous of giving you an authentic mark of this, and I beg that you will accept the Grand Eagle of the Legion of Honour. I also beg you to receive the cross of the Legion which I wear, and which is worn by 20,000 soldiers who have been mutilated, or who have distinguished themselves on the field of honour. The one is a homage paid to your genius as a general, the other to your rare valour as a soldier.

" NAPOLEON."

Certainly the admiration which the Archduke felt for the military genius of the Emperor was now reciprocated.

To KING LOUIS OF HOLLAND.

" PARIS, 3rd April, 1810.

"I do not consider it right that you should issue a proclamation to your people. Simply send a message to the legislative body, which must not be printed, saying that the independence of Holland can exist only as long as it is not incompatible with the interests of France; that it cannot be disguised that Holland is situated at the outlets of France, and that if care be not taken to avoid thwarting the system of France, Holland may lose her independence; that the Emperor, believing himself thwarted as regards the blockade, has determined to unite Holland to France.

" NAPOLEON."

On the 9th orders were given for Suchet to be severely reprimanded for retiring from Valence, against which city he had marched with inadequate means.

On the 16th General Clarke was instructed to write to Marshal Davoust to give orders at Hamburg to threaten, and if possible to take, the rock of Heligoland.

To M. DE CHAMPAGNY.

"COMPIÈGNE, 25*th April*, 1810.

"... I wrote to you to send away the Persian ambassador, but without treating him badly. You must tell him that I do not wish to see him, and that I am displeased to learn that Persia has sold its political interests to the English for a few thousand crowns; that if the Shah writes to renew his relations with me he must first of all drive out the English.

"NAPOLEON."

To THE QUEEN HORTENSE.

"COMPIÈGNE, 26*th April*, 1810.

"MY DAUGHTER,—I have received your letter, and I am glad to see that you have arrived at Amsterdam with your children in good health. I start to-morrow for Antwerp which I shall reach on the 1st May. I am assured that you are very well pleased with the king and with Holland, and this affords me great pleasure.

"NAPOLEON."

During the negotiations, Louis, with the consent of Hortense, had asked for a divorce, and on this relief having been refused, he declined to attach his signature to the dissolution of the Emperor's marriage with Josephine. He accepted, however, an invitation to go to Compiègne, whither Napoleon had repaired to meet Marie Louise, but finding his apartment next to that of his wife, he left the castle in the middle of the night. After his return to Amsterdam he not only lived in a separate part of the palace from his wife, but took good care that this should be known.

To THE EMPRESS JOSEPHINE, AT THE CASTLE OF NAVARRE.

"COMPIÈGNE, 28*th April*, 1810.

"MY FRIEND,—I have received two letters from you. I have written to Eugene. I have ordered a marriage to take place between Tascher and the Princess de la Leyen.

"I shall go to Antwerp to-morrow to see my fleet. . . . Eugene tells me that you wish to go and take the waters. Do just as you please. Do not listen to the gossip of Paris, which is far from knowing the real state of affairs. My feeling towards you does not change, and I much desire to know that you are happy and contented.

"NAPOLEON."

To the KING OF SAXONY.

"ANTWERP, 4th May, 1810.

"I have received your Majesty's letter of the 18th. I shall be pleased with anything which you find useful for the Princess Amelia. In the present position of affairs I cannot offer any political objection.

"NAPOLEON."

The above letter refers to a proposed marriage between the Princess Amelia and the Archduke Charles of Austria.

To M. FOUCHÉ.

"ANTWERP, 5th May, 1810.

"You must deny the report of the recall of Moreau, and state that that general, whose intrigues with the Bourbons are well known, is for ever excluded from France. . . .

"NAPOLEON."

On the 7th Napoleon sent orders to his minister of public worship that no priest was in future to be ordained in the departments of Rome and Trasimene without his permission; that all the foreign priests were at once to leave Rome; that all the bishops were to take the oath of allegiance, and that those who refused were to have their property sequestrated and to be sent to France; that the canons were to be treated like the bishops, &c. And the same day, being determined "to force the priests to take the oath, and to put an end to the ridiculous scenes in Rome," he wrote to his war minister to strengthen the force at the disposal of General Miollis.

To M. DE CHAMPAGNY.

"BERG-OP-ZOOM, 9*th May*, 1810.

"Present a very lucid note to the Prussian ambassador on the affair of the Prince of Hatzfeld, in which you must dwell upon the scandal of this trial, say how it displeases me, and that I recognise in it the hand of that cabal which has drawn down so many misfortunes on the country. You must refer to the treaty of Tilsit, to the manner in which M. de Hatzfeld has conducted himself, and declare that I take him under my special care, and that I shall not suffer any harm to be done to him. . . . You must proclaim everywhere that the enemies of M. de Hatzfeld are my enemies; that those who attack him attack me. . . . You must speak in the same sense to Marshal Kalkreuth. . . .

"NAPOLEON."

A note appended to this letter states that—The Prince of Hatzfeld, who was pardoned by Napoleon in 1806, was living in Berlin, and remained on friendly terms with the French agents engaged in collecting the war contributions in the hope of obtaining some mitigation in favour of his countrymen. These relations, no matter how profitable to Prussia, aroused the suspicions of the king, who ordered the prince to be tried. The intervention of the Emperor put a stop to the affair.

On the 9th May Napoleon wrote another letter to the minister of public worship in which he said that he had ordered General Miollis to be reinforced by three columns; that he supposed by this time all the bishops, vicars, curates, and canons had either taken the oath, or were on the road to France, and that their property had been seized. As for the bishops, he ordered the seizure not only of their ecclesiastical, but of their patrimonial property, and he expressed his determination to reduce the number of sees in Rome and Trasímene where there were thirty sees for 700,000 inhabitants, whereas in some of the French sees there were over a million inhabitants. He declared that he would send 100,000 men to Rome if necessary, just to show that he could unmake, if he could not make bishops.

To KING LOUIS OF HOLLAND.

"BERG-OP-ZOOM, 9*th May*, 1810.

"I reckon that you will have ten vessels in the roads by the month of June, and yet I have heard of no movement in Holland. Think how important this is for the common cause, and keep your engagements.

"NAPOLEON."

The position in which the two brothers stood requires some explanation.

Napoleon had hardly seated Louis on the throne of Holland when he began to quarrel with him. Louis wanted to be something more than a vassal, while Napoleon wanted him to sacrifice all the interest of the Dutch to France. Louis was to close his ports to England, and see his commerce ruined; to lose his colonies, to maintain French troops, to build ships for the French Emperor, and to fight against all the Emperor's foes. In 1808 Napoleon offered Louis the throne of Spain, which Louis refused in consequence of the stratagems by which the drivelling Charles IV. had been deprived of his crown. A few months later Napoleon asked Louis to cede him Brabant and Zeeland in return for the Hanse towns, just as he afterwards asked Joseph to cede him the provinces of the Ebro in exchange for Portugal, and Jerome a portion of his kingdom in exchange for Hanover. Louis indignantly refused to acquiesce in the dismemberment of Holland. Angry remonstrances were frequently addressed to him on the subject of the non-observance of the continental blockade, which Louis never could or never would enforce strictly.

After the peace of Vienna Napoleon determined to dethrone Louis, and he accomplished his purpose in his usual crafty manner. Louis was invited to Paris. Being aware of what was in store for him he wished to refuse, but his scruples were overcome by his ministers. He had hardly reached the French capital when Napoleon published a declaration to the effect that Holland was one of the chief arteries of France, and that it was necessary for the two countries to be united. Upon this Louis wished to return to Holland, but he found himself a prisoner. The house of his mother, where he was staying, was surrounded by gendarmes. He managed to send an equerry to Amsterdam with an order not to allow the French troops to occupy the forts, nor to enter the capital.[1] This order was executed, but at the same time the king was advised to submit to the conditions imposed by Napoleon, resistance being considered useless. So affected was Louis by the violent threats of his brother that he was attacked by a nervous fever from which, he said, he unfortunately recovered. Napoleon, he declared, treated him as Popilius treated Antiochus, and enforced submission before granting him his freedom. The conditions upon which Louis was finally released were that he should prohibit

---

[1] When the Emperor heard of this order, learned that his troops had been refused admittance to Bergen-op-Zoom and Breda, and that the war minister, Krayenhof, was fortifying Amsterdam, he flew into a violent passion. In a letter, dated 3rd March, 1810, and addressed to Fouché (letter not mentioned in *The Correspondence*, but quoted by M. Thiers), he said—" Has the King of Holland gone mad? You must ask him if it is by his orders that his ministers have acted, or on their own authority. I shall have them all arrested, and their heads cut off." Louis would not have been at all surprised had his execution been ordered.

all commerce with England, that he should keep up a fleet of fourteen ships of the line and seven frigates, maintain an army of 25,000 men, &c. On the 16th March Louis agreed to the above conditions, ceded to the Emperor a slice of Dutch territory, and consented to seize a number of American ships lying in Dutch harbours. After this he was released, and was allowed to return to Amsterdam.

On the 16th May Napoleon addressed a letter to M. de Champagny, telling him to inform his ambassador at Berlin that he was at liberty to allow M. de Hardenberg to re-enter the cabinet. At the same time the ambassador was to lecture him and Russia in these terms :—" Engagements have been entered into with the Emperor, who desires them to be kept. If, during the war with Austria, the cabinet of Berlin had pursued a firm and loyal policy, it might have freed itself from an enormous burden. If, when Austria declared war, the Prussian ambassador at Vienna had left that capital saying that his master had secret engagements with the Emperor ; if Prussia had placed 15,000 men in the field to join the Saxons and the Bavarians," &c., &c. And after recapitulating a long list of crimes of commission and omission, the ambassador was to insist upon the war indemnity being paid to the uttermost farthing.

To the EMPEROR OF RUSSIA.

"IMPERIAL PALACE OF LACKEN, 16*th May*, 1810.

" Caulaincourt has informed me of all the amiable things which your Majesty has said on the subject of my marriage. I beg you to accept my thanks. My feelings towards you are as unchangeable as the political principles which govern the relations of my empire. Never will your Majesty have to complain of France. The declarations which I made last December form the whole secret of my policy. I shall reiterate them to you at every opportunity. . .

"NAPOLEON."

In reality the czar was deeply offended. He was opposed to an alliance, but was incensed at the way in which the negotiation for the hand of his sister had been both carried on and broken off.

A letter addressed to the minister of finance on the 17th shows that Napoleon made 150,000,000f. by the sale of mortmain property in his Roman departments.

On the 19th M. de Champagny was directed to tell Caulaincourt to deny in conversation the report of a union between a French princess and the Prince Royal of Sweden. We shall see how a French woman afterwards became Queen of Sweden.

On the 19th May Murat was complimented on the courage shown by his navy. He was then told to remember that he had been on the throne for two years, and that for the last year he should have had a ship of the line and a frigate. If that had been the case he would not see Naples blockaded by an English ship *rasé*. "If," added the Emperor, "you understand the interests of your people you will have an 80-gun ship by the end of the year. The Neapolitans would gladly pay 10 per cent. extra in the way of taxes. . . . The English have a squadron at Venice, where I shall soon have five vessels; they have squadrons in the Baltic, on the Dutch coast, off Rochefort, Toulon, Lorient, Cherbourg, and Flushing, where at present I have fifteen ships of war. Should the war continue until 1812 I shall have in my ports and in those of my allies 100 ships. . . . Adopt measures so as to have an 80-gun ship this year, and five by the end of 1812, and then the English will not come and blockade you."

The next day his Majesty wrote to his minister of marine, saying—

"I intend going to Havre. Let me know if the frigate *La Gloire* can be launched while I am there. Let me also know if the two frigates *L'Oder* and *La Perle*, which ought to be finished at Dunkirk, can be launched in my presence.

Let me know also when *L'Iphigénie* will be launched at Cherbourg; when *La Clorinde* and *La Renommée* will be in the roads at Brest; when the *Nestor* will be floated there; *Le Pregel* at St. Malo; *L'Jena* at Rochefort; *Le Wagram* and *Le Spectre* at Toulon.

"Napoleon."

In consequence of Louis not wishing, or not being able, to adhere to his engagements, Napoleon wrote him on the 20th May (letter not given in *The Correspondence*), saying —"The die is cast: you are incorrigible. Advice and affection having failed, I must resort to threats and force. What are these prayers and mysterious fasts which you have ordered? Louis, you do not wish to reign any longer; your actions reveal your sentiments better than your letters. Listen to a man who knows more of the world than you do. Return to the right road. Act like a Frenchman, or your own people will drive you from the country; you will leave Holland an object of pity, and you will be the laughing-stock of the Dutch. It is with reason and with political acumen that states are governed, and not with a vitiated and lymphatic temperament." Poor Louis, previously taunted with sacrificing the interests of his Catholic subjects, was now accused of bigotry. As for the dilapidated state of his health, the fruit of youthful indiscretions in Italy, Napoleon was never tired of raking up that misfortune to which he attributed all the backslidings of his brother.

To MARSHAL BERTHIER.

"Dieppe, 27*th May*, 1810.

"Write to the King of Spain, saying that I am sorry to see this extensive arming of Spaniards, which is only fit to prolong resistance and to cause the blood of French soldiers to flow; that when one has been so often deceived it is difficult to understand so much obstinacy. Write to Massena that the English army is 23,000 strong, and that of the Portuguese 22,000; that he must therefore have more troops than are necessary to beat the English, should they try and hinder the siege of Ciudad-Rodrigo. . . . Write to the King of Spain that as the English alone are to be feared, he should place Regnier with the second corps under the orders of Massena to manœuvre on the right bank of the Tagus.

" NAPOLEON."

Massena had over 50,000 men under his orders without Regnier's corps. Napoleon had himself frequently ordered Joseph to raise Spanish troops.

That all the Spanish troops in the French service had not the good luck to escape like Romana's corps is shown by the following letter.

To GENERAL CLARKE.

"HAVRE, 29*th May*, 1810.

"Inform the King of Spain that I cannot send him the regiment *Joseph-Napoléon*, which is animated with so bad a spirit that the officers have demanded its withdrawal from the frontiers of Spain; that he can judge from this fact how impolitic and inconsiderate his Spanish levies are.

" NAPOLEON."

On the same day Berthier was directed to write again to Massena, saying that Wellington had only 24,000 men and the Portuguese 25,000. "But," added Napoleon, "I do not wish to enter Lisbon at present, because I could not feed the city, whose immense population draws its provisions by sea. Let Massena employ the summer in taking Ciudad-Rodrigo and Almeida. . . ."

Berthier was also to send to the *Moniteur* an account of the fall of Leridon, and to levy a contribution of several millions upon that place.

To the EMPRESS.

(*Letter not dated.*)

"My Friend,—I have received your letter. Eugene will give you news of my voyage and of the empress. I approve of your taking waters, and I hope that they will do you good.

"I greatly wish to see you. If you are at the Malmaison at the end of the month I will pay you a visit.

"My health is good. Let me know the name under which you will travel. Do not doubt the sincerity, &c.

"Napoleon."

To M. FOUCHÉ.

"St. Cloud, 3rd *June*, 1810.

"I have received your letter of the 2nd June. I am aware of all the services which you have rendered me, and I believe in your attachment and your zeal; however it is impossible for me to allow you to keep your portfolio. The post of minister of police requires an absolute and entire confidence, and that confidence can no longer exist, because you have compromised my tranquillity and that of the state, and this is not to be excused by the legitimacy of the motives.

"A negotiation was opened with England; conferences took place with Lord Wellesley, and that minister knew that he was spoken to on your behalf; he must have thought that it was on mine also; hence a total change in all my political relations, and, if I were to permit it, a stain upon my character, which I cannot, and will not, tolerate.

"Although I do not distrust your attachment and your fidelity, I am, however, obliged to keep up a constant supervision, which fatigues me. . . .

"Napoleon."

The crime of Fouché, in a few words, was this. Napoleon had put forward his brother Louis to appeal to England to make peace, as unless peace were concluded the French Emperor would inevitably annex Holland, which would be a terrible blow to Great Britain. Negotiations were opened with the Marquis of Wellesley through the medium of the Dutch banker Labouchère, who was to point out among other things that in refusing to make peace England had already lost Spain, Portugal, Naples, and Trieste, and would soon lose Holland, the Hanse towns, and Sicily. The terms upon which peace was indirectly offered were of course quite unacceptable. Fouché took it into his head to negotiate on his own account, and sent an Irish officer called Fagan to London with far more acceptable terms than those offered by M. Labouchère, but the British Government did not consider that Fagan had sufficient authority to negotiate. When Napoleon learned that Fouché had been meddling in this way he was highly incensed, although naturally nothing could have eventually come of the Fagan negotiation without the consent of the Emperor. Perhaps there were other reasons mixed up with the disgrace of the minister of police. Fouché had made friends with Talleyrand, he was on good terms with Napoleon's brother, and he was suspected of having warned Lucien of the wrath that was coming, and of having thus enabled him to make his escape from Rome, and to throw himself into the arms of the English. Napoleon at first thought of having Fouché executed for the crime of *lèse majeste*.

A second letter, written on the same day, informed the fallen minister that the Emperor conferred upon him the governorship of Rome; and on the 5th June the Emperor wrote to Maret, Duc de Bassano, to go and see the Duc d'Otrante, and to ask him to give up all the documents, whether written in visible or in invisible ink. Maret, too, was to persuade Fouché to leave the police office at once, and afterwards to turn the conversation on Rome, and to try and persuade him to start for the Holy City before the 15th, his presence being much required there.

To M. DE CHAMPAGNY.

"St. Cloud, 14*th June*, 1810.

"I have read your report on the subject of the dispute between my consul and the Dey of Algiers. My agent seems to me very culpable; he should not compromise my interests for such trifles. Make known to him my displeasure. Let M. Thainville settle this affair. I will not quarrel with the dey about such stupidities. . . .

"NAPOLEON."

To GENERAL CLARKE.

"St. Cloud, 17*th June*, 1810.

"Make me a report on the conscripts who have not joined. We might send them to dangerous posts. Would it not be well to despatch them to Corsica, and to form a corps of 6,000 or 7,000 men for the conquest of Sardinia? It would be sufficient to appoint a good general and good colonels to command them.

"NAPOLEON."

To M. FOUCHÉ.

"St. Cloud, 18*th June*, 1810.

"I wrote to you yesterday for the letter which M. Fagan brought back from Lord Wellesley. I write to you again to-day to let you know that you must hand to me, with that letter, all the documents, without exception, concerning Ouvrard, Labouchère, and Fagan. . . . I have the right of insisting, and it is important for me and for you that I should have all the papers in this affair. . . .

"NAPOLEON."

Fouché, Duc d'Otrante, was at the Chateau de Ferrières when this angry note reached him.

To the EMPEROR OF RUSSIA.

"St. Cloud, 20*th June*, 1810."

"Prince Kourakine has handed me the letter which your Majesty has been good enough to write in order to congratulate me on my marriage. This minister of state has equally expressed to me, on the part of your Majesty, your good wishes for my happiness and for that of the Empress, my well-beloved spouse and companion. . . .

"I sincerely share the desire of your Majesty to force England to conclude peace. The intimate union of the continent, and especially the assurance which you have given me to co-operate in every way to attain so desirable an end, make me hope that our united efforts will be crowned with success. . . .

"Napoleon."

For a moment the Emperor conceived hopes of being able to grow his own cotton. On the 24th June he addressed a note to Champagny, saying:—"Bring the letter of M. Otto to the cabinet council to-morrow, and also specimens of the cotton which were inclosed." It seems that a Dr. Angelo of Vienna had proposed to manufacture cotton goods out of thistles.

On the same day his Majesty wrote another letter to his minister for foreign affairs, saying that he had ordered Oudinot to march upon Amsterdam. Instructions were to be sent to the French ambassador, Serurier, to insinuate that there remained only one way of getting out of the difficulty. "Let my troops," said Napoleon, "be received in triumph at Amsterdam; let the city give my soldiers a grand banquet, and let the king and the court display good feeling towards France; this will be the only way to efface the insult offered to my eagles at Haarlem. . . ."

On the 23rd June, Napoleon, to his great indignation, learned that his *chargé d'affaires* had been slighted by

King Louis at a diplomatic audience, and that a coachman in the livery of the French embassy had been beaten in a squabble. According to treaty the number of French troops in Holland was limited to 6,000 men, who were to be engaged in protecting the littoral. Napoleon now sent 20,000 men into the country because a Dutch officer had refused to allow a French patrol to pass at Haarlem. Finding the French troops closing round him, Louis wished to summon the nation to arms, to break the dykes, and to defend Amsterdam as Saragossa had been defended. The Dutch, however, were not inclined to put the country under water, and to sacrifice what little wealth and freedom remained to them, because one Bonaparte bullied another. The consequence was that Louis determined to abdicate in favour of his son, Napoleon Louis, and to seek safety in flight, a step which he knew would incense the Emperor by depriving him of one excuse for seizing on Holland. The Emperor had always declared that Louis was the source of all evil. Louis therefore made up his mind to leave the country, saying, "We shall see what he will do now." About the same time Lucien fled from Rome, preferring to fall into the hands of the English to falling into the clutches of his terrible brother; while Joseph appealed with increasing persistence to be released from his unenviable position at Madrid.

To GENERAL CLARKE.

"ST. CLOUD, 24*th June*, 1810.

"You will give the following instructions to the Duc de Reggio (Oudinot):—As soon as he has assembled a sufficient number of troops at Utrecht to march upon Amsterdam, he must write to my *chargé d'affaires* that the French troops have been insulted; that the gates of Haarlem were closed to them; that he is to demand reparation for this insult; that the French eagles can go into all friendly and allied countries; that for the last fifteen years French troops have been in every portion of

Holland, and that therefore a gratuitous insult has been paid to the French troops; that the Emperor is much offended, and has ordered additional forces into Holland; that his instructions did not order him to enter Amsterdam, but that the challenge offered to the French troops, and the intrigues of England tending to arm the Dutch against the French, provoked the order which he received to present himself before Amsterdam; that it is for the Dutch to say if they desire to treat us as friends or as enemies, and if they wish to accept the perfidious counsels offered to the king in order to ruin Holland. . . .

"NAPOLEON."

To M. GAUDIN.

"ST. CLOUD, 1st *July*, 1810.

"You will receive from the office of the secretary of state a decree annulling that which appointed Fouché to the government of Rome. Inform General Miollis that it is my intention to leave him at the post which he fulfils so well, and that I reckon upon his zeal.

"NAPOLEON."

When this decision was taken, Fouché thought it only prudent to leave the country, and go into voluntary exile, thinking his Majesty quite capable of carrying out his first intention.

On the 8th July the Emperor wrote to General Clarke and to Admiral Décrès, saying that he had made up his mind to annex Holland, and instructing those ministers to adopt certain military and naval measures. He then wrote to the ex-consul, now Prince Lebrun, saying:—

"MY COUSIN,—I require your services in Holland. Have your travelling carriages prepared, and come to Rambouillet as speedily as possible for instructions. It is indispensable that you should leave Paris to-morrow evening for Amsterdam."

On the day following Napoleon wrote to the President of the Government Committee which had been formed at Amsterdam :—

"I have received the letter written to me by the council. I much regret what has taken place. I cannot consent to the Grand Duke of Berg, my nephew and ward, becoming King of Holland. . . . Inform the inhabitants of Holland by means of a proclamation that the circumstances of Europe, that their geographical situation, and the pretensions of our common enemies make it my duty to put an end to these provisional governments which for the last sixteen years have tormented that portion of the empire (!). The inhabitants of Holland shall be the objects of my care. I shall rejoice in their prosperity as in that of my good city of Paris. The vast field which I open to their industry, from Amsterdam to Rome, will permit them to await the time marked by destiny for opening up to the commerce of my subjects the countries illustrated by your ancestors, and which have raised so high the honour of Dutch and Batavian names."

And on the 10th his Majesty announced to Prince Lebrun, lieutenant-general of the Emperor in Holland, that he had just despatched Comte Lauriston to Amsterdam to bring back the Grand Duke of Berg to Paris. He also impressed it upon the mind of Lebrun that the first thing he would require in Holland would be a good minister of police.

On the 13th the Emperor wrote thus to the Queen Hortense :—

"I see that you have received letters from Holland. There is no news of the king; no one knows whither he has retired, and it is impossible to account for this piece of folly. I send you some letters, which I think you should write to the President of the Government Council. . . .

"NAPOLEON."

These letters were to say that her Majesty had placed her affairs and those of her son in the hands of the Emperor, who was the head of the family. Of course the docile Hortense obeyed: it is true that she had had more than enough of her husband and of Holland, and was enchanted to regain her freedom.

To GENERAL CLARKE.

"RAMBOUILLET, 15*th* *July*, 1810.

"I am informed that English prisoners are being enrolled in the Irish legion. I wish all these prisoners to be sent back. I will not have any English soldiers; I prefer that they should remain prisoners and answer for my prisoners in England; and then most of them desert.

"I beg you will take measures to put a stop to the recruiting of Spaniards in the Neapolitan and Portuguese regiments, and that of Germans and Irish in the Polish regiments. It is useless to augment the number of my soldiers, especially of men who all desert in Spain.

"NAPOLEON."

To ADMIRAL DECRÈS.

"RAMBOUILLET, 16*th* *July*, 1810.

"I have read with interest the bases of the budget of 1810, for the large ports.

"It appears to me that *Le Pacificateur*, *L'Auguste*, *L'Illustre* and *Le Conquérant* might be launched in May, 1811, and *Le Trajan*, *Le Gaulois* and *La Superbe* in July, so as to have nineteen vessels at Antwerp by October. . . . It results from your report that I shall have twenty-four ships before the end of the year, and sixty-six by the 1st January, 1812. . . . I suppose that I shall have twenty in Holland, that will make eighty-six, which, with the two of Italy and the one of Naples, will make eighty-nine. The budget of 1811 must be so arranged as to have twenty more in France, and four or five in Naples and Italy. In this way I shall have from 110 to 115 ships at the end of 1812. . . .

"NAPOLEON."

To M. DE CHAMPAGNY.

"ST. CLOUD, 19*th July*, 1810.

"Insert some articles in the papers on the successes of the Russians in Turkey, and on the peace which is about to be concluded on condition of the cession of Moldavia and Wallachia, and the confiscation of vessels said to have come from Teneriffe, but which in reality come from England.

"Make known my intentions as regards Turkey to Caulaincourt. Write to him that I shall be pleased to see Turkey conclude peace by ceding the left bank of the Danube; but that Russia would violate her engagements with me should she keep anything on the right bank, and if she interfered with the Servians. You will write this in cipher, letting Caulaincourt know that as I would see with pleasure Russia settle matters with Turkey, so would it displease me were she to keep anything on the right bank; that a single place kept by Russia on the right bank of the Danube would destroy the independence of the Porte, and would entirely change the state of affairs. . . .

"NAPOLEON."

To THE EMPRESS JOSEPHINE.

"ST. CLOUD, 20*th July*, 1810.

"MY FRIEND,—I have received your letter of the 14th. I see with pleasure that the waters did you good, and that you liked Geneva. My health is pretty good. The conduct of the King of Holland has afflicted me. Hortense is soon coming to Paris. The Grand Duke of Berg is on the road, and I am expecting him to-morrow. Adieu, my friend.

"NAPOLEON."

To MADAME MÈRE.

"St. Cloud, 20*th July*, 1810.

"Madame,—I hasten to inform you that the King of Holland is at Tœplitz in Bohemia. As you must have experienced some uneasiness on his disappearance, I do not lose a moment in sending you this news to tranquillise you. His conduct can be explained only by the bad state of his health.

"Your very affectionate son,
"Napoleon."

The two brothers did not meet again until 1814 when Napoleon, on the solicitation of Marie Louise, consented to receive the runaway, not as King of Holland, but as a French prince.

To the EMPEROR OF AUSTRIA.

"Paris, 21*st July*, 1810.

"Sir, my Brother and Father-in-Law,—Allow me to send your Imperial Majesty a porcelain cup from my manufactory of Sèvres upon which the portrait of Louise is painted. I hope that this present will be agreeable to your Majesty, and that you will find it well done. . . .

"Napoleon."

To COMTE DE MONTALIVET.

"St. Cloud, 25*th July*, 1810.

"Having suppressed most of the convents in Rome, and wishing as far as possible to maintain the rank and importance of the population of that great city, I desire to establish manufactories there, and to encourage the cultivation of cotton. I am assured that the soil of Rome is good for that culture, and that there are a great many watercourses, where the convents stood, which can serve as motive power for machines. Adopt measures in order to arrive at this result. It is my intention to place a sum of 500,000 francs at your disposal for this object.

"NAPOLEON."

To carry out this idea of making Rome the rival of Manchester, a competent person was to make a report, and was to answer the following questions:—

1st. Why have the environs of Rome been left uncultivated?

2nd. Why are they unhealthy?

3rd. What remedy can be applied?

4th. In what condition is the draining of the Pontine marshes? What works have been accomplished? What is the system which has been pursued, and what is that which ought to be pursued?

TO M. DE CHAMPAGNY.

"ST. CLOUD, 26th July, 1810.

"Have a courier ready to convey my letter to the Emperor of Austria. Write to M. Otto to demand the arrest of Pozzo di Borgo as having been condemned to death by default for having betrayed France in favour of England. In reality I shall be satisfied with demanding his expulsion from Austria. Write to M. Otto to keep an eye upon M. de Razumowski, and to insinuate, as a piece of advice, that I should like to see him turned out of Vienna. . . .

"NAPOLEON."

There was a sort of vendetta between the two Corsicans, Napoleon and Pozzo di Borgo, which commenced in the days of Paoli, and when the latter preferred leaving the island with Sir Gilbert Elliot to acknowledging the French Republic. After remaining eighteen months in England, Pozzo di Borgo took service in Russia, but retired to Austria on the signing of the Treaty of Tilsit. He now fled from Vienna, and had to go to Constantinople to find a safe issue from the Continent in order to return to England.

To the Emperor of Austria.

"St. Cloud, 26*th July*, 1810.

"Sir, my Brother and very dear Father-in-law,— I have received the letter of your Imperial Majesty of the 15th. I beg you to receive my thanks for the amiable things which it contains. . . . Count Metternich, the Prince Schwartzenburg, and the subjects of your Majesty who were in Paris during that painful circumstance are deserving of all praise, and their conduct has given me great pleasure. I desire to give the Legion of Honour to several of them, and I have charged Count Metternich to obtain the permission of your Majesty.

"I do not know if the Empress has informed you that the hopes we have of her being *enceinte* increase every day, and that we have all the certainty which is possible after two months and a half. Your Majesty will easily understand all that this adds to the feelings inspired by your daughter, and how much these new ties increase my desire to be agreeable to her. . . .

"Napoleon."

On the 29th July, Napoleon sent his compliments to Massena on the taking of Ciudad Rodrigo, adding that he thought Almeida might be taken towards the end of August, and that then Massena could march on Lisbon. He was to deliver battle against the English if he liked. The Emperor was however opposed to Badajos and Elvas being besieged as both places were strong, and once the English beaten and re-embarked they would fall of themselves.

In a letter addressed to General Clarke from Trianon on the 4th August the Emperor wrote: "I see that the five Portuguese regiments forming ten battalions have their battalions organised *à la Française*, six companies to each;

but that out of these companies the grenadier and voltigeur companies are with the thirteenth provisional demi-brigade. The thirteenth provisional demi-brigade, coming from Metz with two marching battalions, is therefore composed of thirty companies. . . .

On the 5th August Napoleon wrote to the King of Saxony asking for some information of a military character with regard to the Duchy of Warsaw. He concluded his letter thus: "As I desire to have all this information secretly and without allowing any one to suppose that I am occupied with these matters, I consider it more simple to write to you direct. However, your Majesty will observe that this is merely a matter of precaution, because my relations with Russia continue to be excellent."

The above letter was one of the first symptoms betraying the intention of a war with Russia.

On the 9th August the Emperor wrote this short note to the Director General of Customs in Paris: "In the middle of July a vessel left Ostende for England. Who could have authorised the Director of Customs to allow this vessel to pass? Summon this director to Paris to give an account of his conduct, and send me a report on the matter."

And on the 14th August the Director-General received another letter to this effect: "Let me know how it comes that the *Hercule* of 120 tons, flying the French flag, laden with elephants' teeth, mahogany, &c., arrived at Dunkirk on the 17th July. Who allowed the introduction of this merchandise? Who authorised the admission of the *Conciliateur* which arrived at Genoa on the 11th July with a cargo of ebony, &c.? Also *La Miséricorde*, which discharged on the 11th July at Marseilles a cargo of sulphur, quinquina, &c.; and *La Conception* laden with oils, cottons, &c.?" and in fact the Emperor had to complain of numerous irregularities which greatly disturbed his blockading proclivities.

On the 10th August Napoleon addressed a letter to

Berthier, who, although in Paris, was acting as chief of the army of Spain. In this letter his Majesty directed that the following note should be sent to General Kellermann: "At a moment when his Majesty is collecting in Paris in a single body the archives of the German Empire, those of the Vatican, of France and of the United Provinces, it may be interesting to search what has become of the archives of Charles V. and of Philip II., which would so nicely complete this vast European collection. These archives should be under the care of the governor of Old Castile. This is what the historian Robertson says in his *History of America*:—

"By a singular arrangement of Philip II. the records of the Spanish monarchy are deposited in the *Archivo* of Simancas near Valladolid, at the distance of 120 miles from the seat of government and the supreme courts of justice. The papers relative to America, and chiefly to that early period of its history towards which my attention was directed, are so numerous that they alone, according to one account, fill the largest apartment in the *Archivo*, and, according to another, they compose 873 large bundles. . . ."

The archives were duly sent to Paris, but they were restored to their rightful owners, like so much other plunder, when the allies occupied France.

To GENERAL CLARKE.
"ST. CLOUD, 19*th August*, 1810.

"I have received no details respecting my army of Catalonia. I am ignorant of the manner in which Macdonald has made his movement, what troops he has taken with him, and what cantonments he has left behind him. My army of Catalonia is the only one of which I have no news. . . ." "NAPOLEON."

The fact is that matters were not going on well in that quarter.

To GENERAL CLARKE.

"ST. CLOUD, 22nd *August*, 1810.

"I have received your letter of the 17th, in which you tell me that 200 Englishmen have been removed from the Irish regiment. I believe that I informed you before that I did not wish this regiment to be recruited any longer and that I even proposed to disband all these auxiliaries. Send me a list of the number of Irish who remain, indicating the depots from which they came, and with what English army they were acting when they were taken prisoners. . . Spaniards, Germans, Swiss, Italians, and even French who have been captured while serving against me must not be sent back to Spain. . . ."

"NAPOLEON."

By a note addressed to the Minister of Marine on the 28th August, on the subject of an exchange of prisoners, we find that the French claimed to have in their depôts—

English	10,526
Irish Legion	932
Hostages	500
Spaniards	38,355
TOTAL	50,313

And the English claimed to have—

Frenchmen	43,774
Dutchmen	103
Danes	2,294
Russians	302
TOTAL	46,473

The French Government constantly insisted upon having Frenchmen in exchange for any prisoners they might offer England, whereas England wished to have Englishmen first, on the ground that good French soldiers and sailors were worth more than untrained Portuguese and Spaniards.

To the Minister of Public Worship.

"St. Cloud, 28*th August,* 1810.

"It appears that the number of *curés* who have refused to take the oath in the departments of Rome and Trasimene is 500, and that the number of those who have taken the oath is 900. I think that the 500 *curés* could be dispensed with, and that the 900 *curés* will be sufficient.

"Napoleon."

Few days passed upon which Napoleon did not issue some order for the confiscation of colonial merchandise. On the 29th August, however, he wrote a letter to Champagny, in which he proposed not only to the King of Saxony and the princes of the Confederation of the Rhine, but also to Prussia and to Russia to lay a heavy tax on all the colonial merchandise in their respective countries:

"This," wrote Napoleon, "will create large revenues for those countries. You will take care to make known that this customs measure does not mean to say that colonial merchandise can enter, but only that what exists should pay this contribution. . . . Prussia would gain several millions in this way. . . . The loss will fall upon English commerce and upon the smugglers. . . Reiterate the order for all the colonial produce in the towns on the Oder to be seized, and write to my agents in Frankfort and other commercial towns to let you know the quantity of colonial merchandise in those towns and the place where it can be seized.

"Napoleon."

Talleyrand, having tried to make friends, received the following letter dated from St. Cloud 29th August:—

"I have received your letter which was very painful to me. While you were at the head of the Foreign

Office I closed my eyes to a great many things. I therefore regret that you should have taken a step which recalls so many *souvenirs* which I desire to forget.

"NAPOLEON."

TO THE EMPEROR OF RUSSIA.

"ST. CLOUD, 29*th August*, 1810.

"I cannot allow Prince Kourakine to leave without reiterating to him my feelings towards your Imperial Majesty. Those which I bear your Majesty, as well as the political considerations of my empire, make me desire more and more every day the continuation and the permanence of the alliance which we have contracted. On my side it is proof against all change and no matter what event. I have spoken frankly with Prince Kourakine upon several questions of detail. May I beg your Majesty to accord him your confidence, especially when he speaks of my friendship for you and of my desire to see the alliance which binds us eternal?

"NAPOLEON."

Oh the 2nd September the Emperor, in a letter to Marshal Davoust, said that he had seen with pleasure the seizure at Mecklenburg of twelve ships laden with colonial merchandise. "Let it all be sent to Cologne," he said, "and be confiscated." And the marshal was instructed to act upon this principle, that all colonial merchandise, no matter whether it arrived on board Danish, Swedish, American, or Russian ship and accompanied by a certificate of origin, was good prize.

On the same day his Majesty refused to purchase the wooden hut at Saardam which Peter the Great inhabited for two years. King Louis had announced his intention of purchasing it, but did not. However, the Emperor accorded a pension of 100 francs a month to Widow Mallard, the nurse of Louis XVI., and a similar pension to Widow Laurent, the nurse of the unfortunate monarch's daughter.

On the 6th September the Emperor wrote to Prince Lebrun for maps and papers concerning the island of Java, as it was his intention to send out a large number of frigates to that colony.

Java was the last colony which remained to France, nor did she keep it long.

To the PRINCESS OF PONTE CORVO.

"ST. CLOUD, 6*th September*, 1810.

"MY COUSIN,—I have received your letter of the 4th. You must have long ago been persuaded of the interest which I take in your family. I have no doubt that the noble sentiments with which you have inspired your son will render him worthy of the high destinies to which he is called. "NAPOLEON."

To CHARLES XIII., KING OF SWEDEN.

"ST. CLOUD, 6*th September*, 1810.

"Count Rosen has handed me your letter of the 21st. Your Majesty informs me that the Diet has appointed the Prince of Ponte Corvo Prince Royal of Sweden, and you ask me to allow him to accept. I was little prepared for this news, since your Majesty had informed me that you wished to propose for election the brother of the late Prince Royal. I, however, appreciate the sentiments which have induced the Swedish nation to give this mark of esteem to my people and my army. I authorise the Prince of Ponte Corvo to accept the throne to which he has been called. "NAPOLEON."

To the EMPRESS JOSEPHINE.

"ST. CLOUD, 14*th September*, 1810.

"MY FRIEND,—I have received your letter of the 9th, and am pleased to learn that you are in good health. The

Empress is in fact four months gone in the family way; she is very well, and much attached to me. The little Princes Napoleon (the two sons of Louis—Napoleon Louis and Louis Napoleon) are staying at the pavilion in the park. My health is good enough. I wish to know that you are happy and satisfied. . . . "NAPOLEON."

To MARSHAL BERTHIER.

"ST. CLOUD, 17*th September*, 1810.

"Exactions of all kinds are committed in Spain, and a traffic is made of the liberation of prisoners. Send an officer with a letter to General Kellermann. Write at the same time to Massena to have the individuals guilty of these crimes arrested. Send officers to examine the garrison of Ciudad Rodrigo, and especially the commandant of artillery, who was asked for 200,000 reals to let the garrison go. Let General Becket inquire into this affair. It is high time to put an end to this brigandage. Massena, in one of his letters, says that he has forwarded a list of the contributions levied by Marshal Ney, and which have not been paid in. You have not laid that list before me; make me a report upon it. "NAPOLEON."

There is something grotesque in Massena accusing Ney of plundering.

To MARSHAL BERTHIER.

"FONTAINEBLEAU, 18*th September*, 1810.

"The rumour of the pretended marriage of Prince Ferdinand (Prince of Asturias) with an Austrian princess is much believed in.[1] It is important that you should

---

[1] Comte Miot de Melito, in his *Memoirs* (vol. iii. p. 179), refers to this projected marriage. The fact is that Napoleon more than once thought of getting out of his Spanish difficulty by means of a matrimonial alliance, which would allow him to come to some arrangement with Ferdinand. It was with this view that Talleyrand had been ordered not to let his captive commit himself at Valençay.

write to the commanders of the various army corps in Spain, warning them that this report is nothing but a piece of Parisian gossip; that they should deny with indignation the very idea of a retrograde step. That it has never been a question of such a thing.

"NAPOLEON."

To MARSHAL BERTHIER.

"FONTAINEBLEAU, 19*th September*, 1810.

"To-morrow you must send an officer with a letter to Marshal Massena, telling him to attack and to overthrow the English; that Lord Wellesley has not more than 18,000 men, of which 15,000 are infantry and the rest cavalry and artillery; that General Hill has not more than 6,000 men, and that it is ridiculous to think of 25,000 Englishmen holding the balance against 60,000 Frenchmen; that in not feeling his way, but in attacking boldly after having reconnoitred, he will make them experience severe checks. . . . Marshal Massena has four times more artillery than he requires against the enemy. I am too far away, and the position of the enemy changes too often, for me to be able to give advice as to the manner of attack; but it is certain that the enemy is not in a position to resist. According to authentic news received from spies in London, if the 4,000 men at Cadiz are joined to the English army in Spain, it is only 28,000 strong.

"NAPOLEON."

The above letter led to the battle of Busaco, when Wellington was attacked by Massena, Ney, and Regnier, who after a sanguinary struggle were beaten off with a loss of nearly 5,000 men *hors de combat*. Among the wounded was General Foy. After this repulse, Massena, finding it to be a losing game to "attack boldly," began to feel his way, and to try and turn a position which he had failed to carry in a front attack. Wellington, after having inflicted this blow on a superior force and proved that resistance was not out of the question, retired on the celebrated lines of Torres Vedras, against which Massena, the "spoilt child of victory," Duc de Rivoli, Prince d'Essling, was destined to dash in vain.

To M. DE CHAMPAGNY.

"ST. CLOUD, 20*th September*, 1810.

"Write to Prussia, and speak to M. de Krusemark here, saying that I should like to see the Prussian Government lay a duty on the export of cereals. England is in want of corn, and it will be useful and agreeable to Prussia to levy this contribution from her. Explain this theory to my *chargé-d'affaires* and to my consuls. Let it be equally understood at Dantzic that this duty should be levied in all the ports of the Baltic.

"NAPOLEON."

To MARSHAL DAVOUST.

"ST. CLOUD, 20*th September*, 1810.

"On Sunday I shall hold a parade in Paris, at which will be present the Portuguese legion quartered at Meaux, a battalion of the rear guard of the army of Spain, the Dutch Guard, and my French Guard. My Guard will offer a dinner to all the Portuguese soldiers, and yours must give a dinner to the officers.

"NAPOLEON."

To GENERAL CLARKE.

"ST. CLOUD, 21*st September*, 1810.

"The idea of sending Spaniards to Corfu is bad. Give orders for the Spaniards to be sent to Toulon. . . . At Corfu they would consume provisions, and would betray us on the first opportunity. They must be sent into the interior. . . .

"NAPOLEON."

To GENERAL CLARKE.

"PARIS, 23rd *September*, 1810.

"I have read with surprise a letter from the major of the Irish regiment. I never ordered that the Irishmen who fought for me at Flushing, and who were wounded in my service, should be sent back among the prisoners. . . . I can therefore understand nothing of this gossip. It is contrary to my desire that deserters and Irishmen who have served me should be placed among the prisoners. I do not know what this major means.

"NAPOLEON."

Everything was evidently not working well in Holland, as may be gathered from the following letter addressed to Prince Lebrun on the 25th September:—

"You speak to me of the complaints of the people of Amsterdam, of their uneasiness, and their discontent. Do the Dutch take me for a Grand Pensioner Barnevelt? I shall do what is suitable for the welfare of my Empire, and the clamours of madmen, who think that they know better than I do, inspire me only with contempt.

"NAPOLEON."

In a letter to Berthier of the 29th September, Napoleon ordered the King of Spain to be informed that he was forming an army of the centre to reinforce the army in Spain. Marshal Soult, too, was to be directed to keep on the heels of General Romana and to prevent him from crossing the Tagus. Before this order could have reached Soult the Marquis of Romana had managed to join Wellington with 5,000 men. Unfortunately this gallant Spanish general, who was so highly appreciated by the British commander and by all who knew him, died shortly afterwards of heart disease.

To the EMPEROR OF AUSTRIA.

"FONTAINEBLEAU, 30*th September*, 1810.

"SIR, MY BROTHER AND VERY DEAR BROTHER-IN-LAW,—I have several times seen Count Metternich, and have spoken to him of the friendship I bear your Imperial Majesty. I hope that he will return to Vienna fully persuaded that I take a lively interest in you and in your monarchy. I have been highly satisfied with my stay here. Our present relations reassure me perfectly as to the intentions of your Majesty. I no longer attach any value to the execution of the secret articles of the treaty of Vienna relative to your army. I desire that you will see in my abandonment of the articles a wish to please you and to give you fresh proofs of my esteem and consideration.

"NAPOLEON."

To GENERAL SAVARY.

"FONTAINEBLEAU, 1*st October*, 1810.

"I beg that you will continue to take measures for procuring me all the works published in England, either concerning my policy or on the affairs of the day. I derive very important intelligence from them.

"NAPOLEON."

In spite of remonstrances, the Emperor would continue to read hostile criticisms in the English papers, which invariably threw him into ungovernable fits of fury.

Stringent orders were sent to the Viceroy of Italy with regard to the execution of the decree of August, and he was ordered to see the tariff on colonial produce levied on all such merchandise, not only in warehouses but in shops, and at the same time " not to vex citizens!" He was also directed to despatch 6,000 troops into the Italian cantons of Switzerland, in order "to sequestrate all the colonial merchandise, and to lay a duty on all goods prohibited in Italy, and which are there for the purpose of being introduced by contraband." The Italian *chargé d'affaires* in Switzerland was to be informed that this measure had been rendered necessary by the smuggling which went on in the cantons, and that this occupation would last until peace was concluded with England ; that "this is one of the hostile methods which I employ against England in Mecklenberg and the German ports, and that it does not touch the real neutrality of Switzerland. . . . You must arrest all the scamps banished from the kingdom of Italy, and all the Englishmen you find in that country. . . . . The generals whom you despatch on this duty must issue no proclamations and commit no follies. You must order them to confiscate all the English merchandise, and to lay a duty on all colonial produce.

"I do not wish to address myself direct to Switzerland. There will be no harm in a quarrel between you and that country; afterwards I shall be referred to, and that will deaden the shock; but it must appear as if the blow came from you. You must write in this sense to the *chargé d'affaires* of Italy and of France, and you must say that the government has been driven to take this step through necessity. Besides, you must allow these cantons to enjoy their constitution, and you must not impose any new taxes. The troops must be provisioned by you, and you must place no Frenchmen in the columns. I am assured that there is a large quantity of English merchandise in the Valais custom-house. Order the same operation in the Upper Valais."

And writing on the 6th October to the King of Saxony, the Emperor said—" I regret to see that the pay is several months in arrear. The duty on the colonial merchandise should produce a considerable sum in Saxony and the grand duchy of Warsaw. There is a great deal at Leipsic. . . . . I am on good terms with Austria and with Russia, but this latter power hates the grand duchy so intensely that we must be on our guard. . . . ."

And on the 7th Napoleon addressed instructions to Champagny, who was to insist upon Bavaria executing the tariff, especially upon the Swiss, Austrian, and Bohemian frontiers.

And, evidently losing patience, his Majesty wrote to his foreign minister, to this effect, on the 7th :—" Switzerland is encumbered with colonial produce ; this state of affairs cannot go on. Write to my *chargé d'affaires*, to demand— 1st. That all English and colonial merchandise be sequestrated provisionally, and without delay. 2nd. That all English merchandise being prohibited, all that is sequestrated must be confiscated. 3rd. That all colonial produce seized must be subjected to the same duty as in France. . . ."

To M. DE CHAMPAGNY.

"FONTAINEBLEAU, 8*th October*, 1810.

"The information which Caulaincourt has given you on the subject of the Russian army will enable you to get up the case against Russia. Your correspondence with Warsaw, Bucharest, and other points bordering on Russia, will permit you to rectify this case. I believe that in this manner I can be made acquainted with the force of the Russian army and its movements. You must write to M. Alquier at Stockholm to furnish you with information on the subject of the Russian regiments in Finland.

"NAPOLEON."

To THE VICEROY OF ITALY.

"FONTAINEBLEAU, 12*th October*, 1810.

"The map of the *étapes*[1] of France is no longer sufficient for my daily use. Have one made, which will include Spain, Portugal, Italy, Naples, the Illyrian provinces, Holland, and Germany, as far as the Inn and the Vistula. I require such a map at every moment.

"NAPOLEON."

[1] Halting places.

To M. DE CHAMPAGNY.

"FONTAINEBLEAU, 13*th October*, 1810.

"I send you a draft of instructions for M. de Nerciat. I wish this agent for the present to visit only Syria and Egypt; he must pay attention to St. Jean d'Acre, Jaffa, Rosetta, Alexandria, and the citadel of Cairo, and he must study the political situation of the different parties in Syria and Egypt. . . .

"NAPOLEON."

To M. DE CHAMPAGNY.

"FONTAINEBLEAU, 13*th October*, 1810.

"I send you a letter from General Rapp. I beg that you will have an interview with Prince Kourakine; that you will inform him that a great many vessels laden on English account sail for Russian ports, and that if the Emperor confiscates them he will be doing a thing very useful to the cause of the Continent, and very damaging to England. Speak to him of the sad position in which England finds herself, and point out that she will be obliged to sue for peace if Russia does not open her ports to her. . . .

"NAPOLEON."

To M. DE CHAMPAGNY.

"FONTAINEBLEAU, 17*th October*, 1810.

"I forward a letter, which has just fallen into my hands. Write to M. Otto (ambassador at Vienna) to forewarn him on the subject of the false rumours it contains. Speak in the *Moniteur* of the presents which I made M. de Metternich on his departure, which consisted, I think, of some Gobelin tapestry.

"Send me the draft of a bulletin to forward to my ambassadors, informing them of the truth concerning the false news spread with regard to Spain and the pretended marriage of the Spanish prince, Ferdinand, with a princess of Austria.

"NAPOLEON."

To GENERAL CLARKE.

"FONTAINEBLEAU, 17*th October*, 1810.

"If there are any monks among the Spanish prisoners, you must make them throw off their frocks on crossing the frontier, and have them dressed with coats and mixed up with the other prisoners.

"NAPOLEON."

To THE EMPEROR OF RUSSIA.

"FONTAINEBLEAU, 23*rd October*, 1810.

"Your Majesty has sent me such handsome horses, that I cannot delay thanking you.

"The English suffer greatly from the union of Holland, and the occupation of the Mecklenberg and Russian ports. There are failures every week in London, which spread confusion through the city. . . . I have just seized enormous quantities of English and colonial merchandise in Switzerland and at Frankfort. Six hundred English vessels which were wandering in the Baltic were refused in Mecklenberg and Prussia, and sailed towards the states of your Majesty. Should your Majesty admit them the war will continue. . . .

"NAPOLEON."

On the 3rd November the Emperor sent Berthier a series of instructions for his generals in Spain, in which he more than once employed the phrase—"as soon as the English have re-embarked."

Ten days after this letter was written, Massena had to break up his position in front of Torres Vedras, and to fall back upon Almeida and Ciudad Rodrigo.

To M. DE CHAMPAGNY.

"FONTAINEBLEAU, 4*th November*, 1810."

"Send me the draft of a reply to Prince Kourakine, very polite, very moderate, but which nevertheless shall contain those truths which it is fit that Russia should know. You must tell him that his note has been laid before me; that the assurance given by the Emperor of Russia that he is determined to damage English commerce has given me lively satisfaction, that peace or the continuation of war lies in the hands of Russia; that if she really wishes to hinder commerce in colonial goods, England will make peace within a year; but that Russia must speak frankly, and that up to the present she has followed opposing principles; that there is a proof of this; that the colonial produce at the last fair at Leipsic was brought from Russia in 700 waggons; that to-day all the commerce in colonial goods is done, and that 1,200 merchant vessels, under Swedish, Portuguese, Spanish and American colours, which the English escorted with twenty ships of war, have partly landed their cargoes in Russia: that if Russia desires peace with England she has the means of procuring it; let her confiscate all the goods introduced by the English, and let her unite with France in forcing Sweden to confiscate the immense quantity of merchandise which the English have landed at Gottenburg under all kinds of flags; as for the principle advanced, that while making war with England, Russia does not wish to make war with neutrals, that principle is the result of an error. . . .

"NAPOLEON."

Nothing can better show than the above letter the repugnance with which the obligatory allies of Napoleon entered into his continental blockade and colonial produce systems.

To GENERAL SAVARY.

"FONTAINEBLEAU, 4th November, 1810.

"Send *Madame Mère* a passport for King Louis by which he will be able to go to any part of the south of France or of Italy, and to reside there.

"NAPOLEON."

In a letter addressed to the minister of marine on the 6th November, in which the Emperor ordered him to have a thousand masts which had been purchased in Russia sent to Dantzic, his Majesty said—"Dantzic is mine; there is a French government and a French garrison there"—a fact which of course over-rode the clause in the treaty of Tilsit which constituted Dantzic a free town.[1]

On the 7th November the Emperor ordered his foreign minister to send this letter to M. Laforest, at Madrid—

"The Emperor assembled the Spanish nation at Bayonne and presented one of his brothers as king. The Spanish nation, through its deputies, took the oath of allegiance. Thinking that he had rallied the majority of the nation, the Emperor treated with the King of Spain [brother Joseph].

"Since then the entire Spanish nation rushed to arms; the king driven from his capital was merely general of the French armies. Upon this the Emperor entered Madrid by force.

"Since that epoch a great many battles have been fought. Andalusia and even Seville have been conquered; but for all that, not a Spaniard has joined the king; none of the Spanish forces have fought against *the insurrection*, and 400,000 Frenchmen, alone, have had to conquer all the provinces, all the fortresses, all the towns, all the villages; Spain belongs to the Emperor by right of conquest.

"The King of Spain would be nothing were he not the

[1] *Vide* Art. 6.

brother of the Emperor and the commander of the French armies. He would be of so little importance that not a hamlet ot 4,000 inhabitants but would be stronger than him and all his partisans in Spain. His Guard even is French. Not a Spanish officer of name has shed his blood for the king.

"His Majesty has no longer to deal with Spanish affairs according to the treaty of Bayonne. That treaty has not been ratified by the Spanish nation. His majesty regards it as null and void. He declared very plainly on entering Madrid that if the country did not submit, he would himself assume the crown.

"However, his Majesty having read in the English papers the acts of the *insurgents* assembled in the isle of Leon, under the name of Cortes, wishing to give a new proof of his desire to conciliate all parties and ameliorate the position of his brother, sends the Marquis d'Almenara to Madrid to persuade the king and his cabinet to come to terms with the insurgents, and to propose the convention of Bayonne as the basis of the Spanish constitution. The Emperor will consent to recognise this treaty still if the insurgents will recognise it with good grace, and show themselves desirous of sparing the blood which must still be shed."

La Forest was then instructed to proceed by way of insinuation, but his insinuations were only to be made after the French army had entered Lisbon, and the English army had once more sought refuge on board its ships.

The letter then continued—

"I must acquaint you with the real intentions of the Emperor so that you may know how to act in any unforeseen circumstance. His Majesty is sincere; and, if Lisbon has really been taken, and if the cabinet of Madrid can really decide the insurgents, among whom are many reasonable men, to enter into an arrangement, his Majesty, *beyond a rectification of frontiers* which will give him some indispensable positions, will consent to the integrity of Spain, since that will release the greater portion of his troops, and will finish a war which may still cost much blood.

"But, if this attempt does not succeed, as there is reason to think, the Emperor wishes to be able to show—1st, that the Spaniards themselves consider that the treaty of Bayonne no longer exists; 2nd, to make the guilt of the insurgents more apparent, as also the madness of England (which will have reason to repent), and the fault committed by responsible ministers in refusing the integrity of Spain; 3rd, to make the cabinet of Madrid acknowledge that the insurrection has been the real cause of the ruin of Spain, and not the affairs of Bayonne."

To M. DE CHAMPAGNY.

"FONTAINEBLEAU, 12*th November*, 1810.

"It is indispensable to send to my minister at Berne my decree respecting the annexation of the Valais. He must not make it known until General Cæsar Berthier has entered Sion at the head of the French troops and has taken possession of the country. He must say that this measure *proves the independence of Switzerland*, and that the relations between Italy and Switzerland are settled. . . .

"NAPOLEON."

On the 14th November, Berthier was directed to blame Soult for the small amount of energy he was showing and for having fallen back shamefully on Seville instead of following up Romana.

To PRINCE LEBRUN.

"PARIS, 28*th November*, 1810.

"Have all the merchandise of English manufacture in Holland, in the warehouses, shops, &c., burned at once.

"NAPOLEON."

Napoleon, who was continually insisting upon the necessity of Russia closing her harbours to British commerce, had reason to suspect that his dear friend Alexander was growing weary of an alliance which weighed so heavily on his subjects. Accordingly, on the 5th December he instructed his minister for foreign affairs to write thus to Caulaincourt—"that the Russians are constructing works on the Dwina and even on the Dniester, that he must keep his eyes open, and send a report on this matter; that it is impossible to disguise the fact that these works, being field-works, show a bad spirit on the part of the Russians. After having concluded peace with the Porte do they mean to conclude peace with the English, and to violate the treaty of Tilsit?[1] Allow Caulaincourt to say that this would constitute a case of war."

In another letter within the same day M. de Champagny was directed to furnish the Emperor with a report showing the situation of the troops of the Confederation of the Rhine (some 200,000 men) including the grand duchy of Warsaw; and another on the Russian and Austrian armies.

In a message to the Senate of the 10th December, the Emperor, after explaining the reasons which induced him to annex Holland, said—

"I have had executed the plan of a canal which will be made before five years, and which will connect the Baltic with the Seine. Indemnities will be given to the princes who may feel offended by this great measure, which is commanded by necessity, and which will carry the frontiers of my empire to the Baltic.

"Before coming to this determination I warned England. She knew that the only way to preserve the independence of Holland was to cancel the decrees in council [in reply to decrees of Berlin and Milan]. But that Power was deaf to the voice of its own interests and to the cry of Europe.

[1] *Vide* letter of 6th November.

"I hoped to be able to establish a *cartel* for the exchange of prisoners between France and England, and to take the opportunity of the stay of two commissioners in Paris and London to arrive at an understanding between the two nations. My hopes have been deceived. I recognised in their way of negotiating nothing but *cunning*, and bad faith on the part of the English Government.

"The annexation of the Valais is a consequence foreseen by the immense works which I have been carrying on for the last ten years in that portion of the Alps. . . . As long as the war with England lasts the French people should not lay down their arms.

"My finances are in the most prosperous condition. I can meet all the expenses of this immense empire without demanding any new sacrifices on the part of my people.

"NAPOLEON."

To M. DE CHAMPAGNY.

"PARIS, 17*th December*, 1810.

"I send you a report on the losses of Westphalia. You argue as if Hanover belonged to Westphalia. Hanover does not belong to the King Jerome, for that prince not having executed the treaty which he concluded with me, I look upon it as null and void. I therefore consider that I am in possession of Hanover. The population of the kingdom of Westphalia was 1,900,000 inhabitants. I deduct from that kingdom 200,000 souls, a revenue of so much, taxes to such an amount. *Propose to me to give him* [brother Jerome] *in exchange, the portion of Hanover which I do not take.* . . .

"NAPOLEON."

To COMTE BIGOT (*Minister of Public Worship*).

"PARIS, 23*rd December*, 1810.

"The Prefect of Savona writes that the Pope is disposed to come to terms and to play the pope wherever I like.

This is the first time that I have heard such language. If this *exposé* is exact, and if the Pope be sincere, as I desire nothing better than to enter into an arrangement, you can write to M. Chabrol that I have learned from Prince Borghese, and from the minister of police, that in a conference which he had with the Pope, the Pope said that he would act as pope wherever it was wished; that he would exercise his spiritual power only, without hampering the temporal power; in a word, that he wished to come to an arrangement. . . . I shall make no temporal concession, and if the Pope desires an arrangement he must write a letter to the Emperor on the misfortunes of the Church, &c. This letter must be written without bitterness, with Gospel charity. . . . You must add that the Emperor will no doubt return a favourable reply to such a letter. . . .

"NAPOLEON."

M. Chabrol, the Prefect of Savona, was much mistaken if he really announced that Pius VII. was inclined to yield to either artifice or violence.

To MARSHAL BERTHIER.

"PARIS, 26*th December*, 1810.

"Send an *estafette* to Bayonne, and write to General Foy to say that we have news from London of the 22nd, from which it results that on the 3rd December Massena still occupied Santarem, that he had had some affairs with the English advanced guard, which he repulsed, and that Lord Wellington had resumed his position at Torres Vedras. . . . Send General Foy three copies of the *Moniteur* containing the news received from London yesterday.

"NAPOLEON."

Massena appears to have had no idea of the existence of the lines of Torres Vedras until he found himself in front of that impregnable position which he reconnoitred in vain in the hope of finding some vulnerable point. He had written several letters to Berthier imploring reinforcements, but receiving no reply, he imagined that his despatches must have fallen into the hands of the enemy. At that time it required fully 500 men to take a letter from one point of Spain to another. In his difficulty Massena determined to send General Foy to Paris under a strong escort, and that officer, on his arrival, explained to Napoleon how matters stood, and was able to justify his chief in the eyes of the Emperor. General Foy was on his way back to Spain when the above letter was written.

Massena was right in his conjecture, at least as regards some of his despatches. In one of his intercepted letters he gave a very fair account of the battle of Busaco, in which he acknowledged that he had been repulsed in both his attempts to carry the English position, and that he had lost 4,000 men and a large proportion of his best officers. This did not hinder Napoleon, in the *Moniteur*, transforming Busaco into a French victory, where the English were attacked, turned, and hotly pursued; the French loss was reduced from 4,000 to 200 men. The army of Massena suffered the most terrible privations, but people read in the *Moniteur* that it was amply provided with bread, meat, rice, wine, rum, sugar, and coffee!

After breaking up his position in front of Torres Vedras in the middle of November, Massena had fallen back with great skill upon the strong position of Santarem, in which Wellington did not venture to attack him with the force at his disposal.

CHAPTER II.

THE YEAR 1811.

THERE was peace on the Continent in 1811 between the great powers, or rather a truce. In France and Austria it had been fondly hoped that the marriage between Napoleon and Marie Louise would close the era of war, and that Europe would at least be allowed time to recover itself. The realisation of this hope seemed more probable in the month of March when an heir to the imperial crown was born; the very anxiety of Napoleon to have a direct successor, and to found a dynasty, led people to believe that he would change his warlike policy, and not stake his fortunes in the uncertain game of war. It will be remembered why Cambacérès had voted in favour of a matrimonial alliance with Russia; he felt certain that if that alliance were not concluded, the Emperor would march to St. Petersburg. Prince Metternich, too, was of the same opinion. In the correspondence of 1811 we shall find many symptoms of the storm which was gathering in the north; and before the close of the year it became evident that a collision between the French Emperor and the czar was inevitable. Russia was the only power on the Continent which had not been completely subdued, and "Carthage" had still to be destroyed by means of the continental blockade against which Russia seemed inclined to rebel. We shall find

Napoleon, under various pretences, moving troops and sending arms to the north, and Russia recalling divisions from Finland and the banks of the Danube, and concentrating them on the Polish frontier where danger threatened. We shall also find Prussia, goaded to despair, making some show of resistance, but speedily reduced to obedience, and Sweden also exhibiting signs of impatience; she had been plundered by Russia on one hand, and she was being ruined by France on the other. The czar had despoiled her of Finland, and Napoleon had ruined her commerce by forcing her to adhere to the continental system.

Several letters in 1811 show that Napoleon, in spite of the great naval superiority of England, had not renounced all idea of meeting us once more on the ocean. He was indefatigable in building ships and preparing expeditions, especially an expedition to Ireland which would force the British Government to hurry back its troops from Spain, where matters were not faring well. For the moment, however, all his military ports were strictly blockaded, and none of his fleets dared to put to sea.

His Majesty did not write as many letters on Spanish affairs as might have been expected, or else some letters must have been suppressed, especially concerning the battle of Fuentes de Honor, and the removal of Massena, who was replaced by Marmont, whose military capacity was not to be compared to that of "the darling child of victory." The French were surprised at Sabugal and at Arroyo del Molinos, they lost a post at Olivenza, they evacuated Almeida, they were defeated at Albuera and at Fuentes de Honor, and obliged to retire from Portugal.

In 1811 Napoleon found time to occupy himself a good deal with the affairs of the Church. As Lanfrey observes in his message to Parliament of the 29th June, the Emperor referred to his difference with the Holy See without allowing any one to suspect the harsh way in which he had behaved towards the Pope personally.

Napoleon said, "I have united Rome to my empire," and as an excuse for wishing the pontiff to reside in Paris, he remarked that the Pope liked to be in the centre of Christendom. "It was thus that St. Peter preferred Rome to remaining in the Holy Land." Pius VII. was still a prisoner at Savona, and he still refused to consecrate the bishops named by Napoleon. The Emperor imagined to have the bishops consecrated by their various chapters. The pontiff gave the chapters to understand that they were not to elect bishops. The amount of opposition which ensued, greatly incensed the Emperor, who threw the Abbé d'Astros, one of the boldest adherents of the Pope, into Vincennes, where he remained till the fall of the empire. Cardinals di Pietro, Oppizoni, and Gabrielli, who had distributed the papal brief, shared the same fate, while several members of the chapters of Asti and Florence were committed to the cells of Fenestrelle, in which were Cardinal Pacca and a number of other ecclesiastics.

Napoleon thought seriously of deposing the Pope, but he ended by trying what physical suffering would do. Orders were given for Pius VII. to be treated with the greatest severity; his few comforts were suppressed; he was strictly guarded, he was deprived of his carriages, he was forbidden to hold any communication or to correspond with any one outside the walls of his prison; his confessor and his intimate servants were thrown into prison; his papers were seized, his pen, ink and paper, even his breviary and a purse containing a few pieces of gold were taken from him. It may well be asked if Napoleon, when complaining of his treatment at St. Helena, remembered how he had treated a venerable and defenceless old man.

Napoleon next imagined to summon a council, but first of all he got Cardinal Fesch and nineteen bishops to sign a document in which they implored the Pope not to reduce the Church of France to the dire extremity of providing for her own preservation. Three bishops were sent to Savona to try and shake the determination of Pius VII. who naturally insisted that a prisoner and deprived of the aid of his usual counsellors, he could not possibly come to a determination which would greatly modify the constitution of the Church. The bishops however persevered, and after a long struggle, the Pope, driven almost out of his mind, consented, not to sign, but to accept a note giving satisfaction to most of the demands of the Emperor.

Napoleon was not satisfied. The council was summoned, and its first sitting terminated by a solemn oath of obedience to the Pope, and it was with great difficulty that Cardinal Fesch prevented his colleagues from going to St. Cloud to throw themselves at the feet of the Emperor and to implore the liberty of the pontiff. After a time the council, upon the report of the Bishops of Tournay, Bordeaux, and Ghent, pronounced itself incompetent to usurp the rights of the Church. The consequence was that the council was dissolved and the Bishops of Tournay, Bordeaux and Ghent were arrested and flung into Vincennes.

His Majesty now set Savary to work, and such was the terror inspired by the minister of police, that when Napoleon convoked another council in August, the prelates voted a decree to the effect that if before six months the Pope did not consecrate Napoleon's bishops, they were to be consecrated without him. The Pope accepted his Majesty's demands with some slight reserves concerning the Gallican Church, and here the matter remained for a time as the Emperor had to turn his attention from spiritual affairs to those of Russia, where a storm was rapidly brewing. He left the Pope's affectionate letter, accepting the decrees, unanswered until his return from Moscow, and he did not communicate the papal brief to his council of state, hoping to obtain even more than he had done from the unfortunate Pius after the Russian campaign.

Napoleon appears to have written only two letters on the 1st January. In the first he complained to Marshal Davoust, who was in command of the army of Germany, that his ex-Secretary, Bourrienne, civil governor of Hamburg, had gained 7 or 8,000,000 francs by selling licences and by other malpractices. The second letter, addressed to King Jerome, ran thus—

"My brother, I thank you for what you say on the occasion of the new year. I hope that you may have a son this year. It is the best thing I can wish you."

Although General Miollis had exceeded orders in laying violent hands on the Pope, Napoleon was determined not to let his Holiness escape. On the 2nd January he wrote thus to his brother-in-law, Prince Borghese, governor of the transalpine departments.

"It is necessary to send a company of the 4th regiment of artillery to Savona, and to keep the guns of the citadel in good order. I even desire you will always keep 100,000 rations of biscuit in that place so that in case of emergency the garrison may be able to throw itself into the citadel, with the Pope."

To PRINCE EUGENE.

"PARIS, 3rd *January*, 1811.

"They have just discovered a party of the Pope here. An Abbé Gregori and an Abbé Fontana, whom I brought here from Rome, were the intermediaries of a correspondence between the Pope and the Vicars-General of Paris. They have been arrested with their papers; it results that the Pope has been guilty of the most horrible conduct joined to the greatest hypocrisy. . . .

"NAPOLEON."

And on the 5th his Majesty wrote to Barbier to know if there existed any examples of emperors having suspended or deposed popes, and to Comte Bigot to sound the French bishops on the subject of summoning a National Council, and to draw up a report on these matters—" The refusal of the Pope to confirm the bishops; on his bull of excommunication; on his absence from Rome; on the liberty he enjoyed at Savona, on the abuse he made of it; on the letters he wrote to Cardinal Fesch, showing the state of irritation and frenzy with which he is animated; on his letters to Cardinal Maury and to the Grand Vicar of Astros." The Archbishops of Paris, Lyons, Tours, Malines, Toulouse, Turin, and Bordeaux were to be consulted on these matters.

On the 6th January, 1811, Napoleon, in reply to an address on the part of the Chapter of Paris, complained bitterly of the conduct of the Pope, and explained his own deep political designs to his astonished audience: He told them how it was necessary in the struggle which he had undertaken against heretic England, that he should be master of the Adriatic and be able to close all the ports of Italy to that Power. "But," pursued the Emperor, "these great considerations had no influence on the mind of the Pope. He confined himself to replying that he had no reason for declaring against the English; that he was the common father of the faithful; that he should not deprive himself of the means of communicating with the faithful in countries beyond the sea. I could not, however, leave him at the mercy of the English. A long negotiation ensued. . . . He did not confine himself to insults— he excommunicated me, my ministers, and all the persons employed in my government." Napoleon afterwards spoke in violent terms of some letters which the Pope had secretly written and which were circulated through the empire. "These culpable letters were taken from Savona to Lyons," he said, "by a *valet-de-chambre* of Pius VII., and it was a woman who from Lyons brought them even to Paris. The Abbé d'Astros, the Prelate Gregori, and Father Fontana dipped their hands in this intrigue, and that is why I punished them." His Majesty, after speaking at some length in his usual strain, explained the conditions upon which he was willing to release Pius VII. The above is not to be found in *The Correspondence.*

On the 10th January Napoleon announced that he had organised the Grand Army in four corps. The two first, under the orders of Davoust and Oudinot, were on the Elbe; the third, under Ney, was to occupy Mayence, Dusseldorf, and Dantsic. In other words, the Emperor was moving towards the Russian frontier.

King Joseph had sad complaints to make against General Belliard, who had been left in command of Madrid by Napoleon, who on the 17th January wrote to Berthier—"If it be true that the King of Spain has deprived Genera Belliard of the government of Madrid, let it be restored to him without delay: this is my formal order." And his Spanish Majesty consented to reign on such terms!

To COMTE BIGOT.

"PARIS, 29*th January*, 1811.

"I send you back your report on Papal affairs; I find it incorrect. For instance, the union of the Papal States to the Empire did not take place until the Pope was at Savona. You must not speak of the marriage and the legitimacy of the child; that is too absurd.[1] You must say that it was found necessary to remove the Pope from Rome because he wished to excite a revolution, and that I ordered him to be taken to Savona. Say nothing about Grenoble. . . . You must show how the Pope has constantly endeavoured to weaken the power of France, and quote the briefs which I received the day after the victories of Austerlitz and Friedland, in which I was insulted because he thought that I would be beaten. . . .

"NAPOLEON."

In a letter addressed to Marshal Bessières on the 2nd February Napoleon said: "I have appointed Brigadier-General Dumesnil commandant at Vincennes."

[1] The King of Rome, who was expected.

The gallant Dumesnil, nicknamed *Jambe de Bois*, gave serious trouble to the allies when Napoleon abdicated, by refusing to surrender Vincennes until a leg which he had lost in battle was restored to him. The statue of this obstinate warrior now stands in one of the avenues leading to the fort he persisted in holding, and his name is still popular in France.

In a letter to his War Minister, dated the 3rd February, the Emperor wrote: "If I were to have war with Russia, I reckon that I should require 200,000 muskets with bayonets for the Polish insurgents." A good many letters were written at this time about the purchase of arms. Austria had 50,000 French muskets to sell!

On the 9th February Napoleon wrote to General Clarke, complaining of the number of conscripts who escaped service. On the march to Rome twenty-nine out of 100 deserted at Breglio; on the 28th November thirty-eight escaped at a short distance from Toulon, and on the 24th December twenty more, and so on.

To ADMIRAL DÉCRÈS.

"PARIS, 14*th February*, 1811.

"The first time that you write to the Transport Office you may mention that a man named Kolli, who says he is an Irishman, and who was the bearer of a letter written by the King of England and a commission appointing him plenipotentiary minister to Ferdinand VII., is among the prisoners, and that the Emperor would be willing to exchange him for a person of the same rank.

"NAPOLEON."

At this date Ferdinand was supposed to be on the best of terms with his Imperial jailer. He had asked him to remove that scheming monk Don Juan de Escoiquiz, and had written to him assuring him of his "blind obedience," expressing his confidence in that generosity which characterised him, and asking Napoleon to adopt him as his son.

The *Annual Register*, in the State Papers for 1811, gives an account of the Kolli affair, and says that the baron was betrayed by Ferdinand!

On the 17th the Emperor, evidently determined to deal Russia a blow, wrote these two letters to M. Champagny:—

"I desire you to send a courier to Constantinople. Write to M. Latour-Maubourg to make advances to the Porte, and, without compromising himself, to act so that the Sultan may write to me and send me an ambassador; that on my side I will reply and will send an ambassador. While passing through Vienna the courier must hand a letter to M. Otto reassuring him. . . ."

And in the second letter:—

"I beg that you will send a courier to St. Petersburg to-morrow, sending letters of recall to Caulaincourt. You must inform him that after having conferred with the Russian Government he can quit his post on the ground of having obtained leave for two months, or as having been replaced and presenting his letters of recall, according as the Emperor of Russia may deem fit; but in either case he must make known at St. Petersburg that I desire to replace him by the Comte de Narbonne, the Comte de Larochefoucauld, or the Comte Lauriston; that I wish to know which of the three will be most agreeable to the Emperor Alexander. You must give Caulaincourt instructions on the subject of the Oldenburg affair. I did what I could in the way of giving the Czar an exact and real indemnity.

"You must tell Caulaincourt to have a conference with M. de Romanzoff and with the Emperor; to declare to both that I persist in the alliance; that I cannot foresee any possible circumstance for inducing me to make war with Russia unless Russia should side with England; that I have no alliance with any Power, and that my policy remains unchanged."

His Majesty had appropriated Oldenburg a month

before, and was of course well aware of the effect which such an insult would have on the Court of St. Petersburg. The Duke of Oldenburg was the brother-in-law of the Czar, having married the Grand Duchess Catherine, whose hand Napoleon had demanded at Erfurth.

On the 19th the Emperor wrote thus to the Grand Chamberlain :—

"The service of the ushers of the chamber is very badly performed. At the Privy Council which I held yesterday everything was arranged upside down : that is not astonishing; the door of the grand apartments was kept by a valet. The service of the ushers was never worse done. Strike the man called Henri off the list of ushers, and see that the door of my cabinet, and especially that of the grand apartments, is in charge of ushers."

TO M. DE CHAMPAGNY.

"PARIS, 25*th February*, 1811.

"I have read with attention the letters from Stockholm. There is so much effervescence and turmoil in the head of the Prince of Sweden, that I attach no importance to the communication he has addressed to Baron Alquier. I wish nothing to be said about it to the Minister of Denmark, or to the Minister of Sweden, and I desire to ignore it until further orders.[1] . . . Write to my minister in Denmark to tell the Danish Government to keep the fortified places in Norway in good order, . . . to encourage and support Denmark, and say that as long as she acts thus I shall sustain her with the whole force of my empire. . . . Write to my minister at Stockholm that I attach no importance to the overture made by the Prince of Sweden ; that I am sufficiently powerful to stand in need of no one to help me ; that my relations with Russia are excellent, and that

---

[1] Bernadotte, Prince of Sweden, had offered, in the event of war between France and Russia, to invade Finland, and to threaten St. Petersburg, provided that Napoleon would aid Sweden to recover Norway from Denmark.

I have no fear of war with that country; that I am in a good situation as regards Austria ; but, *that as my finances are in so prosperous a condition I have augmented my armies by* 150,000 *men, and that I calculate upon doing the same next year.* He ought, however, to insinuate that as long as the alliance with Denmark lasts, France cannot permit any harm to be done to Norway. This should be said very gently, and some time after the arrival of the courier. He must add that to wish to take Norway would be a piece of folly on the part of Sweden ; that Russia would be no more satisfied than Denmark, as, mistress of Norway, Sweden would be better able to recover Finland. . . .

"NAPOLEON."

In a P.S. the Emperor admitted that he had no system with regard to the countries in question, and directed that Baron Alquier should speak in general terms.

On the same day M. de Champagny was directed to send a courier to Vienna with instructions for M. Otto, who was to speak about the approaching confinement of the Empress, and to express the hope that this event would draw closer the bonds uniting the two empires. M. Otto was also directed to "sound M. de Metternich on the subject of a near war between Russia and Turkey, to know what Austria wishes and is inclined to do. By the treaty of Tilsit, France stipulated the restoration of Moldavia and Wallachia to the Porte. Since then, at Erfurth, the Czar persuaded France to ignore that clause, and to meddle no more with the question. France agreed to this through hatred of Austria, who was then arming, nothing being more opposed to the interests of the Austrian monarchy than the occupation of those provinces by Russia. To-day France regrets to see this large territorial increase on the part of Russia, all the more so because the last ukase will exclude French silks and produce from Moldavia and Wallachia. But it is to be hoped that the Porte will be able to defend the two provinces against Russia for another year. Is it not to be feared that in addition to these provinces the Porte may lose Servia or see Russia establish a hospodar there? France cannot express any opinion contrary to the possession of Moldavia and Wallachia by the Russians without annoying them and driving them to make peace with England, a peace which would inevitably lead to war between France and Russia. Besides, Russia has gone too far to renounce the two provinces to-day in cold blood. Lastly, France has only a secondary interest in Moldavia and Wallachia, whereas they are of first-rate interest to Austria; it is important to know how far Austria is disposed to go, and what she is in a position to do to hinder their union to Russia.

"All this should be said in conversation, vaguely, in order to feel the ground and to form an idea. The union of the two empires, the happy circumstance of the confinement of the Empress, which draws them closer together; it is from this point that you must start in order to try and discover the real intentions of the ministry. The displeasure occasioned by the occupation of Moldavia and Wallachia, does it go so far as to make Austria not fear a war with Russia? Then what is her system in this affair? What hopes does she conceive from the resistance of the Turks? Tell Comte Otto to find out the names and the strength of the Russian regiments in the two provinces.

"NAPOLEON."

Three days after writing the above instructions, Napoleon addressed the following observations to his dear ally of the raft on the Neimen. He began by saying that Caulaincourt being ill he wished to replace him by the Comte de Lauriston, and he was profuse in his expressions of attachment to the Czar, but he added—"I cannot disguise from myself that your Majesty has no longer any friendship for me. You raise all kinds of difficulties on the subject of Oldenburg, when I do not refuse to give an equivalent for that country, which has always been a hot bed of English smugglers, and when the situation of that country rendered it indispensable that I should unite it to my states. The last ukase of your Majesty, in spirit, and especially in form, is directly aimed at France. In other days, before adopting such a measure against my commerce, your Majesty would have given me warning. . . . All Europe views the matter in this light; and already our alliance has ceased to exist in the eyes of England and of Europe. . . . Allow me to say frankly to your Majesty that you forget the benefits you have derived from this alliance; and yet what has happened since Tilsit? By the treaty of Tilsit you should have restored Moldavia and Wallachia to Turkey; yet, instead of restoring those provinces, you have united them to your empire. Moldavia and Wallachia form a third part of Turkey in Europe; it is an immense acquisition which in resting the vast empire of your Majesty on the Danube, deprives Turkey of all force, and, it may be said, annihilates that Power—*my most ancient ally*. However, instead of holding to the execution of the treaty of Tilsit, in the most disinterested manner, and by pure friendship for your Majesty, I recognised the annexation of those fine and rich countries; but, without my confidence in your friendship, several unfortunate campaigns would not have induced France to see her oldest ally thus despoiled. In Sweden, when I restored the conquests which I had made in that country, I consented that your Majesty should keep Finland, which was the third of Sweden, and a province so important for your Majesty, that it may be said Sweden no longer exists. And yet Sweden, in spite of the false policy of its king, was one of the oldest friends of France. Insinuating men, urged on by England, fatigue the ears of your Majesty with calumnies. They say that I wish to re-establish Poland. I was master to do this at Tilsit. Twelve days after Friedland I might have been at Wilna. If I had wished to re-establish Poland, I should have disinterested Austria at Vienna; she asked to preserve her ancient provinces and her communications with the sea, and that her sacrifices might fall on her Polish possessions. I might have re-established Poland in 1810, when all the Russian troops were engaged against the Porte. I might do so at present without waiting for your Majesty to come to terms with the Porte. As I have not done so under any of these circumstances, it must be because the re-establishment of Poland does not enter into my views. But if I change nothing in the condition of Poland, I have the right to insist that no one shall interfere with what I do on this side of the Elbe. However, it is true that our enemies have succeeded. The fortifications which your Majesty is constructing at twenty points along the Dwina, the protests in connection with Oldenburg and the ukase prove it. I feel the same towards you, but I am struck by the evidence of facts and the idea that your Majesty is inclined, on the first opportunity, to make an arrangement with England, which would be equivalent to kindling war between the two countries. . . . I beg your Majesty to read this letter calmly, and to see nothing in it but what is conciliatory, calculated to remove all kinds of distrust, and to re-establish between the two nations that intimate alliance which for nearly four years has been so beneficial."

Up to the very moment of drawing the sword the two potentates who were so recently engaged in dividing the world between them, were profuse in their assurances of friendship but neither deceived the other, and both knew in what these negotiations would end.

On the 2nd March, 1811, the Emperor wrote a letter to Comte Bigot, which is not inserted in *The Correspondence*, saying—" I desire that 100 more of the worst priests be sent from Parma and Placentia to Spezzia, and be there embarked for Corsica. Let the minister of police take measures for sending the necessary funds to Corsica.

Write to General Morand that all these priests must be disembarked at Bastia and united at the same place. . ."[1]

In replying to a deputation from Finistère on the 3rd March the Emperor said: "I shall go to Brest as soon as possible. The power of my people is such that in four years I shall have more than 100 line-of-battle ships and 200 frigates. The sailors of the Adriatic and those of the Baltic already rival my Bretons and Provençals in zeal and courage, in order to contribute to the liberation of the sea, which interests, not only my empire, but all the other nations in the world."

And although trade and commerce were represented as so flourishing, on the 4th his Majesty wrote to Mollien saying: "I authorise you to employ a million [40,000*l*.] in making advances to the manufacturers of Amiens. . . . I authorise you to have purchases made at Rouen, St. Quentin, and Ghent for 2,000,000 by the bank. Follow these operations secretly and with all due prudence."

In a letter addressed to Admiral Décrès on the 8th March, the Emperor thus explained his naval tactics for 1811:—

"I do not wish my squadrons to put to sea, but that they must be always provisioned as if about to sail; that sealed orders, to be opened at a certain distance from land, be frequently despatched to the various ports, so that my admirals themselves may think that they are about to sail. . . . This will oblige the English to blockade me with five squadrons, or sixty vessels." He then spoke of sending 30,000 men to Ireland, of expeditions to Sicily or Egypt, to St. Domingo, Martinique, Cayenne, Surinam,

[1] Number of priests who suffered persecution since *senatus consultum* of 17th February, 1810:—Thirteen Italian cardinals deprived of the emblems of their dignity, and detained in France under the supervision of the imperial police. Nineteen bishops of the Papal States sent from Rome to France under the escort of gendarmes to live there under the same conditions. Similar measures struck a number of canons and grand vicars, and more than two hundred priests were transported to Corsica.

the East and West Indies, and the Cape of Good Hope. He wrote five long letters to Admiral Décrès on the same day upon his naval conceptions, which, however, depended a good deal on the turn taken by affairs in Spain. Once able to withdraw his troops from that country, he would, avoiding the British cruisers, spread 80,000 men over the two hemispheres.

To M. DE CHAMPAGNY.

"PARIS, 10*th March*, 1811.

"Send a courier to St. Petersburg with a letter from General Lauriston to Count Romanzoff, announcing his approaching departure, his desire to be agreeable, and the hope that his mission will meet with the approbation of the Czar. Inform Caulaincourt that the English intend sending a large fleet into the Baltic, and that I have thought fit to reinforce Dantsic with a few companies of infantry and artillery; that the infantry is all Saxon or Polish, that only a portion of the artillery is French... Tell him to say that I am this year forming large camps at Toulon, Boulogne, the Escaut, and at Texel [very far from the Russian frontier]; that the levies are aimed at England; that I have no wish to search a quarrel with Russia, but that I shall be obliged to declare war should she conclude peace with England. . . .

"NAPOLEON."

To GENERAL CLARKE.

"PARIS, 11*th March*, 1811.

"I have received your report on the Irish regiment. Send me a more detailed report, informing me if the officers of that corps are Irish, and if there are means of creating an Irish regiment *principally recruited among Germans*. This regiment might be useful in the event of an expedition to Ireland. . . .

"NAPOLEON."

On the 16th March Napoleon addressed a long note to the ecclesiastical committee, in which he recapitulated the crimes of the Pope. He said: "Bulls and letters have been printed by órder of the Pope and spread through the whole of Christendom; it was not his fault that the scenes of Clement, of Ravaillac, and of Damiens were not renewed; that I was not abandoned by my people and by my armies like Philippe le Long. I am therefore obliged to admit that if the thunders of the Church have had little effect, I have to thank the intelligence of the age, and perhaps the fact that religion has lost a great deal in the minds 'of all the people of Europe. . . .

"I have decided upon assembling a Council of the West, to which I shall summon the bishops of Italy and Germany. . . . I desire to know, 1st, how the convocation should be made, 2nd, what matters should be treated with the view of causing the scandalous struggles between the temporal and the spiritual to disappear, struggles which have been so baneful to religion, for they have occasioned the separation of the Greek Church, of that of England, and of all the northern powers. How shelter my empire from the hatred and enmity of the Court of Rome which will constantly fall on my descendants as it fell on the descendants of Charlemagne. . . ."

On the 19th March M. de Champagny was instructed to give plausible explanations to Prince Kourakine on the subject of the 12,000 men sent to Dantsic and a large number of guns and muskets sent to Dresden.

To THE EMPEROR OF AUSTRIA.

"PARIS, 20*th March*, 1811.

"SIR, MY BROTHER, AND FATHER-IN LAW,—Yesterday at 7 P.M. the Empress sent for me. I found her on a couch beginning to feel the first pains of child-birth. She went to bed at eight o'clock, and from that time until six she suffered severely. The doctor thought that this deliverance would be delayed for twenty-four hours, which made me send away the court, and tell the senate, the municipal body, and the chapter of Paris that they could withdraw. This morning at eight o'clock the *accoucheur* came to me in a great state of mind to tell me that the deliverance would be very difficult and would be attended with great danger for the child. The Empress, very weak from pain, showed the greatest courage, and at nine the faculty having declared that not a moment was to be lost, the deliverance took place, accompanied by great pain, but with complete success. The child is in perfect health and the Empress as well as can be expected; she has slept a little and taken some food. Your Majesty can have no doubt of the satisfaction which I experienced; the hope of this event perpetuating the bonds which unite us is considerably increased.

"NAPOLEON."

A similar announcement was sent to all the members of the imperial family with the exception of the fugitive Louis.

To the EMPRESS JOSEPHINE.

"PARIS, 22*nd March*, 1811.

"MY FRIEND,—I have received your letter and thank you. My son is big and healthy. I hope that he will grow up well. He has my chest, my mouth, and my eyes. I trust that he will fulfil his destiny. I continue to be satisfied with Eugene; he has never given me any pain.

"NAPOLEON."

On the 24th March Napoleon sent pages of instructions to Marshal Davoust, who was commanding at Hamburg, explaining that he expected Russia would force on a war next year when she had finished with the Turks. The marshal was to represent all his military preparations as directed against England, and he was to persuade Prince Poniatowski to form national guards in all the towns in

Poland, and to say that he had 100,000 muskets packed up for arming them.

On the 25th March Napoleon wrote a long letter to M. de Champagny on the subject of Mecklenburg, which country was threatened with the loss of its independence unless it adhered to the continental system and furnished 600 good sailors to France : " I have no need of Mecklenburg," said his Majesty, " but I shall annex it if it does not second me in my three principal means of war against England. I am not obliged to respect any one, since the English respect no one at sea." The same sort of language was to be held to Prussia by Comte de St. Marsan, who was instructed to call on the Prussian Government to prevent smuggling, to intercept all commercial communications with England, and to try and persuade Prussia as delicately as possible to furnish 1,000 sailors. He was also to say clearly that peace would depend on the observation of the treaty of Tilsitt and the execution of the Berlin decree. Similar threats were to be held out to Denmark and Sweden. The ambassador of the latter country was to be told that, "if an American, Danish, Swedish, Spanish, or Russian vessel laden with colonial produce is admitted into any of the ports of Swedish Pomerania, my troops and custom house officers shall at once take possession of that province."

On the 26th March Napoleon directed M. de Champagny to send further instructions to his ambassador at Vienna with regard to Russia. He had no idea of allowing the Russians to establish themselves in Servia, and to threaten the tranquillity of Dalmatia and his Illyrian provinces.

"The influence of the new Servian Government," M. de Champagny was to write to M. Otto, "would extend along the whole shore of the Adriatic to the Mediterranean ; a Grecian sovereignty established in Servia would arouse the pretensions and the hopes of 20,000,000 Greeks from Albania to Constantinople, who, on account of their religion, can rally only round Russia, and the Turkish empire would be wounded to the heart.

"The Emperor wishes you therefore to declare to the Court of Vienna that he will not permit the Russians, after the peace, to preserve any influence in Servia, or to establish a government of their choice there. If you find the Austrian Cabinet favourable, you can even concert measures with it, so that on the conclusion of peace Servia may be restored to the Porte.

"The Emperor Alexander entered into an engagement with the Emperor Napoleon to keep nothing in Servia. The occupation of Belgrade is a violation of this promise. . . ."

This Servian affair was to be kept quite clear from the Moldavian Wallachian affair, concerning which Austria had not yet replied.

On the 27th March the Emperor instructed M. de Champagny to inform Prince Kourakine that the measures taken by Russia necessitated measures on the part of France which "this year cost 4,000,000*l.*; that it was the Czar who commenced. . . ."

To M. DE CHAMPAGNY

"Paris, 2nd *April*, 1811.

"I forward you a report from Marshal Marmont with regard to the request of Prince Schwartzenberg relative to affairs in Illyria. You should see the Marshal in order to draw up a reply, and try if it would not be better to settle the mortmain affairs. Austria can then do what she likes with the Church property on her side, and I shall be able to seize upon all on my side. Matters will thus be equally balanced, and it can be proved in a note that Austria began.

"There is a report that the Emperor of Austria has assumed the title of King of Dalmatia. M. Otto has said nothing about this.

"Napoleon."

On the 2nd April the Emperor addressed a long letter to the King of Wirtemberg asking for a regiment. The kings of Saxony, Bavaria, and Westphalia had contributed one each. The object was to protect Dantsic from the English or any other Power. Napoleon added:—

"I hope and believe that Russia will not go to war. However, since the end of last year, she has raised new regiments, and is marching divisions from Finland, Siberia, and Moldavia, to the frontiers of the Grand Duchy of Warsaw, &c. These are facts. All that is repeated to the Czar for the last six months is false. They have made him believe, for example, that I have asked the Confederation for troops. His commercial ukase proves that his policy has changed; not that he was not at liberty to adopt this measure, but one remarks in it something favourable to England and hostile to France. Now the Emperor alone in Russia was in favour of the alliance against England.

"Under these circumstances your Majesty will not, I am sure, allow me to entertain any doubts with regard to the Confederation, doubts which would entirely upset the system in which you have found tranquillity and happiness. . . . I annexed Hamburg and the Hanse towns because I was unable to count upon them in my system against England. If the princes of the Confederation allow me to entertain the smallest doubt with regard to their intentions, I frankly declare that they will ruin themselves; for I prefer having open enemies to having doubtful friends. As soon as I think I shall have an enemy the more I shall raise an additional 30,000 men."

After pointing to the melancholy fate which overtook the King of Prussia, who wept before Jena, and the Emperor of Austria, Napoleon went on to say:—

"I am not far from thinking that the same fate will befall the Czar. . . . If Alexander desires war, public opinion is in conformity with his intentions; if he does not wish for war, and does not quickly stop the impetus which has been given, he will be carried away by it next year; and thus war will take place in spite of him, in spite of me, in spite of the interests of France and those of Russia. I have seen this happen so often that my experience of the past unveils the future. All this is an operatic scene, the shifting of which is in the hands of the English. If anything can remedy the situation, it is the frankness with which I have explained matters to Russia. . . . Lastly, your Majesty cannot suppose that I wish for war. Why should I wage war? To re-establish Poland? I might have done that after Tilsit, after Vienna, this year. . . . Then I have war with Spain and Portugal, extending over a country larger than France, and occupying a large number of men; then I cannot desire war. And yet I have this year raised 120,000 men, and next year I shall raise 120,000 more. I am forming new regiments, &c., &c., because I suspect that Russia is acting in such a manner that war will break out in 1812. My extraordinary expenditure this year amounts to 4,000,000*l*. Do you think that it amuses me to incur expenses so considerable? But if I do not wish for war, and if I am far from desiring to be the Don Quixote of Poland, I have the right to insist upon Russia remaining faithful to the alliance, and I must take measures not to permit her to come to me when she has concluded the war with Turkey, and to say, 'I am going to withdraw from the alliance, and to make peace with England.' . . .

"NAPOLEON."

Caulaincourt had been recalled from St. Petersburg owing to lukewarmness, and because he evidently disapproved of the policy of his master.

On the 5th April M. de Champagny was directed to send instructions to this effect to Comte Lauriston at St. Petersburg. That the Emperor would not go to war about Poland, nor the ukase which damaged his commerce, but only in the event of Russia seizing upon

Servia, or, tearing up the treaty of Tilsit, concluding peace with England. Napoleon was determined not to allow Greek influence to creep down by way of Montenegro and the Morea to the Mediterranean. He added in his instructions:—

"As for Moldavia and Wallachia, it may be said that Russia holds those provinces from France. The policy of the Emperor at the present moment is not to meddle with them; but no declaration must be made to this effect, because if matters become more embroiled it is probable that Russia will end by losing those two provinces. . . .

"NAPOLEON."

To THE EMPEROR ALEXANDER.

"PARIS, 6*th April*, 1811.

"As soon as I learned that the choice of Comte Lauriston was agreeable to your Majesty, I gave him orders to start. I do not send your Majesty a man skilled in diplomacy, but a man true and straightforward as the feelings I bear you; and yet the news which I daily receive from Russia is not pacific. Yesterday I learned that the Russian divisions in Finland were marching on the Grand Duchy, and that five divisions had left Moldavia and Wallachia for Poland. . . . This is the repetition of what happened in Prussia in 1807, and in Austria in 1809. As for myself, I shall remain the personal friend of your Majesty, even should that fatality which drags Europe along place arms in the hands of our two nations. . . . I shall not be the first to attack, and my troops shall not advance until your Majesty has torn up the treaty of Tilsit. . . . "NAPOLEON."

To THE PRINCE ROYAL OF SWEDEN.[1]

"PARIS, 6*th April*, 1811.

"MY COUSIN,—I have received the letter in which you inform me that the King of Sweden, owing to a serious

[1] Bernadotte.

illness, has decided to hand over to you the administration of the kingdom. This circumstance, painful to your heart, offers you an opportunity of showing the nation over which you have been called to reign what it has to expect from your devotion to its glory and its happiness. I hope that your efforts will be crowned with success. I renew with pleasure my assurances of esteem and friendship.

"NAPOLEON."

To COMTE DE MONTALIVET.

"PARIS, 13th April, 1811.

"I have fixed upon the 2nd June for the baptism of the King of Rome, which will be celebrated in the church of Notre Dame, to which I and the Empress will repair to render thanks to God for his birth. After the ceremony at Notre Dame, I shall dine at the Hotel de Ville of my good city of Paris, and I shall witness a display of fireworks. The same day a *Te Deum* must be sung throughout the whole Empire. I desire *fêtes* and rejoicings to take place at the same time. . . . You must send me a list of the marriages which can be performed in each of the principal towns, endowing poor girls and orphans, and uniting them to old soldiers.

"NAPOLEON."

To MARSHAL DAVOUST, AT HAMBURG.

"PARIS, 16th April, 1811.

"I send you two fine Spanish battalions forming 2,000 men, with a general. The soldiers are good; they volunteered, and have served for two years. I think that they will fight like the Portuguese, and that there will be very few deserters if not sent to the outposts. . . . It is probable that they will be surrounded by pimps. The police should keep their eyes on these battalions; they will catch lots of English agents.

"NAPOLEON."

Lord Londonderry mentions that when Almeida fell, a large portion of the garrison volunteered to serve in the French army, possibly preferring the chance of desertion to a French prison.

On the same day Napoleon sent the King of Saxony several pages of instructions to serve him in the event of war with Russia, and on the 19th he furnished General Clarke with the composition of "The Army of Germany,' which was to be divided into three *Corps d'Observation*, of the Elbe, of the Rhine, of Italy. On the 20th his Majesty called for a return of the numbers of Portuguese in the army, saying, that well fed and well paid they would be useful, but they were not to be left in France, as the Emperor objected to having suspected troops in his rear.

On the 24th April Napoleon addressed instructions to the Minister of Public Worship on the subject of despatching the Archbishop of Tours, and the bishops of Nantes and Treves, to Savona to confer with the Pope. This mission was to be kept secret. If the Pope would confirm the bishops appointed by the Emperor, and if he would take the oath of allegiance to the Emperor, he would be allowed to return to Rome. Should he refuse to take the oath, he might be allowed to go to Avignon, where he would enjoy a revenue of 80,000*l.* a year, on promising to do nothing contrary to the four propositions of the Gallican Church. As for the temporal power, that was dead and gone.

On the 30th April the Emperor, in a letter addressed to M. Maret, Duc de Bassano, who had succeeded M. de Champagny, Duc de Cadore, complained that smuggling was very active in Prussia. He was to speak to the Prussian ambassador about this. He was also to write to Saxony, and to complain that smuggling was tolerated, and to ask how it came that there was an accumulation of English goods at Leipsic The Emperor added :—

"Write to M. St. Marsan that he allows himself to be duped by Prussia; that all these movements of troops along the coasts are useless, as no descent on the part of the English is feared; that if Prussia be arming, it must be against me, and that I shall occupy the country; that Prussia must therefore remain quiet and make no movement until my quarrel with Russia is terminated. . . .

"NAPOLEON."

To MARSHAL BERTHIER.

"ST. CLOUD, 7*th May*, 1811.

"I send you a translation of the English papers. You will see that Wellington passed the Tagus on the 18th April. . . . You will perceive that what I foresaw has happened; that they were simple-minded enough [his generals] to leave a small force at Olivenza, and to allow 300 men to be captured. Olivenza was taken on the 14th. It appears astonishing to me that Soult, who, on the 4th April was aware of the passage of Lord Beresford, did nothing up to the 25th, and did not take measures to relieve Badajoz before the arrival of Wellington.

"NAPOLEON."

That there was a considerable amount of distress in France at this period is shown by many letters. On the 8th May Napoleon directed his new Minister of the Interior, Comte de Montalivet, to double the amount of money given in charity, and to triple it in the dangerous faubourgs of St. Antoine and St. Marceau, also at Lyons and Rouen. Considerable sums were to be distributed at once, and large public works undertaken; large purchases, too, were to be made, especially in the way of furniture, harness, &c.

On the 26th May, the Emperor being then on a tour of inspection, wrote to Berthier from Caen on the subject of the operations in Portugal. He said:—

"Should the English march upon Ciudad Rodrigo, let

Bessières concentrate his forces in order to go to the help of Marmont, and to deliver, at last, a grand battle. You will point out to him that instead of writing every day he writes hardly ever. Recommend Marmont to re-organise his army well, and to deliver battle if the English march upon Ciudad Rodrigo, in which case Bessières can reinforce him with 10,000 men of my Guard; tell him that he should announce my approaching arrival and his march upon Lisbon as soon as the harvest is cut. . . ."

And on the 27th, Joseph being still in Paris :—

"The king can leave when he likes; he is at liberty not to await my return to Paris.

"I require a marshal to command the army of the north. Bessières does not appear to suit the king; I am inclined to replace him by Marshal Jourdan, if that be agreeable to the king and to the marshal. But I cannot change the organisation of the army of the north, which must remain as it is, further than placing it under the orders of a French marshal who enjoys the confidence of the king."

Up to the 1st July the king was to receive 20,000*l.* a month, and for the remainder of the year 40,000*l.* a month. The Emperor had just promised Joseph that he should act as commander-in-chief in Spain.

King Joseph had not gone to Paris for the christening of the King of Rome, as was officially announced, but to endeavour to persuade Napoleon to allow him to reign in Spain, and not to ruin the country and drive the inhabitants to despair. Joseph, in a royal progress, had been so well received that he felt confident of being able to rule if his terrible brother would only cease devastating the country. What his position was before he left for Paris may be gathered from such letters as the following :—

King Joseph, appealing to Berthier for money on the 21st February, said: "I repeat to you that all which is robbed here is afterwards paid for in French blood. I must add that this habit of pillaging causes many of the allied soldiers to desert, and even turns them into brigands."

MINISTER OF WAR TO NAPOLEON.

"PARIS, 13*th March*, 1811.

"I have the honour to lay before your Majesty details concerning the malversations of which several superior officers of the army of Portugal are accused. Follows list of colonels and embezzlements."

JOSEPH TO BERTHIER.

"MADRID, 13*th March*, 1811.

". . . The troops in my service have neither been paid nor clothed for eight months. . . . The contractors have just been given all the objects of value which still existed in the palace of Madrid, and I have been obliged to strip the chapel of my house. . . . MM. Mazzarado and Campo Alange have been reduced to asking me to allow them rations for their families, and I was obliged to refuse, as all the other civil servants would have made the same demand. My ambassador in Russia is a bankrupt; the one in Paris died in the greatest poverty, and I live here amid the ruins of a great monarchy."

And poor Joseph implored permission to send all the thieves back to France.

TO MARSHAL BERTHIER.

"ALENÇON, 1*st June*, 1811.

"I suppose that you send the *Moniteur* to Spain. Inform Marshal Marmont that a battle took place on the 16th at five leagues from Badajoz between Marshal Soult, who is supposed to have had from 25,000 to 30,000 men, and the allies, composed of the Spaniards of Blake and Castanos, and the Portuguese and English of Beresford and Hill. The English say in their newspapers that they lost three generals and 8,000 men, and that Lord Wellington was going to march with 12,000 men to the support of Beresford.

"NAPOLEON."

The battle here alluded to was Albuera, in which the allies suffered very heavily, but at the same time Soult was foiled in his attempt to relieve Badajos. We find no mention in *The Correspondence* of the retreat of Massena from his position at Santarem in front of the lines of Torres Vedras, no mention of the battle of Fuentes de Honor, nor the evacuation of Almeida, which shortly preceded Soult's failure.[1]

---

[1] Michaud, in his *Biographie universelle*, thus speaks of the career of Massena when fighting against us in the Peninsula :—

"Wishing to drive the English out of Portugal, where Junot and Soult had failed, Napoleon in 1810 selected Massena, the most daring and fortunate of his lieutenants, and confided to him an army of 80,000 men. It is even believed that the Emperor held out to him in perspective the crown of Portugal as the reward of success. Massena at first invested Ciudad Rodrigo, which he took, and then laid siege to Almeida, which fell in the middle of September. He then penetrated into Portugal, and found the English army, commanded by Wellington, posted on the heights of Busaco. Instead of turning it, he attacked it in front, and lost between 6,000 and 7,000 men in killed and wounded. His *début* was therefore marked by a blunder. Having at last turned this position he marched upon Lisbon, and Wellington retired before him. Massena thought that he was going to re-embark; but at the sight of the formidable lines of Torres Vedras, which covered Lisbon, he was struck with astonishment, and did not dare to attack. This hesitation made the campaign a failure. All his operations came to naught in presence of the coolness and firmness of his adversary. The country was laid waste; the French army was perishing from hunger and want. At last, after having passed five months near Lisbon, and having in vain offered battle to Wellington, the marshal, seeing his forces disorganised and half exhausted, made preparations to fall back. This retreat was worthy of the high reputation of our troops and of Massena himself. . . . . This campaign cost him 20,000 men. He little expected, when his army was re-organised, reinforced, and once more formidable, to find his prudent antagonist suddenly changed into a daring adversary. His pride,

On the 2nd June, 1811, in a letter to the minister of public worship, not inserted in *The Correspondence*, Napoleon said—

"I have turned the Bishop of Seez out of my house, and I have had one of the canons, named Le Gallois, arrested and sent to Paris. The Minister of State will send you the resignation of the bishop. It is impossible for any one to be more evil-minded. Everything was going wrong in his diocese. . . ."

The facts of the case appear to be as follows :—On the 31st May, 1811, Napoleon, passing through Seez with Marie Louise, was told that the bishop of that place was imbued with royalist proclivities. The prelate was sent for, and after some violent abuse, was ordered to resign, while all his papers were seized. A few hours afterwards the grand vicars and the chapter were sent for, and the Emperor poured forth all the vials of his wrath upon the Abbé Le Gallois, who was said to have exercised great influence over the bishop, whose crime was—1st, that he had ordered vespers to be sung on religious feast days suppressed by the Emperor. 2nd, that he was frequently absent when *rosières* married retired officers. The result of this scene was that the bishop got an attack of paralysis and died before the end of the year, and the Abbé Le Gallois was taken to Paris in custody of two gendarmes, and thrown into the prison of La Force, where he remained for eleven days in solitary confinement, " sleeping on the still warm straw of an unfortunate wretch who had been led to the scaffold." The Minister of Police, in a report upon the affair, to the annoyance of the Emperor, acquitted the abbé. The reply

wounded to see Wellington, after having pursued him, invest Almeida, and carry off his prey under his very eyes, drove him to make two murderous attacks on the English army posted at Fuentes de Honor. He was not more fortunate than at Busaco, and abandoning Portugal he fell into disgrace with the Emperor, who appointed as his successor a less skilful and more unfortunate commander (Marmont)."

of Napoleon was—"He is too clever; he is a dangerous man; let him be confined at Vincennes," and there he remained for nine months. He was then attacked with paralysis, and was removed to a hospice, where he remained till the fall of the Empire.[1]

King Joseph had been anxious to get rid of General Belliard, and to keep Marshal Jourdan, but he was ordered to retain the services of the first, and was obliged to dispense with the services of the second. Now Napoleon was inclined to send Jourdan back to Spain, and wrote—

To MARSHAL BERTHIER.

"ST. CLOUD, 8*th June*, 1811.

" Reply to General Belliard,[2] that *you have laid his letter before me;* that he must have lost his head when he wrote it; that to offer his resignation on account of not obeying orders is equivalent to declaring that he will not obey; that this is to incur the penalty of capital punishment; that his 3,000 men and 1,200 horses might have saved the army of the south; that he is very culpable, ... that there are three or four paragraphs in his letter which are not those of a soldier, that if you had placed them under the eyes of the Emperor, he would have had him arrested and would have made an example of him for this breach of military discipline; that, through respect for his previous services, and owing to the friendship you bear him, you have not informed the Emperor of his uncalled-for expressions, and that you confined yourself to saying that my orders had been carried out; that this affectation of sentiments of honour and personality is the height of ridicule and of military insubordination; that the honour of a general consists in obeying, in keeping his

[1] *L'Eglise Romaine et le Premier Empire*, Comte d'Haussonville, vol. iv. p. 183.

[2] Belliard had seen an immense amount of service, and had saved Napoleon's life at Arcola.

subalterns in the road of probity, in maintaining discipline, in devoting himself exclusively to the interests of his country and his sovereign, and in entirely disdaining private interests; that you see by the tone of his letter that he has unlearned what France is, and that when it is a question of executing the orders of the Emperor *he thinks that he is speaking to the King of Spain.*

" NAPOLEON."

To ADMIRAL DECRÈS.

" ST. CLOUD, 13*th June*, 1811.

"I beg that you will write a letter to the transport office, demanding the return to France of all the prisoners who are in England, captured at Baylen with Dupont's army. Put forward some reasons to show how just this would be.

"NAPOLEON."

Dupont had capitulated to the Spaniards, on condition of being allowed to return to France with his army, it was therefore argued that the English had no right to capture any of Dupont's men returning home by sea.

On the 16th June, at the opening of parliament, Napoleon made a speech to this effect—" The peace concluded with Austria has been cemented by the happy alliance which I contracted. The birth of the King of Rome has fulfilled the wishes, and assures the future of my people."

Turning to religious affairs, and "the pretensions of a small corner of Italy," his Majesty said—" I have united Rome to the empire. I have accorded palaces to the Popes in Rome and in Paris. If they have the interests of religion at heart, they will often sojourn in the centre of affairs in Christendom. . . . Holland has been united to the empire; she is but an emanation of it; without her the empire would not be complete." Then came a few words about the conduct of England, which had obliged him to make sure of the mouths of the Ems, the Weser, and the

Elbe. He had also been obliged to annex the Valais, " in order to conciliate the interests of Switzerland with those of France and of Italy."

As for the English they were accused of all kinds of crimes, and French legislators were informed that "war through every part of the Continent could alone insure the prosperity of England." Then the author of war, in every portion of Europe, declared—" I wish for nothing but what is contained in the treaties which I have concluded. I shall never sacrifice the blood of my people for interests not immediately connected with those of my empire. I flatter myself that the peace of the Continent will not be disturbed.

"The King of Spain came to take part in this last solemnity. I have granted him all that is necessary for his people. . . . Since 1809 most of the strong places in Spain have been taken after memorable sieges; the *insurgents* have been beaten in a number of pitched battles. England understands that this war is drawing to a close, and that henceforth intrigues and gold are not sufficient to feed it. She has been forced, from an auxiliary, to become the chief actor in that war. All her regular troops have been despatched to the Peninsula. English blood has been shed in streams in several actions glorious to the French arms. This struggle against Carthage, which was to have been decided on the ocean, or beyond the seas, will henceforward be decided in the plains of Spain! When England is exhausted, and feels the misfortunes with which she has so cruelly afflicted the Continent for twenty years; when half of her families are covered with mourning, a thunder stroke will put an end to the affairs of the Peninsula, to the destinies of her armies, and will revenge Europe and Asia by bringing this second Punic war to a close."

After this fine flourish came the usual announcement that the country and the finances were in a prosperous condition, and that no new taxes were to be levied.

To M. MARET.

"ST. CLOUD, 21st *June*, 1811.

"I beg that you will hint gently to the Swedish ambassador that I regret to see the Princess Royal arrive in France without having obtained permission; that this is not usual, and that I am sorry she should have left her husband at so critical a moment. You should also speak to the ambassador about the relations of Sweden with England.
"NAPOLEON."

The Princess Royal was Napoleon's old flame, Desirée Clary, the sister of Joseph's wife, who married Bernadotte. Napoleon would probably have liked her to remain at Stockholm to play the spy.

On the 21st June further instructions were sent to Comte Lauriston at St. Petersburg. He was to speak very plainly to the Czar, and to say that France was quite ready for war, and had men under arms and money in her coffers; he was, however, to add that Napoleon desired peace, but was to leave the court of St. Perersburg no hope that his Majesty would allow Poland to be touched; that would dishonour him, and he preferred honour to life.

Writing the next day to M. Maret, the Emperor said that "Russia appears to be frightened since I picked up the glove; but nothing is yet decided; the object of Russia seems to be to obtain, as an indemnity for the Duchy of Oldenburg, the cession of two districts of Poland, which I will not consent to, by honour and because that would altogether destroy the grand duchy." The Minister for Foreign Affairs would write this to the poor King of Saxony, who had been driven from his capital during the war with Austria, and was once more in a dangerous position, and was to add—"Marshal Davoust has 130,000 men in hand, and I wish the Saxon corps to be held in readiness to march, also the three Polish divisions in the Grand Duchy."

At the close of a letter addressed to his minister of war on the 23rd June, the Emperor wrote—

"I wish to see the plans relative to the invasion of Ireland again, so as to force England to withdraw troops from Spain. Nothing ought to be more easy than, towards the end of October, to throw 25,000 men into Ireland."

On the 26th June, M. Maret was instructed to complain to the minister of Naples that the king of that country (Murat) was doing nothing for the common cause, "and yet," added the Emperor, "I have reduced the number of French troops in that kingdom. . . . Point out to Baron Durand the difference between the kingdoms of Naples and Italy, which is also one of my conquests; that the kingdom of Italy brings me in 30,000,000 francs a year, holds 60,000 men at my disposal, spends 3,000,000 francs on the strong places which cover my frontier, has offered me several frigates, has eight ships of the line afloat, and will soon have nine, and furnish over 1,500 sailors." M. Maret was to add in conversation that when Louis was king, Holland was of no assistance, but that now she furnished 10,000 sailors and twelve ships of the line—which was a gentle hint to King Murat.

To GENERAL CLARKE.

"ST. CLOUD, 4*th July*, 1811.

"Send for O'Connor and the other Irishmen in Paris and get up an Irish party. I have at this moment twenty-five ships of war at the Escaut, and nine at Texel. I am inclined to send an expedition of 30,000 men and 4,000 horses to Ireland at the end of October. . . . I will conclude any treaty that the Irish wish. I attach great importance to this. I wish to have a plan and to know how I stand before a fortnight. There is nothing to prevent me getting out of the Scheldt, and the English, having no soldiers in England, will be obliged to recall their troops from the Peninsula. This will take two or three months, and we shall have time to establish ourselves in the country before they arrive.

"NAPOLEON."

On the 12th July, Napoleon, who was then at the Trianon, drew up a note on the completion of the Palace of Versailles in which we find—"His Majesty will inhabit the first floor in the portion built by Louis XIII. The Empress will inhabit the ground floor below the Emperor, and the children of France the other part of the ground floor." His Majesty proposed to lay out over 14,000,000 francs on the necessary additions and embellishments. As a matter of fact, Napoleon never inhabited Versailles, where no French sovereign has taken up his abode since the ill-fated Louis XVI. was dragged from that palace and escorted to Paris by the revolutionary mob which afterwards put him to death.

TO M. MARET.

"ST. CLOUD, 1st *August*, 1811.

"I shall make no difficulty about granting Prussia licences for the exportation of Silesian cloths. Demand that Prussia shall no longer receive any colonial produce coming from Russia. I will willingly give Prussia licences for exporting corn to England on condition of her being paid in money. The duties will go to Prussia, and I shall only have the duty on the licence. The great affair is to prevent colonial produce entering Prussia by way of Russia. . . .

"NAPOLEON."

It was one of the causes of dispute with Russia, that while Napoleon insisted upon her rigorously observing the continental system, he violated the system himself by the sale of licences.

The effect of the system of licences may be thus summed up. The English alone possessed the merchandise required, which they sold to the holders of licences at an exorbitant price. The French purchaser was supposed to offer French goods in exchange, but it frequently happened that the goods thus offered were prohibited in England, and had to be thrown overboard to keep up the exports! Add to the above charges the tax paid for the licence, and the profit of the merchant, and a fair idea may be formed of the price which the consumer had to pay for a pound of sugar or of coffee, and of the encouragement thus given to smugglers. Finding that prohibited goods existed in large quantities in France, Napoleon placed a tax of 50 per cent. on all colonial produce, and ordered goods of English manufacture to be burned, although the loss fell upon French merchants. To see his decrees carried out, forty-one special tribunals were created which punished smugglers, &c., with the penalty of death, of hard labour, and branding, while informers were encouraged by the promise of half the prohibited merchandize they enabled the authorities to seize. The taxes of 50 per cent. was levied on all colonial produce, no matter what its origin, whether it belonged to a person who had purchased a licence, or whether it had been captured by a French corsair and sold. The merchant who could not pay in money had to forfeit half his stock.

According to Miot de Melito, the continental blockade caused such distress in France that complaints arose on all sides and broke forth in murmurs and insulting placards. The Emperor, he says,[1] made the following remarkable reply at this time to a deputation of merchants to whom he granted an audience—reply which is not given in *The Correspondence*—

[1] In a note Comte Miot de Melito says that the effect of the decrees would have been disastrous for England but for the scandalous traffic in licences, which enriched the courtiers, and was said to have swelled the privy purse of the Emperor.

"The decrees of Berlin and of Milan are the fundamental laws of my empire. As for *neutres*, I look upon the flag as an extension of the territory; the power which allows it to be violated cannot be considered as neutral.

"The fate of American commerce will soon be decided; I shall favour it if the United States conform to these decrees; if they do not, their ships shall be driven from my empire.

"The commercial relations with England must cease. I say this firmly, gentlemen; those merchants who have business to terminate and funds to withdraw must do so at once. I gave this advice some time ago to the people of Antwerp, and they find themselves very well off. I wish for peace, but not a patched-up peace; I wish for it in good faith, for I have not forgotten the losses which commerce experienced by the last declaration of war. I should not have made peace at Tilsit; I should have gone to Wilna and further but for the promise of the Emperor of Russia to bring about peace between France and England. Before the annexation of Holland I made new overtures for peace; the English Government would not listen to them.

"The Continent shall remain closed to English importations. I shall remain armed from head to foot in order to cause my decrees to be executed, and to resist the attempts of the English in the Baltic. Some fraudulent practices still exist, but they shall be annihilated. Those who only think of evading the law by means of extravagant operations end by becoming bankrupts. But, if they manage to escape my custom-house officers, my sword shall reach them sooner or later.

"I have an ear in the chambers of commerce; I know that my measures are loudly blamed, and that the merchants say I am badly advised. I cannot be angry with them for their opinions because they are not in a position to see and calculate as I am. Those persons who have just returned from England, and who have seen the effect produced by the interruption of trade with the Continent, cannot help saying—' Perhaps he is right, and will attain his end.'

"In my empire the internal commerce amounts to over 160,000,000*l*. It is upon this basis that its resources and prosperity must be combined. I know that Bordeaux, Hamburg, and other ports, suffer by the interruption of maritime commerce, while the municipal regulations introduced by the Czar will do harm to the manufactures of Lyons. There are individual losses. I endeavour to alleviate them. But the exportations for Russia, which do not exceed 1,000,000*l*., are of little account. Russia has paper money, Austria also; England is swamped with it. France is the richest country in the globe. Her territorial resources are enormous. She has a great deal of money. After an inquiry just made, over 40,000,000*l*. has entered France in the shape of war contributions. I have 8,000,000*l*. in my private treasury at the Tuileries."

Napoleon went on to say that France, thanks to chemistry, would soon be able to do without the sugar and the indigo of India, to talk of building a fleet of 200 line of battle ships, and to indulge in other dreamy speculations.

To PRINCE CAMBACÉRÈS.

"ST. CLOUD, 3*rd August*, 1811.

"I send you the papers relative to the order of the union. The shield and the device do not suit me. A great state cannot take for device—*Fais ce que dois, adrienne que pourra.* That is the device of a doughty knight. A device must be formed showing the advantages of the union of the Baltic, the Mediterranean, the Adriatic, and the Ocean. This great event, which really characterises the empire, might be called the Order of the Union. . . .

"NAPOLEON."

To ADMIRAL DECRÈS.

"St. Cloud, 16*th August*, 1811.

"Which is the best port for assembling my squadron of the ocean? I see only two between which to choose— Brest or Cherbourg. Which of those two ports offers the greatest facilities for invading England or Ireland? Which of the two offers the greatest facilities for sailing to America and India? . . .

"Napoleon."

The Emperor was always most particular in seeing that the lives of his troops were not uselessly sacrificed, and that unhealthy quarters were not occupied.

To MARSHAL DAVOUST.

"St. Cloud, 16*th August*, 1811.

"I send you a letter from a soldier in garrison at Stettin. He says that there are a great many men on the sick list. I thought that the air of Stettin was good. . . . Take care to have my troops quartered in places where no sickness is to be feared. Better fight the most sanguinary battle than leave troops in an unhealthy spot. Remember what happened to Moraud's division after the battle of Wagram.

"Napoleon."

On the 17th August Napoleon wrote to the Minister of Public Worship, giving him instructions for the deputation which was going to Savona to ask the Pope to adhere to the decree of the council which had been assembled in Paris. In order to render this deputation all the more imposing, it was to consist of no less than nine prelates, the Archbishops and Bishops of Paris, Tours, Venice, Treves, Malines, Nantes, &c. "The 'decree,' said Napoleon, extends over all the bishoprics of the empire, of which Rome forms a part, and over those of our kingdom of Italy, of which Ancona, Urbino and Feltro form part. Also over Hamburg, Munster, the grand duchy of Berg, Holland, Illyria, and all the countries united, *or to be united*, to France."

On the 18th August the Emperor received a deputation from the Ionian Islands, at the Tuileries, and in reply to an address said:—

"I have carried out large works in your island. I collected a great many troops there, and ammunition of all sorts. I do not regret the money which Corfu has cost my treasury; it is the key of the Adriatic. I shall never abandon isles which have fallen into the power of the enemy owing to his superiority at sea. In India, as in America (meaning West Indies), as in the Mediterranean, all that is and has been French shall remain French. Conquered by the enemy, owing to the vicissitudes of war, they will return to the empire by other vicissitudes, or by the stipulations of peace. . . ."

"NAPOLEON."

To ADMIRAL DECRÈS.

"ST. CLOUD, 19*th August*, 1811.

"Let me know what day my troops can embark at Cherbourg. When will all the vessels be there? . . . I have a great many relations with Ireland. I already hold the thread which sets a good many things in motion. My agents begin to come and go. . . .

"NAPOLEON."

To GENERAL DUROC, DUC DE FRIOUL.

"ST. CLOUD, 19*th August*, 1811.

"You must inform Comte de Remusat that he has nothing more to say to my wardrobe. Until I have found some one to replace him, you must perform the functions. I send you the budget of my wardrobe which I have drawn up, and an order on Comte Estève for 16,000 francs which I owe. I do not wish to charge this sum to the budget. The treasurer will then pay these 16,000 francs out of my privy purse. Call for a list of my things, and verify it. I think that a further economy can be made. See that the tailor does not do any bad work, and that the budget be not exceeded. The day that new clothes are to be bought you must present them to me so as to see if they fit well, and then they will be received. Settle all this, so that there may be well-established rules for the master of the wardrobe when I appoint one. It seems to me that Comte de Remusat was not appointed by a decree. If there was a decree appointing him, present me with a decree dismissing him. "NAPOLEON."

In the list drawn out by his Majesty one finds nine coats of various description, which were to last each three years. Then forty-eight vests and breeches, at eighty francs (they must be furnished every week, and last three years); two dressing-gowns; forty-eight flannel waistcoats (one every week; four dozen shirts (one every week); four dozen pocket-handkerchiefs (one every week); two dozen pair of silk stockings (one pair every fortnight); twenty-four pairs of shoes (one pair every fortnight), to last two years, and six pairs of boots; four hats. And at the end of a long list, in which the price and duration of each article is minutely given, comes "perfumery, taking out the grease, Eau de Cologne, washing of linen and silk stockings, divers expenses. . . . Nothing is to be spent except after the approbation of his Majesty." The amount to be laid out in perfumery, washing, &c., is left in blank.

Strange contrast with the wardrobe of Frederick the Great.

To GENERAL CLARKE.

"ST. CLOUD, 22*nd August*, 1811.

"I beg that you will have the fortifications of Geneva blown up. Perhaps in a military point of view it would be of interest to keep this place; but, the inhabitants having always exhibited a bad feeling, I have decided upon blowing up the fortifications without delay.

"NAPOLEON."

Just as he ordered the fortifications round Vienna to be blown up after peace had been concluded, although from a military point of view they had little value.

To ADMIRAL DECRÈS.
"ST. CLOUD, 23rd August, 1811.

"The Boulogne flotilla has returned to harbour. It sustained some damage. I think even that a gunboat went down. Write that this should cause no discouragement. These gales are just the things to exercise the crews.

"NAPOLEON."

To MARSHAL BERTHIER.
"ST. CLOUD, 23rd August, 1811.

"Express my displeasure to Marshal Soult for sending me the flags of Albuera by a foreigner. . . . It appears that he was in the Austrian service, and he must therefore have fought against us. It is ridiculous of Soult to send such a man.[1]

"NAPOLEON."

To M. MARET.
"ST. CLOUD, 24th August, 1811.

"It is necessary for you to write again to my minister at Carlsruhe. The Princess Stephanie is wrong to show a preference for Manheim; her duty is to be with her husband. The princess is wrong to wish to dine at five

---

[1] Napoleon himself often employed generals and other officers who had borne arms against him, such as Colli and others, and we shall find him in 1812 recommending the Emperor of Austria to make Prince Schwartzenberg a marshal for services rendered to France in Poland.

o'clock; her duty is to dine at the same hour as her husband; her duty is to do what he wishes, and to be where he is. Instead of encouraging the princess in these little acts of resistance, Baron de Moustier should give her advice through her lady of honour. . . .

"NAPOLEON."

Napoleon had forced Stephanie de Beauharnais into this marriage with the heir to the Duchy of Baden, and it was a long time before the union was attended with domestic felicity.

To M. MARET.
"TRIANON, 25th August, 1811.

"I send you extracts from the English journals. You must show them to Prince Kourakine while conversing with him. After this you must send them to Comte Lauriston, so that he may show them in Russia. You must tell him that we have received news of 150 ships under false American flags having arrived in Russia . . . . that the plans of Russia are unmasked; that she wishes to renew her commerce with England, and that is why she is concentrating troops, and will not terminate the Oldenburg affair.

"NAPOLEON."

To COMTE MOLLIEN.
"COMPIÈGNE, 3rd September, 1811.

"I beg that you will pay 2,500 francs a month to the ex-Queen of Etruria, at her convent in Rome. . . .

"NAPOLEON."

The poor Queen of Etruria, deprived of her kingdom, which was handed over by Napoleon to his sister Eliza, was most cruelly treated. She has left an account of her persecution in a small volume of memoirs, and the tale of her martyrdom is curious if not very interesting.

To MARSHAL DAVOUST.

"COMPIÈGNE, 3rd September, 1811.

"I have received your letter concerning the cheating of Bourrienne at Hamburg. It will be important to throw light upon what he has done. Have the Jew, Gumprecht Mares, arrested, seize his papers, and place him in solitary confinement. Have some of the other principal agents of Bourrienne arrested, so as to discover his doings at Hamburg, and the embezzlements he has committed there.

"NAPOLEON."

Bourrienne had been a fellow student of Napoleon at Brienne, and had for several years acted as his private secretary. He was, however, an incorrigible swindler, and had to be dismissed even from the Imperial service.

To M. GAUDIN (*Finance Minister*).

"COMPIEGNE, 7th September, 1811.

"I send you a memorandum concerning Lippe. . . . I think that we must treat with the Grand Duke of Berg. It was never my intention to leave him all the domain. . . . Everything in the shape of forests and domains should belong to me. If there be any reason for indemnifying the Grand Duke he must be indemnified with *rentes*.

"NAPOLEON."

The Grand Duke of Berg was the second son of Louis, who at this period was seven years of age.

To GENERAL CLARKE.

"COMPIÈGNE, 8th September, 1811.

"I have read with interest the letter of General O'Connor, which I return. It appears very important to me to establish relations with Ireland. Ask for particulars with regard to the state of public opinion at present. I am rather inclined to send 6,000 horses and 30,000 men there.

"NAPOLEON."

To MARSHAL DAVOUST.

"COMPIÈGNE, 14th September, 1811.

"I have sent a courier to Berlin to-day to tell Comte St. Marsau to leave that capital if the Prussians continue their fortifications and provisioning Spandau and Kolberg.

"As soon as Comte St. Marsan leaves Berlin you must march on that city with your army. . . .

"Warn the King of Westphalia, who must unite his troops at Magdeburg.

"Write to the King of Saxony to concentrate his forces at Glogau. . . .

"My resolution is expressed in such strong terms that I hope Prussia will feel her impotency and the folly of her pretentions, and that Comte St. Marsan will not leave. You must not make any preparations which may be considered as a threat. Your troops, however, should be kept on the alert, and have four days' rations on pretext of a review. If you enter Prussia issue no proclamation—say nothing, but take and disarm everything; and, above all, maintain strict discipline. You must try, in this case, to surprise Spandau.

"NAPOLEON."

To MARSHAL BESSIÈRES.

"BOULOGNE,[1] 20th September, 1811.

"Go often to see the King of Rome; see Madame de Montesquiou, and adopt measures for her security. Inform

---

[1] Nothing appears in *The Correspondence* on the subject of a little disaster which befel the Boulogne flotilla in an engagement with the *Naiad* frigate, three brigs, and a cutter, which took place by order of and under the eyes of his Majesty. One praam, with sixty soldiers and fifty-two sailors on board was captured, and the rest of the flotilla, with the admiral, escaping by running under the shore batteries.

Madame de Montesquiou that in the event of anything happening she should address herself to you.

"NAPOLEON."

To PRINCE CAMBACÉRÈS.
"ON BOARD THE 'CHARLEMAGNE,' FLUSHING ROADS,
"25*th September*, 1811.

"I have been for the last two days on board the *Charlemagne*. We were thirty-six hours without communicating with the land, owing to an equinoctial gale. This did not hinder me from eating and sleeping well. The sea was very rough; however, the roads are excellent. If the weather becomes better, I propose manœuvring my squadron to-morrow.

"NAPOLEON."

To THE COMTESSE DE MONTESQUIOU.
"ANTWERP, 30*th September*, 1811.

"I have seen with pleasure your different letters respecting the health of the King. Since you have not gone to Meudon I suppose that the report of the Faculty is opposed to that place. It appears to me extraordinary that this house, so well situated, should not be healthy. . . . I desire the constitution of the King to be formed at an early age by a solid *régime*. However, as regards that, I have full confidence in you, madam.

"NAPOLEON."

To GENERAL SAVARY (*Minister of Police*).
"AMSTERDAM, 23*rd October*, 1811.

"I see with pleasure King Charles IV. leave Marseilles with his household and go to Rome. I authorise you to send some persons to him who enjoy his confidence to make him this proposition. I should like him to take advantage of the remainder of the fine season to start. On the road the greatest honours must be rendered to him, and even, should he visit the fleet at Toulon, he must be received there as a king. The garrisons must furnish him escorts, and the Generals commanding the districts through which he passes must accompany him. From Nice he could go by Tende Pass, from there to Placentia, and thence to Rome. You must assure him that he shall receive the same pension as to-day. If he has debts I cannot pay them, seeing that Spain costs me so much [was in fact a bad bargain even at the low price given for her], and that 80,000*l*. in his situation should be sufficient. As for his residence, he can be lodged in the Borghese palace, or in one of the palaces which I have in that city.

"Arrange this affair delicately. . . . It is well for the Bourbons to be at Rome: their stay there will be useful to the great city.[1] . . .

"The Duchesse de Bourbon, the Duchesse d'Orleans, and the Prince de Conti are very unhappy in Catalonia. As I continue to pay them a pension you might also propose to them that they should go to Rome. They must pass rapidly through the southern provinces, without any honours being paid to them on the road, and you must see that their journey creates no sensation [as was the case with the Pope]. If they can obtain a passport from the English cruisers, which I think possible, they would do better to embark at Barcelona for Civita Vecchia.

"NAPOLEON."

To PRINCE EUGÈNE.

"ROTTERDAM, 26*th October*, 1811.

". . . From this place I intend going to the Grand Duchy of Berg, and afterwards to Fontainebleau. I am extremely satisfied with the Dutch. The only recollection they have preserved of their independence is that which makes them feel the advantages of a union such as uniformity in the law, a system of moderate contributions, and the regular march of affairs. They are more French than any inhabitants of the united countries. As for the

[1] Nearly all the Bonapartes flocked thither after Waterloo.

King [poor Louis] they remember him only as a good sort of man, very changeable, who had very limited views on the subject of administration, and who undid in the evening what he had done in the morning. . . . I acknowledge that I have been agreeably surprised. I have several vessels on the stocks, and the Dutch will be extremely useful for my navy, for they are all sailors; this country is highly interesting.

"NAPOLEON."

With regard to the Dutch it is certain that on the occasion of the visit of the French Emperor and Empress they were guilty of the most base adulation.

TO COMTE BIGOT.

"WESEL, 1st *November*, 1811.

"I return you the letters from Savona. Reply yourself to the Doctor Porta that you have laid his letter before the Emperor; that his Majesty has written in the margin of his letter from Amsterdam that no matter what discussions may have taken place between the Pope and his Majesty, and no matter how animated they may have been, his Majesty will always consider personal services rendered to the Pope as if they were rendered to himself; that the Doctor Porta had merely to make known what he required, and that his salary would be paid to him as when the Pope was at Rome; that in consequence a salary of 12,000f. is allowed to him from the moment he left Rome, which salary will be continued as long as he remains with the Pope. . . .

"NAPOLEON."

Doctor Porta had consented to act as a spy on the Pope and to do what he could to persuade him to accept the terms imposed by Napoleon. This traitor was to receive 40*l.* a month, while only 2*s.* 0½*d.* were to be allowed for the keep of Pius VII. and of each of his attendants.

To PRINCE CAMBACÉRÈS.

"DUSSELDORF, 3rd *November*, 1811.

"I beg that you will see the Queen of Spain and tell her that I wish the Princess of Sweden [1] to leave Paris and return to Stockholm. This is all the more important because the measures being taken by Sweden will probably bring about war between the two countries, and that it would not be right for the princess to be here at such a moment; that I think the princess should lose no time and not await my arrival in order to return to her husband.   "NAPOLEON."

The crime of Sweden was an evident leaning towards Russia and England and violations of the continental blockade. Napoleon therefore instructed his Minister for Foreign Affairs to draw up a general report on the conduct of Sweden, which was a bad sign, and concluded his letter by saying: "I desire to remain at peace with Sweden, but I prefer war to such a peace as this."

The Prussian Government having declared that it was in spite of its orders that General Blucher had executed works at Kolberg, the Emperor wrote thus to M. Maret on the 3rd November: "Write to Comte St. Marsan that he should prevent General Blucher from being employed, and thus put the good faith of the Prussian Government to the test."

To GENERAL CLARKE.

"DUSSELDORF, 3rd *November*, 1811.

"I am waiting with impatience for news from Ireland and I receive none. You must send some more agents there. My means are ready, and if I were sure of finding a party there I would undertake an expedition which might sail at the end of February or the beginning of March. You must despatch agents and complete the Irish regiments.
          "NAPOLEON."

---

[1] Wife of King Joseph and the wife of Bernadotte were sisters.

To KING JEROME.

"DUSSELDORF, *3rd November,* 1811.

"I am informed that you have made a present of some horses to the Prince Royal of Sweden. I desire that you countermand the despatch of these horses. Sweden is behaving very badly, and at any moment we may go to war. These gifts are therefore not proper at the present moment. You do not know to what a man you make these presents. Besides, the sending of horses has always the air of rendering homage. Nothing can displease me more.[1]

"NAPOLEON."

From Cologne, on the 6th November, the Emperor addressed a letter to M. Maret, in which he said :—

"Your language in Paris should be this: That if Russia wishes to disarm, I shall ask nothing better than to disarm also; that this would tranquillise Prussia and reassure every one, but that Russia must reassure us with regard to her manifesto; that this can only be done by terminating the Oldenburg affair. . . ."

Prussia, too, was to be told that she was pursuing a miserable policy which would lead her to ruin, and that she would perish without inspiring esteem: "While in allying herself openly to Russia or any other Power which she supposes going to wage war with France she would, if she succumbed, at all events fall with honour."

"On the 12th November his Majesty wrote to M. Maret telling him to prepare a despatch for Comte Lauriston, informing him of the Emperor's arrival in Paris, of his pacific views, and his desire to see his differences with Russia terminated "this winter." You must tell him," added Napoleon, "that a division of cuirassiers has gone to Erfurth; that the uncertainty of all that is

---

[1] In a letter to the King of Spain, 16th February, 1808, he announced a gift of horses, and in a letter to the Czar, 23rd October, 1810, he thanked Alexander for sending him a similar present.

doing in Prussia rendered this augmentation of cavalry necessary." .... On the same day the Emperor addressed a letter to General Clarke on the subject of Switzerland and his Swiss troops, in which he said: "Switzerland costs me a great deal of money and renders me no service. Up to the present I have been duped." After insisting that the cantons should maintain a force of 12,000 men Napoleon added, that in the event of a war with Russia or with Austria, which would interest the Swiss, they should furnish 16,000 men.

Napoleon then related the following incident to his Minister of War:—

"As I was passing through Givet a detachment of English prisoners set to work to repair the flying bridge. I remarked especially the zeal and activity of eight or ten of them, who threw themselves into a little boat. Give orders for a list to be made of the ten men who most distinguished themselves upon this occasion; let them receive a new suit of clothes and five Napoleons each, with an order to go to Morlaix, where they must be handed over to the Transport Office, making known the cause of their release.... There is an English clergyman there who asked my permission to spend three months in England; grant this to him. He might take charge of the others. I also send you a petition handed to me under the same circumstances by an English lady; send me a report upon this demand."

On the 14th November further instructions were sent to Marshal Davoust on the subject of Prussia and what was to be done in the event of war. Then the Emperor said: "M. Saint Marsan is engaged in negotiating, but there is so much bad faith and uncertainty in the Berlin cabinet that I fear it will be impossible to prevent the ruin of Prussia ... Your corps will be able to reach the Vistula before the Russians because you will be at Berlin before they know anything at St. Petersburg.... The Russians have obtained great successes over the Turks, who behaved like brute beasts. I see that peace is about to be concluded. I have made sure of Austria."

On the 16th November the Emperor wrote to Admiral Decrès on the subject of the Boulogne flotilla, which he intended to keep up as one of the most powerful means of influencing England; it would oblige the English to keep a squadron off Boulogne and to have a reserve force in the Thames and the Downs, he wrote.

To GENERAL SAVARY (*Minister of Police*).

"ST. CLOUD, 20*th* November, 1811.

"You have committed a breach of duty in prosecuting an individual simply because he made some complaints against you; this was all the more unjust, because he told me things which I did not know and which I ought to have known. Taking this man from the present moment under my special protection, no measures must be adopted against him without my special authorisation. I hope that you will not fall again into the same error. All French citizens have the right of appealing to me against no matter who. . . .

"NAPOLEON."

In another long letter to Marshal Davoust, of the 2nd December, the Emperor said:

"The Germans complain that all the reports on the subject of an insurrection in Germany are fomented by the French . . . . and that you said at Rostock that you would know how to prevent Germany from becoming a Spain. This speech has done a great deal of mischief. There is nothing in common between Spain and the German provinces. Spain would have been reduced long ago but for the 60,000 Englishmen, but for those 1,000 leagues of coast which oblige our armies to be always on the frontiers, and but for the 100,000,000 fr. furnished by South America, for England is not in a position to furnish Spain with money. But, as there is no America in Germany, nor sea, nor numerous fortresses, nor 60,000 Englishmen, there is nothing to be feared, even were the Germans as lazy, as idle, as addicted to assassination, as superstitious, as given over to monks as the people of Spain, where there were 300,000 monks. Judge then what there is to fear from a nation so good, so reasonable, so cold, so tolerant, so removed from all excesses that there is not an example of a single Frenchman having been assassinated during the war in Germany...

"NAPOLEON."

To MARSHAL BERTHIER.

"PARIS, 5*th December*, 1811.

"Write to Marshal Suchet to complain that his wife in her letters to Madame de Saligny speaks about military matters; that these details should not be found in the letter of a lady, who should know nothing either of the number of the troops or their movements, but speak of her health, and that is all.[1]

"NAPOLEON."

On the 6th December, in another letter to Marshal Berthier, the Emperor said—"Express my dissatisfaction with regard to the flank march made by General Gerard in presence of the enemy—march of three days—all the more ill combined because the enemy were always in a position to cut him off. . . . It is unfortunate that with an army of 80,000 men those measures dictated by

---

[1] It is rather curious that the widow of Marshal Suchet, the Duchesse d'Albufera, thus ordered to speak only of her health, should be still alive, and residing in Paris in the mansion close to the English embassy, which King Joseph gave her as a wedding present.

prudence were not taken to avoid receiving an affront from a small English corps of 6,000 men. Tell him that my opinion remains the same, that every time that he delivers battle, especially with the English, he must not divide his forces, but present imposing masses. . . . Marshal Soult has the finest army in the world, and yet he holds in check neither General Hill nor the army of Murcia, the whole of which marched to the relief of Valencia. . . ."

To M. MARET.

" PARIS, 16*th December*, 1811.

"M. de Nesselrode will soon be here, and that decides me to raise the conscription. . . . I also desire a communication to be addressed to the princes of the confederation to remount their cavalry and to prepare their contingents. They must give as a reason the Russian levy of four men in every 500, the large number of troops on the frontier, and the decision at which Russia seems to have arrived of making war. . . .

"NAPOLEON."

And on the 20th, his Majesty wrote to his Foreign Minister to inform Baron Bignon that—" in the event of war he is to be attached to the head-quarters' staff, and placed at the head of the secret police, including the spy system in the ranks of the enemy, the translation of intercepted letters, the reports of prisoners, &c. It is therefore necessary for him to organise the secret police at once." A free use was to be made of Poles speaking Russian and acquainted with military matters, and the Emperor said that he would not regret to spend 12,000 francs a month for satisfactory information. "My brother of France," said Frederick the Great, on one occasion, "has twenty cooks and one spy where I have one cook and twenty spies." Napoleon had lots of both.

To Prince Cambacérès.

"Paris, 26*th December*, 1811.

"Comte Auguste Talleyrand, on his marriage, declared to his wife's family that he had a sum of 8,000*l*. which had been given to him by his cousin, the Prince de Benevento (Talleyrand) then Minister of Foreign Affairs. However, the prince insisted upon having bills payable to order for this sum. These bills have since been placed in circulation; they are in the hands of a stockbroker, and must shortly be paid, or Comte Augustus Talleyrand will be dishonoured. I cannot approve of this double dealing. Matrimonial clauses are sacred, and as it was declared that the Prince de Benevento gave 8,000*l*., he should not have exacted bills, and having exacted them, delicacy ought to have prevented him from allowing them to get into circulation. Having made a sacrifice of 88,000*l*. in purchasing the residence of the Prince de Benevento simply to enable him to settle his affairs, that sum must also serve to settle those of Comte Auguste Talleyrand. I beg you to speak to the Prince de Benevento and Comte Auguste Talleyrand on this subject, and to constitute yourself their arbitrator. I wish this affair to take the form of a family, and not a commercial arrangement, which should not exist between men of honour.

"Napoleon."

Comte Auguste Talleyrand was one of the Emperor's chamberlains, and hence this interference on his behalf.

To M. de Champagny.

"Paris, 31*st December*, 1811.

"I have just seen the porcelain service sent to the Empress as a new year's gift. It is very ugly. See that it be prettier another year. Have a breakfast service made, and on each cup the portraits of the Empress and of the six princesses, my sisters and sister-in-law. Have another set made with the portraits of the ladies of honour to the Empress.

"NAPOLEON."

To THE MAJOR-GENERAL.

"PARIS, 31*st December*, 1811.

" General Fournier is granted permission to go home. The major-general must state what county he belongs to so as to hinder him from coming to Paris. It is the corruption of the great city which attracts all these young fellows.

"NAPOLEON."

CHAPTER III.

THE YEAR 1812.

1812 will for ever remain memorable as the year of the Russian campaign and the retreat from Moscow. General Gouiron de St. Cyr traced the conduct of Napoleon in this big war to ambition. Certain it is, however, that the French Emperor, who seldom forgot or pardoned a slight unless it suited his policy, had several pretexts for quarrelling with the Czar. At Erfurth Napoleon threw out a hint that he should like to form a matrimonial alliance with the Russian Imperial family, and the Dowager Empress immediately gave the hand of her only marriageable daughter to the Duke of Oldenburg. During the war with Austria the Czar gave Napoleon very little aid, and after the treaty of Vienna the advances of his Majesty, who demanded the hand of the youthful Grand Duchess Anne were so coldly met, that Napoleon turned to the court of Vienna, and married the Archduchess Marie Louise. The first serious consequence of this marriage was, that Napoleon refused to ratify a decree which had been signed by his ambassador, in which it was proposed to abolish even the name of Poland. When the match with the Czar's sister was broken off, Napoleon assumed a tone of virtuous indignation, and swore to protect Poland, or that portion of the country not in the grasp of Austria and Prussia. This determination was in itself enough to kindle war between the two empires. Again, there was constant bickering going on over the continental blockade, the principles of which Napoleon insisted should be strictly observed by Russia, while he eluded them himself by means of licences. The first act of independence in which the Czar indulged, was the issuing of a ukase, which ordered that all goods manufactured in England should be burned, and also several articles manufactured in Germany and in France, especially cloths and silks. M. Thiers says in his history (vol. xiii., p. 447) that Napoleon, on learning the news, exclaimed—" I would sooner receive a blow on the cheek than see the produce of the industry and labour of my subjects burned." It must be said that he himself acted in the same way with regard to some of the products of Switzerland, his ally, and of Italy, his domain.

Another cause of rupture with Russia is mentioned by Lanfrey (vol. v. p. 501). It appears that in reply to the remonstrances of his finance ministers, Gaudin and Mollien, he replied—"I shall wage this war in a political interest, but also in the interests of my finances. Have I not always re-established them by means of war?" Napoleon recalled Caulaincourt, because he had become too Russian, and replaced him by Lauriston; a similar change was made at the Foreign Office, where the servile M. Maret, Duc de Bassano, replaced M. Champagny, Duc de Cadore, who tacitly disapproved of war with Russia.

In August, 1811, Napoleon, at a grand reception, addressed the most violent reproaches to Prince Kourakine, on the subject of the conduct of Russia—reproaches and invectives similar to those addressed to Lord Whitworth on the rupture of the treaty of Amiens, to Prince Metternich, on the eve of war with Austria, and to Cardinal Consalvi, over the Concordat, to the Portuguese ambassador at Fontainebleau, and to the Neapolitan ambassador at Milan. However, up to the very last moment, both Czar and Emperor denied that their intentions were hostile. Both protested that they were acting on the defensive, and both protested that they would not be the first to strike. It was not until June, 1812, that hostilities commenced. On one side stood France, Austria, Prussia, the Confederation of the Rhine, Switzerland, Poland, and Italy, on the other Russia. The Emperor had reckoned on the co-operation of Sweden and Turkey, but both those powers, exasperated by the perfidy and overbearing conduct of Napoleon, made peace with Russia. Sweden preferred the Czar, who had just plundered her of Finland, to Napoleon, who had encouraged and sanctioned that act, and it was the same with Turkey, in regard to Moldavia and Wallachia. The French Emperor, in permitting Alexander to rob right and left, thought that he was accomplishing a clever political stroke, and creating for Russia two implacable enemies, one on each flank, and lo, both Sweden and Turkey turned against him.

Napoleon was more successful with Austria and Prussia, who signed treaties with him, against their will, it is true. Austria promised a contingent of 30,000 men, who were not to be employed in Spain; and Prussia, several of whose fortresses were to be occupied by the French in case of hostilities with Russia, promised 20,000 men. Lanfrey points out that Russia had no objection to this arrangement, being well aware that when the right moment came she would be able to count upon the courts of Vienna and Berlin, who would be better able to help her afterwards, if not at once exposed to the wrath of Napoleon, especially as the Czar had made up his mind to draw the French into the heart of Russia.

Before war was openly declared, the Emperor, wishing to approach the scene of action, set out for Dresden, where he was met by the Emperor of Austria, the Kings of Saxony and Bavaria, and a crowd of princes who were all more or less his vassals. He was now at the head of an army of 640,000 men, 60,000 horses, and 1,200 guns. Under his standards were arrayed men of nearly every nation in Europe, even men belonging to countries with which he was at war—Spaniards and Portuguese. The fifth corps of the Grand Army was composed of Poles, and was commanded by Prince Poniatowski; the sixth corps was composed of Bavarians, the eighth corps of Westphalians. Other countries furnished divisions or brigades, while the National Guard was organised into Legions and Cohorts for home service.

It is impossible, even at this distant date,to read about the horrors of the Russian campaign without a shudder. As Southey says :—

> "The Emperor Nap he would set off
> On a summer excursion to Moscow.
> The fields were green, and the sky was blue.
> Morbleu ! Parbleu !
> What a pleasant excursion to Moscow."

It would have been more true to have said the Emperor Nap. allowed himself to be lured on to Moscow and destruction. Before taking the field, he had called for, and no doubt studied, the campaigns of Charles XII. If so, the lessons of the past were useless. He must have read such warnings as this, which we take from the pages of Lardner :—

"The advance of the Swedes was soon marked by a succession of triumphs ; and Peter, finding that Charles was resolved to pursue him, and that the invader had but 500 miles to traverse to the capital, an interval unprotected by any places of consequence, with the exception of Smolensko, conceived a masterly plan for drawing him into a part of the country where he could obtain neither magazines nor subsistence for his army, nor, in case of necessity, secure a safe retreat. . . . Charles, heated with victories, and panting for further acquisitions, surveyed the vast empire, upon the borders of which he now hung like a cloud, as if it were already within his grasp ; while Peter, more wary and self-possessed, conscious of the magnitude of the stake for which he fought, and aware of the great difficulties of his situation, occupied himself in making provision against the worst."

Charles, finding the whole country laid waste, paused at Smolensko, beyond which place Napoleon's marshals in vain urged him not to venture. Charles turned off into the Ukraine; Napoleon went on to Moscow: the same fate befell both conquerors. The same policy adopted by Peter, and then by Alexander, succeeded as far as the total destruction of their enemies was concerned.

The Russians attributed the overthrow of Napoleon to Providence, and so did many eminent Englishmen, such as Dr. Arnold. If so, a million of men perished, most of them after the most horrible sufferings, in order that Napoleon might be punished, and in 1813 he was himself thanking the Almighty for the victories of Lutzen, Bautzen, and Wurschen, and having *Te Deums* sung through the length and breadth of France. We have known more than one survivor of the terrible retreat from Moscow, the details of which make the gorge rise. Nor have the Russians forgotten those days of trial. The peasants, especially in the neighbourhood of Moscow, still talk of the invasion of 1812, and, with terrified faces, speak of the French as of an army of giants which suddenly came and devastated the country.

We shall find Napoleon leaving his army, or the remains of it, at Smorgoni, on the 5th December, as he left his army in Egypt, and for the same reasons. His presence was necessary in Paris. This was perhaps true; a Colonel Malet, during the absence of news from the army, by spreading a report of the Emperor's death, had almost managed to upset the regency. Then again it was necessary for Napoleon to keep a sharp look-out upon Prussia and Austria, and by re-organising a new army, to frighten them into being faithful to the alliance as long as possible. When the year ended, Napoleon had not yet heard that the Prussian, General York, who was acting with Macdonald, had gone over to the Russians.

In 1812 Napoleon had not much time to occupy himself with Spanish affairs, where, at the beginning of the year, matters assumed a very sombre hue for the French. Marshal Victor was repulsed at Tariffa. Wellington took Ciudad Rodrigo, and Badajos, and gained the battle of Salamanca, which opened the gates of Madrid for him. Soult was obliged to abandon Cadiz, the seat of the national government, which had been blockaded by land for four years; and the French, too, were driven out of Seville. Towards the close of the year, however, Wellington, for want of siege guns, failed in his attack upon Burgos, and had to fall back from the Spanish capital. As Napoleon learned the result of the battle of Trafalgar just before Austerlitz, so he learned that of Salamanca on the eve of Borodino.

There was not much time left for theological discussion in 1812. The Pope was transferred for safe keeping to Fontainebleau, until the Emperor could find time to take up the thread of the Concordat, and insist on due respect being paid to the liberties of the Galican Church.

No letters appear to have been written upon the 1st January, but on the 2nd the Emperor wrote thus to Marshal Berthier—

"I beg that you will send me a report, destined for publication, on the affair of General Girard. It appears that General Briche was posted on the side on which the enemy advanced, and that he was completely surprised, not having bivouacked, but having slept in a good house, and that the hussars had unsaddled their horses. My object is to make an impression on the minds of the generals and colonels in command of the light troops, and to remind them, in principle, that a colonel of chasseurs or hussars, who, instead of passing the night in his bivouac in continual correspondence with his outposts, goes to bed, deserves death. . . .

"NAPOLEON."

Lord Londonderry gives this description of the affair in question—"Lord Hill passed the night of the 21st at Malpartida, where he obtained information which induced him to hope that he might overtake the enemy and bring him to action. On the evening of the 27th, unobserved by Girard, he reached Alcuerca. He was now within a short league of Arroyo del Molinos, the village where Girard's corps was to pass the night, and the enemy remained in utter ignorance of his proximity until they found themselves attacked on the morning of the 28th. Taken by surprise, they offered, as might be expected, no resolute resistance; and Lord Hill's success was so complete that out of 2,500 infantry, and 600 cavalry, of which the French corps originally consisted, scarcely 500 escaped. General Girard was wounded, and his artillery taken." A foot note says that when the 71st and 92nd Highlanders dashed in upon the astonished Frenchmen, their bagpipes struck up "Hey Johnny Cope, are ye wakin' yet," which must have increased the confusion caused by a howling storm, musketry and artillery fire, and charges of cavalry.

To MARSHAL BERTHIER.

"PARIS, 6*th January*, 1812.

"In the *Rêveries* of Marshal Saxe, amid a great many things extremely *médiocre*, there are some ideas on the way of raising contributions in the enemy's country without fatiguing the army, which appear to me to be good. Read them and put the substance in instructions destined for my generals in Spain.

"NAPOLEON."

According to Marshal Saxe, the best way to obtain provisions in a hostile country, without fatiguing the troops, is to send out circulars saying that at such a date parties will be despatched to collect receipts, and to set fire to the houses of those who cannot produce them. These parties to consist of thirty men, to march at night, and, on pain of death, to do no damage. Before returning to their quarters, the various parties to be mustered and searched, and any man found to have robbed the smallest thing to be hung without pity. In this way the marshal says that the country for 100 leagues round will furnish provisions and money, for none of the inhabitants will be able to sleep in peace without having sent in their contributions.

The next day we find his Majesty obliged to send 2,000,000 francs to Spain; so much to the king; to the armies of the north, the centre, of Portugal; the garrison of Santona, &c.

The want of sugar was so severely felt in France at this period that there appeared a caricature in Paris of the Emperor trying to sweeten his coffee with beetroot, and giving the little King of Rome a piece of beetroot, saying, "Suck, suck, my child, it is sugar."

On the 13th January, Napoleon wrote a long note upon the continental blockade. In the note in question he pointed out that whereas sugar had reached an exorbitant price in Italy, Naples and France, it was much cheaper in the States of the Confederation, which proved that while the laws were observed in the three countries above named, they were violated by the Confederation. He said that Italy and Naples were both aware that if they did not execute the laws of the empire they would be annexed.

The Emperor, after dwelling on the amount of sugar consumed in France, went on to say that he had granted licences for the importation of 45,000,000 lbs. of raw sugar into France, the duty upon which would produce 70,000,000 francs, and that the same system would be applied to tea, coffee, indigo, raw cotton, and other articles.

The destroyer of colonial produce was jubilant over the great activity which this measure would produce in France, and the amount of duty which would be levied, and he artfully explained that his concession would do England no good. He wrote—

"If, after having taken this system into consideration, England adheres to it, she will experience great damage and annoyance, as well as the disappointment of seeing that the activity of our manufactures, and the increased production of our customs more than compensate for this relaxation of the continental system. His Majesty does not consider this as a change of system, but as the consequence of the system. The system was war, the result is victory.

"In fact did we ever say that we would never receive any more sugar, coffee or indigo? No, for we were satisfied with placing a duty on those articles. *It was for England to furnish us*, and we never thought that our navigation and our prizes could supply us; but we said that we would receive these goods only against the produce of French soil, with a high duty, that we would permit them to arrive on board our ships and with our licences only.

"It is evident that the system which has just been established is a permanent system, which may be perpetual; we can always give our wine and our silks in exchange for articles which we have not got; give them, not after the manner of the disadvantageous treaty of Versailles which took into no account the difference between the consumption of 30,000,000 and of 10,000,000 inhabitants, but on a calculation by which the value is multiplied by the quantity, and not based upon one of those elements only. . . .

"Therefore we shall no doubt do good to England, but a good which we cannot help, and in return for which we shall receive three-fold. It would be a bad combination to refuse three for one."

Having thus excused himself in a manner worthy of one of those Jesuit fathers described by Pascal in his *Provincial Letters*, his Majesty went on to explain the nature of his licences, the conditions upon which they would be granted, the harbours which would be thrown open in France, Italy, Naples, Prussia, Austria, Hamburg, Dantsic, &c., and the kind of goods to be imported and transported.

And yet on the 10th January, the Emperor ordered M. Maret to draw up a note explaining the motives which had determined him to occupy Swedish Pomerania, "where not only English smuggling is tolerated, but recent facts show that Sweden takes an active part in it."

To GENERAL CLARKE.
" PARIS, 19*th January*, 1812.

"You have given the command of the department of the Apennines to Adjutant Commander Bourmont, that is to say to an old *Chouan* leader. This measure is ridiculous. That officer should not be employed, or employed only in such a way as to be under supervision. What would my troops think on seeing themselves commanded by such a man?

" NAPOLEON."

On the 25th January, Napoleon wrote a letter to General Lacuée, which was to be kept secret, saying that as soon as war was declared he intended raising 120,000 men who would be obliged to serve as long as the war lasted, but who would not be sent out of the country. They were to protect the interior.

Two days later the Emperor thus explained the situation to brother Jerome, King of Westphalia.

"Some time since, various indications made me fear that the Emperor of Russia no longer entertained the same opinions as at Tilsit. A ukase published in December, 1810, essentially damaged the interests of France and the Confederation, and was advantageous for England. However I refrained from making any complaints, confining myself to friendly representations. In the month of April the Emperor of Russia sent a protest relative to the Oldenburg affair to the various courts. I was all the more astonished at this singular step because, foreseeing the wishes of Russia, I had from the first offered a suitable indemnity to the Duke of Oldenburg. Russia not appearing to accept the indemnity proposed, I pressed her to know what she required. In fact I did everything possible to repair the consequences of an act calculated to excite distrust between the two courts. Instead of explaining herself, Russia weakened her army on the Danube, evacuated the right bank of that river, withdrew a portion of her troops from Finland, and concentrated all her disposable forces on the frontiers of the Duchy of Warsaw.

"The territory of the Confederation was thus threatened to such an extent that I was obliged to order the troops of the Duchy to fall back upon the Vistula so that I might be able to aid them in the event of a sudden attack. From the commencement of these movements on the part of Russia my first care was to provide for the defence of Dantsic, which is one of the bulwarks of the Confederation. This led me to ask for a portion of the contingents and to write to that effect to your Majesty, who sent one of your regiments to that place.

"A short time afterwards an ambassador from Brazil, conveyed by an English frigate, was received at St. Petersburg as the minister of a friendly power, although, in virtue of the treaty of Tilsit Russia should be at war with the House of Braganza. I desired peace; I was interested in preserving it because a portion of my army was employed in Spain; but when Russia supported the violation of treaties by arming I also was obliged to arm. This precaution is more than justified to-day by the extraordinary levy ordered by Russia.

"I have been obliged to concentrate my armies and to replenish my war material. These preparations have taken a year. Now 300,000 men are about to cross through Germany, and to march on the frontiers of the Confederation, not with hostile intentions, but in order that my armies may be as near to the Vistula as the Russian armies.

"When the time comes, I will instruct my Minister for Foreign Affairs to reply to the protest relative to Oldenburg, that the affairs of that country are really foreign to Russia; that the duke, called upon during the last war to furnish his contingent, did not do so; that not having fulfilled his duties, as a confederate he lost all the rights of one; that, through love of peace, however, I offered him a suitable indemnity, and that I am still ready to grant him one.

"While agreeing to this in principle, Russia has not said what she desires, and I am obliged to suppose that she intends asking for Dantsic or some other portion of the territory of the Confederation. If, in fact, she had propositions to make which are not contrary to the treaty of Tilsit and to my principles, would she have armed and would she have refused to explain herself? However, I am far from having lost all hope of peace. But since the Russians admit the fatal proceeding of negotiating with me at the head of a powerful army, it concerns my honour to do the same. I do not wish to commence hostilities, but I shall place myself in a position to repel them. I do not wish to violate Russian territory, but I wish to be ready to make any one repent of a violation of the territory of the Confederation.

"I desire your Majesty in consequence to assemble your contingent so that it may be prepared to take the field on the 15th February next. . . .

"NAPOLEON."

The above is very similar to the letter which the Emperor wrote to Jerome excusing the war with Austria in 1809 and calling upon him for assistance.

To MARSHAL DAVOUST.

"PARIS, 28*th January*, 1812.

"I await with impatience your report upon the colonial merchandise which you have found in Pomerania. You have, no doubt, sent a detachment of custom-house officers there. . . . As you are going to enter Pomerania it will be necessary to close hermetically all the passages between Sweden and the Continent, and that, without doing anything ostensibly, you lay a kind of embargo, so that nothing may enter or leave the country, with the exception of the cabinet couriers which the Swedish Government may wish to send to France; no commercial goods must be allowed to pass.

"NAPOLEON."

To ADMIRAL DECRÈS.

"PARIS, 4*th February*, 1812.

"The reports from Toulon, as well as accounts from England, show that my squadron manœuvred badly, and that it ought to have captured two English frigates which were allowed to escape. Express my dissatisfaction to Rear-Admiral Baudin, and ask for the names of the captains who were the most in advance in this affair. Tell Vice-Admiral Emeriau that the government ought to know everything; that this manner of disguising facts is most reprehensible. You can order that officer to return on board. Tell him that I hope he will redouble his zeal; that I shall be at Toulon when I am least expected. . .

"NAPOLEON."

James, in his *Naval History* (vol. v. p. 331), thus refers to this affair:—

"Is it not a little surprising that, out of upwards of fifty-six sail of the line in commission at the different ports of the French Empire not one squadron, nay, not one line-of-battle ship should have ventured out of sight of her own harbour?

What prevented Vice-Admiral Emeriau going fairly to sea on the 20th November? Where were the Duguay-Trouins, the De Grasses, and the Suffrens, when, on the 6th December, 1811, a French admiral with sixteen sail of the line allowed himself to be driven back into port by a British admiral with twelve?"

To M. MARET.

"PARIS, 16*th February*, 1812.

"M . . is not fit for the Foreign Office. He is said to be imbued with English customs and tastes, and that he likes and prefers the individuals of that nation to other people. This, in a French agent, is very inconvenient. M. . . . does not suit; he lives at Copenhagen with a mistress; he is extremely miserly, and is not fit for that mission. . . .

"NAPOLEON."

To MARSHAL BERTHIER.

"PARIS, 18*th February*, 1812.

"I beg that you will repeat my instructions to Marshal Marmont in the following terms.

"NAPOLEON."

The terms were: "The Emperor is not satisfied with the turn which you have given to the war. You have a superiority over the enemy, and instead of taking the initiative you receive it. You knock your troops about and fatigue them. That is not the art of war. Should General Hill march upon the army of the south that will be the most fortunate thing that can happen; that army is strong and well enough organised to fear nothing from the English, even should they unite four or five divisions."

Then followed instructions for keeping Hill in the south and preventing him from joining Wellington, and—

"The capture of Ciudad Rodrigo was a check for you, but the English are sufficiently acquainted with French honour to know that this success can become dangerous for them; it places them under the obligation of defending that fortress, and in this way they leave you master to select your field of battle, for they will be forced to march to the relief of that place and to fight in a position at a distance from the sea.

"The result of this advantage can be delayed until after the harvest. Then you will be in a position to besiege Ciudad Rodrigo: the enemy will have to fight or to submit to the disgrace of seeing you take that place."

Marmont was then directed to take up his head-quarters at Salamanca, to fortify that town, and to threaten the enemy in all directions. He was told that Soult would be at hand to hold Hill in check, and that it would be madness on the part of Lord Wellington to recall Hill as long as Soult continued to make demonstrations. The instructions went on to say:—

"Lord Wellington can therefore attack you with his corps only, and should he march upon you, you must unite seven divisions at Salamanca with all your artillery and cavalry; that will give you a force of 50,000 men. Leaning upon Salamanca, having all the artillery and ammunition you require, your army 50,000 strong is inattackable, even should General Hill form his junction with Lord Wellington. It would be inattackable, not for 35,000 Englishmen, which is the total strength of the English in Portugal without counting the Portuguese, but for 70,000 Englishmen. A camp selected, a retreat secured, guns and ammunition in abundance, are advantages which you know well how to appreciate.

"However, while you are observing the enemy, I will suppose that Hill has joined Wellington, and that Wellington is much stronger than he is; in that case the cavalry and two divisions can be called up from the army of the north; you can reinforce yourself in a day, and victory will be assured. But once a resolution adopted you must stick to it; you must choose your position in front of Salamanca, and be a conqueror, or perish with the French army on the field of battle selected by yourself. . . .

"When you assumed the command of your army it had just experienced a check by its retreat from Portugal; that country was ravaged, the hospitals and magazines of the enemy were at Lisbon; your troops were fatigued, disgusted with forced marches, without artillery, without military train; Badajoz was attacked; a battle in the south had not caused the siege of that place to be raised. . . ."

Marmont was then complimented for having marched on Badajoz, and having forced the enemy to raise the siege, and to re-enter Portugal. The instructions added—

"Since then, marshal, you have returned to the north, Lord Wellington has fallen back upon the real point of defence of the country, and you are in presence of each other.

"At the present moment your position is simple and clear, and consequently does not require any mental combinations. Place your army in such a manner that in four marches your troops can be concentrated at Salamanca. . . . Should Lord Wellington march upon Badajoz, let him go there; immediately concentrate your army and march straight upon Ameida; send out parties in the direction of Coimbra, and be assured that Wellington will soon turn to meet you. But the English know too well what they are about to commit such a fault. . . . By following these directions, and executing them with rapidity, you will hold the enemy in check; London itself will tremble at the prospect of a battle and the invasion of Portugal, so feared by the English; and then, at harvest-time, you will find yourself in a position to besiege Ciudad Rodrigo, and to take that place in the teeth of the English, or to deliver battle, which is desirable, as they are far from the sea, and if beaten, will be ruined and will lose Portugal."

The above instructions extend over seven closely-printed pages.

To the Emperor of Russia.

"Paris, 24th February, 1812.

"Sir, my Brother,—After the arrival of the courier which Comte Lauriston despatched on the 6th, I made up my mind to talk over the unfortunate matters which have occurred within the last fortnight with Colonel Czernitchef. It remains with your Majesty to bring this affair to an end. I beg of your Majesty never to doubt &c., &c.

"Napoleon."

We shall see presently to what this letter referred.

Note for M. Barbier.

"Paris, 26th February, 1812.

"The Emperor wishes to replace the novels and most of the poetry in his library by historical works. M. Barbier is to make a selection of these works, and in the meantime to procure Pelly's *History of France*, which his Majesty desires to read."

To Comte Daru.

"Paris, 27th February, 1812.

"I send you the papers of the committee of inquiry [on the capitulation of Dupont at Baylen]. I beg that you will read them with care and draw up a report. You must join to the report a demand on the part of Comte Regnaud for the convocation of the High Court. . . . You must lay this before me so that I may adopt a definitive decree.

"Napoleon."

In a second letter to Comte Daru, of the same date, his Majesty said :—

"I have a great many Spaniards; the fact is that in the middle of Germany they are more French than

German. I have no fault to find with the Portuguese in my service, and I hear nothing but good of the Spaniards who have been for a year past in Italy and in Germany."

The Emperor, after going into details of organisation, expressed the conviction that through these men he would be able to gain the affection of the population of Spain.

In another letter to Comte Daru, of the 1st March, the Emperor asked for a list of what men Prussia was to furnish to the Grand Army.

To M. MARET.

"PARIS, 2nd March, 1812.

"It will be necessary to send a courier to Comte Lauriston to-day. Do not speak to him about the espionage of Czernitchef, of which you are supposed to know nothing at present. Explain clearly to Lauriston that in no case must he enter into an engagement on the subject of an interview [like those of Tilsit and Erfurth]; that I shall have pleasure in seeing negotiations opened once my troops are on the Oder or the Vistula; that I do not wish for an interview; that an interview is a matter of which he can make use, but that he must always leave me free to elude it.

"NAPOLEON."

And the next day the Emperor dictated a letter to Prince Kourakine, in which he bitterly complained to the Russian ambassador of the conduct of Colonel Czernitchef, who, though not a political agent, but an aide-de-camp of the Czar, had taken advantage of his position to violate what was most sacred among men. The colonel, in fact, had employed the *concierge* of the Russian embassy to obtain from a clerk in the War Office certain information on the subject of the preparations of the Emperor for a campaign against Russia. The papers thus procured rendered any further doubt in the mind of the Czar as to the intentions of Napoleon impossible.

To COMTE BIGOT.

"PARIS, 3rd March, 1812.

"It is time to finish with this scandal of the Sisters of Charity who have revolted against the Superioresses. It is my intention to suppress the convents which, within twenty-four hours after being warned, have not submitted.

"NAPOLEON."

On the same day Prince Eugene was rated for having allowed the *Rivoli* to leave harbour before making sure that the coast was clear, and that there was no English vessel in the Adriatic. The result of this negligence was that the *Rivoli* got snapped up by a British cruiser, and the French and Italian admirals reverted to their old plan of keeping ships in harbour for English squadrons to blockade them.

Captain Talbot, in his report of the capture of the *Rivoli* 74 by the *Victorious* 74, wrote:—"I feel great satisfaction in saying that the conduct of Commodore Barré during the whole of the action, convinced me that I had to deal with a most gallant man, and in the manœuvring of his ship a most skilful and experienced officer. He did not surrender until nearly two hours after his ship had been rendered unmanageable, and had 400 killed and wounded."

To MARSHAL BERTHIER.

"PARIS, 12th March, 1812.

"Send an aide-de-camp to Marmont, saying that you have laid his last letter before me; that he has not concentrated forces sufficient at Salamanca to accomplish his object; that he must throw a bridge across the Agueda, and that if the enemy leave less than five divisions on the right bank of the Tagus, he should march on Coa and Almeida and ravage the whole north of Portugal; that if Badajos be taken by two simple English divisions, and that he, Duc de Raguse, has detained five English divisions on the right bank of the Tagus, the capture of Badajos will not be imputed to him, but will fall entirely upon the army of the south; that if, on the contrary, the enemy should weaken himself and leave only two, three, or four divisions on the right bank, it will be the fault of the army of Portugal if it does not march against the enemy, invest Almeida, and ravage the whole north of Portugal; that the principal duty of the army of Portugal is to hold five divisions of the English army in check, to take the offensive in the north, or, if circumstances permit, to march upon Almarez, so as to relieve Badajos, with as many divisions as employed by Lord Wellington."

Four days after this letter was written Badajos was invested by the English.

To GENERAL LACUÉE.

"PARIS, 15*th March*, 1812.

"I do not wish to buy any *eau-de-vie* at Vienna; but I authorise you to ask my ambassador, Comte Otto, to negotiate with a contractor for the purchase of two million bottles of Hungarian wine on condition of being delivered at Warsaw at 5*d.* a bottle.

"NAPOLEON."

Before taking the field against Russia another change was made in Spain, where Marmont was getting on worse than Massena had done. Hence the following letter to Berthier, who was once more, however, the major-general or chief of the staff of the Grand Army.

"PARIS, 16*th March*, 1812.

"Inform the King of Spain by a courier, who must start to-night, that I confide the command of all my armies in

Spain to him, and that Marshal Jourdan [whom Joseph had been so sorry to part with] is to perform the functions of chief of the staff. . . .

"NAPOLEON."

In another letter of the same date Berthier was told to "communicate to Oudinot the extracts from the treaty with Prussia relative to the non-occupation of Potsdam. He must therefore march upon Brandenburg by some other road. Also he must occupy neither the palace of Charlottenburg nor the king's palace at Berlin. . . ."

To M. MARET.

"PARIS, 28*th March*, 1812.

"I send you a report on the Russian army furnished by the Prussians. Ask Prince Schwartzenberg to communicate to you the ideas of Vienna upon it. It seems to me that this report gives three divisions too many.

"NAPOLEON."

To MARSHAL BERTHIER.

"PARIS, 30*th March*, 1812.

"Inform Marshal Davoust that I do not suppose that the Russians will move; they must be aware that Austria, Prussia, and probably Sweden are with me; that the Turks are about to make fresh efforts, that the Sultan is going to place himself at the head of the army, and that all this is calculated to hinder them from braving me. . . .

"NAPOLEON."

On the 3rd April Napoleon wrote another long letter to Berthier on the subject of affairs in Spain. Among other things he said, "Tell the King of Spain that he can dispose of the division of his guard and the division of dragoons, which forces, united to those of Soult, will assure the failure of the operations of the English. . . . There is now nothing in Spain but the English army; you must therefore assume the initiative by organising the defence of Salamanca and carrying on the war in the north of Portugal. . . ."

To FRANCIS II., EMPEROR OF AUSTRIA.

"ST. CLOUD, 3rd *April*, 1812.

"The letter of your Imperial Majesty, handed to me by Prince Schwartzenberg, contains assurances of a friendship always dear to me. To multiply and draw closer the bonds which attach me to your Majesty is one of my most ardent and constant wishes, and it is with real satisfaction that I have seen the relations existing between us produce an analogous feeling between our subjects, and establish between them a union which time, far from diminishing, will increase. Your Majesty will find me always ready to join you in cementing this friendship, &c. . . .

"NAPOLEON."

To MARSHAL BERTHIER.

"ST. CLOUD, 4th *April*, 1812.

"The Commandant Bourmont should not be employed at the head-quarters' staff: he can be attached to that of General Junot.

"NAPOLEON."

We shall find Bourmont during the Russian campaign commanding the Spanish regiment Joseph-Napoleon, which appears to have distinguished itself on more than one occasion.

To MARSHAL BERTHIER.

"ST. CLOUD, 6th *April*, 1812.

"I return you the letters of your brother. Reply that cacao, sugar, and coffee are not English merchandise, and ought not to be burned. What ought to be burned are articles of English manufacture. But as there are no custom-houses in Corsica, there will be no harm in allowing coffee and sugar to enter, without, however, permitting it, but in closing your eyes.

" NAPOLEON."

And on the 10th April Berthier was instructed to inform the Duke of Dantsic (Marshal Lefebvre) that the Emperor had given him the command of the division of the Old Guard, and that he was to set out at once for Dresden with his horses and baggage. And on the same day, in a letter to King Jerome, the Emperor said, " My Guard has marched. I do not think that the Russians will stir. The last news from St. Petersburg, of the 29th March, is that they are moving, but that they continue to declare that they will not attack."

To PRINCE EUGENE, AT MILAN.
"ST. CLOUD, 14th *April*, 1812.

" MY SON,—Organise Italy as you did before the last campaign . . . and afterwards come to Paris as speedily as possible. After remaining there three or four days you must repair with all diligence to join your army corps at Glogau.

" NAPOLEON."

On the 17th April the Emperor dictated a letter which M. Maret was to write to Lord Castlereagh. His lordship was to be assured that Napoleon continued to be animated with sentiments of peace and moderation, and therefore desired to make a " new, authentic, and solemn attempt to put an end to the misfortunes of war." After recapitulating what had occurred since the peace of Amiens, M. Maret was to say, " The affairs of the Peninsula and of the two Sicilies seem to be the matters the most difficult to conciliate. I am authorised to propose an arrangement upon the following bases : 'The integrity of Spain shall be guarenteed; France shall renounce all extension of her limits on the side of the Pyrenees; the present dynasty shall be declared independent, and Spain shall be governed by a national constitution of the Cortes.

"'The independence of Portugal shall also be guaranteed, and the House of Braganza shall reign.'"

Murat was to remain King of Naples, and the kingdom of Sicily was to be guaranteed to "the present House of Sicily." Spain, Portugal, and Sicily were to be evacuated by French and English troops, and if England did not accept this arrangement, she was to be held responsible for all the bloodshed which would ensue.

On the 26th the Emperor wrote a long letter to Berthier in which he was informed that his Majesty had given Marshal Victor the command of Berlin, and of the garrisons of Stettin, Kustrin, Glogau, &c., and that it was his intention to occupy Spandau and Pillau. Potsdam was not to be occupied, but Napoleon said—" However, it will be well to accustom the people of Potsdam to the sight of French uniforms, and for a good number of officers to go and sleep there in order to see the town. If curiosity does not induce them to visit the place it will be necessary to persuade them. . . ." Prussia was to be bound hand and foot before the French plunged into Russia.

To the EMPEROR OF RUSSIA.

"St. Cloud, 25*th April*, 1812.

"Having reason to think that your Majesty has left St. Petersburg, and that Comte Lauriston is no longer with you, I entrust my aide-de-camp Comte Narbonne with this letter. He will at the same time be the bearer of important communications to M. Romanzof. They will prove to your Majesty my desire to avoid war, and my constant adhesion to the sentiments of Tilsit and Erfurth. However, your Majesty will permit me to assure you that if the fatality of war should become inevitable between us, that will in nothing change those sentiments with which your Majesty has inspired me, and which are secure from all vicissitudes and all change.

"NAPOLEON."

On the 9th May the Emperor left St. Cloud, and on the 17th he reached Dresden, from which place he wrote the following letter to his brother-in-law, Prince Borghese.

"I have been here for the last two days with the Empress, and the Emperor and Empress of Austria. I propose remaining here a few days longer. All my army is on the Vistula. There is nothing new. Hostilities have not commenced.

"Having learned that there are English vessels off Savona, I think that it will be necessary to place the Pope in safety. In consequence, you will direct the prefect and the commander of the gendarmerie to make the Pope leave with his attendants in two carriages. His holiness will have his doctor in his carriage. Precautions must be taken so that he may pass through Turin during the night, that he does not stop till he reaches Mont Cenis, that he may pass through Chambery and Lyons during the night, and be thus taken to Fontainebleau where orders have been given for his reception. I commend everything to your prudence. . . The Pope must not travel in his pontifical robes, but in the dress of an ecclesiastic. . . .

"NAPOLEON."

After the above letter follow pages of instructions in unbroken array, filled with military details preparatory to taking the field, and then this—

To THE COMTESSE DE MONTESQUIOU.

"KŒNIGSBERG, 16*th June*, 1812.

"I have received your letter of the 6th June. I can but evince my satisfaction at the care which you take of the king. I hope that you will soon inform me that he has cut his four last teeth. I have granted the nurse all you asked.

"NAPOLEON."

To ADMIRAL DECRÈS.

"KŒNIGSBERG, 16th *June*, 1812.

"The conduct of the post captain who was at Lorient is sharply criticised; it is said that he might have succoured the two frigates. Similar suspicions attach to the conduct of the captain of the *Danaé* who might have helped the *Rivoli*. Make a report on these two affairs.

"NAPOLEON."

The two frigates were the *Ariane* and *L'Andromaque*, who with a brig were run ashore to escape capture, and were blown up.

James in narrating this affair says—"A fine French two-decker, with sails bent and top-gallant yards across, in the harbour of Lorient, lay a mortified spectator of this gallant achievement, by which two French forty-gun frigates and a sixteen-gun brig were driven ashore, and destroyed under the fire of a heavy coast battery, by a British seventy-four and a gun brig. Mortified indeed, for in the state of the wind the commanding officer of the port could do no more than send boats to assist in removing the crews" (vol. v. p. 51).

To MARSHAL BERTHIER.

"KŒNIGSBERG, 16th *June*, 1812.

"Write to Marshal Ney that his corps is diverging from the route traced out for it, and commits devastation everywhere. . . .

"NAPOLEON."

And on the 20th June Berthier was told to write to Prince Schwartzenberg saying that as his funds had not arrived from Vienna the French paymaster-general had been directed to place 20,000*l.* at his disposal. The prince was then co-operating with General Regnier with the view of covering Warsaw.

On the 20th June Napoleon issued his first bulletin to the Grand Army, at Gumbinnen. He said that—" Towards the close of 1810 Russia changed her political system; the English *esprit* regained its influence; the commercial ukase was the first symptom. In February, 1811, five divisions of the Russian army left the Danube and hurried to Poland by forced marches, sacrificing Wallachia and Moldavia.

"When the Russian armies were concentrated, there appeared a protest against France [reason of protest not given] which was sent to all the cabinets. Russia thereby announced that she would not preserve even appearances.

"Every method of conciliation was employed by France, but all was useless.

" At the close of 1811 France saw that this must end in war, and she prepared to take the field. . . .

"In March, 1812, a treaty of alliance was concluded with Austria; a month previously a treaty had been concluded with Prussia. . . .

"On the 22nd April the Emperor of Russia assumed the command of his army and left St Petersburg. . . .

"The Emperor left St. Cloud on the 9th May, passed the Rhine on the 13th, the Elbe on the 29th, and the Vistula on the 6th June."

And two days afterwards came this stirring proclamation to the immense host which was on the road to Moscow—

PROCLAMATION TO THE GRAND ARMY.

"IMPERIAL HEAD-QUARTERS, WILKOWYSZKI,
2nd June, 1812."

" SOLDIERS,—The second war of Poland has commenced; the first was terminated at Friedland and Tilsit. At Tilsit Russia swore an eternal alliance with

France, and war with England. To-day she violates her oaths. She refuses any explanation of her strange conduct until the French eagles have repassed the Rhine, thus leaving our allies at her discretion. Russia is carried away by fatality; her destinies must be accomplished. Does she believe that we have degenerated? That we are no longer the soldiers of Austerlitz? She places us between dishonour and war; the choice cannot be doubtful. Then let us march forward; let us pass the Niemen, and let us carry the war into her territory. The second Polish war will be as glorious for the French arms as the first. But the peace which we shall conclude shall put an end to the baneful influence exercised by Russia upon the affairs of Europe during the last fifty years.

"NAPOLEON."

In a letter to Berthier of the same date occurs this passage—"Place General Vedel in command of Wilkowyszki until further orders, this point being important. . . ." It will be remembered that General Vedel was one of the "cowards" implicated in the Baylen capitulation.

On the 1st July Napoleon addressed a long letter to the Czar from Wilna in his usual style, showing the purity of his intentions, and his love of peace, and laying all the blame of the war on Alexander. He complained that the Czar had refused to enter into any explanations until he (Napoleon) had evacuated Prussian territory, "Thus depriving Prussia of that independence which you professedly wish to guarantee, while at the same time you would oblige me to pass under the Candine Forks. I pity the wickedness of those who gave your Majesty such bad advice. No matter what may happen, Russia can never be permitted to hold such language to France; it is at most that which the Empress Catherine might have addressed to the last King of Poland.

"War is thus declared between us. God Himself cannot cause that which has been not to have been. But my ears shall be always open to negotiations for peace, and when your Majesty wishes to shake off the influence of the enemies of your family, of your glory and of your Empire, you will find me always animated with the truest feelings of friendship. A day will come when your Majesty will acknowledge that if, towards the end of 1810, you had not changed but had entered into loyal negotiation for the modification of the treaty of Tilsit, you would have had one of the most glorious reigns in Russia. After startling and reiterated disasters, by the wisdom of your policy you healed the wounds of the State, united immense provinces to your Empire, Finland, and the mouths of the Danube. But I also should have gained much; the affairs of Spain would have been terminated in 1811, and probably peace would before this have been concluded with England. Your Majesty was wanting in perseverance, in confidence, and, allow me to add, in sincerity; you have destroyed your future. Before passing the Niemen I should have sent an aide-de-camp to your Majesty, as in previous campaigns, if the persons who have the direction of the war, and who appear to me, in spite of the lessons of experience, so anxious to fight, had not found fault with the mission of the Comte de Narbonne...."

To MARSHAL BERTHIER.

"WILNA, *4th July*, 1812.

"Write to Marshal Ney that the situation of his army corps seems to me very alarming as regards his artillery. Without artillery his corps would be greatly compromised. ... Tell him to send out detachments of cavalry to make the stragglers join; a great many men who commit crimes will fall into the hands of the Cossacks. ...

"NAPOLEON."

And on the 9th July—"Reply to Prince Poniatowski that you have laid his letter before me, and that I am very dissatisfied to learn that he speaks of pay and of bread when it is a question of pursuing the enemy; that I am all the more surprised at this because he is alone on his side, with a small force, and when the Guard of the Emperor which came from Paris by forced marches, instead of having a half ration, are without bread, have only meat, and do not murmur; that the Emperor sees with pain that the Poles are such bad soldiers, and have such bad feeling as to complain of such privations; that his Majesty hopes he will hear no more of this."

On the same day the Emperor dictated some instructions for Marshal Macdonald. In these he said—" The Hetman Platoff, with his Cossacks and the corps of Bagration which wished to march upon Minsk, have been cut off from that town, and are being pursued by the King of Westphalia (Jerome). The Viceroy (Prince Eugene) is marching on the upper Dvina. The Guard and the head-quarters will leave here in a few days. It is the intention of the Emperor to march upon Moscow and St. Petersburg, and to free all Courland and Livonia of the army which is at Dinabourg. . . ."

And writing to Davoust the Emperor said—"It is probable that I shall march with my Guard and the 4th and 6th corps on Vitebsk, thereby threatening St. Petersburg and Moscow, having you on my right, and you having on your right King Jerome and Schwartzenberg (with his Austrians)." The Emperor then expressed the opinion that his manœuvres would force the Russians to retreat in order to cover St. Petersburg. The King of Naples was to pass the Drowya with the 2nd and 3rd corps, and was to follow the enemy.

On the 10th July Napoleon instructed Berthier to send a brigade of gendarmerie to Voronovo, "to arrest the pillagers of the 33rd, who are committing horrible devastations in that country. . . . Write to the viceroy to leave a patrol and some officers to prevent any of Marshal Davoust's men from passing Soletchniki; these men, under the pretence of looking for the 1st corps, which is at

Minsk, go to Lida to pillage that valley, which is superb. . . ."

On the 14th July the Emperor, in reply to the deputies of the Polish Confederation, said—

"I have heard with interest what you came to say.

"Poles, I should think and act like you; I should have voted as you did in the assembly of Warsaw. The love of country is the greatest virtue of civilised man.

"In my position I have a great many interests to conciliate, and a great many duties to fulfil. Had I reigned at the time of the first, the second, or the third partition of Poland, I should have armed my whole people to support you.

"As soon as victory permitted me to restore your ancient laws, your capital, and a portion of your provinces, I did so without loss of time, without, however, prolonging a war which would have required the shedding of more blood on the part of my soldiers.

"I love your nation. For the last sixteen years I have seen your soldiers at my side in the battles of Italy as in those of Spain. . . . I may add here that I have guaranteed to Austria the integrity of her states, and that I cannot authorise anything which will tend to trouble her in the peaceful possession of what remains to her of her Polish provinces. . . ."

Amid all the turmoil of war Napoleon found time to write the following letter to Comte Collier de Sussy, his minister of manufactures and commerce—"I see with pleasure that the bad times have passed; we have gained some cruel experience, which I owe, in a great measure, to the false information furnished by the Minister of the Interior. If I had listened to him I should have again delayed forbidding the exportation of corn, and we should have no longer been masters of the crisis. It is of great interest that you should take measures for ascertaining our resources exactly so that we may know when to permit and when to prohibit exportation. This is for the future, because for the next two years, no matter how abundant the harvests may be, we shall require corn to replenish our magazines. . . . I intend employing 20,000,000 francs in the way of magazines at Orleans, Cambrai, and near all the large towns of France. . . . Some years ago I ordered the construction of a magazine close to the arsenal,[1] and I know not by what fatality this building gets on so slowly. I beg that you will see the Minister of the Interior in order to hurry on the works. The Arc de Triomphe, the bridge of Jena, the Temple of Glory, the slaughter houses, can be delayed for two or three years without inconvenience, while it is of the greatest importance that the storehouses should be finished. . . ."

The Emperor during the march upon Moscow installed his Minister for Foreign Affairs at Wilna. On the 19th July he wrote a despatch to him, in which he said—"I suppose that I need not tell you to send couriers two or three times a week to Constantinople with bulletins and all the news possible. If I were obliged to enter into such details with you, you would be seconding my intentions very badly. The Turks must make haste to enter Moldavia and Wallachia, and to threaten the Crimea with their fleet. . . . Make the Polish Confederation send an embassy to Constantinople to ask for the guarantee of Turkey. You will see how important this step is; I have always had it in my head, and I do not know how I came to forget giving you orders on the subject sooner. Let this deputation, with a letter from the Confederation to the Grand Seignor, start before a week, and go 'full flight' to Constantinople."

In a letter to Berthier of the 22nd July, the Emperor, while telling him to write to General Regnier that an attack upon Warsaw was not to be feared, added—"The

---

[1] This huge building, known as the *Grenier d'Abondance*, was not finished until 1817; it was capable of containing 45,000 sacks of meal, or sufficient to feed Paris for a month. For some unknown reason this storehouse was burnt down by the communists in 1871.

pretended forces arriving for the Crimea are myths. Tell him that the Grand Seignor has refused to ratify the treaty of peace, and that on the contrary the Russians will be obliged to send fresh troops into Moldavia and Wallachia. . . . Tell him that we are at Mohilef, that we have crossed the Borysthenes, and that we are marching on Vitebsk and perhaps on Smolensko."

To M. MARET.
" BIECHENKOVITCHI, 25*th July*, 1812.

"Marshal Davoust had a battle on the 23rd at Mohilef; I have not yet learned the details. Bagration wished to trample over him and was defeated. A note, written at six in the evening, on the field of battle, said that the enemy had been defeated. To-day we had an affair with his advanced guard, and captured eight guns and 700 men. The Russian army is at Vitebsk. I tell you this for your information, but you need not write anything about it. We are on the eve of great events. . . .

"NAPOLEON."

To THE QUEEN HORTENSE, AT PARIS.
"VITEBSK, 29*th July*, 1812.

"MY DAUGHTER,—I saw with pain, by your letter of the 11th, that Napoleon has been ill, and I learned with pleasure by that of the 14th that he is out of danger. I expected this prompt cure, knowing how easily a mother is alarmed.

"NAPOLEON."

To M. MARET.
"VITEBSK, 31*st July*, 1812.

"I regret to see that there are 3,000 sick men at Wilna who are in great destitution, and have not even straw; and that the magazines contain no stores of any kind. . . . Let the Archbishop of Malines (the Abbé Pradt) know that I am not satisfied with what he wrote to Prince Schwartzenberg on the subject of military operations. . . .

"NAPOLEON."

To COMTE LAPLACE.

"VITEBSK, 1st August, 1812.

"I have received your *Calculation of Probabilities* with pleasure. There was a time when I should have read it with interest; to-day I must confine myself to expressing the satisfaction which I experience every time that I see you bring out new works. . . . The advancement and perfection of mathematics is intimately connected with the prosperity of the State.

"NAPOLEON."

To M. BARBIER, AT PARIS.

"VITEBSK, 7th August, 1812.

"The Emperor desires to have some amusing books. If there be any new novels which are good, or older ones which he does not know, or memoirs of light reading, you will do well to send them, for we have leisure moments here which are difficult to fill up."

A few days later, on the 10th August, we find Napoleon writing no less than seventeen long dispatches, which occupy more than fourteen closely printed pages. The above letter would hardly have flattered Comte Laplace had he seen it.

To M. MARET.

"VITEBSK, 7th August, 1812.

"I beg that you will see if the two or three hundred carts left behind at Wilna, exposed to the air, have been placed under cover in a church or an arsenal. If that has not yet been done the governor should see to it.

"NAPOLEON."

A note in *The Correspondence* informs us that immediately after having dictated the following letter Napoleon threw himself on his bed without signing it, probably overcome by fatigue :—

To M. MARET.

" Smolensko, 18th August, 1812.

"I have this instant returned to my quarters; the heat is excessive, and there is a great deal of dust, which fatigues us a little. We had the whole Russian army here; it received orders to deliver battle, and did not dare. We carried Smolensko by assault. It is a very large town, with a wall and respectable fortifications. We have killed 3,000 or 4,000 of the enemy, wounded the triple, and found here a large number of guns; several generals of divisions were killed, so it is said, here. The Russian army is marching in the direction of Moscow, very much dissatisfied and discouraged. Schwartzenberg and Regnier united have beaten the Russians."

The fact is that Smolensko was held by the Russian rear guard, 30,000 strong, and resisted all the efforts of Napoleon, who attacked the town with 70,000 men, the remainder of the army being held in reserve. Towards evening, after a most sanguinary conflict, the French howitzers set fire to the place, but the Russians still holding out, Napoleon was obliged to withdraw his troops. The next morning one of Davoust's patrols scaled the walls and found Smolensko deserted, not only by the Russian troops but by the inhabitants. The French are said to have lost 15,000 men in these fruitless assaults, and the Russians 10,000. There is nothing in *The Correspondence* on the subject on the check experienced by Murat's advanced guard under Sebastiani, on the 8th, when Platoff, with his Cossacks, defeated 6,000 horse, and took 500 prisoners. It was this little reverse which made Napoleon concentrate and knock his head against the ramparts of Smolensko, out of which the Russians might have been manœuvred.

To the COMTESSE DE MONTESQUIOU.

"SMOLENSKO, 23*rd August*, 1812.

"I have received the portrait of the King, and find it very like him. It furnishes me with an opportunity, of which I avail myself with pleasure, of expressing my satisfaction with the care you take of him.

"NAPOLEON."

To the EMPEROR OF AUSTRIA.

"SMOLENSKO, 24*th August*, 1812.

"Allow me to express to your Majesty my satisfaction with the conduct of the corps commanded by Prince Schwartzenberg, who cannot have failed to send you a report on the success which he recently gained. . . . Having placed the corps of General Regnier under the command of Prince Schwartzenberg, and as I may confide other corps to him, I beg that your Majesty will accord him the rank of Field Marshal.

"I take this opportunity of thanking your Majesty for all you did for the Empress during her stay in Bohemia. She is now at St. Cloud, where every one finds that she is quite well, and has grown much stouter.

"I start to-night for my advanced guard, which is twenty leagues on the road to Moscow. . . .

"NAPOLEON."

Nothing is said about an attack made by Ney on the Russian rear guard at Valtelina, in which there was some desperate fighting, and in which the Russians, with an inferior force, repulsed the enemy with the loss of 8,000 men, and then continued their retreat on Moscow.

To M. MARET.

"Dorogsbouje, 26th August, 1812.

"The enemy, after having constructed fortifications, raised batteries and redoubts, and announced their intention of making a stand here, as usual, failed in resolution. We entered this town, which is considerable enough, as it has eight or ten steeples. The country is good, and we are assured that it remains so as far as Moscow. The heat which we experience is excessive. The weather continues to be very fine. It is said that the enemy are determined to wait for us at Viazma. In a few days we shall be half way between Smolensko and Moscow, and, I think, at forty leagues from Moscow. Should the enemy be beaten there, nothing will protect that great capital, which I shall enter on the 6th September.

"Napoleon."

The country through which the French were advancing was a perfect desert; it had been laid waste by the Russian columns; there were hardly any brooks, the springs were dried up, and the sufferings of the French troops were such that they lost 38,000 men between Smolensko and Moskwa.

To M. MARET.

"Viazma, 29th August, 1812.

"We have reached Viazma. The enemy continue their retreat upon Moscow. I am waiting for news as to the march of the 16th and 22nd Russian divisions, which are coming from Moldavia. I have written to the Emperor of Austria, begging him to reinforce the cavalry corps of Prince Schwartzenberg by 3,000 men, in order to make good his losses. . . .

"Napoleon."

To GENERAL CLARKE.

"GHJATSH, *2nd September*, 1812.

"I have received the report of Marshal Marmont on the battle of Salamanca. It is impossible to read anything more paltry; there is more noise and more clatter in it than in a clock, and not a word to explain the real state of affairs.

"Here is the view which I take of the matter, and the course which you should pursue.

"You must wait until Marshal Marmont has arrived, and has been nearly cured of his wound. You will then ask him to reply categorically to these questions:

"Why did he deliver battle without the orders of his general-in-chief? [King Joseph.]

"Placed by the general dispositions of the army at Salamanca, it was all very well to defend himself if he were attacked, but since he had evacuated Salamanca, and was several marches away, why did he not inform his general-in-chief?

"Why did he not ask for orders as to the course he should pursue in connection with the general system of my armies in Spain?

"This is a case of insubordination which is the cause of all the misfortune. . . .

"How came he to assume the offensive while waiting for the division of dragoons, the thirty guns, and the 15,000 men which the King had in hand, to come up? . . . .

"At the proper time you must let Marshal Marmont know how indignant I am with his inexplicable conduct. . . .

"NAPOLEON."

To the great joy of the Russian nation the command of the army was now transferred from the hands of Barclay de Tolly, who had conducted the retreat from Smolensko in the most masterly style, to those of

Kutusof, who at that moment was labouring under a slight cloud at St. Petersburg. The change was hailed with delight in Russia, by the army and population generally, because Kutusof was a pure Russian, whereas Barclay de Tolly was the descendant of an old Scotch family, who had fought his way up to the highest rank without intrigue or favour. At Borodino Kutusof determined to show fight.

PROCLAMATION.

"THE IMPERIAL CAMP ON THE HEIGHTS OF BORODINO,
"7th September, 1812. 2 A.M.

"Soldiers, here is the battle which you have so long desired! Henceforth the victory depends upon you; it is necessary for us. It will give you abundance, good winter quarters, and a speedy return to the country! Behave as you did at Austerlitz, at Friedland, at Vitebsk, at Smolensko, and the most remote posterity will quote with pride your conduct on this day; let it say of you—*He was at the great battle under the walls of Moscow.*"

Two days afterwards Napoleon wrote as follows to his brother and very dear father-in-law, the Emperor of Austria :—

"I hasten to announce to your Imperial Majesty the happy issue of the battle of Moskowa, which took place on the 7th at the village of Borodino. Knowing the personal interest which your Majesty is good enough to bear me, I have thought it my duty to announce myself this memorable event, and the good state of my health. I set down the loss of the enemy at from 40,000 to 50,000 men; they had from 120,000 to 130,000 men engaged. I have lost between 8,000 and 10,000 men in killed and wounded. I have captured sixty guns and a large number of prisoners. My advanced guard is six leagues to the front.

"I again beg that your Majesty will reinforce Prince Schwartzenberg, so that he may sustain the honour of the Austrian arms as he has already done. . . .

"NAPOLEON."

It appears tolerably certain that although the French won the day the losses were very evenly balanced, and that the captured guns and the prisoners existed only in the fertile imagination of the Emperor.

To M. MARET.

"MOJAISK, 10*th September*, 1812.

"It is supposed that Wittgenstein has left the Drissa in in order to take up a position between Moscow and St. Petersburg. Should this turn out to be true, write to Marshal St. Cyr to pursue him, and to arrive at the same time as the enemy, in order to cover my flank. . . . Write to Prince Schwartzenberg that the enemy has done all in his power to prevent us from reaching Moscow, and that they will do all they can to drive us out;[1] that I am certain that the troops which were at Kief and Mozyr are

[1] The Russians may have done their best to prevent the French from reaching Moscow, but once the enemy in the city they tried to detain them there till the winter season arrived. At a council of war, held after Borodino, Barclay de Tolly and Kutusof both expressed themselves in favour of not defending Moscow, on the ground that it would lead the enemy into a snare, where his destruction would be certain. The Russian army, too, was far inferior in numbers to the Grand Army. The best policy, therefore, was to abandon Moscow without risking another battle, and to await events. When the divisions from Moldavia and Finland arrived the position of Napoleon would become most critical. Of course, had the Russians been aware that the French had not ammunition enough to fight a second battle they would have adopted a bolder plan.

The Grand Army little expected, when it came in sight of the old Muscovy capital, and when, struck by the splendour of the spectacle, the men broke from the ranks, shouting "Moscow! Moscow!" that the city before them was a snare, and that so few of them would return home to say that they had gazed on its minarets.

marching on Moscow; that he must follow the movement of the enemy actively, and not allow himself to be deceived; that if the enemy who are in front of him fall upon me, he must follow and fall upon them. . . . Henceforth the enemy, wounded in the heart, think only of the heart and take no notice of the extremities.

"NAPOLEON."

CIRCULAR TO THE BISHOPS.

"MOJAISK, 10*th September*, 1812.

"BISHOP OF . . . .,—The passage of the Niemen, the Dvina, the Borysthenes, the engagements of Mohilef, of Drissa, of Potolsk, of Dstrovno, of Smolensko, and, finally, the battle of Moskova, are so many reasons for rendering thanks to the God of Armies. It is therefore my desire that you should assemble my people in the churches to sing prayers according to custom and to the rules of the Church under similar circumstances.

"NAPOLEON."

On the 15th September Napoleon was dictating his orders from Moscow, and on the 18th he wrote to his Minister of Foreign Affairs: "We are following the enemy, who are falling back beyond the Volga. We have found an immense quantity of things in Moscow, which *was* a very beautiful city. It will take Russia 200 years to recover from the loss which she has sustained. It is not an exaggeration to set it down at 40,000,000*l*."

A large amount of provisions was found in the cellars at Moscow, but these stores did not last very long, and before many weeks had passed the French troops, laden with spoil and covered with the richest silks and jewels, were half starving.

TO THE EMPEROR OF RUSSIA.

"MOSCOW, 19*th September*, 1812.

"Having been informed that the brother of the minister of your Imperial Majesty at Cassel was at Moscow, I sent for him, and we had some conversation together. I recommended him to go to your Majesty and to acquaint you with my opinions. The beautiful and superb city of Moscow no longer exists. Rostoptchin had it burned. Four hundred incendiaries were caught in the act; they all declared that they were setting fire to the city by orders of the Governor and of the Minister of Police: they have been shot. The fire now appears to be extinguished. Three-quarters of the houses are burned down. This atrocious conduct is without aim. Is its object to deprive us of some resources? But these resources were in the cellars, which the flames did not reach. Besides, why destroy one of the finest cities in the world, the work of centuries, to attain so feeble an end? It is the conduct which has been pursued ever since Smolensko, and which has reduced 600,000 families to mendicity. The pumps of the city were broken or taken away; a portion of the arms in the arsenal were given to the malefactors, and we were obliged to fire some rounds into the Kremlin in order to drive them out. Humanity, the interests of your Majesty and of this great city, demanded that it should be confided to me as a deposit, since the Russian army did not defend it. The administration, the magistrates, and the civil guards should have remained. This is what was done twice at Vienna, at Berlin, and at Madrid. It is thus that we acted at Milan when Suwarrow entered that city. Conflagrations authorise pillage, in which the soldier indulges to dispute what remains with the flames. But I hold it to be impossible, with your principles, your heart, the correctness of your ideas, that you should have authorised similar excesses unworthy of a great sovereign and of a great nation. While carrying away the fire-engines from Moscow, 150 field-pieces, 60,000 new muskets, 1,600,000 cartridges, with powder, saltpetre, sulphur, &c., were left behind.

"I wage war against your Majesty without animosity; a note from you before or after the last battle would have stopped my march, and I should even have liked to have sacrificed the advantage of entering Moscow. If your Majesty retains some remains of your former sentiments, you will take this letter in good part. At all events you will thank me for giving you an account of what is passing at Moscow.

"NAPOLEON."

After Borodino the Czar, foreseeing the fate of Moscow, sent for the English ambassador, Lord Cathcart, and told him to inform his government that twenty such catastrophes would not induce him to abandon the struggle.[1]

The tremendous losses experienced during the campaign—losses which the Czar in his proclamation of the 20th October set down at 150,000 men—were beginning to be severely felt, especially as the Russians were receiving reinforcements from the Danube, and as recruits were thronging from all parts of the empire with the greatest enthusiasm.

On the 23rd September Napoleon wrote to M. Maret from the Kremlin—"I have just raised a conscription of 140,000 men in France, and in Italy one of 30,000. It is only in the Grand Duchy of Warsaw that nothing has been done. As many recruits as possible must be raised, as some of the regiments are in great need of men. Hurry on this levy so that it may take place at once. Horses, too, must be sent in order to remount the Polish cavalry and artillery. Write to Saxony for recruits, and also to all the courts of the Confederation of the Rhine. The battle of Borodino and the entry into Moscow should not weaken the zeal nor send the allies to sleep. . . ."

Another letter to M. Maret, dated the 24th, shows that the Emperor was obliged to send to France for hand-mills to grind corn for his troops; and on the 28th the Minister of Foreign Affairs, still at Wilna, was written to by the Emperor, who said—"I receive no news from Warsaw,

---

[1] Alison's *History of Europe*, vol. xi. p. 104.

very little from Vienna, and none from Constantinople. Nor do I hear anything about America, and yet it is urgent to do something in that quarter."

The next day his Majesty wrote again thus: "I stand in the greatest need of 14,000 horses. I have sent General Bourcier to Wilna, and have placed 160,000*l.* at his disposal. Purchases should be made in Hanover, at Berlin, &c. . . . In the province of Mohilef there are Jews immensely rich; send for the chief ones and see if you cannot deal with them by paying ready money. . . ." And on the 30th—"I send you the treaty between Russia and the Porte, which was found here in the Moscow papers. It appears that you have not yet received it from Constantinople, as you have not sent it to me." The same day M. Barbièr was written to for more books.

From the above letters it is evident that Napoleon was becoming painfully aware of the dangers of his position. However, he still entertained hopes of being able to conclude an advantageous peace, for he was as confident in the charms of his diplomacy as in the strength of his arm. In the meantime 100,000 men from the shores of the Baltic and the banks of the Danube were converging in order to cut off his retreat.

In the beginning of October, while the weather was still "as fine as that at Fontainebleau in September," the Emperor wrote a series of notes which show how clearly he appreciated the difficulties of his situation. He said:—

"The enemy are marching on the road from Kieff; their object is evident; they are expecting reinforcements from the army of Moldavia. To march against them would be to march in the direction of their succours, and to find ourselves deprived of any *points d'appui* during winter cantonments. Moscow having been burned and deserted by its inhabitants must not be taken into account; that city cannot contain our sick and wounded; the resources found there, once exhausted, no more will be forthcoming.

.... Should the army fall back upon Smolensko, would it be wise to go in quest of the enemy, and to expose ourselves to lose, in a march which would resemble a retreat, several thousand men in presence of an enemy acquainted with the country, having a large number of secret agents and a numerous light cavalry? Although the French army is victorious, it would find itself placed at a disadvantage by this movement, and would suffer serious losses."

After considering whether it would be well to return by the same road that he had reached Moscow the Emperor asked himself:—

"What is the object to be fulfilled? 1st, to place the Emperor as near France as possible, and to give the country confidence that the Emperor during his winter cantonments is in the midst of his people; 2nd, to quarter the army in a friendly country, close to its magazines; 3rd, to place ourselves in a position to back up the Emperor's negotiations for peace by threatening St. Petersburg; 4th, to sustain the honour of our arms at the height to which it has been raised by this glorious campaign."

The Emperor then indicated a series of movements calculated to fulfil the above desiderata, and came to the conclusion that the enemy, upon finding St. Petersburg menaced, would sue for peace. For the moment he considered it feasible to form a junction with Macdonald's corps at Riga and to march on the capital.

On the 10th October, M. de Montalivet having asked leave to prohibit the publication of a work attacking the reputation of a member of the Royal Family of England, the Emperor decided that no works should be prohibited but those which were obscene or calculated to disturb the tranquillity of the State.

Three days after writing the above instructions there was a light fall of snow, which showed that the fine weather was at last going to break up. On the same day (13th October) his Majesty was greatly mortified to hear Kutusoff's artillery firing salutes in honour of the capture of Madrid by the English.

To the COMTESSE DE MONTESQUIEU.

"Moscow, 16*th October*, 1812.

"I have received your letter of the 27th September, and thank you for the feelings you express. It is I who am indebted to you for the excellent care which you take of the little king; I am exceedingly grateful for it. It affords me pleasure to hear you speak of the promise he gives.

"NAPOLEON."

To GENERAL KUTUSOFF.

"Moscow, 18*th October*, 1812.

"General Lauriston has been directed to propose to your Highness arrangements with the view of giving the war a character in conformity with established rules, and for taking measures so that the country shall support only such evils as are inseparable from a state of war. In fact the devastation of your own country is as damaging to Russia as it is painful to the Emperor. Your Highness will easily understand how anxious I am to know the final decision of your Government upon this matter."

Marshal Berthier signed the above appeal, "by order of the Emperor"—an appeal which was in fact an attempt to open up negotiations with the Russian commander-in-chief. Some correspondence had passed between Murat and Beningsen on the subject of outposts, and the Czar had severely reprimanded the Russian general, and had issued strict orders that no shadow of an attempt should be made to negotiate with the French. Murat, too, had just been successfully attacked at Winkowo, where the French lost 1,500 men, thirty-eight guns, and a considerable amount of baggage.

On the 18th October Napoleon wrote to Berthier, telling him to inform the Duc de Trevise (Marshal Mortier) that he was going to leave Moscow the next morning in order to pursue the enemy. Mortier was to take up his quarters at the Kremlin, and was to hold the city with 4,000 cavalry on foot (so many horses having died) and other troops. The Kremlin was to be fortified, and the sick were to be transported to the Foundling Hospital. His Majesty added—" To-morrow, after the departure of the army, he must cause the municipality to issue a proclamation warning the inhabitants that the rumours of an evacuation are false; that the army is marching upon Kalonga, Toula, and Briansk, to seize upon those important points, and the manufactory of arms. . . ."

On the 19th, before leaving Moscow, the Emperor wrote three letters. In the first, to M. Maret, he said—" General Sebastiani, posted a league to the left of Murat, with the advanced guard, allowed himself to be surprised by a horde of Cossacks yesterday; he lost six guns. The enemy's infantry then attacked the King of Naples, who, at the head of his carabineers and cuirassiers, broke it and cut it to pieces. General Dery, the king's aide-de-camp, was killed. . . . The army is on the march. It has been decided to blow up the Kremlin, and to pass by Kalonga and by Viazma, so as to be able to go into winter quarters before the hard weather sets in. Everything is going on well."

The two other letters were addressed to Berthier. In the first, the Chief of the Staff was told to inform Murat that the army was getting into motion at 5 A.M.; that he was to hold the enemy in check, and that the Prince of Hohenzollern had just arrived! In the second letter, Napoleon estimated at a thousand the number of sick and wounded he was leaving behind him. He then gave directions for the transport of those who were to accompany the army. Every kind of vehicle was to be placed at the disposal of the staff, with these exceptions—one carriage for the Emperor, one for Berthier, one for the Secretary of State, one for each marshal or commander of an army corps, one for the Quartermaster-General.

Napoleon left Moscow with 106,000 men, but already there was a great lack of horses and much difficulty in carrying away sick and wounded, plunder, ammunition, &c.

Hardly had the French left Moscow when they were obliged to cut their way through the enemy at Malo-Jaroslawitz, and that was not accomplished without tremendous slaughter. The victory remained with the French, but still the results were disastrous, for they were obliged to fall back by the Smolensko road—a line of retreat which was not contemplated, and which had been laid waste already.

To MARSHAL BERTHIER.

"TROITSKOIE, 20*th October*, 1812.

". . . On the 22nd or 23rd Marshal Mortier must set fire to the eau-de-vie stores, the barracks, and to the public establishments, with the exception of the Foundling Hospital. [The French sick and wounded were not to be burned.] He must set fire to the palace of the Kremlin. He must take care to have the muskets broken in pieces, and powder placed under the towers of the Kremlin; all the gun carriages must be broken, as well as the wheels of the ammunition waggons.

"Having accomplished these things, and when fire has been set to the Kremlin in several places, Marshal Mortier must leave it and take the road to Mojaisk. On the road he must burn all the vehicles left behind, bury the dead as far as possible, and break all the muskets. On arriving at the Galitzin palace he must pick up Adjutant Bourmont with the Spaniards and Bavarians who are there. . . . He must remain in Moscow until he has seen the Kremlin blown up. He will take care to set fire to the house of the ex-governor and to that of Razoumovsky.

"NAPOLEON."

It is interesting to read these instructions following so closely on the pathetic letter to the Czar, and the proposals submitted to Kutusoff. One finds in Alison's *History of Europe*[1] that when the Russians abandoned their capital, Count Rostopchin had already set the example of devotion by setting fire to his country palace, applying the torch with his own hands to his nuptial bed; to the gates he had affixed the following inscription :—
" During eight years I have embellished this country seat and lived happily in it, in the bosom of my family. The inhabitants of this estate, to the number of 7,000, leave it at your approach. Frenchmen at Moscow, I have abandoned to you my two houses; here you will find nothing but ashes."

On the 21st, in a despatch to Berthier, the Emperor said :—

"I cannot too strongly recommend Marshal Mortier to place the men still in hospital in the waggons of the Young Guard and in those of the cavalry on foot. The Romans gave civic crowns to those who saved citizens. Marshal Mortier will deserve one for every soldier he saves. Write to him that he must let them ride on his horses and on those of every one else; that this was what the Emperor did at St. Jean d'Acre. . . ."

On the 23rd December, in his twenty-sixth bulletin to the army, Napoleon thus explained the Sebastiani affair :—

" General Lauriston having gone to Russian headquarters on the 5th October, communications were opened between our outposts and those of the enemy, and it was agreed between them that no attack should be made without three hours' notice being given; but on the 18th,

[1] Vol. xi. p. 92.

at 7 A.M., 4,000 Cossacks issued from a wood at half a cannon shot from General Sebastiani. . . . They made a 'houra' on this light cavalry while it was dismounted and while meal was being served out. This light cavalry was able to form only a quarter of a league further on. However, the enemy penetrating by this interval, took twelve guns and sixty-five ammunition- and baggage-waggons."

Then followed a description of how Murat finally repulsed the enemy, "who not only suffered a loss superior to ours, but disgraced themselves by violating an outpost truce."

The Emperor then manifested his intention of marching on the Dwina, and taking up a position which would bring him within eighty leagues of St. Petersburg and of Wilna, which, he said, would offer him a double advantage, and place him at about twenty marches from "his means and his objective."

Referring then to the damage done to Moscow, he said :—

"Out of 4,000 stone houses only 200 remain, and of 8,000 in wood only 500. It was proposed to the Emperor to burn the rest of the city, and the 2,000 villages and country houses by which it is surrounded, so as to teach the Russians to make war according to rules and not like Tartars. The Emperor refused to sanction these measures, which would have so greatly aggravated the misfortunes of that population. . . ."

And his Majesty, after saying that he could not think of punishing thousands of innocent people for the fault of a few wretches, went on to remark that "The inhabitants of Russia are lost in astonishment at the fine weather of the last twenty days.[1] We have the sun and the lovely days of Fontainebleau. The army is in a country which is extremely

[1] The winter set in so much later than usual that the Russians began to fear that the Almighty was in favour of the invader. If the country were rich it yielded little or nothing to the French.

fertile, and which can vie with the richest portions of France or Germany."

To MARSHAL BERTHIER.

"VEREYA, 28*th October*, 1812.

"Reiterate the order to General Marchand to pick up all the sick and wounded at the abbey of Mojaïsk, making use for this purpose of all the carriages and carts without distinction. Give orders to this effect to the staff. I have ordered my grand equerry to take at least 100 of my baggage-waggons.

"NAPOLEON."

On the 2nd November Napoleon, who had already reached Viazona, sent a despatch to M. Maret, saying:—

"Write to Baron Reinhard to show the king (Jerome) how ridiculous it is to transform the principal Protestant church at Cassel into a Roman Catholic chapel; that it is very dangerous to meddle with religious affairs, which only embitters the feeling of the people; that Cassel being a Protestant town he should leave the Protestants tranquil. If words do not prove sufficient, Baron Reinhard must hand him a note stating how dissatisfied I am with a measure which is as rash as it is contrary to sound policy."

On the 2nd November the French rear-guard was attacked at Wiazma, where the Russians inflicted upon it a loss of 6,000 men and twenty-seven guns. Since the retreat began the corps of Davoust had lost 10,000 men by fatigue or desertion, and it was calculated that the Grand Army, since leaving Moscow, had lost 43,000 men. No less than 240,000 men of the main body, under the immediate command of the Emperor, had perished before a fall of snow took place. The corps of Davoust suffered so severely at Wiazma that it had to be replaced by that of Ney.

On the 5th November, after issuing various orders showing that he was being hard pressed by the enemy in his retreat, Napoleon wrote to General Clarke at Paris saying that he regretted to see that the frontier of the Pyrenees had been insulted by Spanish brigands.

On the 7th November Berthier was instructed to write to Marshal Victor, who was to come to the rescue of the Grand Army:—

"In a few days your rear may be inundated with Cossacks; the army of the Emperor will reach Smolensko to-morrow, but worn out after a march of 120 leagues without stopping. Assume the offensive. The safety of the two armies depends upon this; every day's delay is a calamity. The cavalry are on foot, the cold has killed all the horses. March; this is the order of the Emperor and is a matter of necessity."

And on the 12th, the army being still at Smolensko, Berthier received orders to reply to General Bourcier, who had been sent to Warsaw for horses, that 30,000 animals were required.

On the 15th, 17th, and 18th there was much desperate fighting at Krasnoi, during which Marshal Ney and his corps got separated from the main body. During these three days the Russians captured 26,000 prisoners, most of them half-starved wretches who could offer no resistance. In addition to this 10,000 men were killed, while 112 guns were abandoned at Smolensko, and 116 were captured in the field.

On the 19th the French reached Orcha,[1] from which place the Emperor wrote to M. Maret, saying:—

"I am moving in the direction of Borisof in order to

---

[1] When the Grand Army reached Orcha it was but a skeleton. Of the guard that had crossed the Niemen five months before 43,000 strong only 6,000 men remained; Davoust's corps had been reduced from 70,000 to 4.000 men; Prince Eugene's corps from 42,000 to 1,800 men; Ney's corps from 40,000 to 1,500 men. Such was the condition of the Grand Army when Marshal Victor met it on the 23rd November; and the Beresina had still to be passed.

march upon Minsk, or, if the enemy be too strong, on Wilsika and Wilna. . . . Write confidentially to the Minister of Police that I am in good health. I have no news of Marshal Ney, and I despair of him. . . . Inform Prince Schwartzenberg that I am marching upon Minsk, and that I count upon him."

In the evening of the same day the Emperor, in a second letter to his Minister for Foreign Affairs, was able to announce that Marshal Ney had rejoined the army.

On the 22nd the Emperor issued orders that a considerable reduction was to be made in the number of baggage-waggons—waggons to be burned, and the horses handed over to the artillery.

On the 25th November the Emperor instructed Berthier to "inform the generals that I intend forcing the passage of the Beresina to-morrow night with the 2nd corps, the 9th corps, and the Imperial Guard, successively supported by Marshal Ney and the other corps; that as soon as the passage has been forced I shall send orders for them to come to the bridges; that I intend, with the three first corps above named to attack the enemy upon the right bank."

Napoleon, who had successfully concealed his intentions from the enemy, managed with great skill, and, thanks to the devotion and intrepidity of his engineers, to cross the Beresina on the 26th. The passage, however, was not effected without great slaughter and the most harrowing scenes, for the Russian generals, coming from Moscow, from Finland, and from the Danube, were now harassing the French army, which had become little but a mob. It is estimated, in fact, that the loss sustained by the Grand Army in crossing the Beresina amounted to 12,000 men killed, 16,000 prisoners, and twenty-five guns.

To M. MARET.

"STUDIENKA, 27th November, 1812.

"I have just passed the Beresina, but the ice floating down that river makes the bridges very unstable. The army which was opposed to Schwartzenberg wished to dispute the passage; to-night it is concentrated on the right bank of the river at Borisoff. The cold is intense, and the army greatly fatigued. I shall not lose a moment in getting to Wilna, in order to recuperate a little. . . . Have a large quantity of biscuit prepared. I suppose that you have continually sent news of us to Paris. . . . What is Prince Schwartzenberg doing?

"NAPOLEON."

M. Maret did send news to Paris, in which facts were so skilfully disguised that no one had any idea of the terrible disaster which had befallen the Grand Army until the publication of the twenty-ninth bulletin on the 17th December.

To M. MARET.
"RIGHT BANK OF THE BERESINA,
"29th November, 1812.

"I have received your letter of the 25th, in which you say nothing about France, and give me no news of Spain. And yet for the last fortnight I have received no news, no *estafette*, and I am in the dark as concerns everything.

"Yesterday we had a very warm affair against Admiral Tchitchakof and Wittgenstein. We beat the first who attacked us on the right bank. The second, who wished to force the bridges over the Beresina, was held in check. We took 6,000 prisoners, but we have to lament the loss of General Partouneaux's brigade, which, having missed its way, was captured. Marshal Oudinot and several generals were wounded.

"The army is numerous, but disbanded to a fearful extent. It would require a fortnight to get the men back to their colours, and this fortnight where can we find it? Cold and privations have disbanded this army. Shall we be able to hold Wilna? Yes, if we can hold out for a week; but if we are attacked at once, it is doubtful if we shall be able to remain there. Provisions! provisions! provisions! Without that there is no knowing to what horrors this undisciplined mass will not proceed. Perhaps the army will be able to rally only behind the Niemen. In this state of affairs I think my presence in Paris necessary for France, for the empire, and even for the army.

"Several *estafettes* must have been captured, if you have received no news from me since the 11th.

"You must allow no foreign agent to remain at Wilna, for our army is not fit to be seen to-day. You can send those who are there to Warsaw, saying that you are going to that city, and that I am marching there.

                              "NAPOLEON."

And the next day, in another letter, Napoleon called upon M. Maret to send forward provisions to meet him on the road. He said that he had over 40,000 stragglers, who were marching "like vagabonds, or rather like brigands," adding—"If you cannot furnish us with 100,000 rations, I pity Wilna." And—"The army is terribly fatigued, after a march of forty-five days. . . . Prince Schwartzenberg has cruelly compromised me. . . . The operation of the enemy on Minsk, and the shameful inaction of Marshal Victor, who did not attack them, has done us terrible harm. . . . . You say nothing about Paris. I have had no news of Paris for the last twenty days. Where are the eighteen *estafettes* who are missing? How is the Empress?"

On the 2nd December the Emperor gave the following instructions:—

"M. de Montesquieu must start to-morrow for Paris, and hand the inclosed letter to the Empress.[1] When passing

---

[1] Comte Anatole de Montesquieu was just going to cross over the Rhine to Mayence in a boat when an outrider, in the name of the Duc de Vicence (Caulaincourt), demanded it. The count, on the ground that he was charged with an important mission, and was the bearer of

through Wilna he must see the Duc de Bassano (M. Maret) and point out the necessity of taking measures to stop the stragglers, and to feed them, and also of having abundance of provisions ready. He must announce the arrival of 10,000 Russian prisoners, and the victory gained at the Beresina. He must also announce at Kovno, Konigsberg, and at Berlin, and have put in the *Gazettes*, ' M. de Montesquieu, aide-de-camp of the Prince de Neuchâtel, has passed, bringing news of the victory of the Beresina gained by the Emperor; he is carrying to Paris eight standards captured from the Russians, who lost 6,000 prisoners and twelve guns. When this officer left the Emperor was at Wilna, in good health. . . . .' M. de Montesquieu must travel as quickly as possible so as to contradict the false reports which may have been spread. . . . . On reaching Paris he will be in a position to give the Empress good news of the health of the Emperor, and the condition of the army.

" NAPOLEON."

On the 3rd December was issued the famous twenty-ninth bulletin, which created so great an impression wherever it was read, and filled the French mind with gloomy forebodings. It was, in fact, an official acknowledgment of the terrible disaster which had overtaken the Grand Army. It was to this effect :—

" The cold set in on the 7th November, and we lost hundreds of horses every night. . . . The Emperor learned at Smolensko that a change had been made in the line of operations, owing to the arrival of the Russian army of Volhyjnia on our right. No matter how hard it was to

letters to the Empress, refused to cede his bark. At this moment the Emperor himself approached in the dusk, and taking M. de Montesquieu affectionately by the hand, said—" Come, come, don't be angry, we can cross over together." The young officer wished to excuse himself for not having been able to travel faster, but Napoleon was highly pleased at the idea of reaching the Tuileries unexpectedly.

move in such cruel weather it was necessary to do so. The Emperor hoped to reach Minsk, or at least the Beresina, before the enemy. He left Smolensko on the 15th, and on the 16th he slept at Krasnoï; the cold suddenly increased, and the horses perished, not by hundreds, but by thousands. .... This army, so fine on the 6th November, was very different on the 14th—without cavalry, without artillery, without transport; it was necessary to march on, in order to avoid a battle.... Our columns were enveloped by Cossacks, who, like the Arabs of the desert, snapped up every man or cart that strayed; this despicable cavalry, which makes only a noise, and is not capable of breaking a company of Voltigeurs, favoured by circumstances, became redoubtable.[1] .... Marshal Ney, who with 3,000 men formed the rear-guard, blew up the ramparts of Smolensko. He was surrounded, and found himself in a critical position; he escaped from it with that intrepidity which distinguishes him."

Referring afterwards to the passage of the Beresina, the bulletin said:—

"On the 26th at daybreak, the Emperor, having deceived the enemy by various movements made on the 25th, marched on the village of Studzianca, and at once, in spite of the presence of a division of the enemy, had two bridges thrown across the river. Marshal Oudinot passed, attacked and repulsed the enemy, who fell back on Borioff."

The bulletin, after briefly touching upon the fighting at the Beresina, and the further suffering of the French army during its retreat, added—

[1] At Gorodina the Emperor, while reconnoitring, was suddenly attacked by 10,000 Cossacks, under Platoff, who were sweeping down upon a park of forty pieces of artillery. Several of the Emperor's escort were killed, General Rapp was unhorsed, and but for the anxiety of the Cossacks to secure the guns, and their ignorance of the splendid prey within their grasp, Napoleon would have been captured. Hence his irritation against the Cossacks, twenty-two regiments of whom served under their famous Hetman.

"During all these movements the Emperor marched in the midst of his guard, the cavalry commanded by Marshal Bessières, and the infantry commanded by Marshal Lefebvre. . . . Our cavalry was so dismounted that it was only possible to form four squadrons 150 strong, composed of officers who had still a horse remaining. The generals served as captains, the colonels as subalterns. The 'sacred squadron,' under the orders of the King of Naples, and commanded by General Grouchy, never lost sight of the Emperor.

"The health of his Majesty was never better."

To M. MARET.

"MOLODETCHNA, 3rd *December*, 1812.

". . . . We are terribly fatigued and half starved. Send bread, meat, and brandy to meet us. I have 100,000 stragglers who are trying to live, and who are no longer under the colours. This causes us to run horrible dangers. My Old Guard alone maintains its ranks, but hunger is gaining it. My heavy baggage started last night for Wilna. Hold yourself in readiness to come and meet me at Ochmiana. . . . Speak with confidence, and do not let anything transpire. Ten days' repose, and provisions in abundance will re-establish discipline. . . .

"NAPOLEON."

To M. MARET.

"MOLODETCHNA, 4*th December*, 1812.

"I have received your letter of the 2nd December. I see nothing very important in the *Moniteur* on the subject of Spain. The resistance of the castle of Burgos is a fine military affair, but it simply proves that forts are not to be taken without siege guns. Lord Wellington has retired to operate against the army of Andalusia. Should we lose a battle in that quarter, a serious crisis will ensue. If the news of the battle of Hill be confirmed, it will be a great and good piece of news; but this news is not worthy of belief. It is impossible to suppose that the English should have lost their judgment to such an extent as to fight a battle with Marshal Soult before having united their forces.

"I wish you to come and meet me at Smorgoni. . . . Send the American, the Prussian, and the other ministers to Warsaw. . . .

"The army, worn out with fatigue and hunger, is at the last extremity. It is impossible for it to do anything even if it were a question of defending Paris. . . .

"NAPOLEON."

On the 5th December the Emperor wrote to Cambacérès with his own hand, saying, "The quarrels between the ministers of police and of war are ridiculous; I fear that the Minister of Police is in the wrong. You shall soon have further details respecting this affair."[1]

Having made up his mind to leave the Grand Army, or what remained of it, the Emperor gave these instructions to Marshal Berthier—"Two or three days after my departure the subjoined decree must be put in the orders of the day. The report must be spread that I have gone to Warsaw with the Austrians and the 7th corps. Five or six days afterwards the King of Naples must inform the army that having been obliged to leave for Paris I have confided the command to him; that I hope the army will give him its confidence. . . ."[2]

---

[1] The Malet conspiracy.

[2] Baron Paul de Bourgoing has left an interesting narrative of the Emperor's journey from Smorgoni to Paris, which he had from Comte Dunin Wonsowicz, the Polish officer who accompanied his Majesty. The departure took place at 8 P.M. on the 5th December. In the first carriage was the Emperor, with General Caulaincourt; the Mamluke Roustan was on the box. In the second carriage was Marshal Duroc and Comte Lobeau; in the third Lieutenant-General Lefebvre-Desnouettes and three valets! In a sledge was Comte Wonsowicz and an outrider named Amodru. The escort was formed of thirty *chasseurs à cheval* of the Guard. In the middle of the night the party reached Oszimana, about eight leagues from Smorgoni, and found the garrison

To GENERAL COMTE DE NARBONNE.

"SMORGONI, 5*th December*, 1812.

"You must go to Berlin, and before leaving Wilna let me know how things are looking. . . . You will find at Berlin a letter for the King of Prussia, and my instructions for yourself. You must wait at Berlin for orders and write to me every day.

"NAPOLEON."

under arms, expecting to be attacked. Two detachments of Polish light cavalry had just arrived, on their way to reinforce the Grand Army. Napoleon was fast asleep when they arrived at Oszimana, and was in no way disturbed when he was aroused and informed of the presence of the enemy. In spite of the remonstrances of his generals he determined to push on at once; 266 Polish lancers formed his escort. General Lefebvre-Desnouettes and Comte Wousowicz now took their seats on the box of the Emperor's carriage; they held pistols in their hands. and received strict orders from Napoleon to kill him sooner than allow him to be taken prisoner. The party left Oszimana at one o'clock in the morning; they could see the camp fires of the Cossacks, and hear the voices of the sentinels. The night was so bitterly cold that before they had accomplished many leagues of the road only fifty lancers remained. The same cold which killed them kept the enemy in their quarters, and enabled Napoleon to escape the Hetman's Cossacks, as, returning from Egypt, he escaped the British cruisers. When the military post of Rownopole was reached at daybreak, only thirty-six lancers remained. They were replaced by a detachment of the Neapolitan guard, commanded by the Duke of Rocca-Romana, who had his hands frost-bitten. The thermometer had descended to 28° Réaumur. The Emperor reached the third relay, at the town of Miedniki, without encountering any obstacle, and there met M. Maret, his Minister of Foreign Affairs, who replaced General Caulaincourt in the Emperor's carriage, and informed him of the state of Europe. Wilna was soon afterwards reached in safety, but the Emperor considered it prudent only to skirt the ancient capital of Lithuania, in which the enemy had many friends. All danger was not yet over, for at Kowno, close to the Niemen, the party narrowly escaped falling in with a detachment of Cossacks, to which no resistance could have been offered. At Gragow Napoleon was able to procure a more commodious vehicle, which was placed upon skates like a sledge, and in this, with Caulaincourt and Wousowicz inside, and Roustan on the box, he travelled to Warsaw. As soon as the

VOL. III.   O

Prince Eugene having made some objections against serving under Murat, his Majesty, before leaving Smorgoni, wrote—

"MY SON,—I have received your letter. Do your duty, and have confidence in me. I remain the same for you, and know what is good for you. Do not doubt my paternal sentiments."

After this brief epistle there are no more letters until the 11th, when his Majesty wrote thus to M. Maret at Warsaw from Kutno—

"Inform the diplomatic body that I am going to Paris. Announce this by courier at Vienna and Berlin. Austria must send an able minister to Paris. Prince Schwartzenberg can keep the title of ambassador. Let M. Otto try so that the 30,000 men in Transylvania and in Hungary may assume the offensive in Volhynia.

"I was greatly astonished by all the ridiculous things said during an hour by the Abbé de Pradt. I did not make him feel this. He has none of the qualities requisite

carriage had crossed over the Praga bridge, Napoleon got out, and walked to the Hôtel d'Angleterre, where an apartment had been prepared for him. Here he had his interview with the Abbé de Pradt, Archbishop of Malines, his ambassador. The Emperor left Warsaw on the 10th December, and arrived on the 14th at Dresden, where he had a touching interview with his old ally the King of Saxony. From Dresden the Emperor hurried on to Leipsic, where, in addition to French and foreign journals, he purchased some volumes of "frivolous literature." Napoleon journeyed thence to Mayence, and on to Verdun, where he bought some sugar plums for the Empress and for the King of Rome. On the 18th he dined at Château Thierry, and donned his uniform of the grenadiers of the guard. He counted upon arriving at the Tuileries by midnight, but his carriage broke down, and he was obliged to re-enter his capital in a miserable post-chaise. It was half-past one in the morning when the Emperor reached the gate of the Carrousel, and it was not without some difficulty that he obtained admittance, for the sentry had read only the day before, in the *Moniteur*, that Napoleon was at Smolensko. The distance between Smorgoni and Paris had been accomplished in twelve days.

for the post he fills. This abbé is clever only at writing books. You can recall him at once, or on arriving in Paris, and send him back to his diocese."

The abbé in the history of his embassy at Warsaw has left an interesting if rather jaunty and unchurchman-like account of his interview with the god Mars on that occasion. The Emperor exhibited great volubility, and said, among other things—

"Bah! the army is superb. I have 120,000 men. I have always beaten the Russians. . . . We shall maintain our position at Wilna. . . . I shall fight two or three battles on the Oder, and in six months I shall be once more on the Niemen. . . . I left the troops with regret, but it was necessary to watch over Austria and Prussia. What has happened is nothing, it was all the effect of the climate. I shall beat the enemy wherever I meet them. They thought to cut me off at the Beresina; but I soon got quit of that fool of an admiral (I never could pronounce his name).[1] . . . Perhaps they may say that I lingered too long at Moscow. Possibly so; but the weather was fine, and I expected peace; the winter set in before its usual time. I sent for Lauriston on the 5th October to negotiate for peace; I thought of going to St. Petersburg. I had time to winter there or in the south of Russia. The King of Naples will maintain himself at Wilna. Politics are a great drama; he who ventures nothing will win nothing. There is but a step from the subline to the ridiculous. . . . Who would have thought that they would have burned Moscow. . . It was worthy of ancient Rome (*vide* letter to the Czar of 19th September). I shall not go through Silesia—ah! ah! Prussia."

And so on for three hours, says the abbé, who was almost frozen.

[1] "And last of all an admiral came:
A terrible man with a terrible name,
A name which you all know by sight very well,
But which no one can speak, and no one can spell."

To the EMPEROR OF AUSTRIA.

"DRESDEN, 14*th December*, 1812.

"I remain a moment at Dresden in order to write to your Majesty. In spite of great fatigue my health never was better. I started on the 4th, after the battle of Beresina, from Lithuania, leaving the Grand Army under the orders of the King of Naples. In four days I shall reach Paris, where I shall pass the winter months in order to attend to the most important affairs. Perhaps your Majesty will deem it useful to send some one there in the absence of your ambassador (Prince Schwartzenberg) whose presence is so necessary to the army.

"The various bulletins which the Duc de Bassano has not failed to forward to M. Otto will have acquainted your Majesty with all that has happened since I left Moscow. It will be important under these circumstances for your Majesty to mobilise a corps in Gallicia and in Transylvania, and to raise your forces to 60,000 men [just double the number imposed by treaty].

"I have full confidence in the sentiments of your Majesty. The alliance which we have contracted forms a permanent system from which our subjects derive such great benefits that I think your Majesty will do all that you promised me at Dresden, so as to insure the triumph of the common cause, and to conduct us promptly to a suitable peace. You may be persuaded that upon my side you will find me always ready to do everything that can be agreeable to you, and to convince you of the importance which I attach to our present relations. . . .

"NAPOLEON."

It is possible, when the Emperor wrote the above letter to his "very dear father-in-law," that the prophetic warnings of his brother Jerome and of Marshal Davoust may have flashed across his memory. They both warned him that in the event of experiencing a reverse in Russia the whole of Germany would rise against him.

On the 18th December Napoleon, after accomplishing the journey from Smorgoni in twelve days, arrived quite unexpectedly at the Tuileries in the middle of the night; in consequence of his carriage having broken down on the road he had to accomplish the last part of his journey in a country cart. This was anything but a triumphal entry. He at once wrote to Marshal Berthier with his own hand, saying—

"I regret to see that you did not remain a week at Wilna so as to clothe and to rally the army a little. I hope that you have taken up a position on the Pregel; it is impossible to find so many resources on any other line as upon that of Kœnigsberg. I hope that Schwartzenberg and Regnier have covered Warsaw. Prussia is preparing to send reinforcements to cover her territory.

"NAPOLEON."

On leaving Smorgoni the French rear was totally destroyed, and lost twenty-five guns and 3,000 prisoners; the new rear suffered the same fate, and lost sixty-one guns and 4,000 prisoners; at Medniki sixteen guns and 1,300 prisoners were captured by the Russians, who, on the road to Wilna, took thirty-one more guns, and penetrated into the town almost at the same time as the French. Platoff and his Cossacks, too, cut off a column of 1,000 men, and captured twenty-eight guns. The French were unable to make any stand at Wilna, in which town the enemy found 14,000 men and 250 officers, who were incapable of going any further, besides immense magazines.

The next day his Majesty wrote thus to Murat:—

"I have arrived in Paris, and am extremely satisfied with the feeling of the country, which is disposed to make all kinds of sacrifices, and I am occupying myself without cessation in preparing all my means. I have already an army of 40,000 men at Berlin and on the Oder. The King of Prussia proposes to send reinforcements to his army and to recomplete his cavalry without loss of time ; the King of Saxony has similar intentions. Kœnigsberg and the Pregel will offer you resources.

"The Russians boast of all the interviews you have had with the outposts and disfigure them. They have the impudence to declare that all this was to deceive and to lull you to sleep.

"NAPOLEON."

Having received an address from the Senate on the 20th, the Emperor replied in these terms :—

"What you say to me is most agreeable. I have at heart the glory and power of France; but my first thoughts are for all that can perpetuate internal tranquillity and for ever shelter our people from the 'rending' of factions and the horrors of anarchy. . . .

"Timid and cowardly soldiers lose the independence of nations, but pusillanimous magistrates destroy the empire of the laws, the rights of the throne, and social order itself.[1]

"The most noble death would be that of a soldier perishing on the field of battle, if the death of a magistrate perishing in the defence of his sovereign, the throne, and the laws, were not still more noble.

"When I undertook the regeneration of France, I asked Providence to grant me a certain number of years. It is possible to destroy in a moment, but it requires time to rebuild. The greatest necessity for a State is to have courageous magistrates.

"Our fathers had for rallying cry : *The king is dead, long live the king!* These few words contain the principal advantages of the monarchy. . . .

"The war which I am waging against Russia is a

[1] Allusion to the Malet conspiracy.

political war; I have waged it without animosity. I should have wished to have averted the misfortunes it has caused. I might have armed the greater portion of the population against itself by declaring the independence of the serfs; a great number of villages asked me to do this; but, when I became aware of the ignorance of that numerous class of the Russian people, I refused a measure which would have devoted to death, to devastation, and to the most horrible tortures, a great number of families. My army has experienced losses due to the premature rigour of the season."

While busy reorganising the army which was to take the field as early as possible in 1813, Napoleon found time to turn his attention once more to his venerable prisoner of Fontainebleau.

To POPE PIUS VII.

"PARIS, 29*th December*, 1812.

"MOST HOLY FATHER,—I hasten to send you an officer of my household to express to your Holiness the satisfaction I feel with what the Bishop of Nantes tells me concerning the state of your health, for I was very much alarmed for a moment, *this summer*, when I learned that you were very unwell. The new residence of your Holiness will allow you to see us, and I greatly desire to assure you that, in spite of all the events which have taken place, I have always preserved the same friendship for your person. Perhaps we shall be able to arrive at the long-wished-for end, and to settle all the differences which divide the Church and State. On my side I am anxious to accomplish this, and it will depend entirely upon your Holiness. . . .

"NAPOLEON."

On the 30th the Emperor wrote to the King of Naples, at Kœnigsberg, saying :—"I have received your letter of the 20th. I am sorry to see that the cold is so intense. I am very anxious to learn the real condition of the army."

To Marshal Berthier, at Kœnigsberg.

"Paris, 30*th December*, 1812.

"I have received your note upon the *real losses*, over which I shall think seriously... I have just raised 15,000 cavalry and 8,000 artillery horses, in addition to 4,000 animals for the military train... There is a good deal of war material in Prussia, in Dantsic, and the other places. Eblé should pay attention to this. The conscription is excellent this year. On Sunday I had a parade of about 30,000 men.

"Napoleon."

As for the real losses, it appears from official returns that out of the 610,000 men who crossed the Niemen in June, only 18,800 Frenchmen, and 23,000 allies, recrossed that river. Marshal Ney was the last to recross, and it is related that, upon being asked who he was, he replied, "I am the rear guard of the Grand Army."

CHAPTER IV.

THE YEAR 1813.

THE year 1813 was another year of battles and bloodshed. When it opened, the remnant of the Grand Army had not yet made good its escape. It repassed the Niemen on the 30th December, 1812; but from the Niemen it was driven back on the Vistula, from the Vistula to the Oder, and from the Oder to the Elbe. The sixth coalition was now formed, and France, with her allies, such as Italy, the Confederation of the Rhine, and Denmark, found herself confronted by Russia, England, Prussia, Spain, and Sweden. Austria for a time held aloof, playing the mediator and preparing for war at the same time. She had suffered so severely from miscalculating the resources of France and the genius of Napoleon on previous occasions that she long hesitated. Then she feared and doubted Russia. What if she were to join the allies, and France and Russia were to come to terms, as France and Russia had come to terms after Friedland to the detriment of Prussia? The relations between Austria and Russia had not been friendly for some time. After Austerlitz, Austria had concluded a separate peace with France. During the campaign of 1807, Austria held aloof while Napoleon was fighting with the Czar in Poland. In 1809 Russia sided with France against Austria, and in 1810 came the matrimonial alliance, which meant an understanding between

France and Austria and war with Russia. In 1812 Austria furnished a corps of 30,000 men to France. The court of Vienna had therefore good reason to fear that Napoleon might turn the past to account and sow dissension between his father-in-law and the Czar in the event of Austria casting in her lot with the allies. He attempted this when Austria at last declared against him, but the illusions of Tilsit and Erfurth had vanished. There was Moscow to be revenged, and when Caulaincourt was sent to negotiate with the Czar in secret, Alexander received him in presence of the King of Prussia and the ambassadors of England, Prussia, and Austria. It may be said that during the Wagram campaign the Russians gave Napoleon but little support, and that during the march to Moscow and back the Austrians helped the French as little as possible. Still a good deal of distrust existed between Vienna and St. Petersburg, and it was not until August, that is to say, after Lutzen, Bautzen, and Wurschen had been fought, that Austria threw off the mask and joined the sixth coalition. After the three battles above-named, which were all favourable to the French arms, an armistice was concluded at Pleiswitz which brought about a congress, or the semblance of a congress, at Prague. Several French historians have blamed Napoleon for allowing his enemies time to breathe and to bring up reinforcements. But the armistice was as necessary to the French as to the allies; their successes had been dearly purchased; they were sadly deficient in cavalry; and, as Napoleon said himself, he could not follow up his victories, and he was paralysed by the dubious attitude of Austria.

The armistice having been denounced, hostilities were resumed on the 17th August. The Emperor Napoleon threatened at the same time Berlin, Breslau, and Prague, which weakened his centre. However, he foiled the allies in a rash and sanguinary attack upon Dresden, where Moreau fell mortally wounded. The strategy of the allies now consisted in refusing to accept battle where Napoleon commanded in person, and in attacking his lieutenants, and this plan was crowned with success. Macdonald was beaten at Katzbach, Vandamme at Kulm, Oudinot at Gross-Beeren on his road to Berlin, and Ney at Dennewitz, while Davoust was obliged to fall back behind the Elbe. Bavaria now went over to the allies, and was shortly afterwards followed by Baden and Wirtemberg. Then came Leipsic, during which the Saxons went over to the enemy—all but their old king. The disaster of Leipsic brought the campaign of 1813, but not the war, to a close. Not more than a fifth of the French army re-crossed the Rhine, while 120,000 men were left in the fortresses along the Elbe, the Oder, and the Vistula. Rapp was shut up at Dantsic, Davoust at Hamburg, Du Tailly at Torgau, Lemarois at Magdeburg, Lapoye at Wittenberg, Grandeau at Stettin, d'Albe at Custrin, and Laplane at Glogau. On the 9th November Napoleon returned to Paris, and when the year closed the allies were crossing the Rhine and invading the northern departments of France.

In Spain matters went very badly with the French. "In May the British army," as Lord Londonderry says, "was lying between the Agueda and the Tagus, observed by a greatly superior force, and master only of Portugal, from which it seemed competent for an enemy, with a little skill and determination, to drive it. The month of December beheld the English troops victors in five pitched battles, after having swept the whole armed power of France over broad and rapid rivers, across wide and fertile plains, through the passes of the Pyrenees, and back into the hitherto unviolated territory of *la belle France*. . . . Never was such a series of brilliant successes accomplished by a British army as was achieved by Lord Wellington and his companions in the course of that campaign. The strong-holds of Burgos, Pampeluna, and St. Sebastian were incapable of arresting their triumphs. The first was abandoned and blown up ; the second yielded to the slow but sure process of blockade; and the third, in spite of Soult's best efforts, was carried by assault in open day."

The great victory, however, was that of Vittoria, the news of which was hailed with delight in Germany, revived the drooping spirits of the allies, and was so severely felt by Napoleon that he at once sent Soult back to Spain as his lieutenant-general; but Soult was unable to stop the British, who crossed the Bidassoa, and gained the battles of the Nive and the Nivelle.

Austria, as we have remarked, was for some time deterred from joining the coalition lest Russia should conclude a separate peace with Napoleon. Lord Londonderry, after describing the battle of Vittoria, says: "It does not appear to have formed any part of Lord Wellington's plan at this period of the war to carry his victorious arms into the south of France. He felt that an accommodation between Napoleon, the Emperor of Russia, and the King of Prussia, which seemed then not unlikely, might occur, and that would render it impossible for him to maintain himself beyond the Pyrenees."

The reign of King Joseph naturally came to an end with the events above referred to. Forced to take refuge in France, he was soon afterwards ordered by his brother to leave the frontier and to repair to Mortfontaine. The Emperor was about to reopen negotiations with his captive, Ferdinand VII.

When hostilities broke out, the King of Saxony, distracted between his engagements with Napoleon and the increasing enthusiasm of his army and his people for the cause of the allies, was doubtful which side to take. Napoleon, however, after entering Dresden, informed his Majesty that if he did not at once return to his capital he would lose his crown.

On the 13th March a treaty was concluded with Sweden, by which that Power was to furnish 30,000 men to the coalition, and was to receive 1,000,000*l.* a year from

England, and the island of Guadaloupe. A promise of Norway was also held out in the event of Denmark refusing to join the allies, and Denmark did refuse.

After writing several letters to Napoleon, urging him, in the interests of humanity, to put an end to a war which was disastrous to France, to Naples, and to all Europe, Murat, whose letters remained unanswered, reluctantly joined the standard of his imperial brother-in-law; but he deserted the French army after Leipsic, as he had deserted it during the retreat from Moscow, and he soon afterwards entered into negotiations with the court of Vienna, which, being opposed to the return of the Bourbons to Italy, was quite willing to recognise his right to the throne of Naples.

Before the close of the year, too, the Prince of Orange landed in Holland, which country at once began to assert its independence.

No letters on the 1st or 2nd January.

To GENERAL CLARKE.

"PARIS, 3rd *January*, 1813.

"The King of Spain demanding the recall of Marshal Soult, or at least that he may return on furlough, send him by an extraordinary courier a furlough to come back to Paris. General Gazan or Marshal Jourdan can take the command of his corps. You must send these orders by duplicate and triplicate.

"Inform the king that under present circumstances I think he should take up his head-quarters at Valladolid; that the twenty-ninth bulletin will have made him acquainted with the state of affairs in the north, which requires our care and our efforts; that he can occupy Madrid with one extremity of his line; and that he ought to take advantage of the inaction of the English to pacify Navarre, Biscay, and the province of Santander.

"NAPOLEON."

Count Miot de Melito says that the year 1813 opened under very gloomy auspices in Spain. Madrid was sad, the palace was deserted, and the celebrated twenty-ninth bulletin left no doubt as to the extent of the disaster in Russia. On his return from Moscow Colonel Desprez wrote to the king, saying: "The imagination cannot attain the reality of our reverses; in a word, *the army is dead.*" As for Soult, the count says that "he passed through Madrid on the 2nd March, followed by a great number of waggons filled with precious articles. After a short interview with the king he continued his road to Paris."

On the 3rd January Savary informed the Emperor that an armourer called Pauly had made an extremely advantageous discovery in the shape of a musket, with which he fired twenty-two shots in two minutes, in the garden of the Minister of Police. According to the inventor, this musket would not cost more than that in use, it weighed a quarter less, while all the accidents to which the ordinary musket was exposed from wet, &c., would be avoided.

"PARIS, 3rd *January*, 1813.

"Referred to Marshal Duroc to send for the inventor, to examine the musket with the officers of the artillery of the Guard, to have trials made, and to furnish me with a report.[1] "NAPOLEON."

[1] It is a rather remarkable fact that when the *chassepot* was adopted by the French, in 1866, Pauly was still alive, and brought an action against the Government either for infringing his patent or for pirating his invention. Napoleon, in his *Plan for the New Organisation of the Army*, written at St. Helena, said:—"The infantry musket, with the bayonet, is the most perfect arm invented by man. . . . It can be fired sixty times without interruption in thirty or even in twenty minutes. . . . . Skilful mechanics have tried to load the musket by the breech, and to prime it with fulminating powder, so as to do away the flint. The trials have not quite satisfied all the conditions, but everything leads one to hope for success, seeing the progress made by chemical and mechanical arts."

To GENERAL RAPP, GOVERNOR OF DANTSIC.

"PARIS, 4th *January*, 1813.

"I have received your letter of the 22nd. Dantsic should be armed and provisioned so as to be able to remain isolated and blockaded for six months. I have united four army corps, which will make 300,000 men, independent of the Grand Army. Should you ever be surrounded, I shall march myself to your relief.

"NAPOLEON."

To THE KING OF DENMARK.

"PARIS, 5th *January*, 1813.

"A letter from my minister informs me that your Majesty has received no reply to the letter which he wrote, and which I received at Moscow, and to which I replied the next day. My minister having sent me a number of Russian bulletins, I must inform your Majesty that they are entirely false. The enemy were always beaten, and captured neither an eagle nor a gun from my army. On the 7th November the cold became intense; all the roads were found impracticable; 30,000 horses perished between the 7th and the 16th. A portion of our baggage and artillery waggons was broken and abandoned; our soldiers, little accustomed to such weather, could not endure the cold. They wandered from the ranks in quest of shelter for the night, and, having no cavalry to protect them, several thousands fell into the hands of the enemy's light troops. General Sanson, chief of the topographic corps, was captured by some Cossacks while he was engaged in sketching a position. Other isolated officers shared the same fate. My losses are severe, but the enemy cannot attribute to themselves the honour of having inflicted them. My army has suffered greatly, and suffers still, but this calamity will cease with the cold.

"I am raising horses on all sides, independent of those

which, thanks to your Majesty, are arriving from Holstein and Jutland. I am raising 60,000 in my own empire. In the spring I shall march with a larger army than the Grand Army at the opening of the campaign. I enter into these details in order that your Majesty should not be deceived by the false reports circulated with great artifice.

"I have guaranteed Norway and the integrity of your states to your Majesty, and nothing in the world shall make you lose the smallest portion of them.[1] England is occupied in Spain, in Sicily, and in America; Russia will be occupied more seriously than ever on our frontiers; they can do nothing to injure your Majesty. I shall have, as always, a corps of 30,000 men to protect your States, as you also will keep up a corps for the defence of the coasts of the Baltic. I am assured of the good feeling of Austria, and I have no complaint to make of the King of Prussia. Your Majesty need feel no uneasiness; we shall come out of the struggle victorious, and all the efforts of the enemies of Denmark will be vain. I know all the intrigues of England, Russia, and Sweden; but I also know your character and the loyalty of your nation, and I feel no alarm. . . .

"NAPOLEON."

At last the camp of Boulogne was to be broken up.

To GENERAL CLARKE.

"PARIS, 8*th January*, 1813.

"The camp of Boulogne has become useless. Give orders for the troops to be quartered in the town.

"NAPOLEON."

To MARSHAL BERTHIER, AT ELBING.

"PARIS, 9*th January*, 1813.

"I have received your letter of the 1st with the strange news which it contained. . . . These are the measures

[1] On the other hand, England and Russia guaranteed Norway to Sweden as the price of her active co-operation.

VAST PREPARATIONS.

which I have taken. As soon as I heard of the treason of General York, I decided upon making a communication to the nation, which shall be done to-morrow, and on ordering an extraordinary levy. I have formed a corps of observation on the Elbe, which is assembling at Hamburg. This corps will be sixty battalions strong, and commanded by General Lauriston. I have formed a corps of observation in Italy, which is assembling at Verona, and which is forty battalions strong, and is commanded by General Bertrand. I have formed a first corps of observation of the Rhine composed of sixty battalions, and I have given the command to Marshal Marmont, whose head-quarters will be Mayence. I am going to form a second corps of observation of the Rhine, which will also consist of sixty battalions. I have converted the eighty-eight cohorts into twenty-two regiments of the line. . . . I have called up 100,000 men, the arrears of the conscriptions since 1810, so that they will all be men over twenty-one years old. . . . . The conscription of 1814 will be of 150,000 men, and will be raised in the course of February.

"The cantons of France have offered me each three mounted chasseurs, which will make from 12,000 to 15,000 troopers. . . . I have raised 20,000 cavalry horses in France.

"I have accepted the offers made to me of six squadrons of body guards of 200 men each; they will be composed of volunteers from the departments, having each a pension of 40*l.* furnished by their parents. I have passed contracts for 8,000 cavalry horses in France. I have reorganised six battalions of military train. I have raised 12,000 artillery horses. I have reorganised the artillery for the Grand Army and for the other corps. I have reorganised the engineers. I have created a regiment of voltigeurs and of sharpshooters of the Guard. . . . I have at this moment five regiments of the young Guard, forming 8,000 men, under arms. I have called up 3,000 old soldiers, who will shortly arrive at the depots of the old Guard. I have procured a special remount of 3,000 horses for the Guard. I have made an extraordinary recruitment for the cavalry. . . . Everything is in motion here. Nothing is wanting, neither men, nor money, nor goodwill, but we want cadres. . . . The courts of Austria and of Denmark appear to be well disposed.

"NAPOLEON."

And on the 11th Napoleon wrote to Marshal Berthier, saying:—

"Make known to Marshal Macdonald the indignation which the letter of General York has produced throughout the country, and the national movement which it has occasioned. . . . You will have seen all that the King of Prussia did when he learned the treason of General York. . . ."

General York, who had been engaged with Marshal Macdonald in blockading Riga, was cut off by General Diebitch, when the French were obliged to retreat. Upon this the Russian general sent a flag of truce to York proposing a convention, which, after much hesitation, was accepted by the Prussian general, in order to save the remnant of his corps. The convention was signed on the 30th December, and it was stipulated that the Prussian corps should remain neutral for two months, whether the convention were ratified or not.

The King of Prussia, somewhat perplexed at first, seeing the state of feeling all through Germany, refused to ratify the convention, and superseded General York, who, however, did not remain long under a cloud.

To KING JEROME.

"PARIS, 18*th January*, 1813.

"According to custom, I consider it right, on important occasions, to make known our situation to your Majesty.

"Your Majesty has learned from the published reports the victories which I have gained over the Russian armies.

I did not once meet them without beating them. As a general rule the Russian cavalry and infantry did not behave well. The Cossacks are the only troops which, in the kind of warfare suited to them, made a good show. After the fighting at Smolensko and the battle of Borodino I entered Moscow. I found abundance of everything in that great city, the houses all furnished, provisions everywhere, and the inhabitants very well disposed. But twenty-four hours afterwards the flames burst out in 200 places at once. The rich magazines became a prey to the fire. The merchants and the middle classes, seeing their houses in cinders, took to flight, and after four days of prodigious and useless efforts, Moscow, which we could not save, no longer existed.

"The inhabitants of a great number of villages asked me for a decree according them their liberty, and promising to take up arms for me. But in a country where the middle class is so few in numbers, and when, frightened by the ruins of Moscow, the men of that class had fled, I felt that to arm a population of slaves would be to devote the country to terrible misfortunes. I never dreamed of doing this. I merely thought of reorganising my army and of falling back on the Dwina."

Then, after a description of the retreat to Smolensko—

"I reached Krasnoï. The Cossacks, who perceived that we had no more cavalry, flung themselves between our columns. The men left their ranks to go, at night, in search of shelter against the rigours of that fearful climate. I had no cavalry to protect them. However, the enemy vainly endeavoured to take advantage of this state of affairs; he was constantly attacked and beaten. Marshal Ney, who remained three days behind, marched by the left of the Borysthenes, and rejoined at Orcha, without having experienced any loss beyond that of his *materiel*, which he was obliged to destroy. I called in the other corps which remained on the Dwina, and I marched to the Beresina, which I crossed in presence of the enemy.

I beat Tchitchakoff, and afterwards fell back upon Wilna with my army, the command of which I left to the King of Naples, and I returned to my capital.

"Your Majesty can now appreciate the falsehoods told by the Russian bulletins. There was not an affair in which the Russians captured either a gun or an eagle; they took no other prisoners than skirmishers, a certain number of which are invariably captured. My Guard was never engaged, and did not lose a single man in action, and it could not therefore have lost any eagles as the Russians declare. When they relate that they took 4,000 men from Marshal Ney, they tell another falsehood.[1] What they say about the affair of the viceroy and that of Krasnoï, where they say that the Guard was engaged, is but a tissue of impostures and stupidities. No doubt a great many soldiers, officers, and even generals fell into the hands of the enemy because they were sick or had straggled away from the army. . . .

"The Grand Army, which I left between Minsk and Wilna, would have remained at Wilna but for the excessive cold, which induced the King of Naples to go into cantonments this side of the Niemen."

The Emperor then gave a very glowing sketch of the actual state of affairs, and set down the effective strength of the Grand Army at 200,000 men, although in a letter to General Lacué of the 16th he said—"Nothing is to be expected from the Grand Army, for all the men appear to be excessively fatigued; it must therefore be entirely reorganised." His Majesty went on to say—

"Thus, independently of the Grand Army, and without withdrawing any men from the army of Spain, which has an effective of 300,000 men, I have more than 300 battalions, all composed of Frenchmen, and most of them of old soldiers, which could, with two divisions of my

---

[1] It is a well-known fact that the corps of Ney was annihilated, and that the Grand Army lost 900 guns.

Guard, be concentrated in the month of March on the Oder and on the Elbe. With this force in the way of men, with the ordinary revenues of my Empire, which for the present year will amount to 44,000,000*l.*, and having reason to count upon the fidelity of my allies, I flattered myself that I should not be obliged to ask my people to make any new efforts.

"But this state of affairs has just been suddenly changed by the treason of General York, who, with a Prussian corps of 20,000 men, has taken part with the enemy. On this occasion Prussia has given me the strongest assurances of her intentions, which I have reason to believe sincere, but they do not prevent the corps in question having gone over to the enemy. The immediate consequences of this treason are that the King of Naples has been obliged to withdraw behind the Vistula, and that my losses will be increased by the men who are in hospital in Old Prussia. One of the eventual consequences may be that the war will approach Germany. I have taken all the necessary measures for protecting the frontiers of the Confederation; but all the Confederate States must feel the necessity, on their side, of making efforts in proportion to the circumstances. It is not only against the foreign enemy that they have to protect themselves; there is one more dangerous to be feared: the spirit of revolt and anarchy.

"The Emperor of Russia has just appointed Baron Stein Minister of State. He admits into his intimate counsels Stein and all those men who, aspiring to change the face of Germany, have long endeavoured to succeed by revolutionary means. . . .

"NAPOLEON."

Similar letters were addressed to the other royal and princely vassals of the French Empire, who were beginning to perceive the very onerous price which they had to pay for the protection of France!

To PRINCE EUGENE, at Posen.

"FONTAINEBLEAU, 22nd *January*, 1813.

"MY SON,—Take the command of the Grand Army. I am sorry that I did not leave it to you when I took my departure; I flatter myself that you would not have fallen back in such haste, and that my losses would not have been so great. The harm which has been done is without remedy. You must write to me in detail every day.

"As soon as you can do without the Major-General (Berthier), send him back; also Daru, if Dumas is fit for duty.

"NAPOLEON."

To the KING OF SAXONY, at Dresden.

"FONTAINEBLEAU, 22nd *January*, 1813.

". . . The events which have happened since my departure from the army and the treason of General York have damaged our affairs in the north; but I have set in motion such forces that when the good weather comes our enemies, no matter what progress they may make, will be driven back very quickly from whence they came. I receive from the King of Prussia reiterated proofs of his good faith. The King of Denmark assured me a few days ago that he is not to be shaken. Your Majesty ought to have information with regard to the court of Austria; all that the Emperor writes, and all that he causes me to be told, show that I should not only have no anxiety on that side, but that the Emperor is decided to make greater efforts than during the last campaign. . . .

"NAPOLEON."

When the French Emperor wrote the above letter he was evidently apprehensive that the Cossacks were about to pay Saxony a visit. A month later the king was obliged to leave Dresden, not for the first time since he joined the Confederation.

On the 23rd his Majesty wrote a letter on naval affairs to Admiral Decrès, which commenced thus :—

"I cannot make up my mind to diminish my maritime armaments. I am not in a position to place the expenditure of twelve or fifteen million francs in the balance with the reaction which would be produced in the minds of my sailors and of my enemies by a diminution. The only thing to which I can consent is not to augment my armaments in Holland and on the Scheldt. . . ."

To PRINCE EUGENE.

"FONTAINEBLEAU, 23rd *January*, 1813.

"I have received your letter of the 16th. I have already told you that I see the command of the army in your hands with pleasure. I find the conduct of the King of Naples very extravagant, and such that it would require very little for me to have him arrested by way of an example. He is a brave man in the field of battle, but he is totally devoid of combinations and moral courage. I am very anxious to know if any Frenchmen have been left at Thorn. Marshal Ney has written to me. Employ him, for he will be necessary to you.

"NAPOLEON."

To COMTE BIGOT.

"FONTAINEBLEAU, 23rd *January*, 1813.

"You must send a courier to General Miollis to acquaint him with the arrangement which has just been made with the Pope, and furnish him with an analysis of the treaty. He must not have it printed, but only make use of it in conversation. You must tell him that the Pope is going to reside at Avignon, where he will exercise his pontificate as in the past. . . .

"NAPOLEON."

And the Grand Chamberlain was ordered to give a year's wages to each of the domestics of his Holiness by way of a present.

To M. MELZI, Duc de Lodi.

"FONTAINEBLEAU, 25th January, 1813.

"I have just signed a Concordat with the Pope. I hasten to forward a copy of it for you alone, as it is not my intention that it shall be published. The Pope is going to establish himself at Avignon.

"The Minister of Worship being dead, I beg that you will present some one to replace him. I also desire that you will furnish me with your views as to the appointments to be made to the vacant sees, especially to that of Milan. I should like, for this latter see, a bishop of irreproachable morals, of a pure doctrine, and who has given satisfaction under all circumstances. . . .

"NAPOLEON."

To the EMPEROR OF AUSTRIA.

"FONTAINEBLEAU, 25th January, 1813.

"Having had the opportunity of seeing the Pope at Fontainebleau, and having conferred several times with his Holiness, we have come to an arrangement respecting the affairs of the Church. The Pope seems to wish to settle at Avignon. I send your Majesty the Concordat which I have just signed with him. I do not wish this document to be made public at present.

"The thorough acquaintance which Comte Otto possesses of the affairs of England and of America make me desire his presence in Paris. I desire to replace him by the Comte de Narbonne, who enjoys my full confidence, and who has manners which will be agreeable at Vienna. I beg your Majesty to let me know if he will be acceptable.

"The King of Naples, being ill, desired to quit the army; he has been replaced by the viceroy. My troops are in motion [being driven back at all points]. The whole of France is in arms, and your Majesty may feel certain that, with God's assistance, as soon as the fine weather comes, I shall drive out the Russians quicker than they came. All my villages and cantons having offered me a voluntary levy of horses, that alone makes 40,000 horses, the riders having already served, and the horses being over six years old ; and this independent of 20,000 horses procured by requisition, and 20,000 more purchased in the north.

"I have received a letter from the King of Denmark, which is as frank as it is firm. He informs me of his positive intention of remaining true to the alliance, and of turning a deaf ear to the attempts of Russia, Sweden, and England.

"I spoke about Sweden to your Majesty at Dresden ; but the day after my departure M. Sigueul arrived, bringing the unexpected demand that I should allow Sweden to take Norway. I was indignant at a proposal so contrary to my honour, because my alliance with Denmark was not an unknown circumstance. I did not even condescend to make a reply.

"Your Majesty has been informed of the affair of General York. The King of Prussia expresses the most cordial sentiments towards me, but I send Comte Otto a translation of the last English papers, which show what the English contemplate. They wish to treat with the King of Prussia, as well as with Ferdinand VII., and to establish a revolutionary committee to act for him. . . .

" NAPOLEON."

The Emperor was in great hopes that in making his peace with the Church he would secure the hearty alliance of Austria. The position of Pope and Emperor at this period may be thus summed up.

The Pope was very differently treated at Fontainebleau to what he had been at Savona. If still a captive, he was sumptuously lodged and fed, and enjoyed comparative freedom. In the hope that he would consent to reside in

Paris, Cardinal Maury had been ordered to prepare the archiepiscopal palace for his reception; architects were called in to decorate it, the gardens were enlarged, and stables built. The disasters in Russia, and the troubled state of Europe, induced Napoleon to reopen negotiations with the Holy See, in the hopes of conciliating Austria and Bavaria and their Catholic subjects. Several interviews took place between the Pope and the Emperor at Fontainebleau, during which Napoleon consented to modify his previous demands. He no longer insisted upon the four propositions of the Gallican Church, held in horror by Rome. He no longer insisted that the Pope should reside in Paris, or that the Pope should blame the "black cardinals" for not having attended his marriage with Marie Louise. The Pope was no longer called upon to banish Cardinals di Pietro and Pacca for ever from his counsels; concessions were also made on the subject of the confirming of bishops, and the Emperor promised to restore to favour all the cardinals, bishops, and priests who had incurred his wrath. The new Concordat was signed on the 25th January, and by this the Pope agreed to exercise his pontificate in France, and by Art. 3 he was to enjoy a revenue of 80,000*l*. Napoleon at once signified the conclusion of the Concordat to the Emperor of Austria, and in a letter to his Minister of Worship, not inserted in *The Correspondence*, ordered *Te Deums* to be chanted in its honour. The Pope, however, had no sooner signed this document than he repented, and with the advice of Pacca, Consalvi, and the "black cardinals," who had been released from prison, and were allowed to visit him, determined to retract. At this time the Pope was in very feeble health, and it was a matter of great difficulty for him to draw up a retractation; he was under the eyes of the police, and he could write only a few lines a day. However, the instrument was at last prepared in secrecy, and forwarded with trembling. The Pope denied the validity of the Concordat of Fontainebleau which had been extorted from him. The anger of the Emperor when he received the letter of Pius VII., was such that he talked of blowing out the brains of some of the cardinals. It was, perhaps, fortunate for them that he was so soon called away to take the command of his armies in the field.

On the 25th March the Emperor wrote thus to Comte Bigot :—

"The Minister of Worship must observe the most profound secrecy on the subject of the Pope's letter of the 24th, for I wish, according to circumstances, to be able to say that I have or have not received it. You must write to the bishops that as this is Holy Week, and they have duties to perform in their dioceses, they should return to them, with the exception of the bishops of Nantes and of Trèves. . . . The Concordat is henceforth the law of the State. It is a treaty more sacred than all others, having been drawn up by the Pope and the Emperor, and signed by them in presence of four cardinals."

The bishops and archbishops were not to know anything of the protest of Pius VII., but the letter said that they were to go to Fontainebleau, and to present addresses to the Pope, imploring his Holiness to come to an understanding with the Chief of the State.

Not having been able to change the determination of the Pope, the Emperor, on the 2nd April, wrote to Comte Bigot, saying—

"I have ordered that no one shall be admitted to the Pope's mass but the cardinals. I have given orders for Cardinal di Pietro to be carried off secretly at night time, and taken to some town forty leagues from Paris. Orders have been given that no more persons be allowed to come to Fontainebleau. . . . I have signified to the cardinals that they must no longer meddle with anything, and that, as they will not settle the affairs of the Church, they must not disturb those of the State."

The Emperor had just won the battle of Lutzen, when he learned that the Chapter of Tournay had refused to elect a bishop. He at once wrote to his Minister of Worship from Dresden, 14th August—

"I have ordered the Minister of Police to arrest all the canons of Tournay ... and to make the professors of the seminaries swear to teach the four propositions of the Gallican Church, and, on their refusal, to arrest them. ... If I hear of any further act of rebellion, I shall suppress the bishopric. ..."

None of the above letters are published in *The Correspondence.*

TO PRINCE EUGENE.

"FONTAINEBLEAU, 26*th January*, 1813.

"... All your efforts should tend towards preserving Warsaw. The reports which reach me from all sides show that the Russians on the Beresina thought themselves lost; that, but for the unfortunate affair of Partouneaux [who wandered into the enemy's lines, and was captured with his division], Victor would have beaten them as we beat the admiral, and that their army would have been crushed; that they had no intention of marching upon Wilna, and were going to remain at Minsk, when the forced marches which were made, and the measures taken at Wilna, encouraged them to push forward. Since then, the success of the treason of General York has enabled them to cross the Niemen. At present, will they endeavour to reach Warsaw? That is the question.

"NAPOLEON.

"P.S.—I have no doubt that you will hold Posen."

This was one way of flinging dirt at Murat. No one could have been better aware of the falsehood of the above assertions than Prince Eugene himself.

In another letter to the Viceroy, written on the 29th, the Emperor said:—

"I have already told you to assemble an advanced guard of 40,000 men and 6,000 horses, in order to hold

Posen, and to keep up your communications with Warsaw. I should have liked the command of this advanced guard to have been given to Marshal Ney, but since you have sent him to Paris, there remains Marshal St. Cyr. . . . I have ordered my saddle-horses, and the horses of my household, to be assembled and reorganised at Berlin, and I have recommended the announcement of my speedy arrival in that capital [which was already growing too hot for the French garrison]. . . . You will see in the *Moniteur* that the kingdom of Italy is electrified. Milan has offered me 100 horses, and I am assured that the country will furnish 2,000. I have a superb corps of 20,000 men, drawn from the marines, on the march; there is not a soldier but has seen one year's service; they themselves asked to serve. You should say, and yourself be well convinced, that in the next campaign I shall drive the Russians back across the Niemen.

"Send back Marshal Berthier, as his health is not good.
"NAPOLEON."

To GENERAL CLARKE.

"PARIS, 31st *January*, 1813.

"Reiterate orders for the King of Spain to remove his head-quarters to Valladolid, to occupy Madrid only with the extremity of his left, and to send considerable forces to subdue the north of Spain.

"NAPOLEON."

To ADMIRAL DECRÈS.

"PARIS, 2nd *February*, 1813.

"Order Admiral Baste to go to Swedish Pomerania, where he will be, under the orders of General Morand, charged with the command of the flotilla, and to adopt measures for the defence of the isle of Rugen and the coasts. He must visit the mouths of the Oder. . . .

"NAPOLEON."

To M. MARET.

"PARIS, 3rd *February*, 1813.

"The Viceroy writes to me that General Bülow has only 300 cavalry, and that therefore Prussia, instead of joining with us to defend her territory, and to repair the treason of General York, does nothing. There are 2,000 cavalry shut up in the fortresses of Silesia, as if they were afraid of us, instead of aiding us to cover their country.

"NAPOLEON."

On the 8th February the Emperor, in a letter to the Viceroy, said :—" If Prince Schwartzenberg evacuates Warsaw and falls back upon Kalisch, it will be necessary to reinforce the corps of General Regnier."

It was on the 8th February that the Russians entered Warsaw and captured Pillau, while Thorn and Dantsic were invested.

To GENERAL CLARKE.

"PARIS, 9*th February*, 1813.

"You must inform the King of Spain, in cipher and by quadruplicate, that I much regret to see that he has wasted two such important months as December and January, when the English had no power to do anything, and that he did not profit by this circumstance to pacify Navarre, Biscay, and Aragon; that he is always asking for money; that money is there, and that without any excuse he allows the finest provinces to be laid waste by Mina; that I have several times ordered him to go to Valladolid, but that the *nonchalance* with which affairs in Spain are conducted is inconceivable. How comes it, in fact, that he has not kept up his communications? . . .

"There is not a moment to be lost. Let the king go to Valladolid, occupying Madrid and Valentia with his extreme left.

"Write to him that the time lost cannot be recovered; that

affairs will turn out badly unless he displays more activity; that it is necessary to occupy Valladolid and Salamanca and to threaten Portugal; that the English appear to be reinforcing themselves in Portugal either to push forward into Spain or to disembark with 25,000 men on the French coast while I am engaged in the north; that to hinder the execution of this plan it is necessary that the army of Spain should be always ready to assume the offensive, and to threaten Lisbon should the English weaken their forces in Spain. . . .

"NAPOLEON."

To M. MARET.

"PARIS, 10*th February*, 1813.

"Write to M. de St. Marsan saying that the extensive recruiting which is going on all through Prussia, under officers whom the king cannot trust, creates alarm here, and that I desire that everything may remain quiet.

"NAPOLEON."

To PRINCE EUGENE.

"PARIS, 10*th February*, 1813.

"MY SON,—You must cause this recruiting of Prussians to cease, and content yourself with the troops of General Bülow as they are. Issue orders on this subject.

"NAPOLEON."

At the opening of the Legislative Body on the 14th February the Emperor said :—

"The war rekindled in the north of Europe offered the English a favourable opportunity for carrying out their plans in the Peninsula. They made great efforts, but all their hopes were deceived. Their army failed in its attack upon Burgos, and, after experiencing great losses, was obliged to evacuate Spanish territory.

"I myself entered Russia. The French arms were constantly victorious. Nowhere could the Russians resist our eagles. Moscow fell into our power.

"When the barriers of Russia were forced, and when the impotency of her armies was recognised, a swarm of Tartars turned their parricidal hands against the finest provinces of that vast Empire which they had been summoned to defend. In a very few weeks, in spite of the tears and despair of the unfortunate Muscovites, they burned down more than 4,000 of their finest villages, thus gratifying their ancient hatred on the pretext of delaying our march by making a desert round us. We triumphed over all these obstacles: even the burning of Moscow, where, in four days, they destroyed the labour of forty generations, in no way interfered with the prosperous state of my affairs. But the excessive cold of a premature winter brought down a fearful calamity on my army. In a few nights everything changed. I have suffered great losses. They would have broken my heart if I had been accessible to any other feelings but the interest, the glory, and the future of my people.

"At the sight of the misfortunes which fell upon us the joy of England was great; her hopes had no limits. She offered our finest provinces as the recompense for treason; she imposed as a condition of peace the dismemberment of this splendid Empire; in other terms, this was proclaiming perpetual war.

"The energy of my people, their attachment to the integrity of the Empire, and the love they have shown me, have dissipated all these chimeras, and have led our enemies to conceive a more just appreciation of the state of affairs.

"The misfortunes produced by the rigour of the frost have brought out in bold relief the grandeur and solidity of this Empire, founded upon the efforts and the love of 50,000,000 of citizens, and upon the territorial resources of the finest countries in the world.

"It is with lively satisfaction that we have seen the

people of our kingdom of Italy, those of ancient Holland, and of the united departments rivalling the French.

"The agents of England propagate among our neighbours the spirit of revolt against sovereigns. England would like to see the whole Continent a prey to civil war and to all the passions of anarchy, but Providence has itself selected her as the first victim of anarchy and civil war.

"I have signed a concordat with the Pope which has put an end to the differences which had unfortunately arisen with the Church. The French dynasty reigns and will continue to reign in Spain. I am satisfied with the conduct of my allies; I shall abandon none of them; I shall maintain the integrity of their states. The Russians shall return to their fearful climate.

"I desire peace; it is necessary to every one. Four times since the rupture of the treaty of Amiens I have proposed it in the most solemn manner. I shall never make any but an honourable peace, in conformity with the interests and grandeur of my Empire. My policy is not mysterious; I have made known the sacrifices which I am willing to make.

"As long as this maritime war lasts my people must be prepared to accept all sorts of sacrifices; for a bad peace would make us lose everything, even hope.

"America has appealed to arms to cause the sovereignty of her flag to be respected. The good wishes of the world accompany her in this glorious struggle. Should she terminate it by obliging the enemies of the Continent to recognise the principle that the flag covers the merchandise and the crew,[1] and that neutrals should not be subjected to paper blockade, the whole in conformity with the stipulations of the treaty of Utrecht, America will have deserved

---

[1] Had not Napoleon forced Louis to seize all the American ships lying in Dutch ports, and the Czar American vessels in the Baltic, having on board colonial produce suspected of being of English origin?

well of every one. Posterity will say that the Old World lost its rights which were re-conquered by the New World.

"My Minister of the Interior will acquaint you with the situation of the Empire, the prosperous condition of agriculture, manufactures, and internal trade, as well as the constant increase of our population. In no age have the agriculture and manufactures of France flourished to such an extent.

"I require great resources to meet all the expenses which circumstances necessitate ; but by means of different measures which will be proposed to you by the Minister of Finance, I shall not be obliged to impose any new burden on my people."

NOTE DICTATED TO THE GRAND MARSHAL OF THE PALACE.

"PARIS, 23rd *February*, 1813.

"It is my intention to pursue quite another system with my equipages than that followed during the last campaign. I desire the number of persons to be greatly reduced, to have fewer cooks, less plates, dishes &c., no large dressing case, and this as much by way of setting an example as in order to diminish trouble. In the field, tables, even mine, shall be served with soup, a boiled, a roast, vegetable, no desert. In the large cities officers may do as they like.

"I do not wish to take any pages with me ; they are of no use ; perhaps I will take with me those attached to the hunting establishment, who are twenty-four years old and who are accustomed to fatigue.

"Diminish also the number of cantines ; instead of four beds have only two ; instead of four tents have only two, and furniture in proportion."

In a letter to Comte Lauriston, of the 26th February, the Emperor said that he was anxious for news with regard to the Cossacks which had been seen prowling round Berlin. In another letter to the Count, who was in command at Magdeburg, the Emperor said, on the 2nd March, after ordering some strategical movements—" Not having a cipher at this moment I dare not write these plans to the Viceroy, because the Cossacks might intercept my letter; but if the enemy march upon Dresden you must tell him not to be astonished. . . . It is well understood that he must hold Berlin and the Elbe as long as possible."

Several other letters were written on the 2nd March. One to Prince Eugene, in which his Majesty said: " I am sorry that you have dispensed with the services of Marshal Macdonald. His presence at Berlin might be useful; he is accustomed to the police duty of that city and is known to the populace. . . . Make severe examples and maintain tranquillity."

Prince Eugene was at this moment packing up, and on the 3rd he evacuated Berlin, which the Russians entered the next day as liberators.

In a letter to brother Jerome his Majesty said: "As soon as the Emperor Alexander and General Kutusoff enter Berlin or Dresden send the Queen to Paris, but not before."

To his faithful ally, the King of Saxony, the Emperor wrote a long letter, explaining his plans. In this he said :—

" My minister tells me that your majesty desires to go to Baireuth. I need hardly tell you that all France is at your disposal. I have a house at Mayence and another at Strasburg where your Majesty's family would be comfortable."

And in a letter to the King of Wirtemburg asking for troops :—

" I have given orders to allow the Russians to advance, and all my measures are ready for taking the field shortly. However it is necessary to guard the Thuringian mountains so as not to allow the heart of the Confederation of the Rhine to be insulted by Cossack patrols."

And in a letter to the King of Bavaria the Emperor said :—

"All the measures which I have taken have been adopted with a view of allowing the Russians to advance. The more they advance the more certain is their destruction."

A similar assurance was addressed to the Grand Duke of Wurzburg.

In all, Napoleon got through twenty-two letters and despatches on the 2nd March, extending over sixteen closely printed pages.

To GENERAL DUROC.

"PARIS, 4*th March*, 1813.

"I beg that you will let me know if my palaces of Strasburg and of Mayence are in a good condition. They may be useful either for me or for the families of some of the princes of the Confederation.

"NAPOLEON."

On the same day his Majesty fearing lest his coasts might be insulted in his absence, wrote to General Clarke to have an eye to the defences of Brest, Cherbourg, Belle Isle, Aix, Oleron, Toulon, Calais, Ostend, Dunkirk, Havre, &c.

In a long letter to Prince Eugene, dated the 4th, the Emperor thus resumed his directions :—" Remain at Berlin as long as you can. Make examples for the sake of discipline. At the least insult from a town or Prussian village burn it down, even if it were Berlin which behaved badly. . . . In the month of May the three corps of the army of the Maine will join my Guard, a good artillery, and a numerous cavalry, and I shall then drive the Russians over the Niemen. . . ."

On the 5th and the 6th Napoleon repeated his orders to Eugene to remain at Berlin, but if forced to abandon that capital he was to intrench himself in front of Magdeburg; and on the 9th in a long letter exhibiting considerable anxiety and filled with reproaches, the Emperor said—"I have received your letter of the 4th (giving an account of the evacuation of Berlin). I do not know if General Gérard has joined you; I suppose that he had already reached that city when you left it. I am assured that General Gérard has fallen into the hands of the Cossacks, as also my Secretary of Legation. . . . I do not see what obliged you to leave Berlin. . . . Nothing is less military than the course you have pursued. . . . An experienced general would have established a camp in front of Custrin. . . . You tell me nothing in your letters. I have written to you several times that in the present state of affairs I require to know the truth in all its details. . . . It is shameful to say, and no one would believe it, but I am ignorant what general commands at Stettin, and what garrison has been left there. It is the same with Spandau. . . . I order you to inform the chief of your staff that if he does not send me detailed reports every day, independent of your correspondence, I shall make a severe example. I learn what passes from the English papers. . . ."

On the 11th, Napoleon reiterated his dissatisfaction with the conduct of the viceroy, and said—"Our military operations are the object of laughter to our allies of Vienna, and to our enemies of London and St. Petersburg, because the army constantly falls back a week before the arrival of the enemy's infantry, on the approach of their light troops and on mere rumour." His Majesty then informed Prince Eugene that after doing everything to lead the enemy to suppose that he intended to march on Dresden himself, he meant to arrive at Stettin by forced marches with 300,000 men, and to continue his march on Dantsic.

To KING JEROME.

"TRIANON, 12*th March*, 1813.

"It is unfortunate with your intelligence that you will not see that Magdeburg can only be provisioned by means of requisitions, that these means are authorised by a state of war; that they have been constantly employed since the world was the world; that the same expedient was resorted to in Italy, in the campaign of 1809, even for Strasburg and Mayence. . . . Why should I not do for Magdeburg what I did for Mayence? Instead of taking energetic measures, you merely upset all that has been done. Besides, you believe that there are millions at my disposal, while, if you will take up your pen for a moment, you will see how much the 300,000 men whom I have in Spain, all the troops which I have raised this year, and the 100,000 cavalry I am equipping, cost. . . . You always argue. What will be the result of this blundering? that the soldiers will requisition the country themselves, and that there will be insubordination and disorder. Do you suppose that if the Russians visit Westphalia they will pay in ready money? . . . Your country has some experience of war, and knows what that state of affairs exacts. . . . It is shameful that a place like Magdeburg, which is the key of your kingdom, should not be provisioned. All your arguments are nonsense. . . . You must requisition with the greatest order possible and pay in *bons*. . . . I am obliged to fortify Magdeburg at my expense, to arm it at my expense, and to struggle constantly with the Westphalian authorities about measures which have no other object but the defence of their country. Of what use is your intelligence since you take such a wrong view? Why gratify your vanity by vexing those who defend you? "NAPOLEON."

The next day his Majesty wrote to Comte Daru, saying—" The King of Westphalia complains that his people are overwhelmed with taxes. I have some idea of concluding a bargain with the king." . . . And in fact Jerome was just as bitter as either Joseph or Louis in his complaints of the way in which his subjects were ruined by his imperial brother.

To COMTE BIGOT.

"TRIANON, 13*th March*, 1813.

"I return you the letter of the Bishop of Nantes. You must inform him that the form of the oath cannot be changed; that it could only be changed if it contained anything contrary to the mysteries of religion. All the pretensions of the cardinals are ridiculous. You must say that if the Pope ever becomes a temporal sovereign we shall break off relations with him. We should not create a schism by so doing, but we shall never tolerate the influence of a sovereign whose political interests may be different from ours. Since the Pope takes the advice of such men as the di Pietros and the Littas only, you must inform him that he will soon perceive once more the baneful consequences of the incapacity of those men. . . .

"NAPOLEON."

To GENERAL CLARKE.

"TRIANON, 13*th March*, 1813.

"I approve of the measures taken for the defence of the Pyrenees, and for calling out the national guard. Write to the general commanding in Catalonia, to the king, and to General Reille, pointing out the false direction given to affairs in Spain, and the necessity of protecting the frontier.

"NAPOLEON."

To PRINCE EUGENE.

"TRIANON, 14*th March*, 1813.

"I have received your letter from Leipsic. . . . As soon as you receive news of General Morand, let me know, even the rumours which may reach you. By our latest news it appears still undecided whether Prussia will take the field against us. However, after the treason of General York, and the appearance which matters have since assumed, it does not seem that the Prussian cabinet will long remain our ally; but I do not think the Prussians have as many troops as General Regnier. Do not forget that Prussia has a population of only 7,000,000. In the most prosperous times she never had more than 150,000 soldiers which she exaggerated into 300,000. In spite of all the efforts of the king he will certainly not have 40,000 men in May, and of these 25,000 at the most, will be able to take the field, because he will have to protect Silesia, garrison Kolberg, Pillau, and Grandenz. After the battle of Jena, in the winter campaign which ensued all the efforts made by the Prussians failed to produce more than 10,000 men. There are a great many sick in General York's corps. . . .

"NAPOLEON."

By the treaty of Kalisch, signed between Kutusoff and Hardenberg in February, and ratified on the 1st March, the Czar and the King of Prussia agreed to prosecute war against France, the former bringing 150,000 men, and the latter 80,000, independent of the garrisons in the strong places. Neither was to conclude a separate peace, and efforts were to be made to induce Austria to join the alliance, &c. This treaty was to be kept secret for two months, and it was not until the middle of March that the French ambassador, M. de St. Marsan, got wind of it.

On the 15th, in a letter of several pages to Prince Eugene, the Emperor showed that he had studied the *Reveries* of Marshal Saxe to some advantage, for he wrote—

"As for the difficulty of living, you have before you the finest provinces of Prussia from which you can draw what you require in following the principles of military execution, that is to say by pointing out to each village, even at ten leagues distance, the quantity of provisions to be supplied to your camp, and where a village does not execute your order by sending a detachment there to lay it under contribution, and if necessary to burn some houses."

On the 16th March General Clarke received orders to send a second convoy with 160,000*l.* to Spain; and the next day the Emperor wrote a letter to the Queen of Westphalia who had arrived at Compiègne, a fact which irritated him as it caused alarm in Paris, and as he had told Jerome not to send his wife away unless either Alexander or Kutusoff entered Berlin.

On the 18th the Emperor called for papers respecting Sweden, being of opinion that it was high time to publish them and to make a declaration of war. The fact is that Sweden, treated with the most unbearable harshness and arrogance by Napoleon, signed a second treaty with Russia on the 3rd March, and entered the alliance against France in an active manner.

It was not until the 28th March that Napoleon, in a letter to Marshal Ney, who was in command of the 3rd corps at Wurzburg, announced that Prussia had raised the standard and had declared war.

To M. MARET.

"PARIS, 4*th April*, 1813.

"... Write to M. de St. Marsan (French ambassador at Berlin) to return home at once. .... M. de Krusemark (Prussian ambassador in Paris) must leave before Monday; he is a spy whom it is useless to keep here. ... In the last conference which you have with M. Krusemark say that M. de Hardenberg keeps none of his promises. ... It appears that the King is no longer master. ... Write a circular to my ministers in the confederation, and let them dismiss the representatives of Prussia. ...

"NAPOLEON."

It was only on the Emperor refusing in the most positive manner so accord him any pecuniary relief that the King of Prussia consented to sign the treaty of Kalisch which was ratified on the 1st March. This blunder on the part of Napoleon was due to the fact of his doubting the sincerity of Prussia, when Prussia appears to have been sincere. The King of Prussia had exhibited the greatest reluctance to break his engagements with Napoleon, and he did not consent to do so until, as Hardenberg said, Prussia had been driven to despair. Before signing the treaty of Kalisch an attempt had been made on the part of Prussia to draw closer the bonds between the two countries by means of a matrimonial alliance; a marriage between the Prince Royal of Prussia (brother of the present Emperor of Germany) and a princess of the Bonaparte family.[1] The French Emperor, however, would have his pound of flesh, and would listen to no remonstrances. He considered the disasters of the Russian campaign repaired, and they were forgotten.

In several letters written in April, Napoleon expressed his faith in the good intentions and the loyalty of Austria. He was sorry that the King of Saxony had been frightened out of Dresden as Eugene had been frightened out of Berlin, and he complained of the conduct of the Saxon troops. However, on the 8th April he wrote as follows to Frederick Augustus:—

"I have received the letter in which your Majesty announces your safe arrival at Ratisbon. I am only waiting until the 4th corps under General Bertrand has reached Nuremburg, to start for Mayence, and to place myself at the head of the army. I hope with the aid of God to be at Dresden in the course of a few days. . . . I am sorry for the affair of the bridge of Dresden (which had been blown up by Davoust), but that after all is only an affair of a few hundred thousand francs. . . ." And writing to brother Jerome on the 11th, the Emperor said

[1] *Manuscrit de* 1813. Baron Fain, vol. i. p. 212.

—"I send you 20,000*l.* in gold. By the 22nd I shall be at Erfurth with 200,000 men independent of the army of the Viceroy."

To GENERAL CAULAINCOURT.

"ST. CLOUD, 13*th April*, 1813.

"These are the plans for my departure; I shall start with you in a light carriage; the Grand Marshal and the Comte de Lobau in another carriage; Fain and Yvan in a third. The three carriages must be all equally light. In my carriage must be placed a selection of books, maps, sketches, &c. Fain must have in his carriage the reports on the situation of the army, my correspondence, &c. . . .

"NAPOLEON."

To THE EMPEROR OF AUSTRIA.

"ST. CLOUD, 13*th April*, 1813.

"SIR, MY BROTHER, AND VERY DEAR FATHER-IN-LAW.—Prince Schwartzenberg has handed me your Majesty's letter. I had great pleasure in seeing him, and I conversed with him for a long time in the most confidential way. I have been highly satisfied with the conduct of General Bubna during his stay here, and I hope that your Majesty will give him some mark of approbation.

"I am on the point of starting for Mayence whither I had the intention of going on the 20th, but the movements of the enemy on the left bank of the Elbe have decided me to hasten my departure. As soon as I take the field I shall send an order to General Frimont to denounce the armistice.

"NAPOLEON."

To PRINCE CAMBACÉRÈS.

"MAYENCE, 17*th April*, 1813.

"I reached Mayence in forty hours, in good health and without accident. The carriage of the grand marshal has not yet rejoined me. I shall remain here for several days to look after a great many things which are wanting.

"NAPOLEON."

In a letter to Berthier of the 19th, Napoleon wrote:—

"Send a courier to the King of Bavaria. Inform him of the orders which you have given his contingent, and the immensity of our forces. Ask the King why he does not send General Wrede to take the command of his troops. Is that General ill? . . . In writing to the King of Saxony tell him that General Regnier has returned to resume the command of the 7th corps, and that as soon as communications have been re-opened he will go to Torgau: that I desire the King will give positive orders so that all the uncertainties which have recently arisen may cease, and that the fortress and the troops may be placed under my orders without the slightest reticence."

TO THE KING OF SAXONY.

"MAYENCE, 20*th April*, 1813.

"Your Majesty's letter has afforded me great pain. You have no more friendship for me; I accuse the enemies of our cause who are in your cabinet of this. I require all your cavalry and all your officers. I have spoken frankly to you; but no matter how events may end, your Majesty may count upon the esteem with which you have inspired me.

"NAPOLEON."

TO COMTE GERMAIN.

"MAYENCE, 20*th April*, 1813.

"I have received your letter of the 19th. The conjectures made with regard to the fidelity of the King of

Saxony are absurd; neither the opinions nor the probity of that prince are known. You should deny these rumours with all your force. . . .

" NAPOLEON."

The Saxons themselves were certainly hostile to the French, but not so their monarch, who on receiving a letter from the King of Prussia calling upon him to join the coalition and shake off the chains of France, replied on the 16th April, that he intended to respect the engagements he had contracted.

To GENERAL CLARKE.

"MAYENCE, 23rd *April*, 1813.

"Reply to the King of Spain that I gave him the command-in-chief of my army; that I am surprised therefore by his continual complaints that he is not obeyed, that this happens because he confounds the King of Spain with the general-in-chief of my armies; that I shall never allow my armies to depend upon Spanish ministers; that in the present condition of France he must expect nothing from me. . . .

" NAPOLEON."

To GENERAL CLARKE.

"MAYENCE, 24th *April*, 1813.

"I have reason to be satisfied with the intentions of Austria. I do not suspect her preparations; however, it is not my intention to be dependent upon her. The vulnerable part as regards Austria is my kingdom of Italy whither I intend to send the Viceroy as soon as possible. Take measures for forming an army of Italy. . . . Write to Naples so that in addition to his contingent the King of Naples may have a corps of infantry, artillery, and cavalry ready to march.

" NAPOLEON."

The fact is that it was the very ambiguous conduct of Austria, which induced Napoleon to send Prince Eugene back to his viceroyalty in hot haste, nor had he a very lively faith in the fidelity of Murat.

To the KING OF WIRTEMBURG.

"MAYENCE, 24*th April*, 1813.

"I thank your Majesty for the information you have sent me concerning Torgau. If the news of the capitulation be true, I am surprised that the King of Saxony said nothing about it; but there appears to be a great deal of intrigue going on round that respectable sovereign. . . . I beg that your Majesty will let me know what you think of the intentions of Austria. Prince Schwartzenberg brought me the most positive assurances; and the Emperor wrote in the same sense to the Empress. I asked Prince Schwartzenberg if the corps of General Frimont, which is on the Cracovia side, was under my orders; upon his reply in the affirmative, I have warned the Austrian General to hold himself in readiness to denounce the armistice, and in fact I shall send him an order to do this as soon as I pass the Saal.

"A proposal was made by Austria to assemble a congress at Prague. I adhered to this with all my heart, but it appears that Russia has sent no reply.

"Perhaps it would be well for your Majesty and the King of Bavaria to try and induce the court of Saxony to remain faithful to the Confederation. I have not said anything on this subject to the King of Bavaria, who appears to have been very much surprised by the departure of the King of Saxony. . . .

"NAPOLEON."

It was becoming very evident, no matter what the personal feeling of the King might be, that the Saxons themselves had no wish to fight for the French and slavery.

To GENERAL SAVARY.

"ERFURTH, 26*th April*, 1813.

"I do not intend that you should transmit direct to the Empress your memoranda on police affairs. That can have no advantage and has many objections. The Empress is too young to have her mind corrupted or disturbed by police details. . . .

"NAPOLEON."

To M. MARET.

"ERFURTH, 28*th April*, 1813.

"I send you a letter from Comte de Mercy. I am extremely dissatisfied with the manner in which I am seconded by my Minister of Foreign Affairs (M. Maret, Duc de Bassano). You allow the missions at the courts of Bavaria and of Saxony to remain incomplete at a moment so important as this! At Munich where you should have the greatest number of persons possible, you have no one! . . . The King of Saxony has made a convention with Austria respecting the Polish troops so as to allow them to pass through Bohemia on laying down their arms, which is quite opposed to my wishes, and you know nothing of it. Pay more attention to my missions and fill up those of Munich and Dresden at once.

"NAPOLEON."

To PRINCE CAMBACÉRÈS.

"LUTZEN, 1*st May*, 1813.

"I have removed our head-quarters to this place. The enemy wished to prevent us from debouching in the plains of Lutzen where they had massed a strong force of cavalry. Our infantry supported by artillery, repulsed them. The enemy have little artillery, and did not do us much harm.

"The first cannon-shot fired caused us a great loss; Marshall Bessières was killed stone dead. Our whole loss amounted to twenty-five men. I write this in haste so that you may inform the Empress, and let the Duchesse d'Istrie know what has happened. Make the Empress understand that the Duc d'Istrie (Bessières) was a long way from me when he was killed. . . .

"NAPOLEON."

On the 2nd May was fought the terrible battle of Lutzen which ended in a retrograde movement on the part of the allies, but which was by no means the decisive victory which Napoleon claimed in his bulletins. At one moment matters seemed so gloomy that the Emperor made preparations to retreat, and if he afterwards restored the fortunes of the day not only was there no pursuit but at nine o'clock at night he narrowly escaped falling into the hands of a body of Prussian cavalry which made a sudden dash on the French position. The allies confessed to a loss of 15,000 men, but declared that no prisoners, guns, or standards had been captured. Napoleon in his bulletin said—"We have made thousands of prisoners. . . . Our loss amounts to 18,000 killed or wounded. That of the enemy is set down at from 25,000 to 30,000 men. . . The gloomy plots hatched by the cabinet of St. James's throughout the winter have in a moment been undone like the Gordian knot by the sword of Alexander. . . ."

PROCLAMATION TO THE ARMY.

"FROM OUR IMPERIAL CAMP AT LUTZEN,
"*3rd May*, 1813.

"SOLDIERS,—I am satisfied with you! You have fulfilled my expectations. You have made up for everything by your good will and your bravery. On the celebrated day of the 2nd May, you defeated and routed the Russian and Prussian army, commanded by the Emperor of Russia and the King of Prussia. You have added new lustre and glory to my eagles; you have shown all that French blood is capable of. The battle of Lutzen will be placed above the battles of Austerlitz, Jena, Friedland, and Borodino.

In the last campaign the enemy found refuge against our armies by following the ferocious method of his barbarous ancestors; the armies of the Tartars burned the fields, the towns, and even holy Moscow. To-day they arrive in our countries preceded by all that Germany, France, and Italy have in the way of scamps and deserters, to preach revolt, anarchy, civil war, and murder; they have made themselves the apostles of every crime. It is a moral conflagration which they wish to light up between the Vistula and the Rhine, in order, after the manner of despotic governments, to place deserts between them and us. The madmen! they little know the wisdom, the good sense and the attachment of the Germans to their sovereigns. They little know the power and the bravery of the French.

"In one single day you have defeated these parricidal plots. We will drive the Tartars back into their fearful climate, which they ought never to have left. Let them remain in their frozen deserts, the abode of slavery, barbarism, and corruption, where man is considered on a par with the brute!

"You have deserved well of civilised Europe. Soldiers, Italy, France, and Germany thank you!

"NAPOLEON."

Lutzen was a very hard-fought field; and at one period of the day the Emperor thought of retreating. If the next day the allies retired, they left neither prisoners, guns, nor colours in the hands of the victors, and while the French lost 18,000 men in killed or wounded, they lost only 15,000, thanks to their superiority in cavalry.

TO THE EMPEROR OF AUSTRIA.

"PEGAU, 4*th May*, 1813.

"Knowing the interest which your Majesty takes in every piece of good fortune which befalls to me, I hasten to announce the victory which it has pleased Providence to grant to my arms in the field of Lutzen. Although I wished to direct all the movements of my army myself, and was sometimes exposed to the fire of grape-shot, yet I met with no accident, and, thank Heaven, I enjoy the best health.

"I daily receive news from the Empress, with whom I continue to be extremely satisfied. To-day she is my prime minister, and she acquits herself to my entire satisfaction. . . .
"NAPOLEON."

To GENERAL CAULAINCOURT.
"DRESDEN, 8*th May*, 1813.

"Send the inclosed letter to M. de Serra at Prague.

"The Emperor has arrived at Dresden. . . . To-morrow the army will pass the river in pursuit of the enemy Inclosed you will find a letter on the subject of the conduct of General Thielman. . . . You must tell M. Senft that to offend against the principles of the Confederation is to declare war against the Emperor; that the Emperor pities the King; that the interest and friendship which the Emperor bears the King have made him patient up to the present, but that circumstances are so pressing now that you can accord the Court of Saxony only six hours to give satisfaction on the following points: 1st. To order General Thielman to leave Torgau with his troops. . . . 2nd. To order all his cavalry to Dresden without delay. 3rd. The King must declare in a letter to the Emperor that he remains a member of the Confederation . . . that he has no treaty with any power contrary to the principles of the Confederation. . . .

"Unless you obtain satisfaction upon these three points you must inform the King that I shall declare him a felon, beyond the pale of my protection, and that he has consequently ceased to reign. . . ."

This vigorous way of acting was eminently successful for the moment. In a letter to Marshal Ney, dated the

10th May, the Emperor said: "The Saxon General Gersdorf has just brought me a letter from the king, with an order placing Torgau and General Thielman at my disposal.[1] The Saxon cavalry is arriving from Prague, and will be here in three days; I think that the king himself will arrive before them. . . ."

To PRINCE CAMBACÉRÈS.

"DRESDEN, 10th May, 1813.

"We have arrived at Dresden; I am master of both banks and of the strong places on the Elbe. It is probable that I shall march into Silesia.

"NAPOLEON."

After having been long in disgrace, and having nearly lost his head, Fouché now received the following letter :—

"DRESDEN, 10th May, 1813.

"I have informed you of my intention, as soon as I enter the states of the King of Prussia to place you at the head of the government of that country. The victory of Lutzen having allowed me to drive the enemy behind the Elbe . . . I wish you to come to Dresden secretly without losing a minute. . . . The Regent (Marie Louise) alone knows anything of your departure. I am very glad to have the opportunity of receiving from you new services and new proofs of your attachment.

"NAPOLEON."

To THE KING OF SAXONY.

"DRESDEN, 12th May, 1813.

"I learn with pleasure that your Majesty is about to arrive at Dresden. . . . I experience sincere pleasure in

[1] General Thielman had refused to hand Torgau over to the French, and when he at last did so on the positive orders of the King he declined to serve any longer under Napoleon.

being able to reinstal you in your capital, and to restore you your states from which Providence designed me to drive your enemies. . . . "NAPOLEON."

The next day, in a letter to Marshal Ney, the Emperor wrote: "The King of Saxony made his triumphal entry yesterday into Dresden; he is to dine with me to-day."

Several letters show that Napoleon at this moment was ignorant of the position of the allies. He had not been able to ascertain whether the Prussians had fallen back upon Breslau or upon Berlin. He informed Marshal Ney that—"The enemy commit all kinds of horrors, burning villages as they did in Russia: this will be a good lesson for the Germans." And, writing to M. Maret, his Majesty complained of the conduct of the ambassador of the King of Naples at Vienna. He had soon more reasons to doubt the fidelity of his brother-in-law.

We now come to a curious episode in the campaign of 1813—an attempt on the part of Napoleon to negotiate separately with Russia.

INSTRUCTIONS FOR GENERAL CAULAINCOURT.

(Who was sent to the Emperor of Russia.)

". . . On learning the views of the Emperor of Russia we shall come to an understanding. Moreover, it is my intention to make him a bridge of gold in order to deliver him from the intrigues of Metternich. If sacrifices must be made, I prefer making them for the advantage of the Emperor Alexander, who fights me fairly, and for the King of Prussia, than for the benefit of Austria, who has betrayed the alliance, and who, under the guise of mediator, wishes to assume the right of disposing of everything." After dilating on the advantages which Russia would reap by coming to an arrangement, the instructions went on to say—" Russia cannot have forgotten the march of the Austrian contingent during the recent campaign, and the Emperor Alexander should feel flattered at the idea of being able to make peace without the aid of that Power, which, after having shown itself so little friendly during difficulties, is now induced by personal interest to violate its recent alliance with France. Lastly, the Emperor Alexander should joyfully avail himself of this opportunity of revenging himself openly for the foolish diversion of the Austrians in Russia. . . ."

Having penned these instructions, his Majesty wrote two letters :—

TO THE EMPEROR OF AUSTRIA.

"DRESDEN, 17*th May*, 1813.

"SIR, MY BROTHER, AND VERY DEAR FATHER-IN-LAW,—What your Majesty said in your letter on the subject of the interest you bear me greatly affected me. I deserve this in consequence of my loyal feeling towards you. If your Majesty takes any interest in my welfare, you should be careful of my honour. I have decided to die, if necessary, at the head of all that is generous in France, sooner than become the laughing-stock of the English, and to allow my enemies to triumph. Let your Majesty think of the future ; do not destroy the fruit of three years of friendship and renew the plots of the past, which will plunge Europe into the convulsions of war ; do not sacrifice for miserable considerations the welfare of our generation, that of your existence, and the true interests of your subjects, why should I not add, of a part of your family, which is sincerely attached to you. . . . "NAPOLEON."

Count Bubna having arrived to negotiate, Napoleon wrote—"I have received your Majesty's letter. I have conversed with Count Bubna for several hours. I have told him all that I think frankly and truly. I desire peace more than any one. I consent to the opening of negotiations for a general peace and the assembling of a congress. As soon as I know that England, Russia, Prussia, and the allies have accepted this proposition, I shall hasten to send a representative to the Congress. I shall even make no objection to admitting plenipotentiaries from the insurgents in Spain. If Russia, Prussia, and the other belligerents wish to treat without England, I shall consent. . . . Your Majesty will see by this language, which is the same that I have held for the last six months, my desire to spare the effusion of human blood, and to put an end to the ills which afflict so many nations."

When Caulaincourt arrived to treat secretly with the Czar he was received by Alexander in presence of the King of Prussia, and of the ambassadors of England Prussia, and Austria.

No letters seem to have been written by Napoleon on the 20th and 21st May. Upon those two days he was busy fighting a sanguinary battle with the allies at Bautzen. As at Lutzen, the Russians and Prussians, greatly outnumbered, after inflicting terrible losses on the French, fell back unmolested, thanks to their cavalry.

To the Emperor of Austria.

"Wurchen, 22nd May, 1813. 9 P.M.

"I delivered battle to the Russian and Prussian army, intrenched in the camps of Bautzen and of Kochkirch, on the 20th and the 21st. Providence granted me the victory. I hasten to inform your Majesty that my health is excellent, counting upon the interest you bear me.

"Napoleon."

In the bulletin of the 24th, giving an account of Lutzen and Bautzen, the death of Duroc, Duc de Frioul, who fell on the evening of the 22nd, is thus described. He was talking with Marshal Mortier and General Kirgener when a cannon ball shaved the marshal, killed the general stone dead, and mortally wounded Duroc. "As soon as the guards were posted," says the bulletin, "the Emperor went to visit the Duc de Frioul, who showed the greatest *sang froid*. The Duke squeezed the Emperor's hand and carried it to his lips. 'All my life,' he said, 'has been devoted to your service, and I regret it merely because I shall no longer be able to be of use to you.' 'Duroc,' said the Emperor, 'there is another life! It is there that you will wait for me, and where we shall meet some day.' 'Yes, sire; but it will be in thirty years, when you have triumphed over your enemies, and realised all the hopes of your country. . . . I have lived an honest man; I have nothing to reproach myself with. I leave a daughter. Your Majesty will be a father to her.'

"The Emperor, pressing the right hand of the Grand Marshal, remained silent for a quarter of an hour, his head supported by his left hand. The Grand Marshal was the first to break silence. 'Ah, Sire! go away; this sight affects you.' The Emperor, leaning upon Marshal Soult and General Caulaincourt, left the Duc de Frioul without being able to utter anything but these words—'Adieu, then, my friend!' The Emperor retired to his tent and received no one for the rest of the night."

On the 25th May the Emperor wrote to the King of Saxony, saying, among other things, that Oudinot was marching upon Berlin, that Denmark had rejected all the offers of the allies, and complaining that General Thielman, who had lately commanded at Torgau, had gone over to the enemy.

To PRINCE CAMBACÉRÈS.

"ROSNIG, 30*th May*, 1813.

"I am sorry that you did not advise the Empress to pardon the man condemned to death. You acted too much like a magistrate in that affair. . . . Take the first opportunity of making the Empress accord one or two pardons on her own initiative. This can be done without much harm to justice, and it will have a good effect upon public opinion." "NAPOLEON."

To M. MARET.

"NEUMARKT, 31st *May*, 1813.

"The Swedish troops having entered Hamburg, it is right that you should at once send me a declaration of war against Sweden.

"NAPOLEON."

To GENERAL CLARKE.

"NEUMARKT, 31st *May*, 1813.

"The question asked by General Cæsar Berthier as to the conduct he should pursue with regard to Queen Caroline of Sicily is probably an idle one. However, you should reply that in the event of such a case occurring he should treat her with the honours due to her rank, and with the greatest possible consideration; this for two reasons—because she is the grandmother of the Empress, and especially as an unfortunate queen, *persecuted by the English*.[1]

"NAPOLEON."

To GENERAL CLARKE.

"NEUMARKT, 2nd *June*, 1813.

"You will see by the *Moniteur* that negotiations for an armistice are going on. It will probably be signed to-morrow or the day after. This armistice interferes with the course of my victories. I decided upon it for two reasons: my want of cavalry, which prevents me from dealing decisive blows, and the hostile attitude of Austria. That court, under the most amiable, the most tender, and, I may say, the most sentimental pretences, desires nothing less than to force me, through fear of its army concentrated at Prague, to restore Dalmatia and Istria. It also demands the left bank of the Inn, the Salzburg country, and half the Grand Duchy of Warsaw, the other half being given to Prussia and Russia. Austria hopes to

---

[1] This was the Queen of Naples, driven from her throne by Napoleon, and replaced first by Joseph and then by Murat.

reap these advantages by the mere presence of 100,000 men and without hostilities. . . . Redouble your efforts; see that artillery, cavalry, and infantry are ready to march as I have ordered. If I can, I will wait until September, in order to strike heavy blows. I wish to be in a position to crush my enemies. . . .

"NAPOLEON."

Writing on the same day to Prince Eugene the Emperor complained bitterly of the insolence and the perfidy of the court of Vienna.

The armistice was signed on the 2nd June, and on the 3rd the Emperor wrote to General Caulaincourt, his plenipotentiary, a letter in which he said :—

"The fact cannot be disguised that this armistice, as proposed in my ultimatum, is not honourable for me. . . . It is I who abandon everything; the enemy nothing. . . . Does the enemy wish to humiliate me by driving me out of a town (Breslau), which fell into my hands after a battle, by means of an armistice? . . . . Tell the plenipotentiaries, in breaking off negotiations, that my love of peace alone induced me to consent to a disadvantageous armistice; that it was through pure *cajolerie* that I consented to abandon the capital of Silesia; that before a week I shall be in Berlin. . . . Tell them that they will be beaten in the next battle, that I shall remain master of Breslau and of Berlin . . . ."

After insisting for some time that the Oder should form the line of demarcation between the two armies, and that he would not abandon Breslau, Napoleon consented to yield on both points, and ratified the armistice. The Emperor at once sent a telegram to the Empress Regent, saying :—

"An armistice of two months, during which negotiations for peace will be carried on, was concluded the 4th June between the two armies."

To MARIE LOUISE, EMPRESS-QUEEN AND REGENT.

"HAYNAN, 7*th June*, 1813."

"MADAME AND DEAR FRIEND,—I have received your letter in which you inform me that you received the arch-chancellor while in bed. I beg that under no circumstance will you receive, no matter who, when in bed. That is permitted only to persons over thirty years of age.

"NAPOLEON."

To PRINCE CAMBACÉRÈS.

"HAYNAN, 7*th June*, 1813.

"I do not approve of the Empress going to Notre Dame. Those great pomps should be rare, without that they become trivial. If the Empress were to go to Notre Dame for the victory of Wurschen, she would be obliged to go there for all the other victories. As it was right to go there after after the victory of Lutzen, which was unexpected, and which changed the position of affairs, so, this time, it would be useless.

"I desire that in general the *Te Deum* be sung on the Sunday immediately following the reception of the news. Delay is inconvenient; war has its chances. It would be ridiculous to sing a *Te Deum* for a victory when, in the interval, the news of a defeat had arrived.

"NAPOLEON."

To THE COMTESSE DE MONTESQUIOU.

"HAYNAN, 7*th June*, 1813.

"I see with pleasure that my son grows and continues to give hopes. I can but express my satisfaction for all the care you bestow upon him.

"The death of the Duc de Frioul pained me. This was the only time during twenty years that he did not guess what would please me.

"NAPOLEON."

To Prince Cambacérès.

"Bunzlau, 8th June, 1813.

"Caulaincourt has written for some comedians for Dresden. I desire that this should make a noise in Paris, as it will have a good effect in London and in Spain by making it believed that we are amusing ourselves at Dresden. It is not the season for playing, and you must therefore send only six or seven actors at the most, well selected, and capable of performing six or seven pieces. You must also let them travel without fuss, and without making any *embarras* on the road. You must none the less allow demands to be made in Paris as if the whole 'tragedy' were about to start, and let people gossip on the subject. Remusat will choose between the *Comédie Française* and the company of the Feydeau theatre.

"Napoleon."

To M. Melzi, Duc de Lodi.

"Dresden, 12th June, 1813.

"You can write to your nephew through the Minister of Police that if he will give his word of honour not to leave you I will have him liberated at once. . . .

"Napoleon."

General Savary had evidently insisted that the good people of Paris were anxious to see peace concluded, for the Emperor wrote thus to his Minister of Police on the 13th June:—

"The tone of your correspondence does not please me; you bore me continually about the necessity of peace. I know the situation of my Empire better than you do; no one is more interested in concluding peace than myself, but I shall not make a dishonourable peace or one that would see us at war again in six months. . . These things do not concern you. . . ."

To the KING OF DENMARK.

"Dresden, 18*th June*, 1813.

"I have seen with pleasure that amidst the vicissitudes of political events the feelings of your Majesty have remained unchangeable. The evil intentions of Sweden towards me are the result of my constant refusal to adhere to the spoliation of Norway. When recent unfortunate events obliged my troops to repass the Elbe (retreat from Moscow), and your Majesty informed me of your desire to treat with England, I consented; my alliance would have been baneful, and I was the first to desire that everything should be done in order to insure the integrity of your states. . . . But events went further. The troops of your Majesty invaded French territory. Since then explanations have been given which have quite satisfied me. Your Majesty repaired everything by placing your troops at the disposal of my generals.

"However, your Majesty must feel that the relations between states are regulated by treaty, that I cannot consider the last treaty as existing, because your Majesty has since attempted negotiations with England and with Russia, and because your troops have entered my territory. I think that it would be well, therefore, to negotiate a treaty either at Dresden or at Copenhagen based on the relations which at present exist between the two states. . . .

"Napoleon."

An extract from the *Morning Chronicle*, showing that Murat at this moment meditated treason, created an unpleasant sensation in France. On the 22nd June the Emperor directed his Minister for Foreign Affairs to inform the French ambassador at Naples that if an embargo were laid upon any of his corsairs, or if his flag were in any way degraded, he was to leave the city. "Before leaving," added Napoleon, "he must hand a note to the Neapolitan cabinet, saying that I am acquainted with all its intrigues, and that it shall repent some day of the slightest insult to my flag. Tell Baron Durand that I am not satisfied with his want of dignity and energy."

The Emperor at this date accorded an audience to Prince Metternich, Baron Fain's version of which is given in *The Correspondence*. It runs thus :—

"'You here, Metternich!' said Napoleon on seeing him; 'you are welcome. But if you wish for peace why do you come so late (23rd of June, 1813)? We have already lost a month, and your mediation, in consequence of this inactivity, is almost an act of hostility. It appears that it no longer suits you to guarantee the integrity of the French Empire. But why not tell me this sooner? Why not have informed me of this on my return from Russia? I should then have had time to modify all my plans, and perhaps should not have commenced this campaign. In allowing me to exhaust myself by making new efforts you counted, no doubt, that events would have marched more rapidly. Those efforts have been crowned by victory. I gain two battles; my enemies are weakened and recover from their illusions. Suddenly you glide in amongst them; you come to speak to me of an armistice and meditation; you speak to them of an alliance, and everything is thrown into confusion. Without your baneful intervention peace between the allies and myself would have been concluded by this. . . Admit that ever since Austria has assumed the office of mediator she is no longer on my side. You were about to declare war when the victory of Lutzen stopped you; seeing that I was still redoubtable you felt it necessary to augment your forces; you wished to gain time. To-day you have 200,000 men ready; Schwartzenburg commands them; he is concentrating them at this moment behind the curtain of the Bohemian mountains, and because you think yourself in a position to dictate, you come to seek me. I have divined your intention, Metternich. Your Cabinet desires to increase my embarrassments and profit by them in order to recover what it has lost. The great question for you is to know if you can plunder without fighting me, or if you must throw yourself into the ranks of my enemies. Well! let us treat. What do you require?' To this sharp attack Metternich replied with set diplomatic phrase, and talked about a spirit of moderation, the respect which should be entertained for independent states, and some guarantee that peace would not be disturbed. 'Speak more clearly,' said the Emperor, interrupting him, 'but remember that I am an old soldier. I offered you Illyria to remain neutral; will that suffice you? My army is quite strong enough to deal with the Russians and Prussians, and your neutrality is all I ask.' 'Ah! sire,' returned Metternich, 'why will your Majesty remain alone in this struggle? Why not double your forces? You can, sire, for it depends upon you to dispose entirely of ours. We can no longer remain neuter; we must be with you or against you.' At these words the conversation grew calmer, and the Emperor took Prince Metternich into the card-room. After some time had elapsed the Emperor's voice assumed a louder tone. 'What! not only Illyria, but half of Italy, the return of the Pope to Rome! Poland, and the abandonment of Spain! and Holland and the Confederation of the Rhine and Switzerland. And this is the spirit of moderation which animates you! You think only of profiting by every chance; you carry your alliance from camp to camp, and you talk to me of respect for the rights of independent states! You desire Italy, Russia, Poland, Sweden, Norway, Prussia, Saxony, and England, Holland, and Belgium. What you aspire to is the dismemberment of the French Empire. And I, docile to your policy, must evacuate Europe, half of which I still occupy, must lead back my legions behind the Rhine, the Alps, and the Pyrenees; must hand myself over like a fool to my enemies, and trust to the generosity of the conquered. And this when my standards wave at the mouths of the

Vistula and on the banks of the Oder; when my triumphant army is at the gates of Berlin and Breslau, and when I am here (at Dresden) at the head of 300,000 men. You wish me to sign such conditions as these without striking a blow? This pretension is an outrage; and it is my father-in-law who consents to this project! In what attitude does he wish to place me in presence of the French people? He makes a strange mistake if he imagines that a mutilated throne can be a refuge for his daughter and his grandson! Ah! Metternich, how much has England given you for playing this *rôle* against me?' At these words Prince Metternich changed colour; a profound silence ensued, the two walked rapidly up and down. The Emperor's hat had fallen on the floor; they passed and repassed it several times. Under any other circumstances Metternich would have handed it to the Emperor; his Majesty had to pick it up himself. Both were some time recovering their temper. Napoleon renewed the conversation, and in dismissing M. de Metternich took care to tell him that Illyria was not the only concession he would make."

To the EMPEROR OF AUSTRIA.

"DRESDEN, 30*th June*, 1813.

" Prince Metternich has handed me your Majesty's letter. I desire peace. If the Russians show themselves as moderate as I am it will be promptly concluded. If, on the contrary, they wish to force concessions from me which are repugnant to my honour and to the interests of my allies, they will not succeed. Your Majesty knows my feelings towards you. I hope that you will not allow yourself to be dragged into a war which will cause the ruin of your states and which will increase the misfortunes of the world. . . .

"NAPOLEON."

On the same day, in a letter to Admiral Decrès, the

Emperor talked of building twelve ships of the line in the Elbe, "to take part in the vast plan of war against England."

To MARSHAL SOULT.

"DRESDEN, 1*st July*, 1813.

"Start to-morrow before 10 P.M. You must travel incognito, assuming the name of one of your aides-de-camp. You will reach Paris on the 4th. . . . Thence you will continue your road in order to assume the command of my armies in Spain. To avoid all difficulties, I have appointed you my lieutenant-general commanding my armies in Spain and on the Pyrenees. . . . You must take measures to re-establish my affairs in Spain, and to preserve Pampeluna, St. Sebastian, and Pancoro. . . .

"NAPOLEON."

And on the 5th July the Emperor again wrote on the subject of Spain: "I expect news from the army with impatience. . . . I have forbidden the King of Spain to meddle with my affairs. I suppose that Marshal Soult will send Marshal Jourdan home. Unless the losses are more considerable than have been represented I hope that 100,000 men will be concentrated on the Bidassoa, and that Marshal Soult will deliver Pampeluna and drive the English back across the Ebro. . . ."

The news of the battle of Vittoria reached Napoleon and the allies at the same moment, the 30th June, and was hailed with very different feelings in the two camps. It induced Napoleon to listen to the Austrian proposals, and it decided Austria to cast her lot in with the allies. Negotiations were not at once broken off, but it soon became clear that the sword of Wellington had destroyed all chance of peace being concluded at Prague. Soult at once returned to Spain, but with all his ability he was unable to resist the torrent and carry out the orders of his master. Soult reached his post on the 13th July.

King Joseph having written an account of the battle of Vittoria to General Clarke, in which he said that, attacked by forces double as strong as his own, he had retreated upon Salvatierra, received in due time this answer: "It will be painful to the Emperor to know that the enemy did not owe their success to superiority in numbers, but rather to the manner in which the forces were handled. The organisation and strength of the Anglo-Portuguese army are too well known to the Emperor to allow him to have any doubt upon this subject. Your Majesty disposed of four armies, or 118,828 men. Lord Wellington had little more than half that number. I have in vain searched for an explanation of that phrase in your letter in which your Majesty says that you had to deal with double your numbers." Lord Londonderry says of Vittoria: "Since the commencement of the war the allies had never gained a victory so complete as this in every point of view. . . . They had been opposed to the united strength of the French armies and had totally overthrown them; for, with the exception of one body of 15,000 under Clausel which did not come up to the Ebro, and another of which Foy was in command, every disposable soldier belonging to the armies of the south, the north, and of Portugal had been brought into the field." The allies had to detach 7,000 men to observe Clausel, they were much inferior to the French in artillery, and the French occupied a very strong position. Both Napoleon and Joseph exaggerated. The number of men engaged on each side were nearly even.

To COMTE BIGOT.

"DRESDEN, 17*th July*, 1813.

"The Bishop of Nantes was the most enlightened priest of the Empire, the most distinguished doctor of the Sorbonne; he can be placed alongside of the most honoured bishops of the Gallican Church. No one was more penetrated with the true spirit of the Gospel; no one knew better how to respect the rights of sovereigns, and to distinguish the rights of the Church from the monstrous abuses and the foolish and insane maxims of the Court of Rome, maxims to-day so ridiculous, which have caused so much blood to flow, and so many schisms in days of ignorance. If all the theologians, if all the bishops, had practised the spirit of religion as well, and had showed as much intelligence and good faith as he did, Luther, Calvin, and Henry VIII. would not have formed sects, and the whole world would have been Catholic. I desire that at the expense of the imperial treasury a monument be erected in the cathedral of Nantes to this worthy prelate.

"NAPOLEON."

On the 19th July the Emperor informed Marshal Davoust, who was at Hamburg, that he had concluded a treaty with Denmark, who engaged to declare war against Russia, Prussia, and Sweden, as soon as hostilities were recommenced. France on her side was to declare war against Sweden. Denmark was to furnish a contingent of 10,000 infantry, 2,500 cavalry, and 40 guns; also to furnish 10,000 horses, all of which were to be paid for by France.

On the same day the Emperor wrote to Prince Eugene saying that he had just appointed Fouché governor of the Illyrian provinces, which, under the circumstances, was a decided insult addressed to Austria, which did not declare herself for the allies until the 27th. At that date she promised to join the coalition with 200,000 men on the condition of receiving subsidies from England, who had already offered her 10,000,000*l*.[1]

---

[1] Among other conditions it was stipulated that Austria should be restored to the position she occupied before the treaty of Presburg, and that the Pope should be reinstated in Rome. To this last condition, of course, neither Protestant England, Prussia, and Sweden, nor schismatic Russia, had any objections to offer.

To ADMIRAL DECRÈS.

"MAYENCE, *1st August*, 1813.

"If I were at Paris, I should go to Cherbourg to be present at the introduction of the sea. I wish the Empress to go there, and, if she goes, it will be proper for you to accompany her. . . . The marine might order something to do honour to the Empress and to amuse her. It appears to me that the preparations, announced beforehand, would attract a great many persons. . . .

"NAPOLEON."

On the 4th August the Emperor wrote this laconic note from Dresden to Marshal Ney—"Nothing is doing at the Congress of Prague. An English agent is meddling with it. They will arrive at no result, and the allies intend denouncing the armistice on the 10th." Similar notices were forwarded to Marshal Davoust and other commanders.

To ADMIRAL DECRÈS.

"DRESDEN, *5th August*, 1813.

"All the news which reaches me from England, and which I read in the English papers, proves that the English are constructing frigates of a calibre equal to those of America, and that very soon our frigates will be unable to show themselves anywhere. I beg that you will follow up this affair. "NAPOLEON."

To MARSHAL DAVOUST.

"DRESDEN, *8th August*, 1813.

". . . I have already informed you that Marshal Oudinot, together with General Vandamme, General Regnier, and the Duc de Padoue (Arrighi), with an army of 80,000 men, will debouch by Luckau and Bayreuth the day the rupture of the armistice takes place, so as to be within three or four days of Berlin. You perceive it to be necessary that all the forces under the orders of the Prince Royal (Bernadotte), to wit, the Swedish army, the 3rd

Prussian army corps commanded by Bülow, the auxiliary corps in the pay of England, and the Russian division, must not he allowed to march in their entirety against the corps which is to debouch by Luckau. . . .

"Austria is against us. That power has 300,000 men under arms, and will send 120,000 men against Dresden, 20,000 against Bavaria, and 50,000 men against the viceroy. . . . "NAPOLEON."

To GENERAL COMTE DROUOT.

"DRESDEN, 9*th August*, 1813.

"It is necessary for you to present me a project for according gratifications to the actors of my theatre, and to inform the Comte de Turenne that he must take measures to send the actors back to France on the 12th.
"NAPOLEON."

To PRINCE CAMBACÉRÈS.

"DRESDEN, 9*th August*, 1813.

"I have written a line to the Duc de Rovigo (Savary) on the present condition of affairs; see him. I hope to make Austria repent her foolish aspirations and her infamous treason. . . . "NAPOLEON."

To GENERAL SAVARY.

"DRESDEN, 9*th August*, 1813.

"It is probable that by the 12th the enemies will denounce the armistice, and that Austria will declare war against us. That Power indulged in a pleasant dream and thought that it would be able to recover all that it had lost during the last twenty years; it wished even to get back Venice. . . . "NAPOLEON."

Two days later, writing to General Clarke, the Emperor said—"Austria seems decided to declare war against us; she has engagements with England, and has entered into all the views of that Power."

To PRINCE EUGENE, AT UDINE.

"DRESDEN, 12*th August*, 1813.

"The enemies denounced the armistice yesterday; hostilities will recommence on the 17th. I have no news of Austria having declared war, but I suppose that I shall receive news to this effect during the day. . . .

"NAPOLEON."

And before the day was over instructions were forwarded to Marshals Ney and Marmont saying that Austria had declared war. Napoleon said that he intended to take up a position between Gœrlitz and Bautzen with 300,000 men, to see what the Austrians and Russians were after, and to take advantage of circumstances. He asked the marshals for their advice, adding, "I suppose that all this must finish by a great battle."

The Austrian proclamation in which war was declared was looked upon by most persons as a very able and unanswerable document, but such does not appear to have been the opinion of Napoleon.

To PRINCE CAMBACÉRÈS.

"DRESDEN, 12*th August*, 1813.

"The Minister of Foreign Affairs will have informed you that Austria has declared war. Her manifesto is insignificant enough. In plain French it simply comes to this, that she considers the opportunity a good one to recover her influence.

"The negotiations of Prague did not take place. The plenipotentiaries did not exchange powers or even see each other. The affairs of Spain have raised their hopes; English intrigue has done the rest. We shall fight on the 17th.

"I wish the Empress to make her journey to Cherbourg, and not to know anything of this until her return. Let her start on the 17th.

"Call a Cabinet Council to know if it will not be advisable to raise 25,000 conscripts in the departments of Languedoc and Guienne, and to send them to Bayonne to reinforce the armies of Spain. . . .

"NAPOLEON."

Writing to Davoust the next day the Emperor said—"I expect the King of Naples to-morrow, he is coming to assume a command in the army."

To the KING OF WIRTEMBERG.

"DRESDEN, 13*th August*, 1813.

"I have received your Majesty's letter. The Congress of Prague never seriously existed. It was a means chosen by Austria to declare herself. The plenipotentiaries of the various Powers never saw each other; those of Russia and Prussia remained at home and refused to see the French plenipotentiaries; no notes were exchanged, nor was any agreement arrived at with regard to the nature of the mediation. At last on the 12th the mediator declared war against us. His manifesto, although moderate, is ridiculous. . . . It appears that Austria has had serious engagements with the allies ever since February, but she was not strong enough to declare herself. . . . In her manifesto she employs the term 'Empire of Germany.' She was sounded to know if abandoning Poland and ceding Illyria would satisfy her, but she requires Venice, the Inn, Magdeburg, and the dissolution of the Confederation of the Rhine. . .'

"In fact the Emperor of Austria wished for war. He wrote to me, four days before, the most amicable letters; this piece of dissimulation was very useless, for I knew what the Austrians were about ever since Minsk, where Prince Schwartzenberg received orders to act in a sense opposed to the instructions which I gave him. . . .

"NAPOLEON.

"P.S. Your Majesty will do well to arm as much as possible."

To PRINCE CAMBACÉRÈS.

"DRESDEN, 15*th August*, 1813.

"The declaration of war on the part of Austria forebodes some big battles which will necessarily cost a large number of men. The unfortunate and unexpected turn which affairs have taken in Spain requires that the safety of the frontier should be guaranteed. . . . Draw out a plan for raising 60,000 men in the good departments so as to feed the war in the north. . . . Draw attention to the injustice of the pretensions of the enemy in the preamble. . . . As the affairs of Spain render a levy in Languedoc and Guienne urgent, let the Regent (Marie Louise) not lose a moment.

"General Moreau has arrived at Berlin. He left America before hearing the news of the battle of Lutzen, and when those gentlemen thought that they were going to enter France.

"NAPOLEON."

And the next day the Emperor informed the archchancellor that—

"A portion of the Russian and Prussian army has entered Bohemia, which promises well for the campaign.

"Moreau has arrived at the Russian army.

"Jomini, chief of the staff to Marshal Ney, has deserted. He it is who has published some volumes on the campaigns, and for whom the Russians have long been bidding. He yielded to corruption. He is a soldier of little value; he is a writer, however, who has acquired some wholesome ideas on the subject of war. He is Swiss.

"NAPOLEON."

To M. MARET.

"BAUTZEN, 17*th August*, 1813.

"I have long thought that Caulaincourt and de Narbonne allow themselves to be taken in by the honeyed style of

Metternich. The stipulations between the Austrians and the Russians were agreed upon last February, and I am persuaded that the conditions which they wished to impose upon me were then signed. . . .

" NAPOLEON."

In a reply to the Austrian manifesto, dictated by the Emperor, and naturally throwing all the blame of the fresh rupture on the Court of Vienna, Napoleon made use of such language as this—" Austria having declared herself in a state of war, the position is simplified. Europe in this way is nearer peace ; there is one complication the less."

In the midst of graver occupations the Emperor found time to send the following rating to the Comte de Montesquieu, his Grand Chamberlain :—

" LOWENBERG, 23rd August, 1813."

" I was much displeased to learn that matters were so badly managed on the 15th August (the *fête*-day of his Majesty) that the Empress was detained for a considerable time listening to bad music, and that consequently the public were kept two hours waiting for the fireworks. . . . It would have been very simple, at the hour appointed for the fireworks, to have informed the Empress, who would at once have quitted the theatre. There would have been no inconvenience in making the Empress leave the theatre, where she was stifled with heat, a little sooner, whereas there was a great inconvenience in causing a whole population, accustomed to retire at 9 P.M., to wait.

" NAPOLEON."

On the 23rd the Emperor in a letter to Marshal Gouiron St. Cyr said—" If the enemy have effected a grand movement on Dresden, I shall consider it a most fortunate thing, for it will enable me to fight a battle in the course of a few days which will decide many matters."

The French had been forced to fall back upon Dresden, which Napoleon had taken the precaution of having strongly fortified, and where he was about to take his stand at the head of 130,000 men.

On the 25th August, 3 P.M., the Emperor wrote a series of instructions to Vandamme, of much importance to remark, seeing what happened afterwards. The Emperor was at Stolpen, and Vandamme at the camp at Kœnigstein, from whence he was to move upon the Russians and get possession of the important position of Tœplitz, which would enable the Emperor to deal the allies a fatal blow, and to cut off their right wing. Among other orders sent to Vandamme, his Majesty wrote—"It will be necessary for you to drive away all the enemy's vedettes so that they may not see what you are about. To-morrow, at daybreak, as soon as the fog has cleared away, your advanced guard of 12,000 men must seize upon the plateau of Pirna. . . . I shall have the heights of Pirna occupied by the Young Guard. . . . The camp of Pirna will therefore be occupied, the right by 40,000 infantry of the Guard, and 8,000 or 10,000 cavalry, the left by your army corps. If you find that you can fall on the rear of the enemy, do so, and I will support you with the Young Guard. . . ."

To GENERAL COMTE VANDAMME.

"STOLPEN, 26*th August*, 1813. 1 A.M.

"I informed you of my intentions yesterday. The whole army of the enemy presented itself before Dresden yesterday, and Marshal St. Cyr feared that he would be attacked to-day; I am going there. . . . In order to create a diversion you should debouch as soon as possible, and I hope that in the course of the day you will fall upon the enemy's rear and annihilate the division told off to observe you.

"NAPOLEON."

To MARSHAL KELLERMANN, AT MAYENCE.

"DRESDEN, 27*th August*, 1813. 6 A.M.

"Inform the Empress by telegraph that I have gained a great victory over the Austrian, Russian, and Prussian armies, commanded by the Emperors of Austria and Russia, and the King of Prussia. A great many prisoners, standards, and guns were taken. "NAPOLEON.".

Writing to Berthier in the evening, the Emperor said—"The enemy are not retreating, and regard the affair of yesterday merely as an attack which has failed; it is doubtful whether they will retreat to-night. If they stand firm, I shall turn their left to-morrow. The King of Naples is charged with this operation."

Napoleon had a narrow escape, for the allies might have attacked and captured Dresden before his arrival. Fortunately for him, Prince Schwartzenberg determined to wait for Klenau's corps, and lost his opportunity of dealing the Emperor a severe if not a fatal blow. As it was, Napoleon had time to get back to Dresden and to repulse the attack of the allies, who suffered heavily in men and in *prestige*. Moreau, who was struck down while speaking with the Emperor Alexander, and who died a few days afterwards, wrote thus to his wife—

"MY DEAREST,—At the battle of Dresden I had both my legs carried off by a cannon ball. That rascal Bonaparte is always lucky. Amputation has been performed as well as possible. Although the army has made a retrograde movement, it was by no means a reverse, but a plan to draw nearer to Blucher. Excuse my scrawl. I love and embrace you with my whole heart."

To PRINCE CAMBACÉRÈS.

"DRESDEN, 27*th August*, 1813. *Evening.*

"I am so fatigued and so busy that I cannot write to you at length. The Duc de Bassano (Maret) will do this. Affairs are going on well. "NAPOLEON."

On the 29th, orders were given to Murat, Marmont, and St. Cyr to pursue the enemy. Napoleon wrote to Murat saying that Vandamme had attacked the Prince of Wirtemberg near Hollendorf, and had captured four guns and 1,900 prisoners, all Russians.

On the 20th August, Napoleon dictated some notes on the general situation of affairs, and the advantages and disadvantages of various plans which suggested themselves to his fertile imagination. After discussing the idea of going to Prague, he added—

"In marching upon Berlin, on the contrary, I shall at once obtain a great result; I shall protect my line from Hamburg to Dresden; I shall be in the centre; in five days I shall be able to be at the extreme points of my line; I shall disengage Stettin and Custrin; I shall be able to separate the Austrians and the Russians; during the season I shall be able to live at Berlin; potatoes, the great resources of that city, the canals, &c., will feed me, and I shall be able to confine the war to where it is at present. The war with Austria will have no other inconvenience for me beyond the sacrifice of 120,000 men standing on the defensive between Hof and Dresden. . . . The Russians and Prussians in Bohemia will force Austria to resume the offensive. But then I shall have taken Berlin, revictualled Stettin, destroyed the Prussian works, and disorganised the landwehr. Then, if Austria recommences her follies, I shall go to Dresden with my army, and a great battle will terminate the campaign and the war. Lastly, in my position, any plan where I am not myself in the centre is not admissible. Any plan which removes me to a distance establishes a regular war in which the superiority of the enemy in cavalry, in numbers, and even in generals, would completely ruin me."

The opposing forces at the moment the Emperor indulged in such pleasant dreams of success may be set down thus—The Grand Army of Bohemia, which threatened Napoleon's rear, consisted of 220,000 men, of which 40,000 were cavalry and 700 guns. The allies had also 90,000 men in Silesia, and 80,000 in the north. There were 25,000 Austrians observing 26,000 Bavarians under Wrede, and 50,000 more Austrians operating against Prince Eugene in Italy. Wellington with 100,000 men was opposed by Soult with an equal force; the allies in Catalonia, and the French under Marshal Suchet, were 45,000 each. In point of numbers actually in the field the French and the allies were evenly matched, but both Russia and Austria were raising strong reserves, whereas France was exhausted. The French in Germany had the advantage of being commanded by Napoleon. The allies, on the other hand, had all the enthusiasm on their side — an enthusiasm heightened by a desire for revenge, and the knowledge that the impending struggle was one of life or death.

To the KING OF WIRTEMBERG.

"DRESDEN, 30*th August*, 1813."

"... The allied army, commanded by the Emperor Alexander, has been entirely defeated. I captured 30,000 men, 40 or 50 guns, 30 standards, &c. The enemy abandoned more than 12,000 wounded men in the villages. The Prince of Wirtemberg, who commanded a Russian corps, has been beaten by General Vandamme who is marching upon Tœplitz. ... It is difficult to imagine the deplorable condition of the Austrian army; it has been in the field only a few days, and already half the soldiers are almost naked and without shoes. ... You will have seen by the proclamation of Prince Schwartzenberg the pretentions of Austria. ... I am so much attached to the Emperor Francis that I pity him for allowing himself to be led astray by such chimeras. I am highly satisfied with Dresden and all the Saxon villages. ...

"NAPOLEON."

To the King of Naples.

"Dresden, 1st *September*, 1813.

"Marshal Macdonald is to-day at Gœrlitz. Should he continue his retrograde movement, it will be necessary for me to march to his assistance. . . . The misfortune which has happened to the first corps is one which could not have been expected. General Vandamme, who appears to have killed himself, did not place a single sentry on the mountains, nor a reserve anywhere. . . . However, many men belonging to his corps are coming in; nearly all the generals have arrived, and 15,000 men already, so that I think my loss will not exceed from 4,000 to 5,000 men.

"Napoleon."

The misfortune which overtook Vandamme's corps had an immense material and moral effect on the campaign. The allies had been sent reeling back from Dresden; they feared that their retreat would be cut off, and it seemed as if the imperial eagles would once more be seen at Berlin. We have seen the orders sent to Vandamme on the 25th August. On the strength of these he advanced towards Pirna with 27,000 foot, 3,000 horse, and 80 guns, and fell upon Osterman's corps, 17,000 strong, which managed to cut its way to Peterswalde. On the morning of the 29th, Vandamme, counting upon the support of the Young Guard, which was at Pirna, descended from the mountains and attacked the Russians in the plain between Kulm and Tœplitz. Having already inflicted considerable loss on the foe, being two against one, and having to deal with a beaten and dejected enemy, Vandamme attacked with detachments as they came up, and this over confidence proved fatal to him. The Russian Guard offered the most heroic resistance, and this gave time for reinforcements to come up and turn the tide of battle. It is probable that Vandamme would have fallen back at this juncture, had he not still expected the co-operation of the

Young Guard, which was lying close to the scene of action. He now found himself assailed by 60,000 men under Barclay de Tolly, and, when he thought of escaping from his difficulties, he found General Kleist on his only line of retreat with 18,000 men. The consequences were inevitable; Vandamme's corps went to pieces, and he himself was taken prisoner. It is calculated that in the two days' fighting the French lost 18,000 men, 60 guns, and 2 eagles.

Napoleon tried to shuffle out of the responsibility of this disaster, and to throw the whole blame on the shoulders of Vandamme. The fact is that both Vandamme and Napoleon committed the same error: they both underrated the enemy. The Emperor accused his lieutenant (thinking him dead) of having disobeyed orders. He wrote a letter to Marshal St. Cyr—letter omitted from *The Correspondence*—in which he said—" I gave Vandamme positive orders to intrench himself on the heights and encamp his corps there, and to send nothing but detachments down into Bohemia to harass the enemy."

We have seen what the orders of the Emperor were. His admirers have endeavoured to excuse him on the ground that he was taken suddenly ill on the 28th, and in fact he appears to have written no letters or despatches on that day. It was thus that a disaster happened which changed the whole face of affairs.

To MARSHAL BERTHIER.

"DRESDEN, *2nd September*, 1813.

"Write thus to Marshal Ney—'We have just received news from Marshal Oudinot who deemed fit to venture within two marches of Wittenberg. The result of this rash movement is that the corps of General Tauenstein and a strong body of Cossacks are interfering with the communications of Marshal Macdonald. It would be difficult for any one to have less brains than Marshal Oudinot. . . . You must march so as to be at Bayreuth on the 6th. From Bayreuth you will be only three days' march from Berlin. Communications with the Emperor will then be re-established, and Berlin can be attacked on the 9th or 10th. All these clouds of Cossacks and this rabble of bad landwehr infantry will retreat from all sides on Berlin as soon as they learn that you are marching.'"

Ney had succeeded Oudinot in the command of the army of the north, the latter marshal having just lost the battle of Gross-Beeren, which cost the French about 8,000 men and 26 guns, and, in the idea of the Prussians, saved Berlin. Ney did no better than Oudinot.

On the 3rd September, the Emperor, writing to Berthier, said—" The army of Marshal Macdonald is rather put out of countenance. I shall be there at break of day, and shall attack the enemy and put them to flight."

To M. MARET, AT DRESDEN.

"BAUTZEN, 6th *September*, 1812. 2 A.M.

"I have pursued the enemy beyond the Neisse. We enter Gœrlitz at 6 o'clock. As soon as the enemy learned that I was with the army, they took to their heels and fled in all directions. There was no means of catching them. . . . "NAPOLEON."

And his Majesty returned to Dresden swearing that he would not go out to fight again.

On the 10th September the Emperor, in a letter to Berthier, made this passing allusion to the defeat of Ney at Dennweitz—"Marshal Ney and his three corps sustained a check on the 6th while concentrating at Torgau. Marshal Macdonald has taken up his position in front of Bautzen; Prince Poniatowski protects his right. This retreat was not necessary, but it was ordered so as to concentrate our forces." In fact Ney, like Oudinot, was surprised on the line of march, and lost 13,000 men and 43 guns; and still more did this victory encourage the allies in the belief that the charm of French invincibility was broken.

In some instructions given to Captain Caraman on the 14th September, the Emperor said:—

"General Lauriston has been attacked and has suffered some loss; Prince Poniatowski was attacked near Stolpen without loss. Marshal Macdonald did not foresee these attacks, and allowed himself to be ill-treated.... Caraman must remain on the spot all day to see what happens, and how the affair with Lauriston finishes. He must not conceal, with all due reserve, that I consider the marshal badly placed, and that I do not understand his manner of operating...."

And on the same day his Majesty wrote to General Bertrand at Torgau, saying:—

"I see with pleasure by your letter of the 12th that your corps behaved well; but I regret to learn the issue of the battle, which appears to me to have been badly engaged. I shall myself shortly take the command of the fourth corps to try and procure you your revenge."

To M. MARET.

"PETERSWALDE, 17*th September*, 1813.

"I slept here last night. Yesterday I drove the enemy back on Kulm. The cavalry made some splendid charges. We captured the son of Blucher, who is a colonel or a major-general.... I am going to Pirna in the course of the day.

"NAPOLEON."

And from Pirna his Majesty wrote to the King of Naples, on the 19th, a letter in which he said:—

"I descended yesterday into the plains of Bohemia, and obliged the enemy to unmask their forces. They drew up their whole army in battle array, expecting to be attacked. I then drew back my columns.... The weather is fearful. Marshal Berthier is suffering from an attack of gout or of fever."

To MARSHAL BERTHIER.

"PIRNA, 19*th September*, 1813.

"General Bruno was captured, not by 4,000, but by 400 men, while he was quietly sleeping in the town, with his whole force. As long as the light troops perform their duties so badly accidents will happen. Instead of bivouacking in a military position, and changing his camp every day, General Bruno shut himself up in a town. Tell Marshal Victor that I am greatly displeased that he did not give General Bruno proper instructions. I have just dictated an order of the day, informing the army of the fate which has befallen General Bruno. . . .

"NAPOLEON."

Poor Bruno, with 150 Westphalian horse, had been snapped up by the Austrians.

In some notes for the Minister of War, drawn up on the 27th September, at Dresden, General Clarke was directed to say in a report that 200,000 men were asked for so as to impose upon Europe, but that in reality the conscription of 1813 would not be drawn until the next year (1814). He was to say that the Emperor had given Austria no cause to complain; that she did not wish to negotiate at Prague, and that she had long determined upon making war; that England had rejected every proposition of peace; that Russia had shown herself an implacable enemy, and had employed her influence to hinder all negotiation; that after having burned Moscow to the ground, she desired to avenge the evils she had brought down on herself by applying the torch to the towns of the French Empire, and perhaps even to Paris. The present state of affairs was to be attributed to the hatred and jealousy of the other Powers, and to the passions and artifices fomented by England.

On the 2nd October, in a letter written to Marshal Victor from Dresden, Napoleon said:—

"I shall look upon the certainty of the enemy blocking themselves up, with an army of 80,000 men in Leipsic, as a good piece of news; the war would soon be over; but I think that they are too well acquainted with my manner of acting to expose themselves to such an adventurous move. . . ."

Napoleon now vigorously contradicted rumours which were evidently gaining ground concerning the defection of Bavaria. He wrote as follows to Savary, his minister of police in Paris:—

"What does a fall on the Bourse matter to you? Those who have sold stock at sixty, will buy it back at eighty. The less you meddle with such matters the better. . . . If the *rente* were to go down six francs, what would that matter, provided the interest be paid? The only way to aggravate the evil is to give it importance. As I make no loans, and do not require to make any, the stock exchange details in no way affect the administration."

On the 6th October, in a series of instructions given to Comte Daru, the Emperor said that he was about to fight a battle; that Dresden would be held by 30,000 man, but that if he lost the battle the city was to be evacuated, the guns were to be spiked, &c., &c. Napoleon added, however, such reassuring paragraphs as the following:—

"His Majesty will win the battle, and Dresden will continue to be the centre of his operations." And—"As his Majesty thinks that he has eighty chances out of 100 on his side, you must act as if he would succeed."

In spite of the military disadvantages of holding Dresden, Napoleon was very loth to relinquish that capital, being well aware of the bad effect which such a step would have on the members of the Confederation; he had the wolf by the ears.

To the KING OF NAPLES.

"DRESDEN, *7th October*, 1813.

"I wrote to you this morning at one o'clock. I am starting for Meissen. The whole Silesian army has debouched by Wartenburg; there is no force from Dresden to Gorlitz, nor from Dresden to Berlin. Marshal St. Cyr will remain at Dresden. Keep the Austrians in check as well as you can, so that I may beat Blucher and the Swedes before they join Schwartzenberg's corps.

"The King of Saxony, the Queen, and the Princess Augusta are coming to Meissen; they will not remain at Dresden during my absence.

"NAPOLEON."

To PRINCE CAMBACÉRÈS.

"WURZEN, 9*th September*, 1813.

"I have received all your letters, with the exception of that of the 29th, which was intercepted. Marshal St. Cyr is at Dresden, and the King of Naples on the Upper Mulde. I am manœuvring with the remainder of my army to force the enemy to raise the siege of Wittenberg. It is possible that this will give rise to a battle, the success of which I consider certain, and which will exercise a great influence on affairs. The weather is very bad. Berthier is getting better. My health is perfect.

"NAPOLEON."

And to the King of Naples the Emperor wrote saying that he expected to attack Blucher at Duben, where he was assured that the army of Silesia had taken up its position, and also that General Alix had entered Cassel at the head of 6,000 French. His Majesty added—"King Jerome has returned to his capital. Czernitchef made all this noise with 2,500 Cossacks. Do not believe in the reported defection of Bavaria, nor in all the rumours circulated by the enemy."

Napoleon and Blucher crossed each other, and the two armies were thus lying across each other's communications. Blucher and Bernadotte got between Napoleon and the Rhine, while Napoleon got between them and the Elbe.

In the march to Duben Napoleon very nearly cut off Sacken's corps, which had to beat a hasty retreat.

On the 10th October the Emperor wrote no less than nine despatches to Berthier, five to M. Maret, two to Murat, and one each to Marmont, Reynier, Bertrand, and Arrighi, despatches which show great uncertainty as to both his own movements and those of the enemy. To M. Maret he wrote—" In the event of it being impossible to hold Dresden, Marshal St. Cyr can retreat upon Torgau. . . . If there be a battle, and I beat the enemy, the Austrians will recross their frontiers, and I shall approach Torgau to put myself in communication with the King of Naples, and to pay a visit to Berlin with him. . . . I intend falling on the enemy's line of operations should there be no battle. . . . I am very anxious to receive information from Leipsic respecting the movements of the enemy, and to know if they are advancing or retiring. . . It is my intention, if the King of Naples is obliged to evacuate Leipsic, to repass the Elbe with my whole army, driving the armies of Silesia and Berlin to the right bank, and taking my time to destroy them."

To General Arrighi (Duc de Padoue), commanding the 3rd cavalry corps, the Emperor wrote—" Tell the King of Naples that Leipsic must only be abandoned in order to avoid being obliged to fight with inferior forces. . . . At the last moment you must tell the magistrates of Leipsic to behave well; that all that they see is the result of manœuvres to force the enemy to fight a battle which they have always avoided, and that this will finish with a peal of thunder for the enemy."

Napoleon was highly elated at this moment by a success obtained by Ney at Dessau, which threw open to him the road to Berlin. Murat, too, had the best of an encounter with Wittgenstein, and the Austrians, with the Emperor, had been forced to fall back upon Frohburg. However, with all this, the allies were now advancing in such masses from various quarters that the French were forced back upon Leipsic. A variety of minor engagements preceded the great battle where, as Berenger sang,

> "Leipsic hath seen our eagles fall
> Drunk with renown, worn out with glory."

In one severe cavalry affair, in which the Prussian cuirassiers overthrew the French horse, the King of Naples had a narrow escape, and had to save himself by flight.

Napoleon was more than ever anxious to play a bold game, and to carry the war into Prussian territory, but his marshals unanimously opposed this plan, fearing that, with their 250,000 men, they would be cut off from France by 400,000 allied troops. Notwithstanding the murmurs of the army and the remonstrances of the staff, it was with the greatest difficulty that Napoleon was induced to relinquish his idea of visiting Berlin. In the end, however, the defection of Bavaria, and the probable defection of Wirtemberg, Baden, and Darmstadt decided him to fall back on the Rhine, and to recall Reynier and Bertrand, who were preparing to march upon the Prussian capital.

On the 13th October, 5 A.M., the Emperor wrote to Ney saying—"I have ordered my Guard to fall back upon Duben, so that I may march upon Leipsic to-morrow. I have ordered Marmont there, and with the King of Naples that will make 90,000 men. . . . There will undoubtedly be a great battle at Leipsic." Similar orders were sent to Macdonald, Reynier, Bertrand, and Sebastiani, and orders were given that the ranks should be only two instead of three deep. It was found that a great number of men were in hospital from wounds in the hand, which the Emperor supposed to have been self-inflicted. Dr. Larrey, however, the surgeon-in-chief, reported that the men in the front ranks were frequently wounded, when in the act of loading, by their comrades behind them. Napoleon accepted this explanation, and ordered the third rank to be done away with. The Emperor was in hopes, too, that this change of formation would deceive the enemy as to his numbers.

On the 15th October the Emperor, in a bulletin to the army, said—" After having seized upon all the enemy's bridges, the Emperor intended to pass the Elbe, to manœuvre on the right bank of that river from Hamburg to Dresden, to threaten Potsdam and Berlin, and to take Magdeburg for the pivot of his operations. But on the 13th the Emperor learned that the Bavarian army had joined the Austrians and threatened the Rhine. This inconceivable defection caused the defection of other princes to be foreseen, and determined the Emperor to fall back upon the Rhine." In fact, the Emperor found himself, as he said, with two more armies against him— that of Bavaria, and the Austrian force which had been engaged in observing it.

On the evening of the 16th came another bulletin, in which Napoleon said that Prince Schwartzenberg, the commander-in-chief of the allied army, had announced a decisive battle for the 16th, and which gave a description of the first day's fighting at Leipsic, with the result of which he appeared satisfied. He created Poniatowski a marshal. During the day the Emperor had sent news to the King of Saxony that he had beaten the enemy, and told him to have the bells of the city rung in honour of his victory. In fact, the look-out was so gloomy that Napoleon ought at once to have prepared to retreat. If the allies had made little impression on the positions where he commanded in person, the corps of Ney had suffered a severe repulse, and Bernadotte, Beningsen, and Colloredo were expected to join the enemy the next day with 100,000 men.

Late in the day General Meerfelt fell into the hands of the French, and as soon as the firing had ceased Napoleon sent for this officer in the hope of being able, through him, to open up separate and confidential negotiations with the Emperor of Austria. It was Meerfelt who had been sent to solicit the armistice of Leoben, who had conducted the negotiations which ended in the treaty of Campo Formio. It was Meerfelt who, after Austerlitz, had negotiated the peace of Presburg. And now, a prisoner, it was the French Emperor who was soliciting his good offices.

Napoleon, who sent Meerfelt back to his camp with a message for his master, was under the impression that the Emperor of Austria might be persuaded to come to terms with his son-in-law; but the war had escaped from the hands of monarchs.

On the 20th Napoleon, before making his escape from the city of Leipsic—an escape accomplished with great difficulty—wrote at 7 A.M. to General Bertrand, who was at Weissenfels, a series of orders, adding—" Write to Erfurth to communicate with Marshal Kellermann, who must make known by telegraph, that after a number of engagements, in which we sustained the glory of our arms, I am marching in the direction of the Saal; that the Emperor's health is good." This was his Majesty's description of Leipsic. In the afternoon he himself reached Weissenfels, whither he was followed by the remnant of his army.

On the 24th the Emperor, having reached Erfurth, drew up a bulletin, in which he attributed his retreat to want of ammunition, which obliged him to fall back on his magazines at Erfurth or Magdeburg to replenish. He chose the former place, so as to be the better able " to appreciate the influence of the defection of Bavaria." He then added—" This circumstance obliged the French army to renounce the fruit of two victories in which, with so much glory, it had beaten a vastly superior force—all the armies of the continent." The Emperor spoke in bitter terms of the treason of the Saxons, and made the most of the blowing up of the bridge over the Elster, which had so disastrous an effect after the battle. " The losses," he said, " occasioned by this unfortunate event amounted to about 12,000 men. The disorder into which it threw the army changed the face of affairs; the victorious French army reached Erfurth as if it had been beaten. . . . The French army, after such brilliant successes, has lost its victorious attitude. We found everything that we required at Erfurth."

From Erfurth the French, hotly pressed by Blucher, fell back to Gotha, whence the Emperor wrote thus to his sister, Pauline Borghese :—

"I have received your letter of the 13th. My expenses have been considerable this year, and will be so for next year. I accept the gift which you wish to make; but the goodwill and the resources of my subjects are such that I think I shall have means to meet the enormous expenditure which will be caused by the campaign of 1814 and 1815. If the European coalition against France lasts beyond that date, and that I have not obtained the amount of success which I have a right to expect from the bravery and the patriotism of the French, then I shall make use of your gift, and of all the gifts which my subjects may feel inclined to offer.

"NAPOLEON."

Now the Emperor, on his return to Paris, at once held a Council of State, and exposed the true position in which he stood. He said that France would have to make vast sacrifices. He himself took 1,200,000*l.* from his vaults in the Tuileries to be applied to the public service, and taxation was greatly increased.

To Cambacérès the Emperor wrote upon the same day, saying :—

"I have nothing to add to my bulletins, which you can communicate to the Empress. I am going to Mayence, and I shall concentrate my army on the frontier. The inconceivable and unexpected treason of Bavaria disarranged all my plans."

His Majesty then dwelt on his want of men and money. He was bent on raising another 100,000 men over twenty-two years of age.

"When all Europe is in arms," he wrote; "when everywhere married and unmarried men are being enlisted;

when every one is rushing to arms against us, France will be lost unless she does the same."

To PRINCE CAMBACÉRÈS.
"FRANKFORT, 31*st October*, 1813."

"I have arrived here. The Bavarians and Austrians, 60,000 strong, posted at Hanau, tried to cut me off from France. I gave them a good drubbing, and captured their guns, standards, and 6,000 prisoners. . . . My health was never better. I am going to Mayence.
"NAPOLEON."

Marshal Wrede, who commanded in this battle, was able to bring only 45,000 men into action, with which he endeavoured to stop the French army in its retreat. That army had been reduced to 80,000 men, many of them stragglers; but still Napoleon had with him his Guard, which had not suffered much during the campaign, and Bertrand's corps, which had not been engaged at Leipsic. The losses were heavy on both sides, and the French, although victorious, were unable to carry off their wounded, 3,000 of whom remained in the woods of Hanau.

To MARIE LOUISE, EMPRESS, QUEEN, AND REGENT.
"FRANKFORT, 1*st November*, 1813."

"MADAME AND VERY DEAR WIFE,—I send you twenty standards captured at Leipsic and Hanau; it is a homage which I have much pleasure in rendering to you. I desire that you will see in it a mark of my great satisfaction with your conduct during the regency which I confided to you.
"NAPOLEON."

To PRINCE CAMBACÉRÈS.
"MAYENCE, 6*th November*, 1813."

"I have received your letter of the 3rd. My presence here is still necessary for the reorganisation of the army. As soon as affairs will permit me to leave I shall return to Paris. "NAPOLEON."

The same day Napoleon gave orders to General Clarke for reconstructing the fortifications of Geneva, which had been blown up by his orders; also a letter, in which his Majesty talked of withdrawing 16,000 cavalry from Spain, as he had no longer any intention of carrying on offensive operations in that country.

The Emperor was back at St. Cloud on the 10th November. On the 12th he wrote to Prince Eugene, saying that he was sorry to learn that he was on the Adige, and asking what resources it would be possible to draw from Italy. He said that he himself was engaged in raising 600,000 men.

To the Senate his Majesty made this brief speech at the Tuileries on the 14th November :—

"Senators, I accept the sentiments which you express.

"All Europe was marching with us a year ago; to-day all Europe is marching against us. The fact is that the opinion of the world is formed by France or by England. We shall therefore have everything to fear without the energy and the power of the nation.

"Posterity will say that if great and critical circumstances arose they were not too much for France and for me."

To GENERAL CLARKE.

"ST. CLOUD, 14*th November*, 1813.

"I am not aware if Belfort is in a state of defence. If so, have it armed, as well as all the castles along the Swiss frontier. Not that I have any reason to distrust the Swiss, but because in the present state of the Empire it is necessary to arm on all sides.   "NAPOLEON."

To GENERAL CAULAINCOURT.

"ST. CLOUD, 15*th November*, 1813.

"Give orders that if ever the English arrive at the castle of Marracq (near Bayonne) it be set fire to; also to all the houses which belong to me, so that they may not sleep in my bed. . . .   "NAPOLEON."

To M. FOUCHÉ, at Bologna.

"St. Cloud, 15*th November*, 1813.

"I beg that you will hasten to Naples to make the king feel the necessity of marching on the Po with 25,000 men; you must also inform the Queen of this, and you must do all you can to let the country be beguiled by the fallacious promises of Austria and the horrid language of Metternich. . . .

"NAPOLEON."

Napoleon had considerable doubts with regard to the fidelity of his brother-in-law—doubts not a little increased when Murat left him after Leipsic on the ground that his presence was absolutely necessary at Naples.

To COMTE DE SUSSY.

"St. Cloud, 20*th November*, 1813.

"The movement of the English upon Bayonne has opened up a portion of the frontier. I learn that they have already landed a certain quantity of their merchandise near St. Jean-de-Luz. I suppose that you have removed your custom-house line. This matter deserves your attention.[1]

"NAPOLEON."

The continental blockade was strong in death.

The King of Bavaria having endeavoured to induce his son-in-law to desert the cause of Napoleon, as he himself had deserted it, Prince Eugene informed the Emperor of the overtures which had been made and indignantly rejected. Napoleon wrote back—"I recognise in this the policy of Austria; it is thus that she makes so many traitors."

[1] The harbour of St. Jean de Luz was no sooner in the hands of the British than it was crowded with ships of all nations, for it was declared a free port, even for French vessels.

Before long Napoleon doubted the fidelity of even Eugene.

At this period M. de St. Aignan, the French Minister at Gotha fell into the hands of the Prussians, and was taken to Frankfort, which place Prince Schwartzenberg, followed by the allied sovereigns, reached on the 4th November. He was present on the 9th November at a conference between Count Nesselrode, Prince Metternich, and Lord Aberdeen, in which the Austrian minister exposed the conditions of peace which the allies would accept.

On the 1st December Napoleon dictated the following reply, which was to be sent to Prince Metternich by Caulaincourt, who had just succeeded M. Maret as Minister of Foreign Affairs.

"It appears from the verbal communication of M. de St. Aignan, that the general bases of the allies are a peace founded—first, on the equilibrium of Europe; second, on the recognition of all the nations within their natural limits; third, on the recognition of the independence of all the nations without any one being able to arrogate to itself any right of supremacy or suzerainty, under no matter what form, on land or on sea.

"It is therefore with lively satisfaction that I am directed and authorised by the Emperor, my master, to declare to your excellency that his Majesty adheres to the bases which M. de St. Aignan has communicated. They will entail great sacrifices on the part of France; his Majesty will make them without regret, provided similar sacrifices be made by England, so as to conclude a general peace on land and sea, which your excellency assures me is the desire not only of the continental powers but of England."

The allies had not only made proposals of peace, which would have left France with the Rhine, the Alps, and the Pyrenees for her frontiers, but the Emperor of Austria had written a private letter to Marie Louise, in the hope that she might induce Napoleon to listen to reason. England was prepared on her side to make great sacrifices, and to do nothing hostile to the dynasty of Napoleon. The French Emperor resorted to delay, in order to gain time. With marvellous activity he prepared for the defence of his empire.

On the 3rd December, in a letter to Prince Eugene, the Emperor said—" The King of Naples writes to me that he will soon be at Bologna with 80,000 men. . . . It is a great consolation to me to have nothing to fear for Italy."

To General Clarke on the 4th :—" Everything announces that the war is about to become serious on the side of Holland."

On the 27th November the Prince of Orange, coming from England, had disembarked from the *Warrior*, and had been hailed with even greater enthusiasm than that which not long before had greeted Napoleon and Marie Louise. In a very short time the tricoloured flag waved only over some of the forts on the southern frontier.

On the 15th December, the Emperor, having learned that the Nassau regiment and the Frankfort battalion employed with the army of Spain had deserted, gave strict orders for all the troops of the Confederation to be disarmed.[1]

On the 16th, his Majesty, in a letter to General Lebrun, Duc de Plaisance, governor of Antwerp, said :—" General Lefebvre Desnoëttes will leave here to night by post to put himself at the head of his division. Two other divisions of the guard will concentrate at Brussels. Marshal Mortier, with the old general, is marching on Namur. . . . Show coolness and energy."

Admiral Allemand, the most energetic and brutal of French admirals, was to take up his head quarters at Flushing, and to co-operate with the land forces.

---

[1] The Nassau and Frankfort regiments came over to the allies just after the repulse of the desperate attack made by Soult on Wellington when he had forced the passage of the Nive. They were received with great joy, drums beating, and arms presented, and were at once despatched to join the allied army in Germany.

On the 17th, in a long letter to Comte de Montalivet, the Emperor expressed his astonishment that there should be 21,200 persons out of work in Paris, while difficulty was experienced in getting work done for the army. However, he would double or triple his orders sooner than allow men to remain without employment. There was no difficulty in finding work for tailors and shoemakers, &c., &c., but his Majesty had to ask for a report to see what could be done for the silversmiths, clockmakers, jewellers, and such like.

On the 19th, at the opening of Parliament, the Emperor pronounced a discourse, in which he said that—"Brilliant victories illustrated the French arms during this campaign; defections without example rendered those victories useless. Everything turned against us. France even would be in danger but for the energy and union of Frenchmen.

"Under these great circumstances my first thought was to call you to my side. My heart required the presence and affection of my subjects.

"I have never been seduced by prosperity. Adversity shall find me superior to its strokes.

"I several times gave peace to the nations when they had lost everything. With a portion of my conquests I raised up thrones for kings who have abandoned me.

"I had conceived and executed great plans for the prosperity and welfare of the world. Monarch and father, I feel all that peace adds to the security of thrones and of families. Negotiations were opened with the allies. I adhered to the preliminary bases which they presented. I was in hopes that before the opening of this session the congress of Manheim would have assembled; but new delays, which cannot be attributed to France, have delayed this movement."

Napoleon, after reiterating his desire to conclude peace, said that he had been obliged to increase his army, and that he would require money. Denmark and Naples alone, he added, had remained faithful to the alliance.

To ELIZA NAPOLEON, GRAND DUCHESS OF TUSCANY.

"PARIS, 25*th December*, 1813.

"MY SISTER,—You must not give any muskets to the Neapolitans. Send the muskets which are at Leghorn and Porto Ferrajo, in all haste to Alexandria, to arm the conscripts. The intentions of the King of Naples appear extravagant. . . . Should the King declare war, France is not yet dead, and a piece of treason so infamous, should it exist, will fall upon its author. I reckon upon your firmness. Allow the King to throw you into prison, or to kill you, but do not permit him to insult the nation.

"NAPOLEON."

"P.S.—I have arranged matters with the Spaniards. It is useless to publish this, but you can let it transpire. This will set free my armies of Aragon, Catalonia, and Bayonne."

To M. MELZI, DUC DE LODI, GRAND CHANCELLOR OF THE KINGDOM OF ITALY.

"PARIS, 25*th December*, 1813.

"I suppose that Pallafox wrote to you on leaving Vincennes. I have sent him to Prince Ferdinand, and thence he went to Madrid. I have settled matters with the Spaniards. I have still 200,000 men there. It will be useless to publish this news, but you can communicate it to the Viceroy."

The way in which matters were arranged with the Spaniards was this. The Emperor opened negotiations with his captive, through M. Laforest, and received the following artful reply from Ferdinand, dated November 21st, 1813 :—" Sire, I feel highly flattered at the honour paid to me by your Imperial Majesty, and your desire to treat with me in order to terminate the misfortunes of Spain. I continue to remain under the tutelage of your Majesty, for whose person I profess both love and respect, but I can do nothing without the consent of the Spanish nation. Your Imperial Majesty would do better to come to terms with the Regency. I have spent five years and a half here very pleasantly, and would willigly pass the remainder of my life at Valençay." However, through the instrumentality of the Duke of San Carlos, a treaty was concluded with Ferdinand. The French Emperor agreed to recognise him as King of Spain, to respect Spanish territory, and to withdraw his troops. Ferdinand, on his side, engaged to maintain the integrity of Spain, to conclude a convention by which Spain was to be evacuated simultaneously by the French and English forces, and to marry King Joseph's eldest daughter. Ferdinand knew that this treaty would never be sanctioned by the Cortes, and he sent San Carlos to Spain to say that he would himself declare it null and void as soon as he crossed the Pyrenees, on the ground that it had been extorted from him by force.

On the 26th December, the Emperor, in a letter to Marshal Mortier, said that the enemy, debouching by Bâle, were marching on Belfort. On the 30th his Majesty, in reply to an address of the Senate of the most laudatory character, said :—" You have seen by the documents which I have communicated to you, what I have done to obtain peace. The sacrifices contained in the preliminary bases which were proposed by the enemy, I accepted them without regret ; but my life has only one object, the welfare of the French. However, Bearn, Alsace, Franche Comté and Brabant are invaded. The cries of that portion of my family rend my soul. I call upon Frenchmen to aid Frenchmen ! I call upon the Frenchmen of Paris, of Brittany, of Normandy, of Champagne, of Burgundy, and the other departments to help their brothers ! Shall we abandon them in their misfortune ? Peace, and the deliverance of our territory, should be our rallying cry. At the sight of the whole nation in arms, the foreigner will flee or sign peace on the bases which he himself proposed.

It is no longer a question of recovering the conquests we have made."

Such was the gloomy document which closed the eventful year of 1813. Out of 400,000 men with whom he commenced the campaign, only 80,000 recrossed the Rhine in November, and it was with this force and raw levies that he was preparing to fight Europe, and even attacking the allies on the Rhine. *The Correspondence*, though it speaks of the Senate and its report, makes no mention of the report of Lainé in the Lower House, which ably exposed the sufferings entailed upon the country by a series of sanguinary and useless wars. His report, adopted by a large majority, was not allowed to be printed, and it caused the dissolution of the Chamber.

CHAPTER V.

THE YEAR 1814.

FRANCE was about to suffer the horrors of invasion. She had carried fire and the sword through every country on the Continent, and now, for the first time since the beginning of the Revolution, the sacred soil was going to be violated. In 1814 Schwartzenberg and his Austrians debouched into France by way of Switzerland; the English had crossed the Pyrenees, a large force of Russians and Prussians pushed forward from the east, and another host of Germans and Swedes, under Bernadotte, approached from the north. It was almost too much to hope that an exhausted France would be able to resist so mighty a torrent as that which now threatened to overwhelm her. Napoleon in 1814 stood in much the same position as did Frederick the Great in 1756—a position which Macaulay has thus described:—" No such union of the Continental Powers had been seen for ages. A less formidable confederacy had compelled Louis XIV. to bow down his haughty head to the very earth. A less formidable confederacy has within our own memory subjugated a still mightier empire and abased a still prouder name... The people whom Frederick ruled were not 5,000,000. The populations of the countries leagued against him amounted to at least 100,000,000. ... Above all Frederick was one and his enemies were many. In their camp would inevitably be found the jealousy, the dissension, the slackness inseparable from coalitions; on his side were the energy, the unity, the secresy of a strong dictatorship. Small as the king's army was when compared with the 600,000 men which the confederates could bring into the field, celerity of movement might in some degree compensate for deficiency in bulk. It was just possible that genius, judgment, resolution, and good luck might protract the struggle during a campaign or two. . . ." The Senate, at the close of 1813, had voted Napoleon 300,000 men, but when he took the field on the 25th January he was fearfully over-matched, and yet he was more than once on the point of driving the allies out of the country. If there was no absolute dissension in the confederate camp Austria was at first very lukewarm, having views of her own, and it was the same with Bernadotte. The military errors, too, committed by the allies gave Napoleon a fine opportunity for a display of his genius and for turning to account the advantages enumerated by Macaulay. With 60,000 men he rushed against the allies and beat Blucher at St. Dizier and Brienne on the 27th and 29th January; then he experienced a check at La Rothière on the 8th February, but repaired it a few days later at Champaubert and Montmirail; he triumphed again at Vauchamps, at Montereau, at Craonne, and at Rheims. At Bar-sur-Aube, however, at Laon, and at Arcis the French arms were not fortunate. Unable to arrest the advance of the allies in front, Napoleon conceived the bold idea of marching to St. Dizier to cut off their communications, leaving the road to Paris open. His knowledge of the Austrian generals led him to suppose that directly they found their rear threatened they would become terribly alarmed and would at once fall back. The allies, however, pushed forward to Paris, which Mortier and Marmont in vain endeavoured to defend. Marmont then forsook his old chief and treated with the enemy. On the 11th April

Napoleon signed his abdication and on the 13th he took the poison at Fontainebleau, which he had always carried about him since he was nearly snapped up by the Cossacks during the retreat from Moscow, but its strength having wasted away it had little effect. On the 20th April he bid farewell to his Guard and set off for Elba.

Among other matters which aided in the downfall of Napoleon was the defection of Murat, who thought to save his crown by coming to terms with the Austrians. Soult was unable to prevent Wellington from entering Bordeaux on the 12th March, and Angereau, who displayed very little energy, failed to prevent the Austrians from entering Lyons on the 21st, while General Maison was driven out of Belgium.

During all these battles, or up to 19th March, the Congress of Chatillon had remained sitting, and frequent and ineffectual attempts, perhaps not very sincere on either side, were made to bring hostilities to a close. When French prospects looked bright Napoleon talked arrogantly of dictating terms of peace on the Vistula, and the allies reduced their demands; but when the Empire was down they insisted upon her being reduced, not to her natural limits of the Alps and the Rhine, as demanded at Frankfort, but to her frontiers of 1789. Napoleon indignantly rejected this proposal. "Abandon the conquests which were made before me," he exclaimed; "leave France smaller than I found her? Never!"

Marie Louise played the part of Regent during the stormy time which preceded the abdication of Napoleon, and after the abdication she and the King of Rome were sent to Vienna, where her return was hailed with the same enthusiasm as had been exhibited four years previously when Berthier arrived to demand her hand. While Napoleon on his road to embark for Elba narrowly escaped being torn to pieces, crowds flocked round the carriage of Marie Louise during her journey to welcome her home. What Napoleon most dreaded occurred—both wife and son fell into Austrian hands—and after leaving Fontainebleau all communication was cut off between the Emperor and the Empress.

On the 4th January appeared a decree ordering a *levée en masse* in the departments through which the enemy were pushing forward. Nine generals were appointed to direct this movement; they were to raise free corps and to give commissions to partisans who were to act on the flanks of the enemy and do them all the damage possible.

To GENERAL CAULAINCOURT.

"PARIS, *4th January*, 1814.

"I consider it doubtful if the allies are acting in good faith, and if England desires peace. For myself I desire it, but solid and honourable. France without her natural limits, without Ostend and Antwerp, would not be on an equal footing with the other states of Europe. England and all the Powers recognised these limits at Frankfort. The conquests of France within the Rhine and the Alps cannot be considered as a compensation for what Austria, Russia and Prussia have acquired in Poland and Finland, and England in Asia. The policy of England and the hatred of the Emperor of Russia will carry the day with Austria. I have accepted the bases of Frankfort, but it is probable that the allies have other ideas. Their propositions have been merely a mask. . . . It is not certain that you will be received at head-quarters; the Russians and the English wish to prevent all conciliation and explanation with the Emperor of Austria. You must try and fathom the views of the allies, and you must let me know day by day what you learn, so that I may be in a position to furnish you with instructions. Do they wish to reduce France to her ancient limits? This would be to degrade her. They are mistaken if they think the misfortunes of war can make the nation desire such a peace. . . . Italy is intact, the Viceroy has a fine army. Before a week I shall have assembled a sufficient force to fight several battles, even before the arrival of my troops from Spain. The depredations of the Cossacks will arm the inhabitants and will double our forces. If the nation seconds me the enemy will march to their destruction. Should fortune betray me my mind is made up; I do not care for the throne. I shall not disgrace the nation or myself by accepting shameful conditions. You must find out what Metternich wishes. It is not in the interests of Austria to push matters to extremes. . . . "NAPOLEON."

In some instructions which were appended to this letter the Emperor said:—"The independence of the whole of Italy is of the greatest importance to France, comprising even Rome and Genoa." Holland, he said, should be left to France, or at all events have a government not attached to England by any family alliance. "If the independence of Italy be recognised the Emperor will give her Corfu. This should suit Russia and England. . . . There must be no question about Elba or Corsica, which must remain French. . . . If we cannot help it we must allow the Pope to be replaced at Rome, but he must recognise the Concordat of 1813 and the arrangements since made in France for the clergy. . . . If Italy is partitioned Tuscany should be given to King Joseph. If they do not leave the King of Westphalia his states in Germany he must be accorded an indemnity in Italy. The Princess Eliza must keep Lucca. . . . All this is included in the bases of Frankfort which I accepted. Anything else must be rejected on the ground that the above conditions were offered by all the cabinets, even by that of England. Without Mayence and Antwerp, France would be nothing but a second-rate Power, which would be contrary to the interests of Austria. . . ."

Joseph on his return from Spain was very badly treated by his brother, who was some time before he would allow him to go to Paris. However a reconciliation took place.

To KING JOSEPH.

"PARIS, 10th *January*, 1814.

"I have had it placed in the orders of the palace that you shall henceforth be announced as *King Joseph*, and the Queen as the *Queen Julie*, with all the honours, and in the manner usual with French princes. . . . I authorise you to wear the uniform of the Grenadiers of my Guard, such as I wear myself. I think that it will not be suitable for you to wear any foreign decorations. . . .   "NAPOLEON."

There was some little difficulty about this affair of a ludicrous nature. Joseph, although he had been bundled out of Spain in the most hopeless manner, wished to preserve his royal titles, while Napoleon having concluded a treaty with Ferdinand VII. could not possibly allow his brother to appear at the Tuileries as King of Spain.

To Marshal Mortier who was in command of the Old Guard at the important strategical position of Langres, the Emperor wrote on the 10th saying, "I send you a letter from the Commandant of Belfort. Try and inform him by means of peasants that he must hold out to the last extremity, and that every effort will be made to succour the place."

In the Franco-German war of 1870, Belfort was one of the only places in France which offered a successful resistance to the Germans, and the result of this resistance was that France was allowed to retain it much to the annoyance of the military party in Germany.

To MARSHAL MACDONALD.

"PARIS, 10th *January*, 1814.

"You must leave garrisons in all the places, call in General Sebastiani and your cavalry, march upon the

Meuse and manœuvre on Blucher's right flank in the direction of Namur.

"Marshal Marmont will manœuvre round Metz. Marshals Ney and Victor will guard the passes of the Vosges. Marshal Mortier is at Langres. The Emperor is assembling an army of 100,000 men in front of Paris. So that should the enemy neglect the forts to march upon Paris, which is not probable, your corps and those of Marshals Marmont, Victor, Ney, and Mortier will be able to join the reserves before the enemy.

"But you will feel how important it is to stop, or at least to delay the march of the enemy. . . . Employ the wood-rangers, the rural police, and the national guards to do them all the harm they can.

"NAPOLEON."

On the 12th January the Emperor wrote a long note on the forces of the allies, and his own forces. Bulow, he said, was invading Belgium with 20,000 men (9,000 being English under General Graham). Then the army of Silesia 40,000 strong, after having left 10,000 men to observe Mayence and other places, was marching on Metz, while Prince Schwartzenberg was advancing with 100,000 men, but he would be obliged to leave half this force behind him to observe Besançon, Belfort, &c. In the opinion of the Emperor, Blucher and Schwartzenberg would not be able to muster more than 80,000 men between them to march on Paris. "This operation is then a piece of madness, but it must be taken into consideration," summed up Napoleon, who added—" If Spanish affairs take a good turn that will be an immense weight in the balance, and will entirely change the face of affairs, for the army of Lyons could reinforce the army of Paris with 30,000 men.

"No matter what happens proper measures must be adopted, and in no case must Paris be abandoned."

Orders were to be given for the fortification of the capital.

The real strength of the opposing forces appears to have been:—

Schwartzenberg	261,000 men.
Blucher	137,000 ,,
Bernadotte	174,000 ,,
Russian, Prussian, and Austrian reserves	235,000 ,,
Austrians in Italy under Bellegarde	80,000 ,,
British and Portuguese in France	78,000 ,,
Anglo-Sicilian and Spanish armies in Catalonia	62,000 ,,
TOTAL	1,027,000 ,,

The French could oppose to this formidable host but 381,700 men, 100,000 of whom were shut up in various fortresses on the Elbe, and the Oder in Italy and in Holland. With such a disparity of force the plan of the allies was not such a piece of madness as Napoleon made it out when using his own figures.

In some general instructions which Napoleon wrote to his Marshals on the 13th giving them permission to issue proclamations in order to counteract the "invectives" of the enemy's generals, he said:—" They must declare that a force of 200,000 National Guards has been formed in Brittany, Normandy, Picardy, and the neighbourhood of Paris, and is marching on Châlons, independent of an army of reserve of the line of 100,000 men ; that peace having been concluded with King Ferdinand, *and the Spanish insurgents*, our troops of Arragon and Catalonia are marching upon Lyons, and those of Bayonne on Paris ; in fact they must predict to the enemies that the sacred territory which they have invaded will consume them."

To PRINCE METTERNICH.

"PARIS, 16*th January*, 1814.

"PRINCE,—The delays which have taken place in the negotiations are due neither to France nor to Austria, and yet France and Austria suffer the most from them. The allied armies have already invaded several of our provinces.

If they advance, a battle will become inevitable, and surely it behoves Austria to weigh and calculate the results of this battle whether lost by the allies or by France.

"Writing to a minister so enlightened as you are, Prince, I have no need to develop those results. I shall confine myself to glancing at them, being sure that their *ensemble* will not escape your penetration.

"The chances of war are uncertain. By degrees, as the allies advance they enfeeble themselves, while the French armies are receiving reinforcements, and in advancing they give the nation a double courage, for henceforth it is evident that it is called upon to defend its greatest and dearest interests. Now the consequences of a battle lost by the allies would weigh upon none of them so heavily as upon Austria, since she is the principal Power among the allies, and one of the central Powers of Europe.

"In supposing that fortune should continue to favour the allies, it remains for Austria to consider with attention what the situation of Europe will be the day after a battle lost by the French in the heart of France; and if such an event would not produce results diametrically opposed to that equilibrium which Austria aspires to see established, to her policy, to the personal affections, and to the family of the Emperor Francis.

"Then Austria protests that she desires peace, but by continuing hostilities does she not place herself in a position to be unable to accomplish this end?

"All these considerations lead me to think that in the present position of the respective armies, and during this severe weather a suspension of arms might be reciprocally advantageous. It might be established by a convention or by a simple exchange of declarations. It might be limited to a fixed or be for an indefinite period.

"This suspension of arms appears to me to depend more especially upon Austria since she has the chief direction of military affairs.

"And I have reflected that in one way or the other, the interest of Austria is that matters should not be pushed to extremes. It is chiefly owing to this persuasion that I write to-day confidentially to your Excellency.

"If I am mistaken, if this advance, absolutely confidential, should have no effect, I beg of your Excellency to consider it null and void.

"You have shown me so much personal confidence, and I myself have such great confidence in the straightforwardness of your views, and in the noble sentiments which you have always expressed, that I venture to hope that a letter dictated by this confidence, if it does not attain its object will remain a secret between your Excellency and myself.

"NAPOLEON."

On the 17th the Emperor directed Berthier to say that he highly disapproved of Marshal Victor having abandoned Nancy when his Majesty had ordered him not to leave the Moselle without fighting. The letter also said :—" You have fatigued your troops by too long marches, and you have emboldened the enemy. This will oblige Marmont and Mortier also to make a retrograde movement and will greatly damage our affairs."

To PRINCE EUGENE.

"PARIS, 17th January, 1814.

"You will have seen, by the various documents which have been published, all the efforts made to obtain peace. I have since sent my Minister of Foreign Affairs to the enemy's outposts. They put off receiving him and yet they march forward.

"Fouché will have told you that the King of Naples has joined our enemies. As soon as your receive the official news it will be important for you to march to the Alps with your whole army. You may leave Italians in garrison at Manuta and other places, taking care not to leave behind the silver and other precious goods belonging to my household.

"NAPOLEON."

To MARSHAL BERTHIER.

"PARIS, 18*th January*, 1814.

"Write to Marshal Marmont to hold his own at Metz as long as possible, and to let you know the strength of York and of Sacken. A great many inhabitants and soldiers must have seen them pass and must have a tolerable idea of their strength and their position.

"NAPOLEON."

On the 24th January the Emperor, before quitting Paris, appointed Marie Louise Regent and King Joseph his Lieutenant-General, and gave him the command of the National Guard.[1] In a series of instructions he explained his own position and that of the enemy, who were pushing forward upon Langres, St. Dizier,

---

[1] Comte Miot de Melito has left an interesting account of what happened at the Tuileries on the 23rd January, when Napoleon gave a grand audience. He says:—"The Emperor came with the Empress and the King of Rome. He presented them one after the other to the officers of the newly re-organised National Guard, and asked them to watch over the safety of what he considered the most dear, repeating several times, 'You will answer for them, will you not? You will defend them?' He pronounced these words with a warmth and an amount of feeling which made a deep impression upon all who heard him. There was a moment of enthusiasm, and cries of 'Vive l'Empereur!' 'Vive l'Imperatrice!' and 'Vive le Roi de Rome!' were heard on all sides. In this animated address the Emperor did not indulge in any hope of peace; on the contrary, he allowed the possibility of the enemy arriving under the walls of Paris to be distinctly seen. . . . But what struck me most was the language of the French. Never had it been more obsequious. M. de Laplace approached me and spoke of his deep attachment to the Emperor, and his confidence in him, in the most feeling manner, expressing at the same time his indignation against the Bourbons. . . .

M. de Laplace a few months afterwards threw himself into the arms of the Bourbons.

and Dijon. "The measures I have taken," he said, "appear sufficient to keep the enemy at a distance from Paris and to insure the tranquillity of the capital." On the 26th his Majesty was writing from Châlons-sur-Marne. "At Vitry," he wrote to Berthier, "take 200,000 or 300,000 bottles of wine or brandy for the troops and distribute them to-day and to-morrow. If there be no other wine but champagne in bottle take it; it is better that we should have it than the enemy." On the evening of the same day we find some despatches dated from Vitry-le-François.

To GENERAL CLARKE.

"ST. DIZIER, 28*th January*, 1814.

"On the 27th I marched upon St. Dizier, which was occupied by the enemy. I drove them out, captured some guns, killed a few men, and took a few prisoners. I learned here that Blucher with 25,000 men had gone to Brienne, where he arrived to-day. I have had the line of operations cut, caused Bar to be occupied, and am starting in pursuit of Blucher. If he stands there will possibly be an affair to morrow at Brienne.

"NAPOLEON."

On the 31st the Emperor wrote to his War Minister from Brienne, and said :—" I had a very warm affair on the 29th at Brienne. I attacked the armies of Blucher and of Sacken—80,000 infantry and a strong body of cavalry. I attacked them with 10,000 men just after having made a long march. At the beginning of the action I had the good fortune to seize upon the castle which dominated everything. As the attack did not begin until an hour before night-fall we fought all night. Blucher was beaten and had 3,000 or 4,000 killed or wounded, and lost 500 or 600 prisoners. He has been obliged to call in all the detachments which were marching on Paris and to fall back upon Bar-sur-Aube. I pursued him in that direction for two leagues. . . . If I had had old troops I should have done better . . . but with the troops I have we must consider ourselves lucky with what happened. . . . I am impatiently expecting the divisions of the army of Spain. . . ."

There were strange ups and downs in those days. On the same day that the above letters were dictated Napoleon wrote thus to his Police Minister Savary: "I highly approve of what General Miollis has done in giving passports to the quondam Director Barras, allowing him to return to France." Barras who had formerly given Napoleon not only Josephine for a wife but the command of the army of Italy.

To KING JOSEPH.

"PINEY, 2*nd February*, 1814.

"It seems that the allies have selected the 3rd February for the opening of the Congress at Châtillon; that Lord Cathcart will treat for England with a dozen Englishmen, Stadion for Austria, Humbolt for Prussia, and Razoumosky for Russia. . . . I shall be to-morrow at Troyes.

"NAPOLEON."

To GENERAL CAULAINCOURT.

"PINEY, 2*nd February*, 1814.

"The troops of the enemy behave horribly everywhere. All the inhabitants seek refuge in the woods. No more peasants are found in the villages. The enemy eat up everything, take all the horses, cattle, clothes, and all the rags of the peasants; they beat every one, men and women, and commit rape. The picture which I have just seen with my eyes should make you understand easily how much I desire to extricate my people as soon as possible from this state of misery and suffering, which is really terrible. This should also make the enemy reflect, for the Frenchman is not patient; he is naturally brave, and I expect to see the people organise themselves into bands. You should draw a very energetic sketch of these excesses. In towns like Brienne, of 2,000 souls, there is no one!

"NAPOLEON."

The horrors of war seem to have been brought home to the Emperor for the first time when he saw this desolation of desolations at Brienne, which was utterly wrecked.

To GENERAL CAULAINCOURT.

"TROYES, 4*th February*, 1814.

"The report of Prince Schwartzenberg is a piece of folly. There has been no battle. The Old Guard was not there; the Young Guard was not engaged. A few guns were taken from us by charges of cavalry. But the army was marching to cross the bridge of Lesmont when this happened, and two hours later the enemy would not have found us. It appears that the whole army of the enemy was there, and they look upon this as a battle .... they had to deal with a force of only 15,000 men, and we held the field of battle all day.

"The letter which M. de Metternich has written to you is perfectly ridiculous, but I recognise in it what I have perceived for a long time, that while he thinks that he leads all Europe every one leads him. . . .

"NAPOLEON."

The affair above alluded to was the battle of La Rothière, much slurred over in French history. The allies had been warned at Brienne of the presence of Napoleon, and had rapidly concentrated over 80,000 men, with which force they attacked the French on the 1st February. The struggle was a severe one, but when night fell Napoleon had to return with his shattered army to Brienne with a loss of 6,000 men and 73 guns. Baron Fain says that the Emperor ordered a retreat upon Troyes by the bridge of Lesmont, and that while the army accomplished this movement, favoured by the obscurity, Napoleon greatly feared that a night attack would spread confusion through his ranks.

On the 5th the Emperor wrote another letter to Caulaincourt, dated from Troyes at 1 A.M. In this he said: "I remained at Troyes to-day thinking that I should have news of the Congress. It seems that you did not begin until the 4th. If they desire peace, and if this again is not a mask to prolong hostilities unanimously, things must be arranged promptly, for in a few days there will be a general engagement which will settle everything. I am going to Nogent to meet 20,000 men of the army of Spain, who will arrive to-day or to-morrow."

Napoleon, when he wrote this letter, had no intention of risking a general engagement. He considered it more prudent to abandon Troyes and to fall back on Nogent. Everything was going wrong and bad news was pouring in from Italy and from the north, and Blucher was marching on Paris. As for the Congress, it increased its demands, and would no longer grant the conditions of Frankfort. The blunders of the allies in dividing their forces and the military genius of Napoleon, which once more shone forth as brilliant as ever, soon changed the aspect of affairs.

To GENERAL CLARKE.

"TROYES, 6*th February*, 1814.

"I am much surprised that Marshal Suchet should not have despatched the troops which I demanded from Lyons. They ought to have arrived and I hear no more of them. If the marshal has taked upon himself not to execute orders he is very culpable. . . .

"NAPOLEON."

Writing the same day to King Joseph on this and other subjects, his Majesty said: "I have been very much put out, for I wished to attack the Emperor Alexander to-morrow at Bar, and to have beaten him. He appears to me to have made some false plans. However, I sacrifice everything to the necessity of covering Paris. . . In the event of anything unforeseen happening the idea of putting King Louis at the head of Paris seems to me a good one. . . . Have all the valuable furniture, and everything which can be regarded as a trophy, removed from Fontainebleau. . . ."

The greatest uneasiness prevailed in Paris, for Napoleon had sent only one bulletin from the front, and that was not of a cheering character.

To PRINCE CAMBACÉRÈS.

"NOGENT, 7*th February*, 1814.

"I see that instead of sustaining the Empress you discourage her. Why do you lose your head like that? What are these *Misereres*, and these prayers of forty hours at the chapel? Have people in Paris gone mad? The Minister of Police says and commits follies instead of informing himself of the movements of the enemy. . . .

"NAPOLEON."

On the same day, writing to King Joseph, the Emperor said—

"The Empress had the intention of going to St. Genevieve; I fear that that will have a bad effect, and create no other result. Put a stop to these prayers of forty hours, and the *Miserere*. If these monkey tricks are continued we shall all be afraid of death. Long ago it was said that priests and doctors render death painful. The moment is no doubt difficult, but up to the present I have done nothing but gain advantages. . . . It is possible that parties of cavalry may be seen at Soissons. The enemy has an immense cavalry, with which they inundate France. . . . "NAPOLEON."

"P.S.—Keep the Empress gay; she is dying of consumption."

On the 8th the Emperor wrote another reassuring letter to King Joseph, adding a postscript in which he said:—

"Have an article inserted in the *Moniteur* about Chatillon, saying that the six members of the Congress dined with Lord Castlereagh, and that it was remarked that the greatest politeness existed between the ambassadors, and especially between those of France and England, who were most attentive to each other."

In a third letter to his brother of the same date the Emperor said—

"I have received your letter of the 7th, which much astonished me. I have read the letter of King Louis. I have replied with regard to the eventuality of Paris; you have no need to return to that. That finale will affect more people than us. When it comes I shall no longer exist, consequently it is not for myself that I speak. I have given you orders for the Empress, for the King of Rome, and our family. Be sure that should the case happen, what I have predicted will infallibly come to pass.

"King Louis speaks of peace; this is giving advice in very bad season. Besides, I understand nothing of your letter. I thought that I had explained matters to you; but you remember nothing, and you are of the same way of thinking as the first man who speaks to you and who reflects an opinion.

"I repeat to you that Paris shall never be occupied during my life.

"I have a right to be aided by those who surround me, because I have aided them.

"If by any chance I should march on the Loire I shall not leave the Empress and my son behind, because both of them might be carried off to Vienna. . . . I must acknowledge that your letter has pained me, because I see that your ideas are shallow, and that you allow yourself to be influenced by the gossip of a crowd of unreflecting persons. If Talleyrand has anything to do with this idea of leaving the Empress in Paris in the event of our troops

GLOOMY FOREBODINGS. 307

evacuating the capital, it is treason. I tell you again to distrust that man. I know him for the last sixteen years; I have even shown him some favour, but he is surely the greatest enemy of our house now that fortune has for some time past abandoned us.

"Should the news of a battle lost, or of my death, arrive, send the Empress and the King of Rome to Rambouillet; order the Senate, the Council of State, and all my troops to assemble on the Loire, and leave a prefect and an imperial commissioner or a mayor at Paris.

"I informed you that Madame and the Queen of Westphalia[1] might remain in Paris as well as the vice-reine of Italy. But never allow the Empress or the King of Rome to fall into the hands of the enemy.

"Be certain that from that moment Austria would cease to take any interest in us, and would carry off the Empress to Vienna on the pretence of rendering her happy, and France would be obliged to adopt the suggestions of the Regent of England and of Russia. By this our party would find itself destroyed by that horrible league between the Republicans and the Royalists. . . .

"However, it is possible that I may beat the enemy, who are approaching Paris, and then all this will not take place. It is also possible that I may conclude peace in a few days. . . . It is in the interest of the country that the Empress and the King of Rome should not remain in Paris, because the interests of the country cannot be separated from their persons, and that since the world was the world I have never seen a sovereign allow himself to be captured in an open town. That unfortunate King of Saxony allowed himself to be taken at Leipsic; he lost his states, and was made prisoner. . . . If I live I must be obeyed, and if I die my son and the Empress Regent should, for the honour of France, not allow themselves to be captured, but retire to the last village with the last soldiers. Remember what the wife of Philip V. said. What would be said of the Empress? That she abandoned the throne of

[1] Napoleon's mother, and the wife of King Jerome.

her son and ours. And the allies would prefer to finish matters by leading their prisoners to Vienna. I am surprised that you cannot understand this. I see that fear has turned the heads of every one in Paris.

"The Empress and the King of Rome once in the hands of the enemy, you and all those who would defend yourselves would be rebels.

"As far as I am concerned, I would sooner see my son slain than brought up at Vienna as an Austrian prince; and I have a sufficiently good opinion of the Empress to feel persuaded that she thinks in the same way, as far as it is possible for a woman and a mother to do so.

"I never saw *Andromaque* represented without pitying Astyanax surviving his family, and without regarding it as a piece of good fortune that he did not survive his father.

"You do not know the French nation; the results of what will happen during these great events is incalculable. As for Louis, I think that he should follow you.

"NAPOLEON."

Two other letters Napoleon wrote to his brother Joseph on the 8th. The first ran thus:—"Have the inclosed letter placed in the hands of the Empress Josephine. I have written to her to write to Eugene. Tell her to send you her letter, and that you will forward it by *estafette*."

The fifth letter was as follows:—"I have just written to the War Minister relative to the evacuation of Italy, and to the King Ferdinand. . . ."

Joseph, in his letter of the 7th, had urged upon Napoleon the necessity of coming to terms with the enemy.

As regards Italy, the Emperor, on account of the defection of Murat, gave orders for all the French soldiers to be withdrawn from that country. His Majesty was beginning to doubt the fidelity of Eugene, and hence the letter which his mother was to write to him.[1]

---

[1] The following correspondence relates to this subject. Josephine at once wrote as follows to her son, Eugène de Beauharnais:—

"Do not lose an instant, my dear Eugène; no matter what the

On the subject of King Ferdinand the Emperor wrote thus to General Clarke :—" As for King Ferdinand, we hear nothing more of the treaty. . . . If the king wishes to go to Barcelona he can do so *incognito*. The fortresses will be handed over to him in return for the French garrisons, who must be sent back."

On the 8th Napoleon also wrote to Commissioner Daure, saying :—" The army is dying of hunger in spite of all your reports. Twelve men died of hunger, although everything was 'put to fire and blood' on the march in order to obstacles, redouble your efforts to carry out the orders of the Emperor, who has just written to me on the subject. His intention is that you fall back upon the Alps, leaving only Italian troops in Mantua and the other fortresses. His letter concludes thus : 'France before everything. France has need of all her children.' Hasten hither, my dear son, and never will your zeal have better served the Emperor. I can assure you that each instant is precious. I know that your wife is about to leave Milan. Tell me if I can be of any use to her. Adieu, my dear Eugène, I have only time to embrace you and to implore you to come quickly."

Prince Eugene replied to his mother :—

"MY GOOD MOTHER,— I received your letter of the 9th on returning from an expedition, during which I beat the Austrians. It perfectly astonished me. I have replied to the Emperor. I did not expect, after such a length of time, to be obliged to give the Emperor proofs of my fidelity and devotion."

To the Emperor and to the War Minister the Viceroy answered on February 18th :—

"SIRE,—I have received a letter from the Empress Josephine, reproaching me with not having promptly executed the orders transmitted by the Duc de Feltre. Your Majesty seems to think that I need more than my devotion towards your person, and my love of my country, to excite me to fall back upon France under present circumstances. Your Majesty must pardon me if I tell you that I have not deserved these reproaches, nor the little confidence you have in sentiments which will always most powerfully influence my actions. Your Majesty's orders expressly stated that I was to retreat on the Alps should Murat declare war. This order was conditional, and I should have been culpable had I executed it before the condition was fulfilled."

procure provisions. However, if I refer to your reports the army is well fed. Marshal Victor has nothing: General Gérard has nothing; the cavalry of the guard are dying of hunger...."

On the 9th Napoleon addressed five despatches to King Joseph, and on the 10th he wrote to him thus:—

" To-day I attacked the enemy to Champaubert. They were twelve regiments strong, and had forty guns. The general-in-chief Olsoufief, and all his generals, colonels, cannon, ammunition waggons and baggage, were captured. We count 6,000 prisoners, 40 guns, and 200 waggons. The remainder were thrown into a pond, or killed on the field of battle. This corps is entirely destroyed.

"We are marching upon Montmirail, where we shall arrive at ten this evening. I shall be there myself to-morrow morning before daybreak in order to march against Sacken with 20,000 men. ... I am close on the enemy's heels. ... I flatter myself that Sacken is destroyed; and if fortune favours us to-day affairs will be changed in the twinkling of an eye; for it is in Sacken's corps that the strength of the Russian army lies, since he has ten divisions, or sixty regiments. Blucher is cut off from Sacken; he has two divisions. ... I think that we have to regret 200 men.

"NAPOLEON."

The surprise of the Russians and the success of Napoleon's cross march had a wonderful effect, and completely revived the drooping spirits of the French, who were fast losing their confidence in the genius of their leader. Champaubert restored the prestige of Napoleon, and rendered all the chances of the campaign uncertain. His Majesty, as usual, exaggerated the losses of the enemy, which seem to have been 3,000 out of 5,000 men, and twelve guns. He now began to speak of dictating terms of peace to Alexander on the banks of the Vistula.

BRILLIANT SUCCESS.

To KING JOSEPH.

"FARM OF ÉPINE-AUX-BOIS, 11*th February*, 1814.

"Berthier sent you a courier from the field of battle. I have since despatched the young Montesquiou. It is 8 o'clock, and before going to sleep I send you two words to inform you that the affair of yesterday was decisive. The enemy's army of Silesia no longer exists. I have completely routed it. We have taken all its guns and its baggage, and made thousands of prisoners—perhaps over 7,000. There are 5,000 or 6,000 enemies lying on the field of battle. All this was obtained by bringing into action only the half of my Old Guard, which accomplished more than could be expected from men. The enemy have fled in disorder in the direction of Chateau Thierry. . . . These two days change the face of affairs. Sacken was killed, and a great many of their generals captured. I think that as night fell York's corps came up; it shared the fate of the Russians. I have written to the Empress to fire sixty rounds. . . . I think that these two days will remove all danger from Paris, for the army of Silesia was the last army of the allies. . . .

"NAPOLEON."

To MARSHAL BERTHIER.

"FARM OF ÉPINE-AUX-BOIS, 12*th February*, 1814.

"Write to Marshal Marmont that the enemy have fallen back upon Chateau Thierry; that we have repulsed them on all sides. . . . The cavalry of Marshal Marmont should commit fearful havoc with the rear guard, seeing that their cavalry is in front, and that those people are not accustomed to see their rear compromised. Let Marmont publish proclamations saying that sixty Russian regiments have been destroyed, and 120 guns captured; that it is time for the French people to rise and fall upon the enemy; that the Emperor is pursuing them; let them arrest the Cossacks. . . .

"NAPOLEON."

Further information was addressed to King Joseph on the same day from Chateau Thierry, whence the rear guard of the enemy had been pursued, for a large portion of the sixty regiments entirely destroyed still remained, although in a bad plight. His Majesty wrote :—

"Having cut the enemy off from the road to Châlons the whole army was obliged to cross the Marne in order to reach the road to Soissons. I snapped up their rear guard, composed of four Russian battalions, three Prussian battalions, and three guns. To-day we have captured 2,000 prisoners. Marmont is marching from Etoges on Epernay or Châlons. If Macdonald, as I hoped, had operated on the right bank of the Marne, not a man would have escaped. However, we have made between 8,000 and 10,000 prisoners, amongst them five or six generals. We have taken nearly all their artillery, all their baggage, and killed an enormous lot of men. This army, which was 35,000 strong, is certainly not over 12,000 to-day. The enemy have been thrown into horrible confusion. . . .

"NAPOLEON."

The loss of the allies at Montmirail was very heavy, although exaggerated by Napoleon in his letter to Joseph. They acknowledge having lost 6,000 men, seventeen guns, and five colours during the two days, and the pursuit would have been continued had they not blown up the bridges after crossing the Marne. Marmont was unable to obey the orders of the Emperor, having been repulsed by Blucher.

Describing this affair to Savary, Napoleon wrote :—" The last army of Russia is destroyed. My Old Guard and Horse Guards performed miracles; the dragoons distinguished themselves. I did not bring into action more than 2,000 men of the Old Guard. What they did can be compared to the romances of chivalry, and to the men in armour of those days where one beat 300 or 400. The enemy must have been struck with a singular terror. Redouble your efforts to arrest all stragglers; let the hospitals at Paris be thrown open to the sick, and let care be taken that this multitude of men from the army be not allowed to remain there uselessly."

There is a strange contrast between the beginning and the end of this letter.

On the 13th the Emperor, who could not get across the Marne to finish the destruction of Sacken's totally annihilated regiments, wrote to King Joseph from the farm of Lurmont, saying :—" During the whole of yesterday the enemy attacked Nogent. Marshal Victor had crossed over to the right bank, and had left only 1,200 men in the town under the command of General Bourmont. This Bourmont is the famous Chouan with whom I am much pleased. The enemy wished to enter in close column ; they were repulsed in three consecutive assaults, and lost 2,000 or 3,000 men. Bourmont was slightly wounded, but our loss was light. Then the enemy, in a rage, brought up mortars and set fire to the town, but to no purpose.... I tremble lest those scamps of Russians should set fire to Fontainebleau by way of reprisal."

Nogent was evacuated the next day, and Fontainebleau fell into the hands of the Cossacks on the 14th.

To M. FOUCHÉ, DUC D'OTRANTE, AT FLORENCE.

"CHÂTEAU THIERRY, 13*th February*, 1814.

" I have received your different letters. The conduct of the King of Naples is infamous, and there is no name for that of the Queen (Sister Caroline). I hope to live long enough to be able to revenge myself and France for such an insult and for such fearful ingratitude. . . .

" NAPOLEON."

And orders were given to Caulaincourt to "prepare the documents concerning this strange war" between Napoleon and his brother-in-law.

On the 14th Napoleon wrote to Marshal Mortier, who was in command of the Old Guard, saying :—" It is 3 A.M., and I am just starting for Montmirail to fall upon Blucher, who has debouched with 10,000 men to attack Marmont, who in presence of a superior force has fallen back without fighting on Fromentières. I hope, therefore, to obtain a success to-day, for I have concentrated 30,000 men." The Emperor wrote in the same manner to King Joseph and to General Clarke.

To KING JOSEPH.
"MONTMIRAIL, 14*th February*, 1814. 9 P.M.

"I send you a line to let you know the happy issue of the battle of Vauchamps. General Blucher, who was separated from his army, and who had his head-quarters at Vertus, had been joined by Kleist's corps, twenty-four battalions strong, and by a new Russian corps of twelve battalions, or 20,000 men. He marched on the 13th against Etoges and Champaubert. Marmont, who was informed of this movement, retreated. I started at three this morning from Château Thierry, and arrived at Montmirail when the enemy were nearly at the gates. I attacked the enemy, who had taken up a position in the village of Vauchamps. I beat them, and took 8,000 prisoners, three guns, and ten colours. Their loss in dead and wounded must be more than 4,000 men. I have lost in killed or wounded only 300. This grand result was obtained because the enemy had no cavalry, whereas I had from 6,000 to 8,000 excellent troopers. . . .

"NAPOLEON."

Blucher was in pursuit of Marmont with 20,000 men when he suddenly found himself in presence of Napoleon, and at once determined to retreat. As usual, the Emperor exaggerated his triumph, but it was signal and complete. It was only after the most desperate fighting, and with a loss of 6,000 men, fifteen guns, and two colours, that

Blucher, with his shattered columns, found shelter behind the Marne from Grouchy and his cavalry.

In a letter to King Joseph on the 15th the Emperor said that the peasants had picked up 40,000 muskets thrown away by the enemy, and that he was moving in the direction of Meaux, for it was now necessary to look after the Austrians, who were approaching Paris sluggishly from another quarter; and that Bulow also was abandoning Belgium and the north in order to march upon the capital.

On the 16th the Emperor wrote to the King from Meaux, as follows:—" I am going to Guignes, and I shall attack the enemy to-morrow. Send me in all haste what remains of the Old Guard, horse and foot, to repair the losses which have been sustained. . . . I missed a fine stroke yesterday; 6,000 Bavarians were at two leagues from me. The enemy manœuvre with such ignorance that I hope in the course of a few days to obtain excellent results."

The allies, at last aware of the error they had committed in separating their armies, now proposed to fall back on Troyes to concentrate; and with the view of gaining time to execute this movement a flag of truce was sent in to say that they were surprised at the offensive movement made by the French army, as they had agreed to the terms of peace proposed by Caulaincourt at Chatillon—proposals to which Napoleon would gladly have adhered but for his success at Champaubert. In reply, Napoleon wrote to Caulaincourt, who was still at Chatillon, dwelling upon the immense advantages he had gained since the opening of the campaign, adding—" I am ready to cease hostilities and to allow the enemy to return home tranquilly, if they will sign the preliminary bases of the propositions of Frankfort. The bad faith of the enemy, and their violation of the most sacred engagements alone cause delay, for we are so near to each other that if they will permit you to correspond with me directly, they can have replies to your despatches in twenty-four hours. Besides, I am going to approach nearer still."

On the 18th Napoleon informed King Joseph that:—
"Prince Schwartzenberg has just given sign of life. He has sent to ask for a suspension of arms. It is difficult to be cowardly to such a degree; he has constantly refused in the most insulting terms all kinds of suspensions of arms, and even to receive my flags of truce after the capitulation of Dantzic and Dresden—a horrible thing, without example in history. These wretches at the first check fall on their knees. Fortunately the aide-de-camp of Prince Schwartzenberg was not allowed to enter my quarters. I merely received his letter, to which I shall reply at my leisure. I shall consent to no armistice which does not purge the territory."

Napoleon then gave his reasons for being willing to treat before Champaubert:—"You can conceive," he wrote, "that being on the eve of a battle, in which I was determined to conquer or die—in which, if I were beaten, my capital would have been taken—I would have consented to everything so as to avoid this great chance. I owed this sacrifice to my self-love, to my family, and to my people. But since they refused to treat, the battle has been fought, and as my capital is no longer threatened I owe it to the interest of my empire, and to my glory, to negotiate a real peace...."

And so it went on; each side, when matters went badly, wished to negotiate, and each party raised its pretensions to an unacceptable degree as soon as it triumphed.

To PRINCE EUGÈNE.

"NANGIS, 18*th February*, 1814.

"I see with pleasure the advantages which you have obtained; if they had been a little more decisive we should have been able to keep Italy.... I have destroyed the army of Silesia, composed of Russians and Prussians. I began yesterday to beat Schwartzenberg. In four days I have taken from 30,000 to 40,000 prisoners, five generals, 600 officers, from 150 to 200 guns, &c. I have lost hardly any one. The cavalry of the enemy is very low. . . . Should fortune continue to favour us, and the enemy be driven across the frontier, we shall be able to preserve Italy. Perhaps the King of Naples will then change sides.

"NAPOLEON."

Writing to Caulaincourt on the 19th the Emperor said :—" It is false what they tell you. The Austrians have been beaten in Italy, and, far from being at Meaux, I shall soon be at Chatillon.[1] In this situation I reiterate my orders, to do nothing without learning my intentions. . . . As soon as I reach Troyes I will send you a counter project. I thank heaven that I have the note of the allies, for it will make the blood of every Frenchman boil with indignation. This is why I wish to draw up my own *ultimatum*. . . . I am so upset by the infamous proposals which you have sent me, that I consider myself dishonoured at being placed in a position to have received them. I will let you know my intentions from Troyes or Chatillon. . . ."

And on the same day his Majesty wrote as follows to Police Minister Savary :—

" The journals are edited without intelligence. Is it proper at the present moment to say that I have few men, and that I have conquered the enemy because I have surprised them, and that we were one against three ? You must have lost your heads in Paris to say such things, when I am constantly giving out that I have 300,000 men, when the enemy believe it, and when you ought to declare it to satiety. This is how you destroy the good resulting from victory with a stroke of the pen. You should read over these things yourself ;

---

[1] Sacken did reach Meaux, and the sound of his guns was distinctly audible in Paris ; it is true that he fell back as soon as he learned that Napoleon was on the move with the intention of attacking Blucher.

it is not now an empty question of glory; it is one of the first principles of war to exaggerate your forces. But how can poets, who endeavour to flatter me, and to flatter the national self-love, be made to understand this? ....

"NAPOLEON."

To PRINCE EUGÈNE.

"CHÂTEAU DE SURVILLE, 19*th February*, 1814.

"It is necessary that the vice-reine should go to Paris without delay in order to be confined, it being my intention that, under no circumstances, shall she remain *in a country occupied by the enemy*. . . . I have beaten Wittgenstein at the action of Nangis, where I took 4,000 Russian prisoners, with guns and flags; and above all I seized upon the bridges of Montereau before the enemy could burn them.

"NAPOLEON."

The above letter, which greatly annoyed the Viceroy, was written under these circumstances. Prince Eugène had been obliged to fall back upon the Mincio, and was uncertain where he would be able to make a stand; he consequently wrote to Marshal Bellegarde, asking permission for his wife to remain in Milan for her confinement, and to be allowed to rejoin him afterwards. The Austrian commander at once granted the request, and forwarded the following letter from the Emperor of Austria to the Princess Augusta, dated from Troyes, in Champagne:—

"MADAME, MY COUSIN,—Marshal Bellegarde having acquainted me with your determination to remain momentarily at the château of Monza, I beg to assure your Imperial Highness that this general has perfectly acted up to my intentions. I have given orders for the formation of a guard of honour for your Imperial Highness, who will enjoy the most entire liberty in all things, and I only regret, madame, the motives which force you to come to a determination which, under other circumstances, I should consider extremely flattering. I beg you, &c. &c.

"FRANCIS."

When Prince Eugene communicated Napoleon's letter to his wife she expressed her indignation in these terms:—

"I am highly indignant, and feel no longer astonished that people abandon the Emperor. Was any one ever more ungrateful? .... It is clear that the family of the Emperor, and perhaps the Emperor himself, are jealous of you. The King of Naples will be pardoned for his treason, but you will never be pardoned for the reputation and esteem you enjoy. I know not where all this will end, but it is sure our lot will never be fixed as long as it depends on the Emperor. This certitude, however, should not hinder us from following the path of virtue and honour to the end of our lives. . . . Were I to fall into the hands of the enemy they could not treat me worse than the Emperor, who has plunged a dagger into my heart. Do not fear telling me to start. If I could go with you to America I would willingly do so, for I am disgusted with the grandeur of the world," &c.

The consequence was, that the Princess Augusta threw herself into Mantua, and she was confined just as Marshal Bellegarde, who had laid siege to that place, was firing a salute in honour of the capitulation of Paris.

To KING JOSEPH.

"MONTEREAU, 20*th* *February*, 1814.

"The Duc de Bassano (M. Maret) will send you a copy of the proposals of the allies. You will see by them that your sermons are out of place, and that I do not require to be preached to in order to sign an honourable peace if that be possible.

"He will also send you an intercepted letter from the Duc d'Angoulême. . . .

"NAPOLEON.

"P.S.—The Emperors had selected their quarters at Fontainebleau for the 18th, but on the same day they left Bray in hot haste for Troyes, on which place the allied armies are retiring."

To KING JOSEPH.

"NOGENT, 20*th February*, 1814. 6 P.M.

"I have just arrived at Nogent. The enemy after Montereau fell back upon Troyes with the greater portion of their army. They enjoyed great luck, for the frost enabled them to march across country; but for this half their baggage and their artillery would have been captured. The enemy committed at Montereau, Bray, and Nogent unspeakable horrors; this should be made known in Paris. The Emperor of Austria has not left Troyes. . . .[1]

"NAPOLEON."

In several letters Napoleon complained in bitter terms of the horrors committed by the enemy. On the 21st, in a letter to Savary, he said:—"My hair stands on end at the crimes committed by the enemy, and the police should collect the facts. Women of sixty and young girls of

---

[1] That the French troops also committed great excesses at this date may be gathered from the following proclamation, dated the 8th February, and which, though not to be found in *The Correspondence*, is quoted by Alison (vol. xii. p. 491), who says that it was due to the destruction of a castle in the neighbourhood of Nogent which belonged to the Emperor's mother. Greatly incensed at the universal pillage indulged in, Napoleon issued this proclamation:—

"The Emperor has to express to the army his displeasure at the excesses to which it abandons itself. Such disorders are always hurtful; but they become criminal when committed in our native country. From this day forth the chiefs of corps and the generals shall be held entirely responsible for them. The inhabitants are flying on all sides, and the troops, instead of being their country's defenders, are becoming its scourge."

twelve have been ill-used. They plunder, rape, destroy, and burn everywhere. The Russian officers declare their intention of going to Paris, and of reducing the capital to ashes. The Prince de ―――― has covered himself with mud. . . ."

To MARSHAL AUGEREAU.

"NOGENT, 21*st February*, 1814.

". . . . What! six hours after having received the first troops coming from Spain you were not in the field! Six hours' repose was sufficient. I won the action of Nangis with a brigade of dragoons coming from Spain, which, since it left Bayonne, had not unbridled its horses. The six battalions of the division of Nismes want clothes, equipment, and drilling, say you. What poor reasons you give me there, Augereau! I have destroyed 80,000 enemies with conscripts having nothing but knapsacks! The National Guards, say you, are pitiable; I have 4,000 here, in round hats, without knapsacks, in wooden shoes, but with good muskets, and I get a great deal out of them. There is no money, you continue; and where do you hope to draw money from? You want waggons; take them wherever you can. You have no magazines; this is too ridiculous. I order you twelve hours after the reception of this letter to take the field. If you are still Augereau of Castiglione, keep the command; but if your sixty years weigh upon you, hand over the command to your senior general. The country is in danger, and can be saved by boldness and goodwill alone. . . .

"NAPOLEON."

Augereau was in command of the army of Lyons, and the Emperor thought that by operating on the rear of the allies, and threatening their communications, he would frighten the Austrians nearly out of their lives. The Austrians, too, were under the impression that Augereau had a much more formidable force under his orders than was the case.

To FRANCIS, First Emperor of Austria.

"Nogent, 21st *February*, 1814.

"Sir, my Brother, and very dear Father-in-Law,—I did all that I could to avoid the fighting which has taken place. Fortune has smiled upon me. I have defeated the Russian and Prussian armies commanded by General Blucher, and since then, the Prussian army commanded by General Kleist. In this situation, and no matter what the prejudices of your head-quarters, my army is more numerous in infantry, cavalry and artillery than that of your Majesty; and if the assurance of this fact be necessary to influence your determinations, I have no objection to let it be seen by a man of sound judgment such as Prince Schwartzenberg, Count Bubna, or Prince Metternich. I consider it my duty to write to your Majesty, because this struggle between a French army and an army chiefly Austrian appears to me to be opposed to your interests and to mine. Should fortune betray my hopes, your situation will be all the more embarrassing. If I beat your army, how will you retire from France, whose inhabitants are exasperated to the highest degree by the crimes of all kinds committed by the Cossacks and the Russians?

"In this state of affairs I propose to your Majesty to sign peace without delay, on the bases which you yourself laid down at Frankfort, and which I and the French nation adopted as our *ultimatum*. I say more; these bases can alone re-establish the European equilibrium. If other conditions were imposed upon France, peace would be of short duration.

"The plenipotentiaries of the allies at Chatillon have presented a note, the knowledge of which would fill France with the greatest indignation; it is the realisation of the dream of Burke, who wished France to disappear from the map of Europe. There are no Frenchmen who would not prefer death to conditions which would render them the slaves of England, and would strike them out of the list of the great Powers. Your Majesty cannot approve of these conditions, which are certainly not in the interest of your monarchy. One can understand that England should wish to destroy Antwerp, and put an everlasting obstacle to the re-establishment of the French fleet! But you, sire, you, what interest can you take in this? Your Majesty, by the bases which you proposed at Frankfort, became a maritime Power. Do you wish your flag to be insulted and violated by England, as it has constantly been? What interest can your Majesty have in placing the Belgians under a Protestant prince, one of whose sons will ascend the throne of England?

"However, these hopes, these projects, are beyond the power of the coalition. The battle about to take place against the army of your Majesty, were it lost, could be repaired, for I have resources enough in Paris to fight two more; and if Paris were taken, the rest of France would never support the yoke proposed in the treaty which the policy of England seems to have inspired. The convulsions of the nation would quadruple the energy and strength of our resistance.

"Never will I yield up Antwerp and Belgium. A peace founded on the bases of Frankfort can alone be sincere, and place France in a position to turn her attention solely to the re-establishment of her marine and her commerce. If your Majesty persists in subordinating your own interests to the policy of England, and to the resentment of Russia; and if arms will only be laid down on the fearful conditions proposed by the Congress, the genius of France and Providence will be on our side.

"This thirst for vengeance on the part of the Emperor Alexander is not justified. Before entering Moscow I offered him peace. At Moscow I did all I could to extinguish the fire lighted by his orders.

"Besides, 200,000 men are in arms in Paris. They have learned by what the Russians have done how fallacious are their promises. They know the lot that awaits them. . . .

May I be permitted to tell your Majesty that, in spite of all you have done since the invasion of my territory, and the little attention you have paid to the bonds which unite us and the mutual interests of our states, my feelings towards you have not changed, and that I cannot see with indifference that if you refuse peace, this refusal will render your own life unhappy, and will produce misfortune for all, whilst with a word you can stop everything, conciliate everything, and restore durable tranquillity to the world? If I had been sufficiently cowardly to accept the English and Russian proposals, you should have dissuaded me from it, for you must know that what degrades 30,000,000 men cannot be durable. . . .[1]

"I presume that your Majesty will not ask why I address myself to you. I cannot address myself to the English, who aim at the destruction of my marine, or to the Emperor Alexander, who is animated with feelings of passion and vengeance. I can therefore address myself to your Majesty alone, lately my ally, who, looking at the force of your army and the size of your empire, is considered the chief Power of the coalition; lastly, to your Majesty, who, no matter what your momentary feelings may be, has French blood in your veins.

" NAPOLEON."

To GENERAL CLARKE.

"CHARTRES, 23rd *February*, 1814.

"Write to Marshal Soult that with his fine troops he ought to beat the Duke of Wellington, but that under present circumstances a little more decision and vigour are necessary. " NAPOLEON."

[1] It is a pity that Napoleon did not reflect upon this before, in opposition to the advice of Talleyrand, he imposed degrading conditions upon Austria, as well as upon all the other countries which he overran and subdued, and also before he imposed his continental system, which was degrading for every country in Europe. That Napoleon was right in what he now said was proved by the alacrity with which his yoke was cast off as soon as an opportunity offered.

In a letter to King Joseph, of the same date, the Emperor scolded him for taking so gloomy a view of affairs. He afterwards said—"As for the idea of doubling the National Guard, since you disapprove of it, I renounce that measure. If I had listened to my ministers I should not have created a National Guard, and I should have distrusted Paris. . . . I have had Augereau written to. I have told the Empress to speak to his wife. I think that you will do well to speak to her also, and to get the 'ladies of the palace' to speak to her. He must march; let him do as I do, and gain honour. The enemy are falling back in all directions, and seem no longer to dream of Paris. Prince Liechtenstein, aide-de-camp to Prince Schwartzenberg, with whom I have had a long conversation, has allowed it to escape that the allies are greatly frightened by the movement of Augereau."

It is certain, to judge from an extract from a letter addressed to Comte de Montalivet, Minister of the Interior, that Napoleon was now well aware of the state of public opinion, which was decidedly in favour of peace. He wrote, on the road to Troyes, on the 24th:— "I have received your letter. If the French were as despicable as you suppose I should blush for shame. You and the Minister of Police know no more of France than I know of China." And he added—"Orleans was threatened yesterday; to-day Platoff is turned, and will perhaps escape with difficulty. Thus at any moment all these alarms may disappear." Napoleon, on his side, was endeavouring to excite resistance by continually referring to the horrors committed by the enemy, and warning the country what it might expect at the hands of the Cossacks. At the same time he had resumed his old confidence, for the main body of the allies was retiring in disorder before him. On the 24th, in fact, the Emperor received from Prince Schwartzenberg proposals for an armistice. These proposals he accepted; Lusigny was the place appointed for the negotiations, and the following instructions were given to General Flahault, who was charged to represent France:—"Flahault will go to Lusigny to negotiate, conclude, and sign an armistice between the two armies. It must be understood that during the conferences there is to be no armistice. . . . I cannot agree to an armistice until I am certain of peace. I cannot be certain of peace until the allies have consented to the bases proposed at Frankfort. . . . General Flahault must speak with politeness but firmly, and say—We know the forces of the enemy, but they do not know ours; every day we receive 10,000 men from Paris clothed and equipped, 2,000 being for the cavalry; our army is 300,000 strong. The Old Guard, which is composed of men who have at least sixteen years service, has been tripled, and formed into three divisions of sixteen battalions each; all the men who had left the Guard have been called upon to rejoin, and it now consists of 30,000 men. It is true that we have 50,000 men who are not in uniform, but their effects are about to arrive. . . . The horrors committed by the Cossacks have excited the population to the highest degree, and the whole country is in arms. Therefore we believe that all the chances are in our favour, and it is only our determination to make peace on the bases of Frankfort which can induce us to agree to a suspension of arms. . . ."

On the evening of the same day Napoleon wrote to King Joseph, saying:—"I have entered Troyes. The enemy besiege me with demands for an armistice. . . . I have had several cavalry affairs, and have captured 2,000 prisoners and eight guns. I have written to the Empress to have a salute of thirty guns fired in honour of these little events and the delivery of the capital of Champagne. . . . If I had had twenty boats to cross the Seine the Austrian army would no longer exist. A few days ago the enemy thought that I had no army; now their imagination runs wild, and 400,000 men are not sufficient for me. . . . This is what comes of terror. It is necessary for the Paris newspapers to write in the sense of these fears. The newspapers are no more history than are the bulletins. One should always lead the enemy to believe that one has immense forces. . . ."[1]

On the 25th the Emperor, writing from Troyes, sent instructions to General Clarke for Marshal Soult to resume the offensive and to fall upon one of the wings of the enemy. "Should he have only 20,000 men, by selecting the right moment and acting with boldness, he should," said his Majesty, "gain an advantage over the English army. He has talent enough to understand what I mean."

Blucher was once more to be placed, thanks to the Czar, in command of a formidable army, which was to march upon Paris. It had been agreed that the army of Silesia, reinforced by the corps of Winsingerode, Woronsow, and Bulow, detached from the forces under the command of Bernadotte, should push forward to the French capital.

In another letter, written by Napoleon on the 24th February, he said to King Joseph—"As soon as I can make out what Blucher is after I shall try and fall upon his rear. . . . It is said that Bernadotte is at Cologne. Could you not, on your own account, send some one to him to point out the madness of his conduct and to induce him to change it? Try this, but without mixing me up in the matter." Joseph and Bernadotte were brothers-in-law.

And the next day, in another letter to King Joseph, the Emperor said—"It appears that the allies have not yet ratified the treaty with the King of Naples. I beg that you will send some one in hot haste to the king; that you will write to him frankly on the iniquity of his conduct, offering to be his intermediary. . . . I need hardly tell you what to say. The English themselves do not

[1] In a letter from Napoleon to Joseph, 10th December, 1809, which is given in the *Memoirs of King Joseph*, the Emperor said : "Military men whose opinion is of value judge from what they know, and pay little attention to orders of the day, proclamations, &c."

acknowledge him as king. There is still time to save Italy and to re-establish the viceroy on the Adige. Write also to the queen on her ingratitude, which disgusts even the allies. . . ."

On the 27th Napoleon wrote thus to Caulaincourt, who was still at the Congress of Châtillon:—"I am going to Arcis-sur-Aube, as Blucher, York, Winzingerode, and other reinforcements are marching on Ferté Gaucher. I am going to fall upon their rear. . . . You must say that I am at Bar-sur-Aube, for it is of the greatest importance that the enemy should not know that I am between Bar-sur-Aube and Vendeuve."

On the 2nd March the Emperor forwarded to Caulaincourt a declaration which he was to make at the Congress, and in which Napoleon repeated that in no case would France renounce her natural limits—the Rhine, the ocean, the Alps, and the Pyrenees. The instructions were long and arrogant, but at the same time Caulaincourt was told that he might tone them down.

On the previous day the allies had signed the treaty of Chaumont to this effect, that if Napoleon did not accept the terms which had been offered to him, viz., the reduction of France to the limits of the old monarchy, as before the Revolution, the four allied powers of Austria, Russia, Prussia, and England should each maintain 150,000 men in the field, and that England should provide an annual subsidy of 5,000,000*l.* to be equally divided between the three Continental Powers, &c., &c.

This treaty virtually dissolved the negotiations at Lusigny and the Congress at Châtillon, for Napoleon obstinately refused to entertain the idea of accepting the France of Louis XIV.[1]

---

[1] Concerning this Congress of Châtillon, Lord Holland, who was certainly no adversary of Napoleon, has written as follows in his *Reminiscences* (p. 294) :—"I have seen the official correspondence with Caulaincourt when he was employed at Châtillon in 1814. It gave me the highest opinion of the abilities, integrity, and pacific

To GENERAL CLARKE.

"JOUARRE, 2nd March, 1814.

"Write to Marshal Soult that with troops like his he should beat the enemy, if he will only exhibit pluck and place himself at the head of the troops. Let him understand that we have reached a period when more than ordinary resolution and vigour are required. If he manœuvres with activity and sets the example of being the first at the post of danger, he should, with the troops he has, beat double the number of the enemy.

"NAPOLEON."

To VICE-ADMIRAL DÉCRÊS.

"JOUARRE, 2nd March, 1814.

"I have seen with pleasure the conduct of the three ships. It is my intention to give the crews forty decorations of the legion of honour, twenty-five of them for the *Romulus*. Express my satisfaction to the officers in command.

"The English papers talk of some rich prizes captured by our frigates which sailed from Nantes; it appears that one of these was recaptured on arriving in French waters.

"NAPOLEON."

His Majesty, as far as the navy was concerned, had to be thankful for small mercies.

principles of the negotiator. It did not, I confess, raise my opinion of the Emperor Napoleon. It was full of subterfuge and artifice on the part of the Government. There seemed an intention not only of violating faith with the confederates, but in case of need of disavowing and sacrificing the honour of the negotiator, who was serving his country with zeal, talent, and fidelity. Caulaincourt reasonably and honestly endeavoured to work on the predilections of Austria to procure good terms of peace for Napoleon, but that prince and his immediate advisers were more disposed to avail themselves of any favourable disposition in Austria to sow dissensions."

According to James a French squadron of three ships of the line and three frigates had gone out of Toulon to meet a seventy-four expected from Genoa. This squadron was chased by Admiral Pellew's fleet, and the leading British vessel, the *Boyne*, ninety-eight, engaged the *Romulus*, the enemy's rear ship. The *Romulus*, however, managed to effect her escape, although she lost seventy men in killed or wounded, and the *Adrienne*, who was also under fire, eleven. "The *Romulus*," says James, "was undoubtedly manœuvred in a very skilful manner, and her captain, whose name we regret not being able to give, deserves credit as well for that as for not striking his colours to so powerful an adversary as the *Boyne*." The *Romulus*, be it mentioned, was protected by the French batteries, and ran so close in shore that the *Boyne* could not cut her off.

In a second letter written to King Joseph on the 2nd March the Emperor said :—" The bridge at La Ferté will be re-established this evening. At midnight I shall be in pursuit of the enemy. They are said to be in difficulties in the mud. . . . I ask night and day for pontoons; this is my great want, for the army of Schwartzenberg would have been destroyed if I had possessed pontoons at Méry, and that of Blucher if I had possessed them here. I am preparing to carry the war into Lorraine, where I shall rally all the troops who are in the fortresses of the Meuse and the Rhine."

On the 4th March Napoleon in another letter to his brother complained bitterly of the inactivity of General Maison in Holland, and of Marshal Augereau at Lyons. Writing to the Minister of War, too, he said : "I see that Marshal Soult has allowed his position to be forced. Let me know how many troops he has under his orders. I cannot conceive such results. Send instructions to Marshal Moncey and General Dejean to make a flank march to cover the Garonne. The English will not advance as long as they fear being cut off. I cannot conceive how, with troops like his, Marshal Soult has been beaten. Write to him strongly and firmly. He already committed a great fault in allowing himself to be attacked. . . ."

It was not until the 4th March that Napoleon took any notice of the engagement at Bar-sur-Aube. He then wrote to King Joseph complaining of the false rumours circulated, and adding: "The fact is that Bar-sur-Aube was not a position to hold. It was necessary to advance or to retire. After the movement which I made on the Marne it was necessary to retire. We had an affair in which we lost 700 or 800 men, but the enemy lost double that number, and we evacuated the town during the night." The fact is that as soon as Napoleon left Troyes a force of 35,000 men, under Generals Wittgenstein and Wrede, fell upon Oudinot, who had only 17,000 men under his command. The French made a gallant resistance, but they were driven out of Bar-sur-Aube with a loss of 3,000 men. The loss of the allies was nearly as heavy.

A few days afterwards Schwartzenberg inflicted a sharp defeat upon Marshal Macdonald, driving him out of Troyes with the loss of 3,000 men and nine guns.

To MARSHAL BERTHIER.

"FISMES, 4*th March*, 1814."

"Write to Soissons to inform General Moreau, who commands there, that I have reached Fismes, and to tell him to send me news of Marshals Marmont and Mortier, who were to march upon Soissons. He must also tell me what he knows of the movements of the enemy.

"NAPOLEON."

Alas, Soissons had capitulated on the 3rd, and on the 4th, the day upon which the above letter was written, Blucher, who was in great difficulties and threatened with utter destruction, managed, thanks to the capitulation of

Soissons, to get across the Aisne and effect his junction with Bulow and Winzingerode. This Soissons incident had an immense influence on the fate of the campaign. Baron Jean Claude Moreau was condemned to death by court-martial, but the sentence was not carried out.

To KING JOSEPH.

"FISMES, 5*th March*, 1814.

"Put the following note in the *Moniteur*.

"'The Emperor had his head-quarters on the 5th at Berry-au-Bac. The army of the enemy under Blucher, Sacken, York, Bulow, and Winzingerode were retreating; but for the treason of the commandant of Soissons, who opened its gates, they were lost. General Corbineau entered Rheims on the 5th. We have beaten the enemy in the actions of Lizy-sur-Ourcq and of May, capturing 4,000 prisoners, with guns and baggage.'

"NAPOLEON."

In a second letter of the same date the Emperor said :—

"The general who commanded at Soissons had the infamy to evacuate the place without firing a shot. He withdrew with all the honours of war; he is now at Villers-Cotterets. I have sent orders to the War Minister to arrest him, to have him tried by court-martial, and executed. He must be shot in the middle of the Place de Grève, and a great deal of importance must be given to this execution. Five generals must be appointed to try him. This affair has done us incalculable harm. I should have been at Laon to-day, and the army of the enemy would have been dispersed. . . ."

On the evening of the 5th Napoleon wrote to General Clarke, saying :—

"Winzingerode's corps wished to hinder us from passing the Aisne, but we crossed the handsome bridge at the double at Berry-au-Bac. We captured Prince Gargarine, who commanded the rear guard. This is a little set off for the great harm done by the treason of the commandant of Soissons."

The next day his Majesty, in a letter to the general, said :—

"You all think in Paris that France is lost ; but when one sees the disposition of the peasants and of the people one does not share this idea. It would be impossible to be more satisfied than I am with all the peasants, who only ask for vengeance and to rush to arms. . . . The army which is at Troyes experienced no check. The action of Bar-sur-Aube was an ordinary one, where the enemy lost as many men as we did. . . . The enemy have lost heavily; the peasants kill a great many men. . . . Order General Maison to take the field. Reiterate orders to General Durutte at Metz, to General Morand at Mayence, and to other generals to do the same."

TO KING JOSEPH.

"L'ANGE GARDIEN, 8*th March*, 1814.

"Yesterday I beat Winzingerode, Langeron, and Woronsow, united, with the remains of Sacken's army. I made 2,000 prisoners. The battle of Craonne is glorious. Marshals Victor and Grouchy were wounded. I have 700 or 800 killed or wounded. The loss of the enemy is from 5,000 to 6,000 men. . . .[1]

"NAPOLEON."

---

[1] The following letter describes the effect which the movements of the allies created in Paris, which was evidently alive to the danger of the situation :—

JOSEPH TO NAPOLEON.

"PARIS, 9*th March*, 1814.

"I received news of the victory of Craonne from Marshal Macdonald. . . . Detachments of the enemy have advanced even to Coulommiers.

"Yesterday the funds fell to fifty-one francs. The movements of the enemy against Marshal Soult cause the greatest alarm for Bordeaux, which would easily become the focus of a civil war.

"After the new victory which you have gained you might sign a

Such was the brief and false account given by the Emperor of one of the most stubborn fights on record. The Russians had 21,000 and the French 29,000 men engaged. Napoleon in this case did not over-estimate the loss of the enemy, but he greatly under-estimated his own. The Russians occupied a very strong position, and before they retired from it upon Laon the French had lost, not 700 or 800, but 7,000 or 8,000 men.

His Majesty does not appear to have written any letter on the 9th March, but on the 10th, having reached Chavignon, he bethought himself once more of Pius VII., and sent the following orders to Savary:—

"... Write to the officer of gendarmes, who is attached to the Pope, to take him by Asti, Tortona, and Placentia, to Parma, where he must hand him over to the Neapolitan outposts. The officer must inform the Holy Father that I have consented to his demand to return to his See, and that I have given orders for him to be handed over to the Neapolitan outposts."[1]

This was a bad symptom.

glorious peace with our ancient limits. ... There would be nothing dishonouring, as France would lose no territory. ... After having saved France from anarchy and from Europe coalesced against us, you will become the father of your people, and you will be as beloved as Louis XII., after having been as much admired as Henri IV. and Louis XIV. In order to accumulate so much glory it is necessary only to desire the welfare of France and your own."

The Emperor sent no reply to this last appeal.

A few days before Joseph had written thus to the chief of the staff:—

JOSEPH TO BERTHIER.

"5th March, 1814.

"... The news you send is always good, and a great deal of it is required to counterbalance the bad effect produced by the retreat of Marshal Soult, of Marshal Oudinot, and the fall of Soissons!"

[1] "The following anecdote," says Colonel Baudus (*Études sur Napoléon*, vol. i. p. 57), "will give an idea of the deplorable state in which the chief of Christendom found himself; at the same time, it will prove into what hands he was exposed to fall when forced to

To KING JOSEPH.
"CHAVIGNON, 10*th March*, 1814.

"The army which I beat at Craonne was the Russian army. It lost heavily, and fell back upon Laon, where it was joined by the corps of Bulow, York, and Kleist, forming the Prussian army. The position of Laon was very favourable to them, and I contented myself yesterday in observing and reconnoitring it. This army is more dangerous for Paris than the army of Schwartzenberg. However, I am going to approach Soissons so as to be nearer to Paris. ... Marshal Marmont, who was marching from Berry-au-Bac to Laon, has arrived. He constantly drove off the enemy, but at night there was a raid made on his corps which threw his infantry into disorder: the soldiers lost their heads, and he was obliged to fall back for several leagues in slight disorder, and abandoning several guns. This is merely an accident of war, but very unfortunate at a moment when I required good luck. It is this which has determined me not to attack to-day. ...

"NAPOLEON."

And the next day his Majesty wrote once more to King Joseph, saying :—

"I reconnoitred the enemy's position at Laon. It was too strong to be attacked without heavy loss. I have therefore made up my mind to return to Soissons.[1] It is

make a long and dangerous voyage. On arriving at a station at the foot of the Alps, where his escort was to be changed, the commandant who had conducted him thus far, in accordance with orders, claimed a receipt from the officer called upon to replace him in this odious mission. This officer, alarmed at the fearful state in which the august captive was handed over to him, and persuaded that he would die on the road, protested against the inhumanity of torturing a dying man ; and resigned himself to take charge of him only after drawing up the receipt exacted from him in these accusing terms—'Received, a Pope in a very bad condition.'"

[1] Evacuated by the allies after Craonne.

probable that the enemy would have evacuated Laon, through fear of being attacked, but for the accident to Marmont, who behaved like a sub-lieutenant.[1] The enemy have suffered enormous losses. Yesterday they attacked the village of Clacy five times, and were constantly repulsed.

"The Young Guard melts away like snow. The Old Guard resists. My Mounted Guard also melts away a good deal. . . . You must give orders for the redoubts at Montmartre to be commenced."

From Soissons, on the 12th, the Emperor with his own hand wrote as follows to King Joseph :—

"I regret that you have spoken to my wife of the Bourbons, and of the propositions which the Emperor of Austria may make to them. I beg that you will avoid these conversations. I do not wish to be protected by my wife. This idea would spoil her, and would make us disagree. And why speak to her thus? Allow her to live as she lives; speak to her only about matters which she must sign, and above all, avoid anything which can lead her to suppose that I can consent to be protected by her or by her father. Never, during four years, has the word Bourbon or Austria been pronounced by me. Besides, that can only disturb her repose and spoil her excellent temper.

"You always write as if peace depended upon me; and yet I have sent you all the documents. If the Parisians wish to see the Cossacks they will repent of it; but still they must be told the truth.

"I have never sought the applause of the Parisians. I am not a character in an opera. Besides, one must be more practical than you are in order to know the opinion

---

[1] Marmont, in this nocturnal attack on his camp, lost forty guns and 131 caissons; not many men were killed, but 2,500 prisoners were made, and the whole corps was dispersed and utterly disorganised.

of Paris, which has nothing to do with the passions of three or four thousand persons who make a great noise. It would be simple, and more expeditious, to declare that you cannot make a levy.

"The Emperor of Austria can do nothing because he is weak and led by Metternich, who is in the pay of England: this is the secret of everything. I embrace you.

"NAPOLEON."

It is estimated that at Craonne, Soissons, and Laon the French lost 16,000 men, and their position was now more desperate than ever.

TO KING JOSEPH.

"SOISSONS, 13*th March*, 1814.

"Before commencing the fortifications of Paris the plan must be known, that which has been presented to me appears to be very complicated; more simplicity is required.

"I receive complaints from all quarters against the mayors and the *bourgeois*, who prevent the people from defending themselves. I see the same thing in Paris. The people possess energy and honour. I fear that there be certain chiefs who do not wish to fight. After the event they will look very foolish at what will happen to them.

"NAPOLEON."

TO KING JOSEPH.

"RHEIMS, 14*th March*, 1814.

"I have arrived at Rheims, which General St. Priest had occupied with three Russian divisions and a Prussian division which had just arrived from Stettin. I beat them; I retook the town, 20 guns, a great deal of baggage, and made 5,000 prisoners. General St. Priest was mortally wounded. What is remarkable is that General St. Priest was hit by the same pointer who killed General Moreau. One may well exclaim, 'Providence! Providence!'

"NAPOLEON."

The capture of Rheims with a dispirited army, which had just met with a heavy reverse, has been justly considered as an admirable military exploit. St. Priest, knowing what had happened to Marmont's corps, insisted for some time in believing that he was being attacked by the remnant of that force; and it was not until he saw the bearskins of the Guard that he became aware of the presence of Napoleon. Taken by surprise and overmatched, the allies seem to have lost 3,500 men, and the French only 800 in this affair.

To MARSHAL MARMONT.

"RHEIMS, 15*th March*, 1814.

"Marshal Mortier writes that—'The enemy are in full retreat, and seem to be falling back upon Laon. I have sent some cavalry to follow their march, which is being made in good order.'. . Send some peasants to try and find out if the enemy are in force at Craonne. . . . Try and recruit men in the villages by writing to the mayors to furnish so many men, and by sending officers and soldiers to recruit. A great many peasants who have been ruined ask for nothing better than to serve. . . .

"NAPOLEON."

The remains of St. Priest's corps did fall back upon Laon, and joined Blucher, who then found himself at the head of 109,000 men, of whom 29,000 were cavalry, and 265 guns.

In spite of his success at Rheims, Napoleon must have considered his position almost hopeless, to judge from the following letter.

To KING JOSEPH.

"RHEIMS, 16*th March*, 1814.

"In conformity with the verbal instructions which I gave you, and with the spirit of my letters, you must, under no circumstances, allow the Empress and the King of Rome to fall into the hands of the enemy. I am going to manœuvre in such a way that you will possibly have no news of me for several days. If the enemy advance upon Paris in such strength that resistance is impossible, send away the Regent, my son, the high dignitaries, the ministers, the officers of the Senate, the Presidents of the Council of State, the grand officers of the Crown, the Baron de la Bouillerie, and the treasure. Do not abandon my son, and remember that I should sooner know him in the Seine than in the hands of the enemies of France. The fate of Astyanax, prisoner among the Greeks, has always appeared to me as the most unfortunate in history.

"NAPOLEON."

To KING JOSEPH.

"RHEIMS, 17*th March*, 1814.

"I have received news that the enemy are falling back in the direction of Nogent. . . . I shall manœuvre according to the intelligence that I receive. . . . See the Regent, Cambacérès, and the War Minister. Find out where the 10,000 men of Marshal Suchet are, and forward 5,000 or 6,000 men by post to the Dordogne. All the forces that can be drawn from Rochefort and the cavalry depots beyond the Loire must be concentrated there, so that, Marshal Soult resuming the offensive and drawing Wellington away, our troops may re-enter Bordeaux. As this is a matter requiring resolution, a safe man must be found to take the command. You might send Suchet himself orders to take the command of the army, which can be called the Army of the Garonne. . . .

"NAPOLEON."

To GENERAL CAULAINCOURT, AT CHATILLON.

"RHEIMS, 17*th March*, 1814.

"I have received your letters of the 13th. I have directed M. Maret to reply to you in detail. I give you authority to make such concessions as may be indispensable for keeping up the negotiations so as to learn the *ultimatum* of the allies; of course the treaty must have for result the evacuation of our territory and the liberation of the prisoners made on both sides.

"NAPOLEON."

On the same day the Emperor wrote to General Clarke to this effect—" To-morrow I am going to march to Arcis-sur-Aube, and from thence to Mèry or to Troyes, in order to fall upon the rear of the enemy. . . . Blucher, who has evidently suffered heavily, will not be able, most probably, to march for two days, and then, as he will have the Aisne to cross, Marmont and Mortier will be there to dispute the passage. The movement which I am making will cause great embarrassment in the enemy's rear. . . ."

What really accounted for Blucher's inactivity was his serious illness—he was unable to mount on horseback during the remainder of the campaign; his army too was suffering from exhaustion and the difficulty of procuring food. In a letter to Winzingerode the old field-marshal said—" The object of our stay here is not a military one. The only design I have in view is to give repose to a harassed army, and, as far as possible, to provide it with bread."

On the 18th the Emperor wrote to King Joseph to tell him that he was marching on Arcis, and that he had opened up communications with Metz and Verdun, which places were going to furnish him with 12,000 men.

TO KING JOSEPH.

"PLANCY, 20*th March*, 1814. 6 A.M.

"Yesterday I crossed the Aube at Plancy, and at once marched upon Mèry. I attacked the town, which was carried at 7 P.M. . . . The Emperor Alexander was at Arcis on the 18th. He remained there only a hour; we were nearly face to face. He returned to Troyes, which was at once evacuated by the general headquarters. . . . The enemy are flying in all directions. . . . Put the inclosed note in the *Moniteur*.

"NAPOLEON."

NOTE.

"The enemy who crossed the Seine at Pont and at Nogent, having learned that the Emperor, master of Rheims and of Chalons, was marching on their rear, commenced to retreat. The Emperor of Russia and the King of Prussia were with the column which was marching from Arcis-sur-Aube to Villenauxe; this column narrowly escaped being cut off. At the approach of the French army the Emperor of Russia hastily fell back on Troyes, from whence the headquarters of the Emperors were removed to Bar-sur-Aube."

To MARSHAL BERTHIER.

"CHÂTEAU DU PLESSIS, 23*rd March*, 1814. 3 A.M.

"Send a gendarme in disguise to Metz, one to Bar, and another to Nancy, with letters to the mayors. Tell them that we are marching on the rear of the enemy; that the moment has come to rise *en masse*, to sound the tocsin, to arrest the commandants and the commissioners of the enemy, to fall upon the convoys, &c. . . .

"NAPOLEON."

The fact is that, on learning the approach of Napoleon, the allies, thanks to the energy displayed by the Czar, at once concentrated, and the consequence was that the French Emperor, instead of falling on the rear of a flying enemy, speedily found himself, not only confronted, but attacked, by the grand allied army. A desperate engagement ensued, which lasted with varied success on each side all through the 21st. The battle may be said to have been drawn; the losses on both sides were equal, but on the 22nd Napoleon fell back, and this retrograde movement, which strongly contrasted with the news forwarded to Paris, greatly damaged the prestige of the Emperor.

Napoleon had no time for writing on the 21st, but on the 22nd he wrote to Clarke telling him to give orders for a convoy of eighty waggons, on the road to Arcis, to stop at Sézanne; that the enemy were at Arcis, and that he was marching to St. Dizier, where he was about to try and stop the advance of Schwartzenberg by throwing himself on his rear and threatening his communications.

Upon the same day the Emperor, much perplexed, wrote a second letter from Sézanne to the Minister of War, saying—" My outposts are in the vicinity of Vitry; it is said that the town is well fortified and prepared to defend itself. In that case I shall throw a bridge over the river at Frignicourt, and shall march on St. Dizier."

The commandant at Vitry having declined to surrender that town in spite of the threat of the garrison being put to the sword, Napoleon turned aside and continued his fatal march on St. Dizier, leaving 180,000 men between Paris and himself, for Blucher at this moment formed his junction with Schwartzenberg.

On the 23rd March, at 10 A.M., the Emperor sent a despatch to Marshal Ney in which he said—" Having learned that the Emperor Alexander slept at Montierender, I am going to St. Dizier, because I suppose that it is at that point that he wishes to attack us. . . . If the enemy wish to interfere with my movement, it is upon St. Dizier that they will march to-morrow."

The allies adopted a very different resolution, that of pushing forward to Paris.

On the 23rd the Emperor also wrote to the Treasurer of the Crown telling him to pay the Empress Josephine in future by instalments, 15,000 francs a month, and to pay all salaries over 120*l.* a year in the same way. " I suppose," he added, " that you have ceased paying for building, furniture, &c."

For several days Napoleon was in ignorance of the

intentions of the allies. On the 27th he announced to Berthier his intention of attacking Vitry and carrying that place by assault. After this letter comes a silence of three days during which Napoleon was hurrying back to defend the capital, only to hear at ten o'clock on the evening of the 30th, on approaching Fontainebleau, that Paris had capitulated. He at once determined to try and re-open negotiations.

To GENERAL CAULAINCOURT.

"LA COUR DE FRANCE, 30*th March*, 1814.

"We order the Duc de Vicence, our Master of the Horse and Minister of Foreign Affairs, to go to the allied sovereigns and to the general-in-chief of the allied armies, to recommend our faithful subjects of the capital to them.

"We invest him for the present with power to negotiate and to conclude peace, promising to ratify anything that he may sign for the good of our service.

"In case of necessity, we also invest him with military powers. . . .

"NAPOLEON."

In a letter to Berthier, dated from Fontainebleau, 31st March, Napoleon instructed the Marshal to write to the Prefect of Orleans—" To announce the unfortunate news of the occupation of Paris by the enemy, which my arrival would have prevented had it been delayed for three hours. Warn him of the concentration which is about to take place at Orleans, and direct him to prepare provisions for the troops. . . . Send a courier this evening to Tours [1] to announce our plans to King Joseph and to his ministers. . . ."

On the 1st April the Emperor, who still dreamed of resisting, wrote a series of military orders. There is no

[1] Whither Joseph had fled with Marie Louise, the King of Rome, &c.

letter or despatch in *The Correspondence* on the 2nd April, but on the 3rd we find under—

ALLOCUTION TO THE OLD GUARD.

"Officer, sub-officers, and soldiers of the Old Guard! The enemy stole three marches upon us. They have entered Paris. I offered the Emperor Alexander a peace purchased by great sacrifices; France, within her ancient limits, giving up all ideas of conquest, and losing all that she gained since the Revolution. Not only did he refuse it, he went further; at the suggestions of some perfidious *émigrés*, whose lives I spared, and whom I loaded with favours, he has authorised them to wear the white cockade, and soon it will be substituted for our national cockade. In a few days I shall march to attack Paris. I count upon you." (There was silence. The Emperor resumed.) "Am I right?" (Suddenly there were shouts of "*Vive l'Empereur! À Paris!*" Then the Old Guard were silent, thinking it useless to reply.) "We will go and prove that the French know how to be masters at home; that, if we have long been masters abroad, we shall always remain so in our own country; and, finally, that we are capable of defending our cockade, our independence, and the integrity of our territory."

To MARSHAL BERTHIER.

"FONTAINEBLEAU, 4*th April*, 1814.

"Send orders to Marshals Marmont, Mortier, Oudinot, and Serrurier, and to Generals Belliard, Gérard, Sorbier, Sebastiani, &c., &c., to come to the palace this evening at ten o'clock, and to adopt measures so that they may be back at their posts before daybreak.

"NAPOLEON."

DECLARATION OF THE 4TH APRIL, 1814.

"The allied Powers having proclaimed that the Emperor Napoleon is the sole obstacle to the re-establishment of peace in Europe, the Emperor Napoleon, faithful to his oath, declares that he is ready to descend from the throne, to leave France, and even to die, for the welfare of the country, which cannot be separated from the rights of his son, those of the Regency, of the Empress, and the maintenance of the laws of the Empire."

On the 5th the Emperor issued a series of orders to Berthier in connection with his proposed march upon Paris; but they could not be executed in consequence of the defection of Marmont, who was in command of the sixth corps. Later on in the day he issued this proclamation—

TO THE ARMY.

"The Emperor thanks the army for the attachment which it has shown to him, and chiefly because it recognises that France is on his side and not with the people of the capital.[1] The soldier follows the fortune and the misfortune of his general; his honour is his religion. Marshal Marmont has not inspired his comrades with these sentiments; he has gone over to the allies. The Emperor cannot approve of the condition upon which he has taken this step; he cannot accept life and liberty at the hands of a subject.[2]

"The Senate has permitted itself to dispose of the French Government: it forgets that it owes to the Emperor the power it now abuses; that it was the Emperor who saved a portion of its members from the storms of the Revolution, and who drew from obscurity and protected the other portion from the hatred of the nation. The Senate makes use of the articles of the Constitution in order to overthrow the Constitution. It does not blush to

---

[1] The allied troops had just been received with the greatest enthusiasm in Paris, where they were hailed as liberators, amid shouts of "Vive Alexander!" and "Vive le Roi de Prusse!"

[2] Marmont, previous to his defection, obtained the assurance that the life of the Emperor was in no danger, and that there was no intention of treating him with harshness.

reproach the Emperor, without remarking that, as the first body in the State, it took part in all that has happened. It has even been bold enough to accuse the Emperor of having altered official documents; every one knows that he did not require to resort to such artifices; a sign was an order for the Senate, which always did more than was desired of it. The Emperor was always accessible to the remonstrances of his ministers, and he expected from them, on the present occasion, the most undeniable justification of his measures. If enthusiasm was mingled with addresses and public discourses, then the Emperor was deceived; but those who held this language should attribute to themselves the consequences of their flattery. The Senate does not blush to speak of libels published against foreign governments; it forgets that they were drawn up in its centre. As long as fortune showed itself faithful to their sovereign, these men remained faithful, and no complaints were made respecting an abuse of power. If the Emperor had despised men, as he is reproached with doing, every one will acknowledge to-day that there exist good reasons for his contempt.[1] He holds his dignity from God and from the nation: they alone can deprive him of it; he has always considered the throne as a burden, and, when he accepted it, it was in the conviction that he alone was able to fill it worthily.

"The welfare of France appeared to be linked with the destiny of the Emperor. Now that fortune has decided against him, the will of the nation can alone persuade him to remain upon the throne. If he is to consider himself as the sole obstacle to peace, he will willingly make this last sacrifice to France. He has consequently sent Marshal Ney, Marshal Macdonald, and General Caulaincourt to Paris to open negotiations. The army may rest assured that the honour of the Emperor will never be in contradiction with the welfare of France."

[1] " Plus vil que le pourceau qui dans l'égout se vautre,
    Son sénat, qui l'avait adoré, l'insultait."—VICTOR HUGO.

ACT OF ABDICATION.

"The allied Powers having proclaimed that the Emperor Napoleon Bonaparte is the only obstacle to the re-establishment of peace in Europe, the Emperor Napoleon, faithful to his oath, declares that he renounces, for himself and his heirs, the thrones of France and Italy, and that there is no personal sacrifice, even that of his life, which he is not ready to make in the interest of France.

". Done at the Palace of Fontainebleau, 11th April, 1814."

No more letters until the 19th, with the exception of the following, written on the 13th, to one of his favourite aides-de-camp :—

"GENERAL CORBINEAU,—I cannot leave you without expressing the satisfaction I have constantly derived from your services. You will uphold the good opinion I have formed of you by serving the new sovereign of France with the same fidelity and the same devotion which you have shown towards me.

"NAPOLEON."

"FONTAINEBLEAU, 19*th April*, 1814.

"MY GOOD LOUISE,—I have received your letter, and see all your pain, which increases mine. I perceive with pleasure that Corvisart encourages you. I am infinitely obliged to him; he justifies by this noble conduct the high opinion I always entertained of him. Tell him this from me, and let him send me frequent bulletins concerning your state of health. Try and go as soon as possible to the waters at Aix, which, they tell me, Corvisart has advised you to take. Take care of yourself and preserve your health for [blank in the text], and for your son, who requires your care. I am about to start for the island of Elba, from which place I will write to you. I shall do all in my power to see you again.

"Write to me often, and address your letters to the

viceroy and to your uncle, if, as they say, he has been made Grand Duke of Tuscany.

"Adieu, my good Marie Louise.

"NAPOLEON."

It is strange that Napoleon should have written the above letter on the day he endeavoured to poison himself!

TO THE EMPRESS MARIE LOUISE.

"FONTAINEBLEAU, 20*th April*, 1814. 9 A.M.

"MY GOOD FRIEND,—I am starting in order to sleep at Briare this evening. I shall leave that place to-morrow morning, and shall not stop until I reach St. Tropez. Beausset, who will hand you this letter, will give you news of me, tell you that I am in good health, and that I hope your health will hold up, and that you will come and join me. Montesquieu, who started at 2 A.M., should have arrived. I received no news of you yesterday, but I hope that the prefect of the palace will overtake me this evening and give me some. Adieu, my good Louise. You can always reckon upon the courage, the calm, and the friendship of your husband.[1]   "NAPOLEON."

FAREWELL TO THE GUARD.

"SOLDIERS OF THE OLD GUARD,—I bid you farewell. For the last twenty years I have constantly found you on the road of honour and glory. Recently, as in the days of prosperity, you showed yourselves to be models of bravery and fidelity. With men like you our cause was not lost; but war would have become interminable; there would have been civil war, and France would have been all the more unfortunate. I have therefore sacrificed all our interests to those of the country. I leave. You, my friends, must

---

[1] A note in *The Correspondence* says that the above letter was confided to M. de Beausset, one of the prefects of the palace, who, being unable to overtake Marie Louise, kept it. It is in Napoleon's handwriting, and forms part of a collection of autographs belonging to M. de la Jarriette.

continue to serve France. Her happiness was my only thought; it will always be the object of my wishes. Do not pity my fate; if I have consented to survive, it is to be useful to your glory: I wish to write the great things that we have done together! Farewell, my children! I would willingly press you all to my heart; allow me at least to embrace your standard! . . . " (At these words General Petit, seizing an eagle, advanced. Napoleon received the general in his arms and kissed the colours. The silence which this grand scene inspired was broken only by the sobs of the soldiers. Napoleon, making a visible effort to stifle his emotion, continued with a firm voice:)

"Farewell once more, my old comrades! Let this last kiss pass into your hearts!"

"*20th April*, 1814."

To GENERAL COUNT DALESME.[1]

"FREJUS, *27th April*, 1814.

"Circumstances having induced me to renounce the throne of France, sacrificing my rights to the interests of the country, I reserved for myself the sovereignty of the island of Elba, which has met with the consent of all the Powers. I therefore send you General Drouot so that you may hand over to him the said island, with the military stores and provisions, and the property which belongs to my imperial domain. Be good enough to make known this new state of affairs to the inhabitants, and the choice which I have made of their island for my sojourn in consideration of the mildness of their manners, and the excellence of their climate. I shall take the greatest interest in their welfare.[2]

"NAPOLEON."

---

[1] Commandant of the island of Elba.

[2] Perhaps Joseph Philip Arrighi, canon of Pisa and Florence, and vicar of Ajaccio, Elba, and Piombino, had seen this letter when he

To BARON CORVISART.

"FREJUS, 28*th April*, 1814.

"I have received your letter of the 22nd April. Your conduct during recent times, when so many others behaved badly, has given me great pleasure. . I thank you, and this confirms the opinion I had conceived of your character. Give me news of Marie Louise, and never doubt my feelings towards you. Do not give yourself up to melancholy.

"NAPOLEON."

And on the 29th Napoleon wrote this brief note to M. Aune, who was attending Pauline Borghese at the castle of Luc in the Var—

"Your conduct towards my sister, and the attentions which you bestowed at a critical moment[1] on him who wished to make France the first nation in the world, but who did not succeed, fully entitle you to my gratitude.

"NAPOLEON."

Having been landed at Elba from the *Undaunted*, Captain Usher, the Emperor at once began to organise the island and to address letters and orders to General Count Drouot, the governor, and to General Count Bertrand, Grand Marshal of the Palace, in the same imperious penned the following pastoral with which he greeted Napoleon on his arrival at Elba. He wrote:—

"Divine Providence, who in His benevolence disposes irresistibly of things, and who assigns to nations their destinies, has pleased that in the midst of the political changes of Europe we should become in future the subjects of the Great Napoleon. The island of Elba, already celebrated for its natural productions, will henceforth be illustrious among the nations of the earth, owing to the homage rendered to its new prince, whose glory is immortal. The island of Elba assumes a rank among the Powers, and its little territory is ennobled by the name of its sovereign. Proud of this sublime honour, it receives into its bosom *the anointed of the Lord* and the other distinguished persons who accompany him."

[1] When poison was taken at Fontainebleau.

style as if they had been dictated at the Tuileries or St. Cloud.

In a long letter to General Drouot dated Porto Ferrajo, 7th May, his Majesty thus expressed himself—" You must find out from the sub-prefect in what the civil government of the country consists. Have the flag of the island run up in all the parishes on Sunday, and make a kind of holiday of that day. . . . The hoisting of the flag should be announced to Naples, Rome, Tuscany, and Genoa." And the Emperor then entered into a number of military, naval, and civil questions. The Grand Marshal was to settle the household expenses every week, even "a leaf of salad or a bunch of grapes should be mentioned." Under the head of "military organisation" are numerous details. The whole force at the disposal of the Emperor consisted of 1,523 men : or, first battalion 404 men ; battalion of Elba 400 men, Guard 400, Poles 80, gendarmes 19, veterans 20, gunners 109, sailors 100. It was the intention of Napoleon to lay in a store of meal, rice, biscuit, oil, and salt meat, together with wine and brandy, so as to be able to stand a siege at Porto Ferrajo.

To GENERAL BERTRAND.

"PORTO FERRAJO, 10*th June*, 1814.

"It is my intention to appoint the mayor of Porto Longone commandant of my palace at Porto Longone. He must perform the functions of commandant, *concierge*, keeper of the robes, and overseer of the gardens. He will receive a salary of 600 francs. . . .

"NAPOLEON."

In another letter dated Porto Ferrajo, 17th June, the Emperor said—"As the theatre is to be demolished some day, it is not my intention to do anything which will greatly increase the expenses ;" and a few days later— "I return you the plan of the house. . . . There is not room on the first floor for more than three apartments ; a large apartment of eight rooms, one of six rooms for the Empress, and another of three rooms. . . ."

NOTE FOR THE GRAND MARSHAL.

"Porto Ferrajo, 17*th July*, 1814.

"Write to my brother Lucien that I have received his letter of the 11th June; that I am pleased with the sentiments which he expresses; that he must not be astonished if he does not receive a reply from me, because I write to no one. I have not written even to Madame [his mother]."

In a letter of the 28th the Emperor said—"I keep up three schooners with sixteen sailors each, and a brig which has sixty. This naval force is necessary to watch the coasts, and to drive off the Algerian corsairs. . . ." And on the same day—"As I am not yet sufficiently well lodged to give *fêtes*, I shall await the arrival of the Empress and the Princess Pauline, whom I expect in the first days of September, to have fireworks. I wish the parish to pay the expenses of a ball to be given in the public square, where a ball-room in wood can be constructed, and the officers of the Imperial Guard be invited. In the neighbourhood of this ball-room an orchestra must be established for the soldiers to dance to, and the parish must take care to have some barrels of wine for them to drink. I also wish the parish to arrange the wedding of two young people whom it must endow. The Grand Marshal and the authorities must be present at this marriage, which must take place after high mass."

To GENERAL COMTE BERTRAND.

"Porto Ferrajo, 9*th August*, 1814.

"Colonel Laczinski, who is going to leave to-day for Leghorn, will go from there to Aix, and will take with him a letter from me to the Empress. Write to Meneval to inform him that I expect the Empress at the end of the month, that I wish her to send me my son, and that it is singular that I have no news of her, which comes from letters being intercepted; that this ridiculous order is probably due to some subaltern, and cannot come from her father; at all events, that no one has any authority over the Empress and my son. "NAPOLEON."

In another letter to General Bertrand the Emperor gave orders for the captain of the Guard, who was leaving the island, to "seize every opportunity of writing to Meneval and to Madame de Brignole, to give them news of me, to say that Madame Mère has arrived, and that I expect the Empress in September. . . . Give a month's leave to Captain Hureau, whose wife is in the service of the Empress. Let him sail this evening, go to Aix, or wherever the Empress may be. . . . I will receive him at four o'clock, and will give him instructions and letters."

To GENERAL COMTE BERTRAND, GRAND MARSHAL OF THE PALACE.

"LA MADONE, 23rd *August*, 1814.

" I arrived here at nine o'clock ; it is now five, and I am going out shooting. One does not feel the heat here. Two shutters are wanting for my bedroom ; try and send them to-morrow. Also send me two lanterns to put at the door of my tent. There are three iron beds here. I have ordered one to be brought from Marciana for Madame. There are fifteen mattresses, with blankets and sheets, which is all that is required. Madame can come to Marciana, if she likes, and lodge in the house of the mayor. She might start on Thursday, at 5 A.M. . . . Send on a *valet de chambre*, a footman and a lady's maid, a cook and Cipriani, to get her house and her breakfast ready. In the mayor's house Madame will have a room for herself and one for her ladies, one for her maids and one for her men servants. If the Sieur Colonna accompanies Madame he will be lodged in the town. In this house there is sufficient furniture. I have had a chest of drawers placed in her apartments. There is enough linen for both of us. Major Roul will be attached to me as orderly officer. His pay will be 200 francs a month. He will accompany Madame, as well as the chamberlain, Ventini. I think there are things enough for Madame's kitchen and mine. There are also candles and lights enough. The kitchen can be established in the house. Send three curtains for Madame's room. The rods are here. Send us also fire-irons, tongs, shovels, &c. I think those people are right who say that it is necessary to have fires of an evening.

"NAPOLEON.

"P.S. The *valet de chambre* has some stuff for making curtains, which he is going to take to Madame's house."

To GENERAL BERTRAND.

"LA MADONE, 26*th August*, 1814.

"I think that I asked you to write to the Princess Pauline not to bring her piano master with her, but only a good singer and a good songstress, seeing that we have here a good violin player and a good pianist.

"NAPOLEON."

And on the same day to the same address :—

"One of my mules was recently drowned, which is a loss; this was due to there not being a small pump in the stable; have one of those in store repaired."

It is difficult to imagine what kind of stable this could have been.

On the 28th the Emperor, seemingly in high glee, wrote to the Grand Marshal of his palace, saying—" Send off Beausset's courier, and tell De Beausset that I received news of the Empress up to the 10th, that I should have been charmed had he come on here, that it would not have been much out of his way. Tell him that the Empress should write to me through M. Senno of Genoa. M. de Beausset will be the bearer of the inclosed letter to the Empress."

After reading the above, one is at a loss to know how it came that M. de Beausset kept the letter which the Emperor wrote to Marie Louise on the 20th April, as he was leaving Fontainebleau.

To GENERAL BERTRAND.

"LA MADONE, 2nd *September*, 1814.

"Write to the Princess Pauline that I have received all the letters from Naples; tell her that I feel much hurt that my letters should have been forwarded open, as if I were a prisoner; that I find this conduct ridiculous and insulting. . . .

"NAPOLEON."

To GENERAL BERTRAND.

"PORTO LONGONE, 9th *September*, 1814.

"I thank you for the pamphlets which I have just received; make a collection of those which are *for* and those which are *against;* one of these days I will run over them all.

"I have received a very tender letter from the King of Naples; he pretends having written to me several times, but I doubt it; it appears that affairs between France and Italy turn his head and make him tender.

"Send me a list of the persons whom the Princess Pauline is bringing with her. . . .

"NAPOLEON."

To FERDINAND JOSEPH, GRAND DUKE OF TUSCANY, AT FLORENCE.

"PORTO FERRAJO, 10th *October*, 1814.

"SIR, MY BROTHER, AND VERY DEAR UNCLE,—Not having received any news of my wife since the 10th

August, nor of my son for six months, I send you this letter by the Chevalier Colonna. I beg your Royal Highness to inform me if you will permit me to send you a letter every week for the Empress, and if you will send me in return news of her and the letters of Madame de Montesquiou, the governess of my son. I flatter myself that in spite of the events which have changed so many individuals, your Royal Highness retains some friendship for me. . . .

" NAPOLEON."

During the remainder of the year no letters of interest were written by the Emperor, or at least none have been made public, but it is certain that active negotiations were being carried on in his name for his return to France, chiefly through the instrumentality of his sister, Pauline Borghese.

CHAPTER VI.

THE YEAR 1815.

WHEN the year 1815 opened Napoleon was still at Elba, carefully concealing his intrigues and his intentions; the Congress of Vienna was sitting, and the question of removing the French Emperor to a greater distance from the Continent had been more than once raised; it was contemplated sending him to the Canary Islands, to St. Lucia, or to St. Helena. The Czar, however, was opposed to a violation of the treaty of Fontainebleau. On the 7th February the news reached Vienna that Napoleon had secretly left Elba, and this intelligence, communicated to the Congress by Prince Metternich, fell upon it like a thunderbolt, and hushed all its dissensions. It was instantly determined to wage war against Napoleon; the treaty of Chaumont was revived and ratified on the 25th April. The allies agreed not to lay down arms until they had completed the destruction of the common enemy.

They at once prepared to invade France with an overwhelming force. In round numbers they set on foot 700,000 men. Schwartzenberg commanded the army of the Upper Rhine, 260,000 strong; Blucher had under his orders 150,000 Prussians and Saxons; Wellington had nearly an equal number of English, Belgians, &c.; while the Russians, under Barclay de Tolly, numbered 160,000. The Swiss, the Spaniards, and the Portuguese were anxious to co-operate, and La Vendée was in a blaze. To meet all these difficulties, Napoleon, who arrived in Paris on the 21st March, after a triumphal march from the Gulf of Juan, set to work to reorganise his army with marvellous rapidity. Siborne says that he never worked greater wonders during his wonderful career than when preparing for his last campaign. He proposed to have an army of 560,000 men by the 1st June, and 800,000 by the 1st October; he calculated too that the National Guard reorganised throughout the country would yield 2,250,000 men for home service. It is true that this gigantic scheme was only partially carried out. All old soldiers were called upon to rejoin, even those beyond the Rhine, and who had served the French Empire in the days of the Confederation. Paris was fortified on the north side, but not on the south.

A good deal has been written about the enthusiasm with which Napoleon was greeted on his arrival in France, but that enthusiasm was almost entirely confined to the lower orders and to the soldiery. The middle classes had an instinctive dread that matters would terminate badly, and that the allies could make France pay dearly for this escapade. Comte Miot de Melito, who was sent into the provinces to observe the feeling in the country, was obliged on his return to make an unfavourable report. He told the Emperor that he had everywhere found the women opposed to him, and he submitted that it would be of immense importance to procure the return of the Empress. The fact of the women being against him, Napoleon said, was because he had never permitted them to meddle with his affairs. There were other reasons, the *bella matribus detestata*; a sufficient number of children had already been sacrificed to the Minotaur. Then the women were influenced by the priests, and the priests were opposed to the persecutor of the Church.

The crowning feature of 1815 was the brief and decisive campaign which lasted only a few days, and which ended in the total overthrow of the most remarkable man the world has ever seen. Napoleon broke into Flanders on the 15th June at the head of 122,000 men—said to have been the finest army that ever marched out of France. He defeated, but did not route the Prussians at Ligny on the 16th. He himself made the fatal mistake of overrating his success, and supposing at first that Blucher had fallen back on Namur with the intention of re-crossing the Rhine. On the 17th, Napoleon, after wasting many hours, sent Grouchy in pursuit of the Prussians, and marched himself with about 80,000 men to attack the Duke of Wellington. Beaten on the 18th the Emperor fled, and did not draw rein till he reached Philippeville, ten leagues from Mont St. Jean. Passing through Charleroi, he was at Laon on the 20th, and from that place dictated his last bulletin.

After several futile attempts to regain power, and then to secure the throne for his son, the Emperor went to Rochefort with the intention of going to the United States. The Minister of Marine, Admiral Decrès, had placed two frigates at his service, but there were eleven English vessels cruising off the port, and so Napoleon surrendered himself to Captain Maitland.

Both during his stay at Elba and afterwards, no correspondence was permitted between the Emperor and Marie Louise. On landing in the gulf of St. Juan he wrote a note to Marie Louise to join him, and he afterwards appealed to the Emperor of Austria, but in vain, to have his wife and child restored to him. For some time Napoleon thought that he would be able to secure at least the neutrality of Austria, but this was not to be.

The Congress of Vienna had busied itself considerably with putting down the slave trade. On the 29th March Napoleon, by an imperial decree, abolished that infamous traffic.

NOTE FOR THE BALLS TO BE GIVEN DURING THE CARNIVAL.

"PORTO FERRAJO, 3rd *January*, 1815.

"Sunday, the 8th, there will be a ball in the grand saloon. It is necessary that the invitations should be made out to-morrow, and the list submitted to his Majesty. The invitations should extend all over the island, without however comprising more than 200 persons. They must be issued for nine o'clock. There will be refreshments without ices, seeing the difficulty there is in procuring them. There will be a supper served at midnight. All this must not cost more than 40*l*.

"Sunday, the 15th, the Academy can open its theatre and give a fancy ball. The 22nd following I can give another ball. The 29th the theatre can give a second fancy ball. During the holidays there can be two fancy balls given, one at the theatre, and one at the palace...."

General Bertrand having submitted for the approbation of his Majesty a bill for eight blinds for the drawing-room of the Princess Pauline, Napoleon decided—

"PORTO FERRAJO, 31*st January*, 1815.

"Not having ordered this expense, which has not been carried to the budget, the princess must pay it. It will be the same with all expenses of this kind made before they have been approved.

"NAPOLEON."

The princess having furnished the linen, the whole expense was about 2*l*. 10*s*.

On the 3rd February came another note of considerable length which began thus—"I see that the Cardinal proposes an expenditure of 5,600 francs for the opera of Porto Ferrajo. Inquire if the band of the guard could not form the orchestra, and Gaudiano be leader; that would reduce the expense to 2,600 francs a month. The note gives a list of four men only, who cannot form a company. There must be women; the Cardinal announced several...."

By a note of the 16th February it appears that the military estimates of Elba, in 1814, amounted to 689,317 francs 78 centimes.

To GENERAL LAPI.

"PORTO FERRAJO, 26*th February*, 1815."

"I am leaving the island of Elba. I have been extremely satisfied with the conduct of the inhabitants. I confide to them the safety of this country, to which I attach a great importance. I cannot give them a greater mark of confidence than in leaving my mother and my sister in their care, after the departure of the troops. The members of the Junta, and all the inhabitants of the island, may count upon my affection and upon my special protection.

"NAPOLEON."

Having thus taken farewell of Elba, his Majesty, somewhat prematurely, set sail for France, and once more, as on his way to Egypt and back, escaped the English cruisers. His return to France had a magical effect on the Congress of Vienna, where all differences respecting Poland and Saxony were at once laid aside, and where preparations were made and engagements undertaken to meet the common danger. It was at once felt by all the assembled sovereigns and diplomatists that a firebrand had been let loose, and that there would be no peace in Europe with Napoleon on the throne.

TO THE FRENCH PEOPLE.

"GULF OF JUAN, 1*st March*, 1815."

"FRENCHMEN,—The defection of Marshal Augereau delivered Lyons, without defence, to our enemies. The army which I confided to him was strong enough to beat the Austrians, and to fall upon the rear of the left wing of the army which threatened Paris.

"The victories of Champaubert, Montmirail, Chateau Thierry, Vauchamps, Mormant,[1] Montereau, Craonne, Arcis-sur-Aube, and St. Dizier, the insurrection of the brave peasants in Lorraine, Champagne, Alsace, Franche Comté and Burgundy, and the position which I had taken up on the rear of the enemy, separating them from their magazines, their artillery reserves, and their baggage, placed them in a desperate situation. The French were never on the point of becoming more powerful, and the pick of the enemy's army was lost beyond resource. It would have found a grave in the vast provinces which it so ruthlessly sacked, when the treason of Marshal Marmont handed over the capital and disorganised the army.

"The unexpected conduct of these two marshals who betrayed at the same time their country, their prince, and their benefactor, changed the destiny of the war. Such was the disastrous situation of the enemy, that at the close of the action before Paris they had no more ammunition, owing to having been separated from their reserve parks.

"Under new and important circumstances my heart was broken, but my soul remained unshaken. I consulted only the interests of my country; I exiled myself to a rock in the middle of the sea; my life had been and might again be useful to you. I did not permit the great number of citizens who wished to accompany me, to share my fate; I believed their presence useful to France, and I took with me only a handful of gallant men necessary for my protection. . . . "NAPOLEON."

A somewhat similar appeal was addressed to the army. In it the Emperor said—

"SOLDIERS,—In my exile I heard your voice. I have arrived after overcoming numerous obstacles and perils.

"Your general, called to the throne by the voice of the

[1] Better known as Nangis.

people and raised upon your shields, is restored to you; come and join him. Throw away the colours which the nation has prescribed, and which for twenty-five years have served as a rallying point for the enemies of France! Show that tricoloured cockade which you wore in our days of splendour!

"We must forget that we have been masters of the continent; but we must not permit any one to meddle with our affairs. Resume the eagles which you had at Ulm, at Austerlitz, at Jena, at Eylau, at Friedland, &c., &c. Do you think that this handful of Frenchmen, to-day so arrogant, will be able to support their view? They will return whence they came.

"Your rank, your fortune, your glory; the rank, the fortune, and the glory of your children, have no greater enemy than these princes whom the foreigners wish to impose upon us. . . .

"Soldiers, come and range yourselves under the standard of your chief; his existence is composed of yours; his interests, his honour, and his glory are yours. Victory will march at double quick time. The eagle with the national colours will fly from steeple to steeple to the towers of Notre Dame. Then you will be able to show your scars with honour; then you will be able to boast of what you have done; you will be the liberators of the country. . ."

Another proclamation was addressed to the Imperial Guard, in which the Bourbons were accused of having forgotten nothing and learned nothing, and of having carried to England the patrimony of the army, amounting to 16,000,000*l.*

Similar language was employed by the Emperor in replying to the congratulatory addresses presented to him on his road to Paris; at Gap on the 6th March, Grenoble on the 9th, Lyons on the 18th, &c., till he entered "his good city of Paris" on the 21st, without having encountered any resistance, in spite of all the armies sent forth to arrest his triumphal progress. Everywhere the troops melted away from their leaders, such was the fascination once more exercised by the name of Napoleon, and then many of the leaders, like Marshal Soult and Ney, went with the current.

On the 21st March, at noon, the Emperor held a review of the army of Paris, and said:—" Soldiers, I came to France with 600 men because I counted upon the love of the people and upon the *souvenirs* of the old soldiers. I was not deceived in my expectation. Soldiers, I thank you. The glory of what we have just done belongs to the people and to you; mine is reduced to having known and appreciated you.

"Soldiers, the throne of the Bourbons was illegitimate, because it was re-erected by foreign hands. . . .

"Soldiers, we are going to drive these auxiliary princes of the foreigner from the country; not only will the nation second us with its wishes, but it will follow our impulse. . . We do not wish to meddle with the affairs of foreign nations, but woe to those who meddle with ours."

The Emperor then presented the battalion which had accompanied him to Elba, and the army swore allegiance. There could be no mistake about the enthusiasm of the army, but there was very little enthusiasm beyond the soldiery and the lower classes. The body of the nation held aloof, and contemplated the return of Napoleon with feelings of distrust and apprehension.

To M. FOUCHÉ, Duc d'Otrante.[1]

"PARIS, 21*st March*, 1815.

"According to the first information which I have received, the Duc de Bourbon has gone to La Vendée,

---

[1] After Napoleon landed, Fouché, seeing that resistance would be useless, told Louis XVIII. that he intended to take office under the Emperor, but that he would correspond with him (the King). More than once, during the Hundred Days, Napoleon was on the point of having Fouché shot as a traitor, and he was only prevented carrying his threat into execution by Carnot, who showed him that such a

where he is organising some Chouans; the Duc d'Orleans has gone to Besançon, and the King appears to be in the direction of the Somme... Send agents in these three directions....
"NAPOLEON."

General Caulaincourt, Duc de Vicence, wished to refuse the foreign office, but it was thrust upon him. On the 23rd March the Emperor wrote to him thus: "I desire to have an analysis of all the despatches written by M. de Talleyrand and by the King (Louis XVIII.) against the King of Naples, so as to be able to communicate them to him."

This note is important as showing that Napoleon evidently made an attempt to work upon the feelings of his brother-in-law, whose subsequent action he strongly condemned.

To GENERAL COMTE BERTRAND, GRAND MARSHAL OF THE PALACE.
"PARIS, 23rd *March*, 1815.

"Send Bernotti with the news to the island of Elba. Write to Lapi to have the tricolour hoisted. Have all my things which are worth being removed sent here. I attach great importance to my Corsican horse, if he be not sick. The yellow travelling carriage, the big carriage, and the gala carriages are worth bringing back, as well as the body linen. I make a present of my library to the town, also my house, which can serve as a casino.
"NAPOLEON."

General Clarke having left Paris with the Bourbons the war office was handed over to Marshal Davoust.

measure would lose him the support of the Jacobins. His Majesty put the matter off for a more convenient season, which never arrived. Had Napoleon returned in triumph from Waterloo no mercy would have been shown to Fouché, and of this the ex-regicide priest was perfectly well aware.

To Marshal Davoust.

"Paris, 27*th March*, 1815.

"Send me a plan for enabling Soissons, La Fère, and Chateau Thierry to resist a sudden attack. It appears that the Duc d'Angoulême was at Avignon on the 23rd I suppose that events in Paris made him feel the necessity of falling back. However, as he has Spain behind him, it will be necessary to disperse this gathering. . . .

"Napoleon."

His Majesty wrote no less than five letters to his War Minister on the 27th. He also wrote a despatch to Marshal Ney, who, after having promised Louis XVIII. to bring Napoleon to Paris in an iron cage, now joined his old master.

To Marshal Suchet, at Strasburg.

"Paris, 27*th March*, 1815.

"I have received your letter of the 14th. You know the esteem which I have always borne you since the siege of Toulon. Your patriotic conduct during recent circumstances has given me great pleasure. I shall be glad to see you in Paris in order to renew the expression of my sentiments.

"Napoleon."

On the 28th was issued a decree, the first article of which ran thus :—" The Emperor calls upon all the sub-officers and soldiers who, for no matter what reason, have left the army, to rejoin their corps and to hasten to the defence of their country. He gives them a special promise that as soon as the existing peace has been consolidated those men who have rejoined owing to the present decree shall be the first to obtain leave to return home."

On the same day the Emperor wrote to Caulaincourt ordering him to have a history written of the various treaties concluded during his reign, such as Campo Formio, Luneville, Amiens, Presburg, Tilsit, Vienna, and the affair of Bayonne! His Majesty added :—

"It is necessary that you should send articles every day to the *Moniteur* dated from various countries to make known what is going on; for example, the differences between Sweden and Denmark with regard to Pomerania; the differences with Saxony, with Bavaria, with the Prince of Orange, who will not cede his states in Germany, &c. You must also satisfy public curiosity and draw attention to the avidity of the various Powers.

"NAPOLEON."

TO THE KING OF NAPLES.

"PARIS, *March*, 1815.

"I have arrived. I have traversed France. The army and the people of country and of town came out to meet me. I entered Paris on the 20th March at the head of the 'camp of Essonne,' upon which the King counted. He retired to Lille, and then went to England with his whole family.

"All France, with the exception of Marseilles, of which I have no news, has hoisted the national colours. There is enthusiasm everywhere. The old soldiers are hastening in crowds to rejoin their colours, and the provinces are ready to make any sacrifices.

"I have an army in Flanders, one in Alsace, one in the interior, and one which is forming in Dauphiny.

"Up to the present I am at peace with every one.

"I shall support you with all my forces. I count upon you. As soon as Marseilles hoists the tricoloured cockade send some ships, there, so that we may correspond, for I fear that correspondence by way of Italy may become difficult. Send me an ambassador; I will send you one shortly on board of a frigate.[1]

"NAPOLEON."

This letter was entirely in the handwriting of the Emperor.

On the 31st March the Emperor wrote to his Chancellor of the Exchequer for information concerning the finances.

---

[1] Murat had no sooner learned that the Emperor had made his escape, and had reached Lyons, than he took up arms against Austria with the idea of making himself master of Italy. The Austrians at first, taken by surprise, fell back upon the Po, but they soon rallied and inflicted a crushing defeat on the Neapolitan army. The consequence was that Murat lost his throne, and had to fly for refuge to France. This affair is enveloped in some obscurity. Who instigated this sudden attack on the part of Murat, who had cast in his lot with the allies the year before? Was it Fouché, as some people say? Napoleon sent him word as he was leaving Elba that he would obliterate the past from his memory, and would guarantee him his throne in exchange for his alliance; but at the same time he begged of him not to molest the Austrians, with whom he intended to negotiate. The position of Murat, too, was excellent with Austria. In a minute on the Congress of Vienna Prince Metternich said: "France shows a natural interest to resume her old influence in Italy through the reestablishment of the dispossessed branches of the Bourbons in Parma, and especially in Naples; while it is the duty of Austria first of all to consolidate her own power and then to preserve Parma, which a recent and formal convention has assured to the Empress Marie Louise; lastly, to support the King of Naples, whose cause she has espoused for the wisest and most powerful motives." Prince Metternich also said, in a memorandum, that Austria had signed a treaty with the King of Naples, which had been approved of by England, promising him aid and protection against all his enemies. It is difficult to suppose that Murat could have fallen on the Austrians without having been secretly prompted to do so. He was beaten, and was, of course, disavowed. At St. Helena Napoleon said: "It was the destiny of Murat to damage us—he first of all worked our ruin by abandoning us in 1814, and then by embracing our cause too warmly in 1815."

In consequence of the economy of the Bourbons, the financial condition of France was in a comparatively prosperous condition when Napoleon returned, and he was soon able to lay hands on over 3,000,000*l*. With this sum, and with money borrowed at various rates of interest reaching as high as 17 per cent., the Imperial Government managed to struggle on until Waterloo.

To the EMPEROR OF AUSTRIA.

"PARIS, *1st April*, 1815.

"SIR, MY BROTHER AND VERY DEAR FATHER-IN-LAW,—At the moment that Providence restores me to my capital, the most earnest of my wishes is to see once more the objects of my most tender affection—my wife and my son; as the long separation which circumstances have occasioned has made me experience the most acute feeling which ever afflicted my heart, and as the virtuous princess whose destiny your Majesty united to mine must also be impatient for our meeting. If the dignity of the conduct of the Empress, during the time of my misfortune, has increased the tenderness of your Majesty for a daughter already so beloved, you will understand, Sire, how much I must desire to see the moment arrive when I shall be able to assure her of all my gratitude. It will be my happiness to see her receive once more the homages of a loving nation which, to-day more than ever, will know how to love and appreciate her virtues.

"My efforts tend solely towards consolidating this throne which the love of my people has preserved for me and restored to me, and to leave it one day, firmly founded, to the child whom your Majesty has surrounded with your parental kindness.

"The duration of peace being essentially necessary to attain this important and sacred object, I have no greater desire than to remain upon friendly terms with all the Powers, and especially with your Majesty.

"I wish the Empress to come by way of Strasburg,

orders having been given for her reception on this line in my states. I am too well acquainted with the principles of your Majesty, I know too well the value which you attach to family affections, not to feel confident that you will hasten, no matter what the plans of your cabinet and of your policy, to aid in the reunion of a wife with her husband, and of a son with his father. . . .

" NAPOLEON."

To GENERAL CAULAINCOURT.

" PARIS, 3rd April, 1815.

" I suppose that you have sent secret agents to Sweden to rally her to our side. I suppose that you have also sent others to Naples, to the Hague, to the Prince of Orange, to the various princes of Germany, to the King of Saxony, and to the Swiss cantons which have remained attached to us.

" The multiplicity of my affairs does not permit me to enter into details; it is for you to take care that, without delay, the courts of Bavaria, Wurtemberg, Baden, the Princes of Hesse-Darmstadt, of Nassau, of Tuscany, Rome, Spain, Portugal, &c., may learn, through frequent insinuations on the part of secret agents, my good intentions with regard to them. Spain is very important. . . .

" NAPOLEON."

CIRCULAR TO THE SOVEREIGNS.

" PARIS, 4th April, 1815.

" SIR, MY BROTHER,—You will have learned my return to France, my entry into Paris, and the departure of the Bourbons. The true nature of these events must now be known to your Majesty. They are the work of an irresistible force, the work of the unanimous will of a great nation which understands its duties and its rights. The dynasty which was forced on the French nation was not suited to it. The Bourbons would associate themselves neither with its feelings nor its customs. France was obliged to separate herself from them. She demanded a liberator; the expectations which led me to make the greatest of sacrifices [to go into exile] were deceived. I returned, and from the spot where I landed the love of my people bore me to the bosom of my capital. The first desire of my heart is to repay so much affection by maintaining an honourable tranquillity. The re-establishment of the Imperial throne was necessary for the happiness of Frenchmen. My fondest hope is to render it at the same time useful in consolidating the repose of Europe. Enough glory has turn about illustrated the standards of various nations; the vicissitudes of fate have seen great reverses succeed to great successes. A fairer arena is now opened to sovereigns, and I shall be the first to descend into it. After having exhibited to the world the spectacle of great battles, it will be more satisfactory henceforth to indulge in nothing but peaceful rivalry, in no other strife but that sacred strife waged for the welfare of the people. . . .

"NAPOLEON."

To M. MARET (*Secretary of State*).

"PARIS, 5*th April*, 1815.

"Send word to Lyons by telegraph that we have entered Bordeaux, which has hoisted the tri-coloured flag. . . . The Duchesse d'Angoulême embarked on the 1st April.[1]

"NAPOLEON."

On the 9th April the Emperor thus addressed his troops in the Carrousel:—"Soldiers, I have just received information that the tri-colour has been hoisted at Toulouse and all through the south. The commandants of Perpignan and of Bayonne declared that they would not obey the orders given by the Duc d'Angoulême to deliver those places to the Spaniards, who have since stated that they

[1] On board an English frigate.

have no desire to meddle with our affairs.¹ The white flag now flies over Marseilles alone. . . ."

The next day his Majesty announced to Admiral Decrès, who was once more Minister of Marine, that Marseilles had accepted the tri-coloured cockade, and the admiral was directed to send a frigate to Porto Ferrajo to bring Madame Mère back to France.

To MARSHAL DAVOUST.

"PARIS, 10*th April*, 1815.

"You must efface Berthier, Marmont, Victor, Perignon, Augereau, and Kellermann from the list of marshals. You must present me a report, so that a pension may be granted to those marshals who have no fortune. . . .

"NAPOLEON."

To COMTE MOLLIEN (*Minister of the Treasury*).

"PARIS, 14*th April*, 1815.

"There are 5 per cents. consolidated due to the Princesse Borghese, to the Princesse Eliza, and to the princes of my House. They should be paid. The 500,000 francs of Prince Louis were given to him in exchange for his property in Holland . . . There can be no doubt about this sum belonging to Prince Louis, and it must be paid. . . .

"Apart from pensions to the house of Spain, there were pensions for the House of Carignan, for the King of Piedmont, and for several princes of the left bank of the Rhine; there was one, I think, for the Princesse d'Orleans. You must make me a report on all this.

"NAPOLEON."

It appears strange that Napoleon should have paid a pension to the Duchesse d'Orleans.²

---

¹ It was not until a month later that Ferdinand consented to join the allies.

² In March 1884 the fact of the mother of Louis Philippe having received a pension from Napoleon was discussed by several Paris

NOTE.

"PARIS, 15*th April*, 1815.

"The Emperor asks the Minister of Foreign Affairs for a report concerning the King of Naples, embracing all the events of the last campaign, and the harm he then did to France.

"The Emperor did not receive any mark of interest from him during his stay in the Isle of Elba. It was not in accordance with the dignity of the Emperor in misfortune to make advances.

newspapers. From that discussion it appears that it was at the earnest entreaty of the Queen Hortense (the mother of Napoleon III.) that the pension was accorded. The Princesse d'Orleans seems to have solicited the intervention of the Queen Hortense in two letters published by a Bonapartist journal. The first ran thus—

"MADAME,—La gracieuse bienveillance que Votre Majesté m'a témoignée me donne l'espoir que vos bons offices obtiendront de l'Empereur une décision qui est devenue si nécessaire et si urgente dans la cruelle position où je me trouve. Je craindrais de fatiguer Sa Majesté l'Empereur par le détail des raisons qui me paraissent de nature à pouvoir influencer sa magnanimité. Je me plais à croire que votre bonté, &c. . . .

"LOUISE-AMÉLIE-ADÉLAIDE DE BOURBON-PENTHIÈVRE."

The second was still more pressing.

"MADAME,—L'intérêt dont Votre Majesté a bien voulu me réitérer le témoignage, dans son aimable lettre du 29 mars, me confirme l'espoir que l'Empereur adoucira ma si cruelle position. Le ministre des Finances l'ayant mise sous ses yeux, il sera bien consolant pour moi de devoir à la générosité de l'Empereur et à votre obligeante entreprise d'obtenir ce que ma position, dont je ne pourrai assez vous exprimer la gêne, sollicite si instamment. Agréez encore une fois, madame, &c. . . .

"LOUISE, &c."

Of course this pension was never paid, but that was the fault of the allies and not of Napoleon. It is strange to reflect that one of the first acts of the nephew of Napoleon I., and the son of the Queen Hortense, on attaining power, should have been to despoil the Orleans princes.

"The palace of Naples was furnished with the most precious objects which the Emperor had collected in his palace of Rome. The only communication into which the Emperor entered with the King of Naples was to ask him to receive Madame Mère. . . . Show that the King of Naples wished to seize upon Italy, and that he attacked the Austrians at a moment when he was entirely ignorant of the situation of the Emperor. This proves conclusively that there was no agreement between them. . . ."

The above note was to form the substance of a letter intended to tranquillise Austria, and persuade her that Napoleon had nothing to do with Murat's aggression; that the Emperor was no firebrand; and that he wished to remain at peace, especially with his father-in-law.

On the 16th April Marshal Davoust was ordered to have salutes of one hundred guns fired at the Invalides, at Lille, at Strasburg, and all the frontier towns, in honour of the surrender of Marseilles to the Imperial troops. The telegram was to be published in profusion. Brest and the other ports were also to fire salutes.

To MARSHAL MASSENA, AT MARSEILLES.

"PARIS, 18*th April*, 1815.

"I have received your letter of the 14th, and have read your proclamation with pleasure. I thank you for having preserved Toulon and Antibes. I shuddered at the passage in your letter where I saw the order which you received from the Duc d'Angoulême to hand over that precious deposit to the English. At the first moment I sent Marshal Brune to command in the 8th division.

"I greatly desire to see you. . . .[1]

"NAPOLEON."

[1] Both Massena and Brune had been for some time under a cloud, and yet they joined their old chief, laying aside their rancour. Before the end of the year the people of Marseilles rose and slaughtered the Mamelukes, much as the rabble of Paris had slaughtered the Swiss Guard, while Marshal Brune was assassinated at Avignon, and his body tossed in the waters of the Rhone.

On the 22nd his Majesty wrote to his Minister of Marine, saying that it was a matter of no importance having no ships ready for sea, but that he could not leave so many gallant officers without employment; it was therefore his intention to raise between 60,000 and 80,000 men along the coast to serve ashore under the said officers.

On the same day the Emperor forwarded to King Joseph a copy of the new Constitution or Additional Act, which he was going to submit to the Chambers, and upon which he asked his brother's advice.

To COMTE CARNOT.

"PARIS, 24th April, 1815.

"It would be well to order in each department the fabrication of a certain number of pikes. Select a model. They will be of use in default of muskets and scythes.

"NAPOLEON."

To MARSHAL DAVOUST.

"PARIS, 26th April, 1815.

"Tell Marshal Suchet, if he is still at Lyons, to remain there, and if he has left send him a courier, so that he may return. I give the command of the army of the Alps definitively to that marshal. . . . Tell Marshal Grouchy that as soon as he has been replaced by Marshal Suchet he must come to Paris. . . .

"NAPOLEON."

On the 30th April was issued a decree for the formation of four armies—Army of the North, Army of the Moselle, Army of the Rhine, and Army of the Alps, and three corps of observation. On the same day his Majesty wrote to Marshal Davoust—"If we have war, and I am obliged to absent myself, I intend leaving you in Paris as Minister of War, governor of Paris, commander-in-chief of the National

Guard, &c. I have no idea of leaving yet, nor do I suppose that the enemy will attack us during the whole month of May. However, I wish you to place the city at once in a state of defence. You will have in Paris thirty batteries of eight guns each. . . . Choose a general officer of engineers. But you must not take Rogniat, nor Haxo, nor Marescot, who are required for the armies. Your infantry will be composed of 90,000 men—30,000 National Guards, 20,000 Marines, 20,000 men from the depots, and 20,000 men detained from the *levée en masse*."

On the 3rd May the Emperor wrote to his Minister of War saying that it would be necessary to raise another 150,000 men in addition to the old soldiers called upon to rejoin their colours; and to the Minister of Marine, rating him for not having appointed the post captains, who were to command regiments, the captains who were to command battalions, and the lieutenants who were to command companies.

To MARSHAL DAVOUST.

"PARIS, 21*st May*, 1815.

"I approve of Marshal Soult receiving a salary of 40,000 francs as Marshal of the Empire, and 40,000 francs as General-in-Chief. I approve of him receiving 6,000 francs a month for staff and office expenses, and 20,000 francs for travelling, which must be renewed by degrees as they are expended.[1]   "NAPOLEON."

---

[1] Soult, after having been made War Minister by Louis XVIII., rejoined his old master, but not before making certain pecuniary conditions of an advantageous nature. The Emperor, perhaps, paid more for Soult than he was worth; he certainly did not approach Berthier as chief of the staff, in which capacity he was now called to act, and after Waterloo he hurried back to Paris instead of remaining with the army. In this, however, he merely imitated his chief. He was proscribed after Waterloo, and took refuge at Dusseldorf, but in 1819 he was allowed to return to France, and his *bâton* was restored to him. He served successively Louis XVIII., Charles X., and Louis Philippe, and died a few months before the declaration of the Second Empire.

In some notes, dictated at a cabinet council held upon the same date, the Emperor said—

"It cannot be disguised that civil war has really broken out in La Vendée, and that military measures must at once be adopted to put down the rebellion. If measures be not taken in Normandy also, plots will soon be hatched in secret against the public tranquillity. . . ."

To MARSHAL DAVOUST.

"PARIS, 27*th May*, 1815.

"It is probable that the Guard will soon march; there will then remain no troops in Paris. It is important that by the 1st June, at the latest, the quartermaster-generals, colonels, majors, captains, &c., of the National Guard should receive their commissions. . . .

"NAPOLEON."

NOTE TO THE MINISTER OF FOREIGN AFFAIRS.

"It is possible that the Chamber may make a motion with regard to the King of Rome, tending to expose the horror which the conduct of Austria ought to inspire. This would have a good effect.

"Meneval should make a report dated from the time of his arrival. He must trace the conduct of Austria and of the other Powers towards the Empress, from her arrival at Orleans until her departure for Vienna; the violation of the treaty of Fontainebleau, since they tore her, as well as her son, from the Emperor. He must direct attention to the indignation shown by her grandmother, the Queen of Sicily, on this subject, at Vienna. He should dwell especially on the separation of the Prince Imperial from his mother and from Madame de Montesquiou, on his tears at leaving her, and on the fears of Madame de Montesquiou for the safety and the existence of the young prince. He must treat this point in a delicate manner. He must speak of the grief experienced by the Empress when she was torn away from the Emperor. She was thirty days without sleeping on the occasion of his Majesty leaving France. He must lay stress on the fact that the Empress is really a prisoner, since they will not permit her to write to the Emperor, and that she has been even obliged to pledge her word of honour that she will never write a word to him. Meneval must embody in this report all the details which he has given to the Emperor."

Baron Meneval quotes an interesting letter, written by Marie Louise while Napoleon was at Elba, throwing light upon the personal feelings of the Empress. She much wished to retain Isabey, the painter, in her service, but Isabey's terms were too high. Her Majesty wrote to the baron on the subject, and said : " Besides, were he to come to Parma for nothing, I should never permit myself to take him without having first of all obtained the consent of the Emperor. You are aware of his prejudices against him, and these I should respect ; although separated from him, I am none the less responsible to my husband for my conduct."

On the 1st June the Emperor met the electors of France at the Champ de Mai, the preparations for the ceremony being much the same as when the unfortunate Louis XVI., on the 14th July, 1790—anniversary of the taking of the Bastille—took the oath to the nation. The new constitution or "Additional Act" was approved of by the immense majority of the electors,[1] and after the announcement of the numbers the Emperor pronounced the following discourse—

" Emperor, consul, and soldier, I owe everything to the people. In prosperity, in adversity, on the battle-field, on the throne, in exile, France has been the sole object of my thoughts and actions. Like the King of Athens I have sacrificed myself for the people in the hope of seeing the

[1] Just as on the eve of the fall of the Second Empire the immense majority of the electors approved of the liberal institutions conceded by Napoleon III.

promise realised that France should retain her natural limits, her honours and her rights. Indignation on seeing these sacred rights, acquired by twenty-five years of victory, disregarded and lost for ever, the cry of insulted French honour, and the wishes of the nation, have replaced me on the throne, which is dear to me because it is the palladium of the independence, of the honour, and of the rights of the people.

"Frenchmen, while traversing, amid public enthusiasm, the various provinces of the empire in order to reach my capital, I counted upon a long peace: nations are bound by the treaties concluded by their Governments, no matter what they may be.

"My whole attention was then turned to the means of founding our liberty by a constitution in conformity with the wishes and interests of the people. I summoned them to the Champ de Mai.

"I shall soon learn that the princes who have disregarded all principles, and who have despised the opinions and the dearest interests of so many countries, wish to declare war against us. They intend to enlarge the kingdom of the Low Countries, and to give it for a frontier all our fortified places of the north, and to reconcile their differences by sharing Alsace and Lorraine between them. It was necessary to prepare for war.

"However, before running the personal risk of taking the field, my first care was to constitute the nation without delay.

"The people have accepted the Act which I have presented to them.

"Frenchmen, when we have repelled these unjust aggressions, and when Europe is convinced of what is due to the rights and independence of twenty-eight millions of Frenchmen, a solemn law, made in the form required by the Constitutional Act, will harmonise the various dispositions of our constitutions.

"Frenchmen, you are about to return to your departments. Tell citizens that circumstances are perilous; that with union, energy, and perseverance, we shall come victorious out of this struggle of a great people against their oppressors; that generations to come will severely scrutinise our conduct; that a nation loses everything when it loses its independence. Tell them that the foreign kings whom I have seated on the throne, or who owe to me the preservation of their crowns, who all, in the days of my prosperity, solicited my alliance and the protection of the French people, to-day direct their attacks against my person. If I did not perceive that it is against the country that they are animated, I should sacrifice this existence to their animosity. But also tell citizens that, as long as Frenchmen accord me those sentiments of love, of which they have given me so many proofs, this rage on the part of our enemies will be impotent.

"Frenchmen, my will is that of the people; my rights are theirs; my honour, my glory, my happiness, can only be the honour, the glory, and the happiness of France."

Here the Emperor, taking the Gospels from the hands of the Archbishop of Bourges, said: "I swear to observe, and to cause to be observed, the constitutions of the Empire." Then followed swearing on the part of the high dignitaries, the Assembly, the National Guard, and the Imperial Guard.

On the 3rd June the Emperor in a letter to Marshal Davoust said:—"Prince Jerome will be employed with the army as Lieutenant-General."

In fact nearly all the Bonapartes had resorted to Paris—Lucien, who had fled from Rome, and had settled in England; Joseph, whose crown had been handed back to its rightful owner; and Jerome, whose crown of Westphalia was past praying for. Of the brothers Louis alone was absent.

To MARSHAL DAVOUST.

"PARIS, 3rd June, 1815.

"Enclosed you will find a copy of the orders which I have given for the cavalry of the army. Marshal Grouchy will command it in chief. Give him a chief of the staff, and a general of artillery. All the generals on the unattached list are at his service. Give Marshal Grouchy orders to be at Laon on the 5th, to pass an inspection of his regiments, to provide for their organisation, and to have cartridges served out so that they may be ready to take the field on the 10th. "NAPOLEON."

And in a letter to Soult of the same date the Emperor said that the enemy were threatening Metz, and that the Imperial Guard would be at Soissons on the 10th, and perhaps at Avesnes on the 13th. His Majesty also wrote this short note to Admiral Decrès :—" You must draw up a report of all the insults which the English have committed at sea since I disembarked. You must refer in detail to the affair of the *Melpomène.*"

This was a terrible affair. The 40-gun frigate *Melpomène*, Captain Joseph Collet, had been sent to convey Madame Mère from Porto Ferrajo to Naples ; when a few miles north of Ischia she fell in with the *Rivoli*, which in the year, 1812, had been captured by the *Victorious*, Captain John Talbot, from Captain Jean Baptiste Barré. It was the *Rivoli* now, a British 74, which captured the frigate sent by Napoleon for his mother. Madame Mère afterwards got clear away from Elba in the *Dryade.*

To MARSHAL DAVOUST.

"PARIS, 6th June, 1815.

" Give orders so that there may be at least 200 guns in position at the different gates and in the works round

Paris by the 12th June. Let me know when the first naval guns will arrive.

"NAPOLEON."

In 1870, too, a number of naval guns were sent to Paris for the defence of the capital, and several of the detached forts were manned by blue jackets.

In the midst of all his preparations for war the Emperor met the representatives of the nation, to whom he addressed the following discourse:—

"For the last three months circumstances and the confidence of the people have invested me with unlimited power. To-day the most earnest wish of my heart is accomplished. I have just founded the constitutional monarchy.

"Men have no power to insure the future; institutions alone can consolidate the destinies of nations. The monarchy is necessary in France in order to guarantee the liberty, the independence, and the rights of the people. . . . My ambition is to see France enjoy all the liberty possible; I say possible, because anarchy always brings back an absolute government.

"A formidable coalition of kings is opposed to our independence; their armies are marching on our frontiers.

"The frigate *La Melpomène* has been attacked and captured in the Mediterranean by an English 74, after a sanguinary combat. Blood has been shed during peace!

"Our enemies count upon our intestine divisions. They excite and foment civil war. There have been gatherings which communicate with Ghent [where Louis XVIII. had established his court], as in 1792 with Coblentz. . . . The finances would be in a satisfactory condition but for the increased expenditure which present circumstances necessitate. . . .

"It is possible that the first duty of the prince may shortly call me to place myself at the head of the children of the nation in order to fight for our country.

"You, peers and representatives, give the nation an example of confidence, of energy, and of patriotism, and like the Senate of a great nation of antiquity make up your minds to die rather than to survive the dishonour and the degradation of France. The holy cause of the country will triumph!"[1]

On the same day the Emperor feeling it so possible that he might have to place himself at the head of his troops, ordered Marshal Soult to start for Lille incognito. He added—" You must come to meet me on the road to Laon, where it is probable that I shall be on the 12th. You must obtain the latest information respecting the position of the enemy; you must try and create a spy office at Lille, and a company of men well acquainted with the roads of Belgium. . . ."

On the 11th June the Emperor, replying to the address of the Lower House, said :—" I shall start to-night to place myself at the head of my armies; the movements of the various corps of the enemy render my presence indispensable. . . . Let us not imitate the example of the Lower Empire, which, threatened on all sides by the barbarians, became the laughing stock of posterity by indulging in abstract discussions while the battering ram was breaking down the gates of the city. . . ."

To MARSHAL DAVOUST.

"PARIS, 11*th June*, 1815.

"Inform Marshal Suchet, by telegraph, that hostilities will open on the 14th, and that he can seize upon Montmelian on that day. If it be indispensable to do so before that date, owing to the movements of the enemy, he is authorised to act. However, it is desirable that he should not take the place before the 15th.

"NAPOLEON."

---

[1] This speech from the throne gave rise to the most adulatory addresses on the part of the Chambers.

In a second letter to the War Minister, the Emperor said :—" One hundred and fifty naval guns have arrived in Paris." In a third letter of the same date :—" Send for Marshal Ney ; if he wishes to take part in the first battles which will take place tell him to be at Avesnes on the 14th, where I shall have my head-quarters." And in a fourth letter :—" Send for Marshal Massena. If he wishes to go to Metz give him the governorship of that place, and the command of the third and fourth military divisions. See that Belliard goes to the army of the north."

Ney joined Napoleon at Charleroi, and the Emperor after a few words of welcome gave him the command of the left wing, and orders to attack the enemy. The arrival of Ney was hailed with delight by the troops, and as the " bravest of the brave " rode through the battalions of Vandamme's corps and those of the Old Guard he was greeted with cries of " *Voilà le Rougeot !* "—nickname he had received owing to his red hair and beard.

Before leaving Paris Napoleon signed the following decree :—

" Art. 1. A pension of 2,000 francs is granted to the widow of General Aubry, of the artillery.

" Art. 2. Our Ministers of War and of Finance are charged with the execution of this decree."

General Aubry was, according to a foot-note in *The Correspondence*, the member of the Committee of Public Safety who in 1795 deprived General Bonaparte of his command in the army of Italy. This is quite a mistake ; the officer referred to above was the Comte Claude Charles Aubry, who distinguished himself at the crossing of the Alps, in St. Domingo, at Essling, at the passage of the Beresina, at Lutzen, and who fell at Leipsic.

The next letter which Napoleon wrote was dated from Laon, 12th June. In it the Emperor urged Marshal Davoust to send him 500 Polish infantry and 500 Polish light horse. His Majesty expressed the opinion that these men sent to the outposts would induce the Poles

POSITION OF THE FRENCH ARMY.

in the ranks of the enemy to desert. On the 13th Napoleon was at Avesnes, at which place he dictated the following order of the day:—

"POSITION OF THE ARMY ON THE 14TH.

"General head-quarters will be at Beaumont.

"The infantry of the Imperial Guard will be bivouacked a quarter of a league in front of Beaumont, and will form three lines—the Young Guard, the Chasseurs, and the Grenadiers. Marshal Mortier must inspect the position of this camp, and see that everything is in its place—artillery, ambulances, military train, &c.

"The cavalry of the Imperial Guard will be placed to the rear of Beaumont, but the most distant corps should not be a league away.

"The second corps must take up its position at Leers, that is to say, as near the frontier as possible. . . .

"The first corps must take up its position at Sobre-sur-Sambre, and will also bivouac on several lines, taking care, as well as the second corps, that its fires cannot be seen by the enemy; that no one leaves the camp.[1] . . .

[1] "During the night of the 13th," says Siborne (vol. i. p. 54), "the light reflected on the sky by the fires of the French bivouacs did not escape the vigilant observation of Zeithen's outposts, whence it was communicated to the rear that these fires appeared to be in the direction of Beaumont; and on the following day intelligence was received of the arrival of Napoleon and his brother Jerome. . . . The vigilance of Zeithen on the 14th, and the arrangements made by Blucher during that night afford a complete refutation of the charge so frequently brought against the allied commanders that the French attack took them by surprise."

"Blucher had already ordered the concentration of his troops upon a first warning received from a drummer of the Old Guard, who deserted on the 13th. The presence of the Old Guard was a certain and sufficient indication to open the eyes of the enemy."—JOMINI, *Campagne de* 1815 (p. 146).

The English did not receive notice of the French irruption so soon, as is shown by the following letter:—

DUKE OF WELLINGTON TO LORD LYNEDOCH.

"BRUSSELS, 13*th June*, 1815.

"We have accounts of Buonaparte joining the army and attacking

"To-morrow the third corps will take up its position a league in front of Beaumont, as near the frontier as possible, without, however, crossing it, nor allowing it to be violated by any of the enemy's detachments. General Vandamme must keep all his men at their posts, and must take care that his fires are not perceived by the enemy. . . . He must be ready to move on the 15th, at 3 A.M.

"The sixth corps will bivouac two leagues in advance of Beaumont, on two lines. . . .

"Marshal Grouchy, with the first, second, third, and fourth cavalry corps, will establish his bivouacs between Beaumont and Walcourt, also causing the frontier to be respected, &c. He must hold himself in readiness to march upon Charleroi the day after to-morrow, at 3 A.M., in order to form the advanced guard of the army. . . ."

To PRINCE JOSEPH.

"AVESNES, 14th *June*, 1815.

"I am going to transfer my imperial head-quarters this evening to Beaumont. To-morrow, the 15th, I shall move to Charleroi, where the Prussian army is; this will give rise to a battle or to the retreat of the enemy. The army is splendid and the weather fine enough; the country is very well disposed. . . ." (Not signed.)

On the same day Napoleon wrote a series of instructions for his War Minister. Suchet was to seize upon Montmelian, and to fortify himself there; the 300 naval guns were to be placed in position in Paris; Lecourbe was to dispute first the passage of the Rhine, then the passage of the Vosges and the Jura; he was to show fight at Belfort, then at Langres, and to defend the Aube, the Seine, and the Yonne. Suchet was to defend Lyons, the Saône, and the Rhone. Rapp was to defend Alsace

us; but I have accounts from Paris of the 10th, on which day he was still there; and I judge from his speech in the Legislature that his departure was not likely to be immediate. I think we are now too strong for him here."—GURWOOD, xii. 462.

On the night of the 13th the Emperor slept at Avesnes.

as well as possible; then the Vosges; after that the Meurthe and the Moselle, and finally the Meuse and the Marne. Having written these gloomy instructions which foreboded defeat, the Emperor thus addressed the army :—

"SOLDIERS,—To-day is the anniversary of Marengo and Friedland, which twice decided the destinies of Europe. Then, as after the battle of Austerlitz, as after Wagram, we were too generous; we believed in the protestations and the promises of the princes whom we left on their thrones! To-day, however, coalesced, they threaten the independence and the most sacred rights of France. They have commenced the most unjust of aggressions. Let us march, then, to meet them. Are not we and they the same men?

"Soldiers, at Jena, against these same Prussians so arrogant to-day, you were one against three; at Montmirail one against six. Let those among you who have been prisoners of the English tell the tale of their hulks and the frightful hardships you suffered.

"The Saxons, the Belgians, the Hanoverians, the soldiers of the Confederation of the Rhine, groan at being obliged to fight for princes who are the enemies of the rights of the people. They know that this coalition is insatiable. After having devoured twelve millions of Poles, twelve millions of Italians, one million of Saxons, six millions of Belgians, they wish to devour the secondary states of Germany.

"The madmen! A moment of prosperity blinds them. The oppression and the humiliation of the French people are beyond their power. If they enter France they will find their graves there.

"Soldiers, we have forced marches to make, battles to fight, and perils to encounter; but with constancy victory will declare itself for us: the rights, the honour, and the welfare of the country will be reconquered.

"For every Frenchman with a heart the moment has come to conquer or to die.

"NAPOLEON."

To PRINCE JOSEPH.

"CHARLEROI, 15*th June*, 1815. 9 P.M.

"MONSEIGNEUR,—The Emperor, who has been on horseback ever since 3 A.M., has just returned overcome by fatigue. He has thrown himself on a bed to take a few hours' repose. He is to be on horseback again at midnight. His Majesty not being able to write to your Highness, has directed me to send you the following information:—The army forced the passage of the Sambre near Charleroi, and placed its outposts half-way between Charleroi and Namur, and half-way between Charleroi and Brussels. We have made 1,500 prisoners and captured six guns. Four Prussian regiments were extirpated.[1] The Emperor lost very few men. But he experienced a loss which he feels deeply; his aide-de-camp, General Letort, was killed on the plateau of Fleurus while commanding a charge of cavalry. The enthusiasm of the inhabitants of Charleroi and of all the country through which we pass is beyond description.

"The Emperor desires that you will communicate this news to the ministers.

"It is possible that an important action may take place to-morrow.

"The First Secretary of the Cabinet,
"BARON FAIN."

General Hulot, who succeeded Bourmont after that officer deserted, says in his report of this affair: "The enemy, on being attacked, fell back from cantonment to cantonment without being broken, and the villages are so close to each other in this country, and the ground offers so many obstacles, that it would have been difficult for a raid, no matter how well conducted, to have succeeded to the extent of dispersing an army."

To PRINCE JOSEPH.

"CHARLEROI, 16*th June*, 1815.

"The bulletin will have acquainted you with what happened yesterday. I am going to transfer my headquarters to Fleurus. We are executing a movement on a large scale. I greatly regret the loss of General Letort. . . . The confiscation of the property of the traitors who are at Ghent (with Louis XVIII.) is necessary.

"NAPOLEON."

To MARSHAL NEY.

"CHARLEROI, 16*th June*, 1815.

"I send you my aide-de-camp, General Flahault, with the present letter. . . . I wish to write to you in detail because it is of the greatest importance.

"Marshal Grouchy is marching on Sombreffe with the third and fourth corps of infantry. I am going to march with my Guard upon Fleurus where I shall be myself before noon. I shall attack the enemy if I meet them, and I shall reconnoitre the road *as far as Gembloux*. There, according to what happens, I shall make up my mind about 3 P.M. or in the evening. . . . As soon as I come to a decision you must be ready *to march upon Brussels*. I will support you with my Guard, which will be at Fleurus or at Sombreffe, and *I should like to be at Brussels to-morrow morning*. [Follow some instructions for the occupation of Quatre Bras.]

"I have determined as a general principle during this campaign to divide my army into two wings and a reserve. Your wing will be composed of four divisions of the first corps, &c., from about 45,000 to 50,000 men. Marshal Grouchy will have about the same force, and will command the right wing.

"The Guard will form the reserve, and *I shall throw myself upon one wing or the other*, according to circumstances.

... You will appreciate the importance which I attach to the capture of Brussels.... So prompt a movement will cut the English off from Mons and from Ostend...[1]

"NAPOLEON."

The battle of Ligny had hardly commenced when Napoleon sent orders to Ney to act so as to envelop the Prussian right, and so much importance did he attach to this diversion that he wrote and sent him word several times that the fate of France was in his hands. (There is no trace of these despatches in *The Correspondence*, but Jomini, in his *Campagne de 1815*, p. 170, quotes one written by Soult at 3.30 from Fleurus to the above effect.)

Ney replied that he had the whole English army on his hands, and that all he could do was to promise to hold it in check. The Emperor, better informed, assured him that he had to deal merely with Wellington's advanced guard, and he once more ordered him to drive back the English at no matter what cost, to seize upon Quatre Bras, and to manœuvre in the direction of Bry and St. Amand.

M. Fleury de Chaboulon, who was acting as secretary to the Emperor, gives the above details in his *Memoirs* (vol. ii. p. 164), followed by a description of Ney's defeat at Quatre Bras. He says:—"Marshal Ney, who had with him only 20,000 men, wished to call up the first corps which he had left in his rear; but the Emperor had sent orders to Comte d'Erlon to join him, and the first corps had already moved off. Ney, when he received this news, was in a cross fire from the enemy's batteries, and was terribly angry. He at once despatched positive orders to Comte d'Erlon to retrace his steps, and Comte d'Erlon unfortunately had the weakness to obey" (p. 167).

Therefore Napoleon, instead of supporting Ney with his Guard as he promised in his letter of the 16th,

---

[1] It was in anticipation of such an attempt as this being probable that Wellington would not concentrate until sure where Napoleon intended to attack.

deprived him of the first corps, which, ordered backwards and forwards, fought neither at Ligny nor at Quatre Bras, which latter place it did not reach until Ney had been driven back to Frasnes.

And on the same day (16th June) the Emperor gave Grouchy orders to march upon Sombreffe, adding—" If the enemy are at Sombreffe I intend to attack them. I will attack them *even at Gembloux*, and also seize upon that position, my intention being, after having made myself acquainted with these two positions, to start to-night, in order to operate against the English with my left wing, commanded by Marshal Ney. . . . All the information I have received shows that the Prussians cannot oppose us with more than 40,000 men."

By the above important orders it will be seen what Napoleon's intentions were, how he miscalculated and how he was foiled. He made sure of Ney being able to surprise and beat the English without any difficulty. He made sure of being able to drive the Prussians back across the Rhine by way of Namur. It was also his intention to succour his wings instead of receiving succour from them. We shall see what happened. The real force of the Prussians at Ligny was about 90,000 men; but Napoleon, as Jomini remarks, at first thought that he had only one corps to deal with. He thought the Prussians were at Gembloux, when they had taken up their position at Ligny, leaving a much smaller gap between them and the English.

ORDER.

"18*th June*, 1815. 11 A.M.

"As soon as all the army is drawn up in battle array, at about 1 P.M., the moment the Emperor gives the order to Marshal Ney, the attack upon the village of Mont-St.-Jean, where the roads intersect each other, will commence. To this effect the battery of twelve belonging to the second corps and that of the sixth will unite with that of the first corps. These eighty guns will open fire on the troops at Mont-

St.-Jean, and Comte d'Erlon will commence the attack by throwing forward his left and supporting it according to circumstances with the divisions with the first corps.

"The second corps will advance by degrees so as to keep on a line with Comte d'Erlon.

"The companies of the sappers of the first corps must be ready to barricade themselves at once at Mont-St.-Jean."

As it turned out the attack was commenced upon Hougomont.

Napoleon had no time to dictate any more letters or despatches until he had recrossed the frontier as a fugitive. He then drew up a detailed account of the battles of Ligny and Waterloo.

LAON, 20*th June*, 1815.

On the morning of the 16th the army occupied the following positions:—

The left wing, commanded by Marshal Ney, and composed of the first and second infantry and the second cavalry corps, occupied the position of Frasnes.

The right wing, commanded by Marshal Grouchy, and composed of the third and fourth infantry and the third cavalry corps, occupied the heights behind Fleurus.

The head-quarters of the Emperor were at Charleroi with the Imperial Guard and the sixth corps.

The left wing had orders to march upon Quatre Bras, and the right wing on Sombreffe.

Marshal Grouchy's columns, while on the march, perceived, after passing Fleurus, the army of the enemy commanded by Field-Marshal Blucher, occupying the tablelands to the left of the village of Sombreffe, with its cavalry stretching along the road to Namur; its right was at St. Amand, which was strongly occupied, having a ravine in front of it.

The Emperor reconnoitred the force, and the positions

of the enemy, and determined to attack at once. It was necessary to make a change of front, bringing the right forward and *pivotant* on Fleurus.

General Vandamme marched upon St. Amand, General Gérard on Ligny, and Marshal Grouchy on Sombreffe. The third division of the second corps, commanded by General Gérard, was in reserve behind the corps of General Vandamme. The Guard was drawn up on the heights of Fleurus, as also the cuirassiers of General Milhaud.

At 3 P.M. these movements were finished. The division of General Lefol, forming part of Vandamme's corps, was the first engaged, and seized upon St. Amand, from which the enemy were driven with the bayonet. It held its own, during the whole engagement, in the cemetery of St. Amand. But this village, which is very straggling, was the scene of several struggles during the evening. The entire corps of Vandamme was engaged, and the enemy brought a large force into action.

General Girard, placed in reserve, turned the village to the right, and fought with his usual valour. The forces on each side were supported by sixty guns.

On the right General Gérard, with the fourth corps, attacked the village of Ligny, which was taken and retaken several times. Marshal Grouchy, on the extreme right, and General Pajol attacked the village of Sombreffe. The enemy displayed from 80,000 to 90,000 men and a great number of guns.

At 7 P.M. we were masters of all the villages situated along the ravine which covered the position of the enemy; but the enemy still occupied the table-land round the windmill of Bussy.

The Emperor marched with his Guard to the village of Ligny; General Gérard ordered General Pécheux to debouch with what remained of the reserve, all his troops having been engaged in that village. Eight battalions of the Guard debouched with fixed bayonets, and to their rear were four squadrons *de service*, the cuirassiers of General

Delord, those of General Milhaud, and the mounted grenadiers of the Guard. The Old Guard charged the enemy's columns, which were on the heights of Bussy, at the bayonet, and in an instant strewed the battle-field with dead. The squadron *de service* attacked and broke a square, and the cuirassiers drove the enemy in all directions. By half-past seven we had taken forty guns, a great many waggons, standards, and prisoners, and the enemy sought safety in a precipitate flight. At ten o'clock the battle was over, and we remained masters of the entire field.[1]

General Lutzow was captured. The prisoners say that Field-Marshal Blucher was wounded. The flower of the Prussian army was destroyed in this battle. It cannot have lost less than 15,000 men. Our loss amounts to 3,000 killed or wounded.

On the left Marshal Ney marched to Quatre Bras with a division, which defeated an English division posted there. But attacked by the Prince of Orange with 25,000 men, partly English and partly Hanoverians, he fell back upon his position of Frasnes. There a series of engagements took place, the enemy vainly endeavouring to force it. Marshal Ney, who was waiting for the first corps, which did not arrive until night, confined himself to keeping his position. A square having been attacked by the eighth cuirassiers the colours of the 69th English regiment fell into our hands. The Duke of Brunswick was killed. The Prince of Orange was wounded. We are assured that the

---

[1] General Gneisenau says in his official report : "Our infantry placed to the rear of Ligny, although obliged to retreat, was not discouraged . . . formed in masses it repulsed all the charges of the cavalry with coolness, and retired in good order. . . . At a quarter of a league from the field of battle the army reformed ; the enemy did not attempt a pursuit. The village of Bry remained in our possession all night, as well as Sombreffe, where General Thielman had fought with the third corps, and from whence he fell back leisurely at daybreak on Gembloux, where the fourth corps, under General Bulow, had at last arrived."

enemy had a great number of generals of note either killed or wounded. The loss of the English is set down at from 4,000 to 5,000 men; ours on this side was very heavy; it amounted to 4,500 men killed or wounded. Night put an end to the combat. Lord Wellington afterwards evacuated Quatre Bras, and fell back upon Gemappe.

On the morning of the 17th the Emperor advanced to Quatre Bras, from whence he marched to attack the English army; he drove it back to the border of the forest of Soignies with his left wing and the reserve. The right wing marched by Sombreffe in pursuit of Field-Marshal Blucher, who was marching upon Warres, where he appeared desirous of taking up his position.

At 10 P.M. the English army occupying Mont-St.-Jean with its centre took up its position in front of the forest of Soignies; it would have required three hours to prepare to attack it; it was necessary to wait till the next day.

The Emperor established his head-quarters at the farm of the Caillou, near Plancenoit. The rain was falling in torrents.

BATTLE OF MONT-ST.-JEAN.

At 9 A.M., the rain having somewhat diminished, the first corps began to move, and took up its position with its left on the Brussels road, and opposite the village of Mont-St.-Jean, which appeared to be the centre of the enemy's position. The second corps rested its right on the Brussels road, and its left on a little wood within cannon shot of the English army. The cuirassiers were in reserve to the rear, and the Guard in reserve on the heights. The sixth corps, with the cavalry of General Domon, under the orders of Comte Lobau, was destined to take up its position to our right rear, to resist a Prussian corps which appeared to have escaped from Marshal Grouchy, and to have the intention of falling upon our right flank—intention which had been revealed to us by the letter of a

Prussian general captured by one of our scouts. The troops were in high glee.

The strength of the English army was set down at 80,000 men; it was supposed that the Prussian corps which might come up in the evening was about 15,000 strong. The forces of the enemy therefore amounted to over 90,000 men, and ours were less numerous.

At noon the preparations were terminated, and Prince Jerome, commanding a division of the second corps, destined to form the extreme left, attacked the wood, a portion of which was held by the enemy. The artillery opened fire; the enemy supported the troops whom they had sent to hold the wood with thirty guns. At one o'clock Prince Jerome was master of the whole wood, and the entire English army fell back behind some rising ground. Comte d'Erlon then attacked the village of Mont-St.-Jean, and his attack was supported by eighty guns. A fearful artillery action took place, from which the English army must have suffered heavily. One of the brigades of Comte d'Erlon's first division carried the village of Mont-St.-Jean; a second brigade was charged by a body of English cavalry, which inflicted a serious loss upon it. At the same moment a division of English cavalry charged Comte d'Erlon's battery on the right, and disabled several pieces; but Milhaud's cuirassiers charged this division, three regiments of which were broken and cut to pieces.[1]

It was 3 P.M. The Emperor moved forward the Guard to draw it up in the plain upon the ground which had been occupied by the first corps at the commencement of the action, that corps having pushed forward. The Prussian division, whose arrival had been foreseen, was now engaged with the skirmishers of Comte Lobau, firing into our right flank. It was necessary, before attempting anything else, to await the issue of this attack. To this effect

---

[1] But not before, as Jomini says, they had thrown the French infantry into confusion, and rendered a portion of their artillery useless.

the whole reserve was held in readiness to march to the assistance of Comte Lobau, and to crush the Prussian corps when it advanced.

That accomplished, the Emperor intended to open an attack upon the village of Mont-St.-Jean, from which he hoped a decided success; but by a movement of impatience, so frequent in our military annals, and which has been so often fatal, the cavalry reserve having perceived a retrograde movement which the English made to shelter themselves from our batteries, from which they had already suffered so heavily, crowned the heights of Mont-St.-Jean and charged the infantry. This movement, which, made at the proper time and supported by the reserves, was to decide the day, made alone and before affairs on the right were terminated, was disastrous. Having no means of countermanding it, the enemy showing numerous masses of infantry and cavalry, and the two divisions of cuirassiers being engaged, all our cavalry rushed at the same moment to support their comrades. There during three hours numerous charges were executed, during which we broke several squares of English infantry and captured six colours—advantage out of proportion to the loss inflicted on our cavalry by grape and musketry. It was impossible to employ our infantry reserve until we had repulsed the Prussian attack on our flank. This attack continued to extend perpendicularly on our right flank. The Emperor despatched General Duhesme there with the Young Guard and several reserve batteries. The enemy were checked, were repulsed, and recoiled; they had exhausted their strength, and there was nothing more to be feared. This was the moment indicated for an attack on the centre of the enemy.

As the cuirassiers suffered from the grape, four battalions of the Middle Guard were ordered to protect them, support the position, and, if possible, disengage a portion of our cavalry and allow it to fall back into the plain. Two other battalions were sent to place themselves *en potence*.

on the extreme left of the division which had manœuvred on our flank, so as to relieve us of uneasiness on that side. The remainder were drawn up in reserve, a portion to occupy the *potence* to the rear of Mont-St.-Jean, a portion on the plateau to the rear of the field of battle which formed our position in case of retreat.

In this state of affairs the battle was won : we occupied all the positions which the enemy had occupied at the beginning of the action ; but our cavalry having been too soon and incautiously employed we could hope for no decisive result. But Marshal Grouchy, having learned the movement of the Prussian corps, was marching on the rear of that corps, and thus insured us a decisive success for the next day. After eight hours of firing, of charges of infantry and of cavalry, the whole army saw with satisfaction the battle gained and the battle-field in our power.

About half-past eight the four battalions of the Middle Guard which had been posted on the plateau beyond Mont-St.-Jean in order to support the cuirassiers, being harassed by the enemy's grape, tried to carry the batteries at the bayonet.[1] Night was coming on ; a charge

---

[1] Colonel Baudus, who was one of Soult's aides-de-camp, has traced a graphic description of the Emperor at this critical moment. In a work on the battle of Waterloo he says :—

"After the disastrous result of this attack there remained only a few regiments of the Old Guard who had not been engaged; these corps were formed into a square to protect the retreat. It was in the middle of one of these squares that the Emperor placed himself: therefore only a small number of officers were admitted, so as not to crowd upon him ; as for myself, I was not allowed in.

"I will not reproach Napoleon with not having exposed himself; he certainly ran great risk where he posted himself so as to follow the execution of his last orders, since I was wounded close to him by the splinter of a shell ; but when he decided upon making that despairing attack he ought to have placed himself at the head of his Guard and have sought death if it did not succeed.

"I examined him attentively during this last act of his military life, and, while thinking of all the misfortunes which this man had drawn

made on their flank by several English squadrons threw them into disorder; the fugitives recrossed the ravine; the neighbouring regiments who saw some troops belonging to the Guard disbanded, thought that it was the Old Guard which had given way. Cries of "*Tout est perdu! La Garde est repoussée!*" were heard. The soldiers pretend even that at several points malevolent persons shouted "*Sauve qui peut!*" However that may be, panic at once spread over the whole field of battle, and a rush was made on the line of communications in the greatest disorder; soldiers, gunners, ammunition-waggons hurried to arrive there; the Old Guard, which was in reserve, was assailed by the fugitives, and was itself carried away by them.

In an instant the army was nothing but a confused mass; the various branches were mixed together, and it was impossible to re-form a corps. The enemy, who perceived this astonishing confusion, let loose their columns of cavalry; the disorder increased; the confusion of night rendered it impossible to rally the troops and to show them their error.

Thus a battle terminated, a day finished, false manœuvres repaired, the greatest success insured for the morrow—all was lost in a moment of panic. Even the household squadrons, drawn up alongside of the Emperor, were overthrown and disorganised by the tumultuous waves, and there was nothing left but to follow the torrent. The reserve parks, the baggage which had not recrossed the Sambre, and everything that was on the field of battle fell into the hands of the enemy. There were not even any means of waiting for the troops on our right; it is well

down upon my country, I experienced so lively an indignation, and so deep a pain, that I should still reproach myself for the anguish I felt lest he should fall into the hands of the enemy had there not been something more than interest for his person in this feeling. I should have considered it a blessing for my country had he been killed, but I should have been grieved to see him fall into the hands of the enemy; this would have dishonoured the army which had thrown itself into his arms with such enthusiasm."

known what the bravest army in the world is when it is clubbed, and when its organisation no longer exists.

The Emperor passed the Sambre at Charleroi on the 19th at 5 A.M. Philippeville and Avesnes were chosen as points of concentration. Prince Jerome, General Morand, and other generals have already rallied a part of the army there. Marshal Grouchy with the right wing is operating a movement on the Lower Sambre.

The loss of the enemy must be very heavy to judge from the number of flags which we captured, and the retrograde movements they made: ours cannot be ascertained until after our troops have rallied. Before the disorder broke out we had already suffered heavily, especially our cavalry, which was so fatally and so gallantly brought into action. In spite of its losses this valiant cavalry constantly kept the position which it won from the English, and did not abandon it until the tumult and disorder of the battle-field forced it to retire. In the darkness, and amid the obstacles which encumbered the road, it was unable to preserve its organisation. The artillery as usual covered itself with glory.

The head-quarter carriages remained in their ordinary position, no retrograde movement having been deemed necessary. In the course of the day they fell into the hands of the enemy.

Such was the issue of the battle of Mont-St.-Jean, glorious for the French arms, and yet so disastrous.

The closing scene at Waterloo and the *sauve qui peut* was thus described in a letter which Jerome Bonaparte wrote to his wife. Perhaps there is a touch of romance in it, as Jerome was fond of swagger. However, he wrote directly after the battle, saying, among other things:—

" The Emperor, hoping that Grouchy would arrive, said ' The battle is won; we must occupy the positions of the enemy; forward!' and all with the exception of six battalions of the Old Guard marched with us. Ney was reinforced by four regiments of the Guard, and reached the English guns. We supported him. Everything was going well, when General Friand was wounded, and, I know not by what fatality, the attack of the Guard failed! The Guard was repulsed, it was necessary to retreat, but it was too late. The Emperor wished to die; we were in the midst of the enemy's fire. Wellington, who had his light cavalry quite fresh, let it loose on the plain at about 8 P.M.; at 9 a panic seized on the army; at 10 there was a rout; our guns had no more ammunition. The Emperor was swept away; no orders were given; we ran till we crossed the Sambre. I reached Avesnes the next day, having been constantly with the rear-guard. At this place I found neither the Emperor nor any of his marshals; they had gone on. I made desperate efforts to rally the *débris* of the army, and I managed to get together 18,000 infantry, 3,000 cavalry, and twelve guns, with which force I reached Laon on June 21. Marshal Soult was there; he thought I was alone, and could not believe I had so large a force; and when one of my orderly officers arrived in Paris, to give an account of this happy news, Marshal Ney, who had been there for several days, declared in the Chamber of Peers that it was impossible. . . . On the day of the battle the Emperor was sublime up till eight o'clock. . . . I press you to my heart, as well as my son. When shall we be united?"

Capefigue (vol. ii., p. 213) says that Napoleon wrote two letters to Joseph after Waterloo, dated from Charleroi; that the first was a long lie about the battle, and was intended for publicity; the second letter, which was confidential, contained the whole truth, but insisted that all was not lost. He spoke of soon having 300,000 men to oppose to the enemy, of raising 100,000 conscripts.

"I am going to Laon," he added, "where I shall find some troops. I have heard nothing of Grouchy; if he be not taken prisoner, as I fear, I shall have 50,000 men in three days; with them I shall harass the enemy, and give Paris and France time to do their duty. The English march slowly; the Prussians are afraid of the peasants. . . . Tell me what effect this horrible battle has produced on the Chamber."

There is no trace of these letters in *The Correspondence*, or in the *Memoirs of King Joseph*. As for Grouchy, he fell back with 32,000 men, in good order, on Namur, where he learned that Napoleon had abdicated for the second time.

As M. Thiers, and other historians nearly as regardless of facts, have blamed Marshal Grouchy, and attributed to him the loss of Waterloo, we give a short analysis of a volume written in 1864 by his son, the Marquis de Grouchy, who was present at Waterloo.

Grouchy's defence amounts to this:—On the evening of the 16th he expected to receive orders to pursue the enemy, but he received none. The Emperor left the field of battle without sending any order to his right wing. He returned to Fleurus, which lies about a league to the south of Ligny. Grouchy was ordered to join the Emperor, and on reaching Fleurus was much astonished, instead of receiving orders to pursue the Prussians, to be told to wait until the next day to learn the intentions of his Majesty. In the meantime Grouchy sent out his light cavalry north and east in order to obtain news of the enemy. At daybreak, on the 17th, Grouchy went to head-quarters, but the Emperor, who was unwell, was sound asleep, and Soult, in spite of the solicitations of Grouchy, refused to disturb him. He waited in the ante-room until 8 A.M., when the Emperor sent him word that he was going to visit the field of battle, and that he (Grouchy) was to join him. Napoleon remained on the battle-field until one o'clock, and on leaving it said to Grouchy, " Go in pursuit of the Prussians, complete their defeat by attacking them as soon as you come up with them, and do not lose sight of them. I am going to unite Marshal Ney's corps to the troops I have with me, and to attack the English if they make a stand on this side of the forest of Soignies. You must correspond with me by the paved road "—*i.e.*, the road from Namur to Quatre Bras.

Now the Prussians, without being disorganised or demoralised, had fallen back from Ligny at 9 P.M. on the 16th. They, therefore, had fourteen hours' start of Grouchy, *who was not to lose sight of them*. Grouchy pointed out this and other facts to the Emperor. He said, too, that many of his men had taken their firelocks to pieces, and were washing them, and that detachments had been sent out in quest of provisions for the men, and forage for the horses. He could not, therefore, march directly. He then expressed fears that with 30,000 or 32,000 men he would not be able to force Blucher to alter his line of march, or to complete the defeat of an army of 90,000 men which had repulsed the last charges of cavalry made against it, and had even, for a short time, resumed the offensive. Grouchy begged the Emperor as he was going to fight the English not to order him beyond the sphere of operations, and not to send him in the direction of Namur and Liège. Napoleon, much annoyed at these observations, reiterated his orders, saying :—" March in the direction of Namur, for, according to all probabilities, the Prussians are falling back on the Meuse; it is, therefore, in that direction that you will find them, and it is in that direction that you should march." This error explains the supineness of Napoleon, for if the Prussians were retreating on Namur they were marching straight away from the English army. It also proves that he had a very incorrect notion of the situation, considered that the Prussian army was demoralised, and was falling back on its basis, and that Grouchy would have nothing to do but to harass its retreat. This fatal mistake was the cause of the delay which gave the enemy a start of fourteen hours.[1]

[1] The fact is, that Napoleon had lost the Prussian army as he lost the Russians after Austerlitz and the allies after Lutzen, not knowing whether they had fallen back on Berlin or Breslau.

Grouchy has been blamed for not having marched to the scene of action, as Gérard and Excelmans implored him to do when they heard the battle raging at Waterloo. Grouchy's defence is that the firing did not astonish him, for the Emperor, when he detached him, said that he was going to fight the English; that Napoleon gave him no orders to join him; that if he had attempted this cross march he could not have reached the field of battle until late in the evening, with only a portion of his corps, and without his artillery, and at the same time he would have exposed his flank to Thielman, and have been unable to stop Bulow or even Blucher.

At 10 A.M. on the 18th, Soult wrote to Grouchy from the farm of Caillou, saying:—" The Emperor directs me to warn you that he is about to attack the English army, which has taken up its position at Waterloo. Therefore his Majesty desires that you will manœuvre in the direction of Wavres, so as to approach us, establish communications, and pursue the Prussian army which has fallen back upon, and which may have halted at, Wavres, where you should arrive as soon as possible. . . ." It was noon before this despatch was finished, registered, and handed to the Polish aide-de-camp, who had to go round by Gembloux, according to the directions of the Emperor, for fear of falling into the hands of the Prussians; and it was 4 P.M. before Zenowicz was able to hand it to Grouchy, who conceived that he had rightly carried out the orders of the Emperor in marching on Wavres, and not on Namur, and in pursuing the Prussians instead of trying to join him.

Later in the day Soult wrote another despatch to Grouchy, saying:—" The movement on Wavres is in conformity with the instructions given to you by his Majesty. However, the Emperor directs me to tell you to manœuvre in our direction, so as to join us before any corps of the enemy can get between us."—A postscript added:—" General Bulow is going to attack us in flank, therefore do not lose an instant, and you will take him in *flagrante delicto.*" .This despatch did not reach Grouchy until 7 P.M., and this was the first intimation which he received that his presence was required at Waterloo, where he was fully convinced that Napoleon would easily overthrow Wellington and his forces.

Long before receiving this order Grouchy had attacked the Prussians at Wavres, but without being able to drive them out of that place. Unable to pass the Dyle at Wavres, he tried to pass it at Limale, but there again he was foiled. Blucher, in fact, had left Thielman behind with 30,000 men to hold Grouchy and his 30,000 men in check, and with his remaining 60,000 men he had pushed on as best he could to lend a helping hand to Wellington.[1] The fault of Grouchy was, therefore, that with 30,000 men he was unable to prevent a portion of a force three times as large as his own, and which had fourteen hours' start of him, from effecting its junction with the English. The fact is that Grouchy on the 18th could no more accomplish what the Emperor required of him when he found himself in difficulties, than Ney had been able to accomplish, on the 16th. Ney received his orders too late, and then found his hands too full at Quatre Bras to fall upon the Prussian right. Grouchy received his orders too late, and then found his hands too full at Wavres to fall on the English left.

Jomini has blamed Grouchy for having carried out the orders of the Emperor when he found that the Emperor was mistaken in supposing that Blucher, thoroughly demoralised, had fallen back upon Namur, instead of on Wavres; but Napoleon himself did not blame Grouchy until he got to St. Helena. In the twenty-ninth bulletin, written at Laon, there is no question of Grouchy. Before

---

[1] It must be remembered that the Prussians were reinforced by Bulow's corps on the evening of the 16th, just after Ligny had been fought. Grouchy consequently had to pursue a force equal to that with which Napoleon had just been engaged.

leaving France, as we shall see, the Emperor several times attributed the loss of Waterloo to Marshal Ney, never to Marshal Grouchy.

M. Fleury de Chaboulon gives the following account of the bulletin written at Laon, which he wrote at the dictation of the Emperor:—

"When it was terminated he called in the Grand Marshal, General Drouot, and the other aides-de-camp. 'Here,' said he, 'is the bulletin of Mont-St.-Jean; I wish you to hear it read. If I have omitted any essential facts you must remind me of them; I do not intend to dissimulate anything. As after Moscow, I must tell France the whole truth. I might have thrown upon Marshal Ney a portion of the misfortunes of this day; but the harm is done; it is no use speaking about it.' [Nothing about Grouchy.] I read out the bulletin; a few slight changes were proposed by General Drouot, and agreed to by the Emperor; but I cannot tell upon what grounds he was at first loth to acknowledge that his carriages had fallen into the hands of the enemy.—' When you pass through Paris,' said M. de Flahaut, 'it will be seen that they have been taken. If you hide it you will be accused of disguising more important truths.' The Emperor, after raising some objections, finished by yielding."

Napoleon at first thought of remaining at Laon. Some of his comrades said—"If you go to Paris you will be accused of deserting your army again as in Egypt, in Spain, and in Russia." Others, however, insisted that his presence was necessary in the capital, and thither he set out, very uncertain how he would be received.

Capefigue in his *Cent Jours* relates that:—

"On arriving at the Elysée after Waterloo, Napoleon said to Caulaincourt:—' The army had performed prodigies when it was seized with a panic, and all was lost; Ney behaved like a madman; he caused all my cavalry to be massacred. I am quite worn out. I must have two hours' repose before attending to business.' And placing his hand on his heart he added—'I am stifling there.'" No mention was made of Grouchy.

MESSAGE TO THE CHAMBER OF REPRESENTATIVES.

"PALACE OF THE ELYSÉE, 21st *June*, 1815.

"After the battles of Ligny and Mont St.-Jean, and after having provided for the rallying of the army at Avesnes and at Philippeville for the defence of the frontier places and that of Soissons and Laon, I came to Paris to concert measures with my ministers for the defence of the nation, and to arrive at an understanding with the Chambers as to what is required for the safety of the country.

"I have formed a committee consisting of Caulaincourt, Carnot, and Fouché, to renew and to pursue negotiations with the foreign Powers, so as to ascertain their veritable intentions, and to put an end to the war, if that is compatible with the independence and honour of France. But the greatest amount of union is necessary, and I reckon upon the co-operation and patriotism of the Chambers, and on their attachment to my person.

"I send Prince Lucien and the Ministers of Foreign Affairs, of War, of the Interior, and of the Police, to take the present message to the Chambers, and to communicate all the information which they may desire to know.

"NAPOLEON."

The French seem never to tire of Waterloo. It appears a kind of enigma which they cannot explain satisfactorily. The names of the soldiers, the historians, and poets who have dealt with the memorable campaign of 1815 would alone fill a volume, and the *Spectateur Militaire* (1st March, 1884) is still discussing the treason of Bourmont and the operations of Grouchy. Victor Hugo, who gave a very dashing picture of the battle in *Les Misérables*, came to the conclusion that it was neither Napoleon nor Wellington who won the day, but Cambronne. In *Les Châtiments* the poet thus vividly described the *sauve qui peut* which, as Gneisenau said, resembled the flight of barbarians. After some preliminary lines we see that—

> " Derrière un mamelon la Garde était massée,
> La Garde, espoir suprême et suprême pensée !
> * * * * * *
> Comprenant qu'ils allaient mourir dans cette fête,
> Saluerent leur Dieu, debout dans la tempête.
> Leur bouche, d'un seul cri, dit : Vive l'Empereur !
> Puis, à pas lents, musique en tête, sans fureur,
> Tranquille, souriant à la mitraille anglaise,
> La Garde Imperiale entra dans la fournaise."

The Guard melted away like wax, and then—

> " La déroute apparut au soldat qui s'emeut,
> Et se tordant les bras, cria, Sauve qui peut !
> Sauve qui peut ! affront ! horreur ! toutes les bouches
> Criaient ; à travers champs, fous, éperdus, farouches
> Comme si quelque souffle avait passé sur eux,
> Parmi les lourds caissons et les fourgons poudreux,
> Roulant dans les fossés, se cachant dans les seigles,
> Jetant shakos, manteaux, fusils, jetant les aigles.
> Sous les sabres pruissiens, ces vétérans, ô deuil !
> Tremblaient, hurlaient, pleuraient, couraient !—En un clin d'œil,
> Comme s'envole au vent une paille enflammée,
> S'évanouit ce bruit qui fut la grande armée." [1]
> * * * * * *

---

[1] Not long ago, too, we found in *La Revue Historique* the following interesting letter written by the historian Sismondi to his mother with this heading :—

ON LIRA AVEC ÉMOTION LE RÈCIT SUIVANT DE LA BATAILLE DE WATERLOO, D'APRÈS LES PREMIÈRES NOUVELLES ARRIVÉES À PARIS, ET RECUEILLIES PAR L'AUTEUR DE L' " HISTOIRE DES FRANÇAIS : "

"23 *juin*, 1815, vendredi matin.

"Je n'ai point commencé ma lettre au commencement de la semaine, bonne mère ; je fis partir celle de dimanche avec peu d'espérance qu'elle pût faire son chemin. Dans les quatre jours qui suivi-

It was very unlikely that the allies who refused to negotiate before Waterloo would consent to negotiate

rent, la communication fut interrompue de tous les côtés ; de nouveaux désastres, une catastrophe qu'on ne pouvait prévoir, rouvriront peut-être aujourd'hui la communication. L'armée, sous les ordres immédiats de l'Empereur, avait commencé les hostilités le 15, et remporté un avantage brillant à Charleroi le 16. Avec une force d'environ 90,000 hommes, elle attaqua près de Fleurus l'armée combinée prussienne et anglaise ; après le combat le plus acharné et à la fin de la journée seulement, elle coupa sa ligne, repoussa les Anglais du côté de Bruxelles et les Prussiens du côté de Namur. Napoléon avec 50,000 hommes, se chargea de la poursuite des premiers, le maréchal de Grouchy de celle des seconds.

"La journée du 17, qui fut extrêmement pluvieuse, fut employée en marches et petits combats.

"Le 18, Napoléon attaqua Wellington retranché dans la forêt de Soignies, devant Bruxelles. Les forces anglaises étaient doubles des siennes, elles avaient encore l'avantage de retranchements préparés longtemps à l'avance et d'une formidable artillerie.

"Ses généraux jugèrent qu'il y avait très-peu d'espérance de succès ; il voulut tenter la fortune.

"Sa brave Garde, l'élite de la nation, et ce que la France possédait de plus glorieux, le seconda avec ce courage calme et inébranlable que ces vieux soldats portaient empreint sur leur front. La vieille Garde était un corps de 7,000 hommes, dont plus des trois quarts avaient obtenu, par des actions éclatantes, la décoration de la Légion d'Honneur.

"Une batterie effroyable qui était masquée a bientôt labouré leurs rangs. Cette vieille Garde n'existe plus ; ils ont tous péri ; lorsque, après le combat le plus acharné, dans lequel plusieurs des positions anglaises ont été enlevées à la baïonnette, et dans lequel Bonaparte cherchait et appelait. a mort sans pouvoir la trouver, se tenant en dehors et en avant des carrés qui soutenaient le feu le plus violent, une terreur panique, un faux bruit, peut-être une trahison, a tout à coup fait lâcher la pied à l'armée ; mais la vieille Garde, ferme à son poste, et abandonnée seule sur le champ de bataille, a repoussé toutes les instances de Wellington ; aucun d'eux n'a voulu se rendre, et la mitraille n'apportant point encore assez rapidement la mort, le petit nombre de braves qui restaient sans espérance se sont embrassés, puis percés de leurs baïonnettes. C'est sur leur corps qui Louis XVIII. veut monter pour regner.

"Cependant le restant de l'armée, ayant rompu ses rangs, n'a plus pu être reformé ; bientôt ils ont jeté leurs armes pour fuir et, se pré-

after that battle. Nor would they, as the following letter shows.

DECLARATION TO THE FRENCH PEOPLE.

"Frenchmen,—In declaring war in defence of the national independence I reckoned upon the united efforts and the good will of every one, and upon the aid of all the national authorities; I had reasons to hope for success, and I consequently braved all the declarations of the Powers against me.

" Circumstances appear to be changed.

" I offer myself as a sacrifice to the hatred of the enemies of France. May they be sincere in their declarations, that they have borne enmity to my person alone.

" My political career is terminated, and I proclaim my son, under the title of Napoleon II., Emperor of the French.

" The present ministers will form a provisional Government. The interest which I bear my son prompts me to invite the Chambers to organise the Regency without delay.

cipitant dans les chemins comme un troupeau de moutons, entraînant avec eux et devant eux ceux même qui étaient les plus déterminés à tenir, ils ont été poursuivis pendant vingt lieues par la cavalerie anglaise. On ignore encore le nombre des morts et des prisonniers, mais il doit être immense, et surtout la terreur dont l'armée fugitive a frappé la nation ne laisse plus de ressources. Pendant le même temps cependant, le maréchal Grouchy avec son corps d'armée avait battu les Prussiens et occupé Namur. Mais l'empereur ne le savait pas et voyant son armée dissipée, toute son artillerie perdue, il est revenu à Paris, où, après trente-six heures malheureusement perdues en vaines délibérations, il a abdiqué hier l'empire entre les mains des deux Chambres, qui ont nommé une commission de gouvernement provisoire pour négocier avec les puissances et pourvoir en même temps à la défense nationale. Le choix des membres de ce gouvernement provisoire donne l'espérance qu'ils ne voudront pas soumettre la nation à l'ignominie du roi des étrangers, et qu'ils balanceront plutôt entre Marie-Louise et le duc d'Orléans ; mais les représentants sont tumultueux et faibles, ils inspirent peu de confiance. Cependant le désastre public, renfermant une espérance de paix, a fait remonter les fonds d'une manière extraordinaire."

"Let all of you unite for the public safety, in order that France may remain independent.

"NAPOLEON.

"PALACE OF THE ELYSÉE, 22*nd June*, 1815."

The above declaration was forced upon the Emperor by his relations and his friends when they perceived that all was lost, and it was Lucien who wrote it at the dictation of his brother.

Capefigue has given an interesting account of an incident which occurred while the proposition contained in the above declaration was being discussed in the Chamber of Peers. The Imperialists were trying to make out that the situation was by no means so desperate as had been represented. He says that :—

"Marshal Davoust was finishing the reading of a report on the situation of the army, and Carnot was commenting upon it with his usual firmness, when the sound of a hollow voice was heard : it was that of Marshal Ney exclaiming, 'It is not so ; it is false ; they are deceiving you.' After this first extraordinary apostrophe the Marshal, greatly excited, rose, and these were the strange revelations which he made to the peers : 'The news which the Minister of the Interior has just read to you is false—false in every way ! The enemy has triumphed everywhere ; I witnessed the disorder since I commanded under the eyes of the Emperor. After the disastrous results of the 16th and the 18th they presume to tell you that they ended by beating the enemy on the 18th, and that we have still 60,000 men on the frontier. It is false ; and it will be as much as Marshal Grouchy can do to rally 15,000 men, and we have been beaten too thoroughly to be in a condition to resist the enemy. All the generals who are here, and who commanded with me, can attest this. . . . What the Minister of the Interior has said about Marshal Soult is false—quite false ; he has not been able to rally a single man of the Guard. This is our real position. The enemy are at

Nivelle with 80,000 men. When they tell you that the Prussian army is destroyed, that is not true. The greater portion of that army was not engaged. In six or seven days the enemy will perhaps be in the centre of the capital; there is nothing to do but to treat with the enemy.'"

And Marshal Ney, by way of attesting his sincerity, expressed the conviction that he would be shot.

On the 25th June General Bertrand, Grand Marshal of the Palace, was instructed to write to the Imperial Librarian Barbier for "works upon America," a report on everything published on the subject of the campaigns of the Emperor, "and in addition, several works on the United States." The library was to be consigned to an American firm, "who will have it transported to America from Havre."

Having thus shown that it was his intention to make his escape across the Atlantic, Napoleon penned the following farewell address to the army :—

TO THE ARMY.

"LA MALMAISON, 25*th June*, 1815."

" SOLDIERS,—In yielding to the necessity which obliges me to quit the brave French army, I carry away with me the happy certainty that it will justify, by the eminent services which the country expects from it, the praises which even our enemies cannot refuse.

" Soldiers, although absent, I shall follow your footsteps. I know every corps, and none of them will obtain a signal triumph over the enemy without eliciting my admiration. You and I have both been calumniated. Men unworthy of appreciating your labours have seen in the marks of attachment which you have given me a zeal of which I was the sole object. Let your future successes prove that in obeying me you served above all the country, and that if I share your affection I owe it to my ardent love of France, our common mother.

"Soldiers, a few gallant efforts and the coalition will be dissolved. Napoleon will recognise you by the blows you are about to deal. Save the honour and independence of Frenchmen; be to the end the same as I have known you for the last twenty years, and you will be invincible.[1]

"NAPOLEON."

On the 27th June, however, Napoleon, thinking that he might fall upon the Prussians and destroy them before the English could aid them, sent the following letter (which is not given in *The Correspondence*) by General Becker to the Provisional Government:—"In abdicating power I did not renounce the most noble right of a citizen, which is to defend my country. The approach of the enemies to the capital leaves no doubt with regard to their intentions and their bad faith. Under these serious circumstances I offer my services as a general, still looking upon myself as the first soldier of my country."

Capefigue, who gives this letter in his *Cent Jours* (vol. ii. p. 290), says that Fouché, after having negligently read it, threw it on the floor, exclaiming—"This man is then mad! He wishes to compromise everything. Return to the Malmaison, and tell him that he must leave at once; that I can be answerable for nothing that may happen." Blucher, says the same writer, swore that he would hang him at the head of his columns; and his War Minister, Davoust, said to M. de Flahaut—"Well! let him go, or I will seize him myself by the collar."

If anything could excite sympathy for the great soldier whose career was now closed it would be the extraordinary baseness with which he was deserted in his hour of misfortune. Few of his old companions in arms appeared

---

[1] The Provisional Government would not allow the publication of this proclamation.

to realise the beauty of Shakespeare's sublime idea that—

> "He that can endure
> To follow with allegiance a fallen lord,
> Does conquer him that did his master conquer,
> And earns a place in the story."

We find no more written matter until the following :—

To the PRINCE REGENT OF ENGLAND.

"Isle of Aix, 14*th July*, 1815.

"ROYAL HIGHNESS,—Exposed to the factions which divide my country, and to the enmity of the Powers of Europe, I have terminated my political career, and I come, like Themistocles, to seat myself at the hearth of the British people. I place myself beneath the protection of their laws, which protection I claim from your Royal Highness as the most powerful, the most constant, and the most generous of my enemies.

"NAPOLEON."

No notice was taken of this undignified appeal, made when escape was impossible.

INSTRUCTIONS TO CAPTAINS PHILIBERT, *commanding* "*La Saale*," *and* POUCÉ, *commanding the* "*Méduse*."

VERY SECRET.

"The two frigates are destined to take him who was our Emperor to the United States."

Then follow very ample instructions for the comfort and safety of Napoleon, who was to be treated with the greatest honour. If the frigates were attacked, that not bearing Cæsar and his fortunes was to sacrifice itself so as to allow the other to escape.

On the 8th July, the same day that Louis XVIII. re-entered Paris, the Emperor embarked on board the

Saale,[1] but there were eleven English vessels cruising in sight of the port, and after waiting for three days he opened communications with Captain Maitland of the *Bellerophon*, afterwards pretending that good faith had not been kept with him. Napoleon for a moment thought of trying his chance on board a merchant vessel, but the fear of falling into the hands of the Spaniards or the Portuguese made him renounce this idea ; nor did he care to remain any longer in France. The correspondence which ensued between the English naval authorities and Captain Maitland clearly prove that the only promise made to Napoleon before he stepped on board the *Bellerophon* was to take him to England and to treat him with humanity.

PROTESTATION.

"AT SEA, ON BOARD THE 'BELLEROPHON,'
"*4th August*, 1815.

"I here protest solemnly before Heaven and before men against the violation of my most sacred rights, in disposing of my person and of my liberty by force. I came of my own free will on board the *Bellerophon*. I am not a prisoner ; I am the guest of England. I came here myself at the instigation of the captain, who said that he had received orders from his Government to convey me to England with my suite, if that were agreeable to me. I presented myself in good faith, in order to place myself under the protection of her laws.

"As soon as I had placed foot on board the *Bellerophon* I was on the hearth of the British people. If the Government, in giving directions to the captain of the *Bellerophon* to receive me with my suite, wished merely to set me a trap, an ambush, it has forfeited its honour and sullied its flag. Should such an act be consummated it will be all in vain for the English to speak in future of their honesty,

[1] Louis XVIII. returned to Paris the first time on the day Napoleon embarked for Elba.

of their laws, and of their liberty. British good faith will be compromised by the hospitality of the *Bellerophon*.

"I appeal to history. It will say that an enemy who for twenty years waged war against the English people, came of his own accord, in his misfortune, to seek an asylum under their laws ; and what greater proof could he give of his esteem and his confidence ? But how did England reply to this magnanimity ? She feigned to stretch out a hospitable hand to this enemy, and when he trusted himself to her good faith she immolated him !

"NAPOLEON."[1]

At St. Helena, too, Napoleon wrote a series of Observations on the campaign of 1815. There, like Philip's godlike son, he

"Fought all his battles o'er again,
And thrice he routed all his foes, and thrice he slew the slain."

He was very severe on his opponents and lavish of praise as concerned himself. Thus in Observation 2 he says—"The art with which the movements of the various army corps were concealed from the enemy at the opening of the campaign cannot be too much remarked. Marshal Blucher and the Duke of Wellington were surprised ; they saw nothing and knew nothing of the movements operated close to the outposts. To attack the enemy the French might turn their right or their left or pierce their

[1] After this what becomes of the following assertion made by Lord Holland in his *Reminiscences* (p. 196) ?—" The headstrong zeal of Napoleon's adherents has often injured his cause and exposed him to the accusation of perfidy, which he sometimes, but rarely, deserved. Some of them most injudiciously as well as falsely accused Captain Maitland of inveigling the Emperor on board, and of equivocation in interpreting the conditions on which he received him. To neither of these most unfounded charges was Napoleon himself directly or indirectly a party ; and the falsehood contained in them cannot in equity reflect on his personal or political character."

centre." This was why Wellington would not concentrate until he could make out where the blow was going to be struck. To continue—"The Emperor adopted the plan of concealing his movements behind the Sambre and of piercing their line at Charleroi, the point of their junction, manœuvring with rapidity and skill." Not rapidly enough, however, to cut off Zeithen's corps, as he had hoped to do, nor that of the Prince of Orange at Quatre Bras. The fact is that Napoleon had hardly entered Charleroi when he ceased the pursuit of the enemy, much to the astonishment of his troops, and allowed them time to barricade themselves. In the *Drame de Waterloo*, by Pierrat, we find—" Having given his columns orders to stop the pursuit of the Prussians, and while the cavalry of Grouchy and of the Guard defiled on the left bank of the Sambre, the Emperor seated himself in a chair in the entrance of a court-yard in the upper part of Charleroi, where the roads to Brussels and to Namur branch off, and fell sound asleep, nor could the *vivats* of the soldiers as they marched past arouse him from his slumber." At 3 P.M. his Majesty awoke, but more time was lost, because instead of attacking the enemy with his Guard, which was on the spot, he insisted upon waiting for Vandamme to come up. As Damitz, the Prussian historian, says, "the Prussians took advantage of this leisure." *Vide* also Colonel Baudus.

In Observation 3 we find it mentioned that—"The French army did not arrive in front of Waterloo until 6 P.M. on the 17th; without lamentable hesitation it would have arrived there at 3 P.M. The Emperor appeared much vexed, and, pointing to the sun, said—'What would I not give to-day for the power of Joshua to put it back for two hours!'"

But were not all these delays due to Napoleon himself, and did he not again delay attacking Wellington the next morning? We might append the opinion of numerous and competent authorities on this subject. Let the three following suffice :—

"How explain the eight hours lost in examining the field of battle, when it was of such interest to pursue the Prussians?"—JOMINI, *Correspondence avec Grouchy.*

"The inaction of the French army during the 17th and on the morning of the 18th June was the real cause of the loss of the battle of Waterloo."—GENERAL BARON DELORT, *Commentaires sur l'Ouvrage de Damitz.*

"On the 17th we should have moved at break of day, but it was nearly eleven o'clock when the Emperor marched, and, to the great astonishment of his officers he broke up the army into two corps, one of which was to follow the Prussians and the other to attack the English—unfortunate conception which was the cause of all our disasters."—GENERAL LAMARQUE, *Memoires.*

Vaulabelle thinks that the delay of the 17th was caused by Napoleon's uncertainty as to the direction in which the Prussians had retreated.

In Observation 5 Napoleon says that the great fault committed by Grouchy on the 18th was in not arriving at Wavres until 4 P.M. instead of 6 A.M. "Ordered to pursue Blucher, Grouchy lost sight of him for twenty-four hours, from the 17th at 4 P.M. till the 18th at 4 P.M." We have seen that Grouchy could get no orders until after 1 P.M. on the 17th, and that then he was sent in a wrong direction, when the enemy had fourteen hours' start of him.

The following written instructions, too, must be taken into account:—

"LIGNY, 17*th June*, about 3 P.M.

"Marshal, march upon Gembloux with. . . . You must send out reconnoitring parties in the direction of Namur and Maestricht, and you must pursue the enemy. . . . if the enemy have evacuated Namur. . . .

"(Dictated by the Emperor, in absence of the Major-General.)

"THE GRAND-MARSHAL BERTRAND."

In Observation 6 the Emperor says that Blucher, when he heard that the French were at Charleroi, should have concentrated not at Ligny but at Wavres, and that after losing Ligny he should have retreated either on Quatre Bras or on Waterloo. Blucher might have attempted this dangerous operation had he known that he would be granted a respite of fourteen hours. It is true that at St. Helena, according to Las Cases, Napoleon declared the march of Blucher on Wavres to have been "one of those flashes of genius which display a great general."

In Observation 7 Napoleon says that Wellington was surprised, and that he did not know of the French being at Charleroi until 11 P.M. on the 15th. He admits that this was the fault of the Prince of Saxe-Weimar, who ought to have warned the Duke at 6 P.M.

It was at about five o'clock in the afternoon of the 15th that the Duke of Wellington, while at dinner, received information of the advance of the French army (*Siborne*, vol. i. p. 77). In a foot-note the author says—"I had hoped that the statements so erroneously made by some writers, imputing to the Duke that he was taken by surprise, were not countenanced at the present day, since such statements, when submitted to an impartial military investigation, must be found totally groundless. . . ." Adding that some writers were of opinion that Blucher should have concentrated at Wavres, and Wellington at Waterloo, before Napoleon had crossed the Sambre.

The Duke of Wellington is also blamed for having kept his infantry, cavalry and artillery in different cantonments, and for thus allowing his infantry to fight at Quatre Bras without cavalry or artillery.[1] It is true that Picton's men belonging to the 42nd and 44th Regiments had to charge the French cavalry at the bayonet, as the 5th Regiment did in 1811 during the Peninsular War when the French

---

[1] This was partly owing to the fact of 2,000 Belgian cavalry turning tail.

advanced to relieve Ciudad Rodrigo, and as British Infantry did on another occasion.[1]

The Duke of Wellington is also blamed for having fought at Waterloo; for, according to Napoleon, he ought to have supposed that the Prussians, beaten at Ligny, having lost between 25,000 and 30,000 men on the field of battle, having 20,000 men dispersed, and being pursued by from 35,000 to 40,000 victorious Frenchmen, would not be able to render him any assistance. Now, according to the Prussian official returns Blucher lost only 11,706 men killed or wounded at Ligny. Wellington was perfectly well acquainted with the true state of affairs, for Gneisenau, who "made up the pills administered by Blucher," as the veteran field-marshal himself expressed it, rode over to see the British General on the night of the 17th to arrange matters with him. The Duke was therefore perfectly well aware that he would receive assistance during the 18th—assistance which he no doubt required as he could count on only 51,000 of the men under his orders, the remainder being raw levies or disaffected. But from unforeseen difficulties, too, Bulow's corps would have arrived at Waterloo three hours sooner than it did.

"If Marshal Blucher," adds Napoleon, "had encamped before Wavres on the evening of the 17th the Prussians would not have detached any troops to the assistance of the English." That is, Grouchy, with his 30,000 men, who were held in check by Thielman's corps, would have given Blucher's 90,000 men full employment.

[1] Speaking of the 5th Regiment, Lord Londonderry says—"They marched up in line, firing with great coolness, and, when at a distance of only a few paces from their adversaries, brought their bayonets to the charge and rushed forward. This I think is the first instance on record of a charge at the bayonet being made upon cavalry by infantry in line." The same sort of thing happened at Minden in 1759, when six English battalions, mistaking an order to "march on beat of drum," marched, beating their drums, against 10,000 French horse, and defeated them.

"The position of Mont St.-Jean was badly chosen. The first condition of a field of battle is to have no defiles in its rear. ... In spite of the diversion of Bulow and his 30,000 Prussians, the English army would have twice retreated on the 18th had it been possible. Thus, by a strange coincidence, the bad choice of a field of battle, which rendered retreat impossible, was the cause of success."

It was certainly not a greater fault on the part of Wellington to have fought with the forest of Soignies in his rear, than for Napoleon to have fought with a river in his rear as at Essling, Wagram, and Leipsic, and again at Waterloo.[1]

---

[1] Pierrat says that Napoleon at Waterloo "had behind him at Genappe only one outlet by a narrow passage over a river swollen by rain, and across which he had thrown no bridge to serve in case of defeat: he took into no account the nature of the forest of Soignies and the large outlets which ran along it, which ran round it, and which ran through it in the direction of Brussels—issues indicated in the map possessed by Napoleon, who returned to his head-quarters, taxing the English general with incompetence for daring to fight him single handed, and this with a large forest in his rear" (p. 273).

"In the midst of the extreme confusion into which the army was thrown, all the fugitives hurried towards Genappe, which in a moment was encumbered. The Emperor remained there for some minutes in order to try and re-establish a little order; but the tumult, increased by the obscurity of the night, rendered all these attempts useless. Perhaps the best thing to do was to offer no resistance and to retreat as quickly as possible. All the corps, all the branches of the service, were mixed up together: foot soldiers, cavalry, artillery, all rushed along crushing each other mutually. Several waggons and caissons were overturned in the streets and on the bridge. ... It was there that the carriage of the Emperor was captured. ... The Emperor did not hear of this loss [mentioned in the bulletin from Laon] until several days after his arrival in Paris."—GENERAL GOURGAUD, *Campagne de* 1815, p. 127.

General Gneisenau, in his report of the 18th June, says:—"It was at Genappe that the carriage of Napoleon was captured; he had just left it to get upon horseback, and with such precipitation that he forgot his sword and his hat. ..."

In Observation 9 we are told that Wellington should, instead of delivering battle at Waterloo, have fallen back through the forest of Soignies in the direction of the reinforcements which had just landed at Ostend from America, and have there formed his junction with the Prussians. Napoleon would never have ventured through the forest to attack Blucher and Wellington; he would have been obliged to hasten back to Paris to protect it against the Russians and the Austrians, and then would have been the time for the English and Prussian armies to have marched on the capital.

"The English general did not know how to make use of his numerous cavalry," says Napoleon, who in his bulletin from Laon attributed the victory of the English to the cavalry of Vivian and Vandeleur, which were let loose on the plain when all the French cavalry had disappeared.[1]

[1] Many authorities might be quoted in reply to the assertion respecting the handling of the British cavalry. We select the following:—
"The sun had set. There was no reason to despair when the two brigades of the enemy's cavalry which had not been engaged penetrated between La Haie Sainte and the corps of General Reille. They might have been checked by the eight squares of the Guard, but seeing the immense disorder which reigned on the right, they turned them. This fresh force of 3,000 cavalry hindered all rallying. The Emperor ordered his four squadrons *de service* to charge them. These squadrons were too few; it would have required a whole division of the cavalry reserve of the Guard, but unfortunately that division had been engaged on the plateau without the orders of the Emperor. There remained no means of rallying the troops; the four squadrons were overthrown, the confusion only augmented."—GENERAL GOURGAUD, *Campagne de* 1815, p. 104.

"The repeated charges of the Old Guard failed in presence of the intrepidity of the Scotch regiments, and each of the French cavalry charges was repulsed by the English cavalry." — *Prussian Official Report*. By order of Field Marshal Blucher. General Gneiseneau.

"In the first period of the battle the check of d'Erlon's corps was determined by that arm (cavalry) and cost us nearly 5,000 men. In the second the repeated and heroic charges of the squadrons of Milhaud and Kellermann and of the Guard, failed not only on account of the resistance of the infantry, but also owing to the well-timed

Dwelling upon the glorious victory, which he would have gained but for the arrival of the Prussians, Napoleon concludes thus :—

"Imagine the grimace of the people of London on learning the catastrophe which had overtaken its army, and that the purest of their blood had been poured out in support of the cause of kings against that of the people, of privileges against equality, of oligarques against liberals, of the principles of the holy alliance against those of the sovereignty of the people."

Strange language in the mouth of a despot who had made so many kings, oppressed so many people, and who had created a new nobility!

Napoleon also dictated the following account of his last campaign :—

"The Emperor, on the night he arrived in Paris, ordered General Excelmans to follow the military household of the king, to take it, to disperse it, or to drive it across the frontier; but this military household fell to pieces of itself. . . .

"Some days afterwards Comte Reille marched into Flanders with 12,000 men to reinforce Comte d'Erlon, who was in garrison on the frontier. The Emperor then deliberated if, with 35,000 or 36,000 men, he should commence hostilities on the 1st April by marching on Brussels, and rallying the Belgian army to his standards. The English and Prussian armies were weak, disseminated, without orders, without chiefs, and without plans; a number of officers were away on leave; the Duke of Wellington was at Vienna, and Marshal Blucher was at Berlin. The French army might have been at Brussels on

and skilful employment Wellington made of his cavalry. Lastly, in the final catastrophe, this same cavalry played a powerful part, especially the two brigades, 2,500 strong, held in reserve until then."— CHARRAS, vol. ii. p. 101.

the 2nd April. But, first, hopes of peace were entertained; France desired it, and would have greatly blamed any premature offensive movement; second, in order to assemble from 35,000 to 36,000 men it would have been necessary to leave twenty-three strong places, from Calais to Philippeville, to their own resources; this might have been done had public feeling been as good as in Alsace, the Vosges, the Ardennes, or the Alps... third, the Duke of Angoulême was marching on Lyons, the Marseillais on Grenoble. The first news of the re-opening of hostilities would have encouraged the discontented; it was essential above all to drive the Bourbons from the territory of the Empire.

"During May, when France was pacified, when there remained no hope of preserving peace abroad, and when the allied armies were marching on France, the Emperor reflected upon the plan of campaign which he should adopt; several suggested themselves to him.

"The first was to remain on the defensive, allowing the allies to take upon themselves the odium of an aggression, to get in among our strong places, to penetrate as far as Paris and Lyons, and there to begin on those two bases a sharp and decisive war. This plan had many advantages: first, the allies, not being able to take the field before the 15th July, would be unable to reach Paris and Lyons before the 15th August."

Napoleon set down the strength of the allied armies at 600,000 men, but, having to mask forty-two strong places, their numbers would be reduced to 350,000 before they reached Paris. With 240,000 regulars, and with Paris fortified and guarded by 116,000 National Guards, the Emperor calculated that manœuvring between the Seine and the Marne, under the protection of a vast entrenched camp, he would be able to conquer 400,000 men of the coalition. Suchet, too, would be able to hold Lyons with 60,000 regulars and 25,000 National Guards.

The second plan was to attack the allies before they were ready. On this subject the Emperor wrote:—

"1st. If the Anglo-Dutch and Saxo-Prussian armies were beaten, Belgium would rise, and her troops would recruit the French army; 2nd, the defeat of the English army would cause the fall of the British Cabinet, which would be replaced by the friends of peace, liberty, and the independence of nations;[1] this circumstance alone would terminate the war."

But the question was whether 125,000 Frenchmen could beat 241,000 allies? Napoleon said that the strength of the two armies was not represented by the above figures, because if an Englishman and a Frenchman were of equal value, a Frenchman was worth two Dutchmen, two Prussians, or two men of the Confederation. Then the allies were commanded by different generals, and had different interests. According to the Emperor the insurrection in La Vendée, which weakened his army of Flanders by 20,000 men, obliged him to adopt a third plan, and to attack the English and Prussian armies, after separating them on the 15th June.

On the subject of this third plan the most celebrated and impartial of military critics has said—

"In order to appreciate the merit of Napoleon's plan it must be remembered that he was opposed, not to one army under one chief, but to two armies independent of each other, having two bases of operations in entirely different directions; that of the English being Ostend or Antwerp, and that of the Prussians Cologne." (Jomini, *Campaign of 1815*, p. 146.)

We shall dwell no more upon what Napoleon wrote at St. Helena in order to throw dust in the eyes of posterity.[2]

---

[1] All that England was fighting for.
[2] *Vide* the *Memorial of St. Helena*, by Las Cases, and the equally inspired writings of Generals Gourgaud, Montholon, Bertrand, and O'Meara.

Lord Holland mentions that one day "Le Mercier read Napoleon a play on the subject of Peter the Cruel. At the moment of his fall that discomfited tyrant was made to say, '*De tout mon vaste empire, il me reste un rocher.*' Napoleon observed: 'It will never do. You mean to rouse us to indignation, and you put into his mouth a pathetic remark on the contrast between his former elevation and present ruin, that cannot fail to excite the compassion of every well-regulated mind.'"

And many years after, indulging in this excellent bit of criticism, he himself, in a similar position and under similar circumstances, excited almost universal compassion, and the big wars which he had waged made ambition virtue.

Little was heard of Napoleon in his captivity with the exception of his constant squabbles with Sir Hudson Lowe. In 1821 he died, but before dying he made a holograph will at Longwood, dated 21st April, 1821, in which he said:—

"I die in the Roman Apostolical religion, in the bosom of which I was born more than fifty years ago.

"I desire that my ashes may repose on the banks of the Seine, in the midst of the French people I loved so well.

"I have always had reason to be pleased with my dearest wife, Marie Louise. I preserve the most tender affection for her to the last moment. I implore her to watch over my son in order to preserve him from the snares which may environ his infancy.

"I recommend my son never to forget that he was born a French prince, and never to allow himself to become an instrument in the hands of the triumvirs who oppress the nations of Europe; he must never fight against France, or do her any harm. He should adopt my motto, *Everything for the French people!*[1]

[1] While at Vienna the Emperor's son, then Duke of Reichstadt, took Marmont (called a traitor in his father's will) as his military instructor. "The Duke," says the Marshal in his *Memoirs*, "spoke

"I die prematurely, assassinated by the English oligarchy and its hired assassin. The English nation will not be slow in avenging me.

"The unfortunate result of the two invasions of France, when she had still so many resources left, is to be attributed to the treason of Marmont, Augereau, Talleyrand, and Lafayette.

"I forgive them, and may French posterity also pardon them.

"I thank my good and most excellent mother, the cardinal (Fesch), my brothers Joseph, Lucien, Jerome, also my sisters Pauline (Borghese), Caroline (Murat), Julie (Joseph's wife), Catherine (Jerome's wife), and Hortense and Eugène for the interest they continue to feel for me. I pardon Louis for the libel he published in 1820: it is full of false assertions and falsified documents." (*Documents Historiques sur la Hollande.*) [1]

Napoleon went on to justify the execution of the Duc d'Enghien, forgetting that he had often denied that he had

with great ardour and passion of his desire to fight. 'France and Austria,' he said, 'might one day be allies, and fight side by side. It was not against France that he could fight, for his father had forbidden that; it would also be contrary to his feelings and to good policy. . . .' At other times, reflecting in despair, that war could take place only between France and the other powers, he would make such remarks as these—'But would not glory, acquired even at their expense, raise me in the eyes of the French; and if I were called upon one day to govern them, would I not be all the more worthy to do so if I had proved my capacity by my actions?' However, he always returned to the idea that French blood should be sacred to him, and that he ought to obey the strict injunctions of his father."

[1] *A propos* to this incident, Lucien Bonaparte says in his *Memoirs*: —"Publicly accused and even insulted by the Emperor, Louis thought right to justify his conduct in a work which greatly offended Napoleon, although he said nothing, and probably because he said nothing, but the truth. . . . 'I pardon my brother Louis the libel he wrote against me'—according to me really meant—'I do not pardon my brother, and I invite all my friends to share my resentment.' "

ordered that execution. Then came various bequests, such as—

"The antique cameo, which Pius VI. gave me at Tolentino, to Lady Holland.

"To Marchand, my first valet-de-chambre, 15,000*l*. The services he has rendered me are those of a friend; it is my wish that he should marry the widow, the sister, or the daughter of an officer of my Old Guard.

"To Comte Lavalette, 4,000*l*.[1]

"To Larry, surgeon-in-chief, 4,000*l*. He is the most virtuous man I have known."

The same sum was bequeathed to several old comrades like Cambronne, to the children of the brave Labedoyère, &c. In all, the bequests in money were to amount to 240,000*l*.

The will sets forth that the private property of the Emperor, derived from savings from the civil list for twelve years, amounted to over 8,000,000*l*. The smallest objects—nearly all of which were to go to his son—were duly mentioned, such as two flannel waistcoats, six pairs of gaiters, six shirts, two pillow-cases, one pair of braces, four pairs of drawers, one pair of slippers, "my night tables which I used in France, and my silver-gilt bidet," and so on. Marchand was to preserve his hair, and to have a bracelet and a little gold clasp made of it for Marie Louise, who was also to have his lace, &c. Special provision was to be made for the soldiers wounded at Waterloo, and a pension was given to sub-officer Cantillon, "tried on the charge of having endeavoured to assassinate the Duke of Wellington, of which he was pronounced innocent. Cantillon had as much right to assassinate that oligarchist as the latter had to send me to perish upon the rock of St. Helena." The Duke of

[1] Fleury de Chaboulon tells us that Lavalette said to Napoleon as Phocion said to Antipater, "I cannot be your friend and your flatterer;" that he remained the Emperor's friend, and that his advice was often followed.

Wellington was also accused of having violated the capitulation of Paris, of being responsible for the blood of Ney and Labedoyère, and of the pillage of the museums!

The museums had to give up the treasures, of which other countries had been plundered, to their rightful owners. If the robber had to render the prey we believe that nothing had to be restored to England, and therefore the conduct of the Duke of Wellington in this matter was disinterested. As for Cantillon—who could not have been innocent, for in that case he would not have received a bequest—his pension was duly paid until, under the Second Empire, the matter was brought before the House of Commons. Upon this the French Government paid off Cantillon, and washed its hands of him. The legacy contrasted strangely with the conduct of Louis XVIII., who, receiving a number of English officers after Waterloo, could not congratulate them on their victory, but said that he might thank them for their humanity afterwards.

In the Longwood will Louis was merely pardoned, and yet the purple was destined to descend to his third son— the younger brother of that "little Napoleon," whose name appears several times in *The Correspondence* previous to 1806.

Shortly after writing his will Napoleon expired, and it was in this poetical, if overstrained, language that Chateaubriand noticed an event which created a deep impression on the whole civilized world:—

"The solitude of Napoleon in his exile and his tomb has thrown another kind of spell over a brilliant memory. Alexander did not die in sight of Greece; he disappeared amid the pomp of distant Babylon. Bonaparte did not close his eyes in the presence of France; he passed away in the gorgeous horizon of the torrid zone. The man who exhibited such powerful reality vanished like a dream: his life, which belonged to history, co-operated in the poetry of his death. He now sleeps for ever, like a hermit or a pariah, beneath a willow, in a narrow valley, surrounded by steep rocks, at the extremity of a lonely path. The depth of the silence which weighs upon him can be compared only to the vastness of that tumult which once surrounded him. Nations are absent; their throngs have retired. The bird of the tropics, harnessed to the car of the sun, as Buffon magnificently expresses it, speeding his flight downwards from the planet of light, rests alone, for a moment, over ashes the weight of which shook the equilibrium of the world.

"Bonaparte crossed the ocean to repair to his final place of exile, regardless of the beautiful sky which delighted Columbus, Vasco da Gama, and Camoëns. Stretched upon the ship's stern he did not perceive that unknown constellations glittered over his head. His powerful glance for the first time encountered their rays. What to him were stars which he had never seen from his bivouacs and which had never shone over his empire? And yet each one of them fulfilled its destiny; one half of the firmament shed its light over his cradle, and the other half illuminated his tomb."

We have now come to the conclusion of our work, having selected for translation out of the mass of correspondence left behind by Napoleon those letters which appear of interest to-day as throwing some light on his character or on the events of his epoch. After the death of Napoleon Talleyrand said of him:—

"It is incalculable what he produced; more than any other man, yes, more than any other four men, I ever knew. His genius was inconceivable. Nothing could equal his energy, his imagination, his talent, his capacity for work, and his facility for producing. He had also sagacity. He was not so remarkable as regards judgment, but when he would give himself time he knew how to profit from the judgment of others."

The published correspondence of Napoleon, taken alone, testifies to the magnitude of the work accomplished by the extraordinary man who for twenty years filled the world with the noise of his exploits. The first letter printed in *The Correspondence*, addressed by Buonaparte, Commandant of Artillery in the Army of the South, to the Committee of Public Safety, is dated 4th Brumaire, year II., or 25th October, 1793, and the last letter is that which was written on board the *Bellerophon*, on the 4th August, 1815. And between October, 1793, and August, 1815, Napoleon found time, in spite of his incessant campaigning, his daily receptions, his verbal instructions, his study of arduous questions, &c., to write or dictate even more than the 22,066 letters, despatches, orders of the day, &c. &c., contained in *The Correspondence*, which forms no less than twenty-eight volumes in octavo of closely printed matter.

INDEX

VOL. III.

INDEX.

A

ABERCROMBY, SIR RALPH, his success in Holland, i. 241; at Alexandria, i. 214; in Egypt, i. 265; Napoleon on, i. 265
Abrial, citizen, minister of justice, Napoleon's letters to, i. 368, 399
Aboukir, battle of, i. 242, 259, 334
Academy, French, dissolution of, i. 316, 317 n
Aix, Josephine at, i. 206; Napoleon at, i. 269
Aix la Chapelle, Napoleon at, ii. 91, 92
Ajaccio, disturbance in, i. 20, 25, 26
Albuera, battle of, iii. 105
Aldini, Count, ii. 480
Alessandria, cathedral of, destroyed, i. 406
Alexandria, Napoleon's orders from, i. 259, 262, 263; capture of, i. 214; English blockade, i. 343; occupy, ii. 6
Algiers, Dey of, Napoleon's letters to, i. 398, 399; threatened by Napoleon, i. 397
Algesiras, battle of, i. 340
Alison's *History of Europe*, on the retreat from Moscow, iii. 182
Allocution to the old guard, 1814, iii. 344
Almeida, fall of, iii. 101, 105
Alquier, M., Napoleon's instructions to, at Rome, ii. 363
Alvinzi, General, at Pavia, i. 118; attacks the French, i. 129; defeated at Rivoli, i. 130
Amed Pasha, Napoleon's letter to, i. 235
Amiens, treaty of, i. 366, 380, 382, 385, 388; proclaimed in London, i. 382; rupture of, ii. 1, 2, 6; causes of rupture of, ii. 12, 13; Napoleon at, ii. 19
Ancona occupied by the French, i. 378; ii. 201; Napoleon at, i. 137
Andreossi, M. de, ambassador in London, i. 383; ambassador in Austria, ii. 300
Annual Register, quotations from, on treaty of Amiens, i. 366; on the arrest of English in France, ii. 2; on English naval victory, 1804, ii. 101; Lord Lake's march against Daolat Rao, ii. 130; on Captain Wright, ii. 163; on the conscription, 1807, ii. 300
Anspach, Napoleon violates the neutrality of, ii. 110, 154, 161
Aosta, Duke of, accused of aiding the English, i. 353 n
Aranjuez, revolution at, ii. 354
Archives, foreign, sent to Paris, iii. 55
Arcola, battle of, i. 119
Arrighi, General, Duc de Padone, Napoleon's letter to, iii. 276
Arrighi, Canon, pastoral by, greeting Napoleon at Elba, iii. 349, 350 n
Aspern, battle of, ii. 429, 454, 455
Asturias, Ferdinand, Prince of, Napoleon's letters to, ii. 380, 393; conspires with Napoleon against his father the King of Spain, ii. 350—353; his projected marriage with Napoleon's niece, ii. 352, 353, 369; Napoleon's perfidy to, ii. 375, 381, 385; Napoleon's orders for his arrest, ii. 382; receives freedom on concluding a treaty with Napoleon, iii. 288; his letters to Napoleon, iii. 287; after battle of Tudela, ii. 421 n

F F 2

336 INDEX.

Aubry, General, iii. 384

Auerstadt, battle of, ii. 198

Augereau, Marshal, Napoleon's letters to, i. 103; ii. 37, 153; iii. 321; Napoleon's instructions to, ii. 205; *coup d'état* by, i. 125, 172; at Eylau, ii. 298; his inactivity when in command of the army of Lyons, iii. 321, 325, 330; placed under General Moreau's orders, iii. 321; deserts Napoleon, iii. 361

Aulic Council, i. 129, 130, 195, 308.

Anne, M., Napoleon's letter to, iii. 350

Austerlitz, battle of, ii. 109, 170, 181—183, 185; provision made for relations of those who fell at, ii. 186

Austria, Emperor of, Napoleon's letters to, i. 279; ii. 95, 103, 169, 190, 464, 475; iii. 26, 29, 31, 51, 53, 64, 93, 155, 169, 172, 196, 216, 235, 241, 245, 246, 255, 322—324, 369; his letter to Princess Augusta, Eugène's wife, iii. 318; his family recognised as imperial hereditary, ii. 91, 95; Napoleon's mistaken estimate of his popularity, ii. 169 *n*

Austria, Archduke Charles of, Napoleon's letters to, i. 146; iii. 31; defeated at Tagliamento, i. 143; unsuccessful against Napoleon, i. 145, 169; defeats Jourdan, i. 241; to his troops after Austerlitz, ii. 184; his want of vigour in 1809, ii. 429, 430

Austria, Archduke Maximilian of, ii. 451

Austria, troops defeated by Napoleon, 1796, i. 69, 91, 125; receives Venice, &c., i. 126; Napoleon enters territory of, i. 144; wars with France, i. 277, 285, 311; in 1805, ii. 109, 149, 151; in 1809, ii. 447, 452, 454, 469; in 1813, iii. 256, 261; manifesto on the war in 1805, ii. 152; invades Bavaria, ii. 152; endeavours to mediate in 1807, ii. 287; position of, in 1813, iii. 201, 204; proposes a congress at Prague, iii. 238; joins the allies in, 1813, iii. 256, 261; proposed matrimonial alliance with Spain, iii. 68; objections to the marriage of the Arch-Duchess Marie Louise with Napoleon, iii. 4; inconsistency of, iii. 8; misery of the Austrian army in 1805, ii. 161; Napoleon's address to the Austrian generals after the capitulation of Ulm, ii. 159

Autun, Napoleon at, i. 4; Talleyrand, Bishop of; *see* Talleyrand

Avignon, attack on, i. 30

d'Azara, M., Spanish minister, i. 95; Napoleon's violent message to, i. 374

Avesnes, Napoleon at, iii. 385, 386 *n*

B.

Badajoz, treaty of, i. 334, 357, 358, 373; invested by the English, iii. 153

Baden, Princess Stephanie, Napoleon's letter to, ii. 244; Napoleon's complaint of, iii. 119, 120

Bale, treaty of, i. 299; ii. 18

Barbé Marbois, M., minister of the treasury, Napoleon's letters to, i. 390; ii. 133, 206, 212; disgrace of, ii. 190

Barbier, M., librarian to the Emperor, Napoleon's letters to, ii. 400, 452; iii. 81, 150, 167

Bard, taken by Napoleon, i. 305

Bar-sur-Aube, battle of, iii. 291, 331, 333

Barras, citizen director, assists Napoleon, i. 57, 63; fears Napoleon's popularity, while complimenting him, i. 195

Barrère, citizen, in Napoleon's service, ii. 92

Baste, Admiral, ordered to Swedish Pomerania, iii. 221

Bassano, battle of, i. 108

Bastia bombarded by Nelson, i. 42

Batavia, republic of, Napoleon's perfidious treatment of the, i. 367; it receives a new constitution, i. 377; establishes his authority in the, i. 384

Baudus, Colonel, quotations from history by, iii. 334 *n*, 398 *n*, 399 *n*

Bautzen, battle of, iii. 202, 246

Bavaria, king of, Napoleon's letters to, ii. 154, 217; iii. 228; endeavours to persuade Prince Eugène to desert Napoleon, iii. 283

Bavaria, Princess Augusta of, Napoleon's letters to, ii. 210, 252; her marriage to Eugène de Beauharnais, ii. 192, 193; her indignation at Napoleon's orders that she should go to Paris, 1814, iii. 319; letter from the Emperor of Austria to, iii. 318

Baylen, capitulation of, ii. 357, 405

Bayonne, Napoleon at, ii. 354, 380

Beauchamp, citizen, sent to Constantinople, i. 237

INDEX.   437

Beaufrauchet, Madame, pension for, i. 318

Beauharnais, Alexander de, marriage of, i. 4; death of, i. 169

Beauharnais, M. de, ambassador in Spain, ii. 351, 352

Beauharnais, Eugene de, Viceroy of Italy, Napoleon's letters and notes to, i. 205; ii. 134, 136, 138, 152, 193, 204, 206, 209, 226, 228, 231, 242, 250, 304, 305, 312, 325, 326, 335, 343, 367, 368, 371, 373, 394, 400, 409, 425, 435, 443, 450, 481; iii. 64, 66, 81, 124, 156, 194, 214, 215, 220, 221—223, 227—229, 231, 232, 258, 261, 282, 283, 285, 299, 316; his first appointment, i. 169; made Viceroy of Italy, ii. 121, 134; his marriage, ii. 192, 193; birth of his daughter Josephine, ii. 304; appointed to command of the Grand army, iii. 214; evacuates Berlin, iii. 227; urged by his father-in-law to desert Napoleon, iii. 283; correspondence with Josephine about his fidelity to Napoleon, iii. 308, 309

Beaulieu, General, defeated by the French, i. 69, 77, 81; in Venice, i. 93, 94

Beausset, M. de, iii. 354, 355

Belfort in 1813 and 1870, iii. 295

Bellerophon, Napoleon on board the, iii. 416

Belliard, General, severely criticised by Napoleon, i. 266; distinguished afterwards, i. 267; in Spain, iii. 435, 436; Napoleon refuses to accept his resignation, iii. 107; saved Napoleon's life, iii. 107 *n*

Beneventum, seized by Napoleon, i. 370, 395; given to Talleyrand, ii. 235, 237

Bensingen, General, at Eylau, ii. 294, 314, 316

Beresina, passage of, iii. 186, 187

Bergamo, occupation of, i. 126

Bergen, battle of, i. 242

Berlin, Napoleon enters, ii. 267; the decree of, ii. 198, 272; evacuated by the French, iii. 227; the Russians enter, iii. 227

Bernier, Abbé de, i. 285, 291, 394; ii. 17

Bernadotte, General, Napoleon's letters to, i. 159; ii. 314, 326, 446; iii. 99; Napoleon's orders to the division under, i. 151, 152; his marriage, i. 52; Napoleon's praise of, i. 177, appointed French ambassador at Vienna, i 206; a staunch Republican, i. 271; minister of war, i. 319; offered post of captain-geenral of Guadaloupe, i. 383, 384; captures Munich, ii. 156; receives Porto Corvo, ii. 235; Napoleon complains of him, ii. 474; elected Prince Royal of Sweden, iii. 10, 59

Berthier, Alexander, Prince of Neuchâtel, Napoleon's letters and notes to, i. 121, 127, 158, 166, 169, 198, 201, 210, 219, 230, 233, 234, 236, 243, 253, 299, 313, 348, 352, 372, 390; ii. 9, 34, 39, 56, 58, 66, 96, 137, 200, 209, 214, 223, 225, 227, 249, 253, 254, 256, 283, 288, 333, 348, 352, 447; iii. 40, 41, 60, 63, 68, 75, 83, 102, 104, 107, 119, 130, 139, 140, 147, 152—155, 157, 159, 162, 163, 165, 180—182, 184, 186, 192, 197, 200, 208, 210, 236, 266, 270, 271, 273, 299—301, 311, 341, 343, 344; letters from Joseph Buonaparte to, iii. 103, 104, 334; appointed chief of the staff in Italy, i. 67; enters Rome, i. 197; his letter to Napoleon, i. 199; ordered to Alexandria, i. 243; his love for Madame Visconti, i. 244; ii. 223; his marriage, iii. 224; sent to Spain, i. 320; directed to form light companies, ii. 43; his career, ii. 223, 224; his note to Joseph, ii. 299; Prince of Neuchâtel, ii. 332; sent as extraordinary ambassador to arrange Napoleon's marriage with Marie-Louise, iii. 22; his reception by the Emperor of Austria, iii. 30, 31 *n*; signs letter to General Kutusoff, iii. 179

Berthier, Cesar, embezzlements by, ii. 245; in the Ionian Islands, ii. 289

Berthollet, M., ii. 368

Bertrand, General, Napoleon's letters to, iii. 272, 351, 353—355; sent to Prussia, ii. 292; his account of Eylau, ii. 298; on the Danube, ii. 459; grand marshal at Elba, iii. 350—353, 365

Berri, Duc de, marriage of, ii. 328

Bessières, Marshal, Napoleon's letters to, ii. 374, 382; iii. 122; his success in Spain, ii. 401; death of, iii. 239, 240

Beurnonville, Marquis de, Napoleon's instructions to, ii. 21, 42; famous bulletin by the, ii. 38

Bignon, Baron, to organise secret police, 1811, iii. 131
Bigot, Comte, minister of public worship, Napoleon's letters to, iii. 12, 14, 74, 83, 90, 106, 125, 152, 215, 231, 257; *see* Minister of Public Worship, letters to
Billington, Madame; *see* Grassini, i. 313
Bishops, Napoleon's circulars to the, ii. 314; iii. 174; his questions to them, iii. 13; their replies, iii. 14; requires the Pope to confirm his nomination of French, i. 389, 393, 400
Blucher, Marshal, in France, iii. 291, 301, 314, 327, 332, 338; his ill-health, iii. 340; his vigilance, 1815, iii. 385*n*, at Waterloo, iii. 405, 423 *n*
Bologna, Napoleon at, i. 97, 98, 134
Bolton, Lord, on the peace of Amiens, i. 383
Bonnechose, M., quotation from; *see* Protestant
Borghese, Prince, Napoleon's letters to, ii. 475; iii. 81, 158; his letter to Napoleon, iii. 14 *n*
Borghese, Princess; *see* Buonaparte, Pauline
Borodino, battle at, iii. 172, 173
Boulogne, Napoleon at, ii. 36—38, 139—147; disaster to Boulogne flotilla, iii. 122 *n*
Bourgogna, Baron Paul de, account of Napoleon's journey to Paris, after leaving the army on its retreat from Moscow, iii. 192 *n*—194 *n*
Bourrienne, M., iii. 121
Brescia, Napoleon at, i, 89, 90, 104
Breslau, capitulation of, ii. 284
Bressieux, Madame, Napoleon's letter to, ii. 89
Brienne, Napoleon enters, i. 2, 4; masters at, i. 5; Napoleon's letters from, i. 5—7, 9; comrades at, i. 6; examinations at, i. 6; Joseph enters, i. 9
Brienne, battle of, iii. 301, 303
Brueys, Vice-Admiral, Napoleon's letter to, i. 205
Bruix, Admiral, Napoleon's letters to, i. 355; ii. 43; blockaded by the English in Brest, i. 294; instructed to capture English peasants and fishermen, ii. 32
Brune, General, Napoleon's letters to, i. 206, 289, 293, 321, 328; iii. 68; sent to La Vendée, i. 289; in Tuscany, i. 326, 327; Napoleon's instructions to, i. 326, 404; appointed to command of the Italian army, i. 321; his death, iii. 374 *n*
Bruno, General, captured, iii. 273
"Buffons Italiens" to perform in France, i. 371
Bulletins to the army, issued by Napoleon after Marengo, i. 309, 311, 312, 314; in 1805, ii. 155—157, 159—161, 166, 168, 169, 182, 185, 186, 192; in 1806, ii. 199, 259, 261, —265, 267, 271, 272, 275; in 1807, ii. 284, 285, 287, 291, 293, 324 *n*; in 1809, ii. 449—451, 454, 456, 459, 460; in 1812, iii. 160, 189, 190; in 1813, iii. 246, 278, 279
Buonaparte, M. de, archdeacon of Ajaccio, Napoleon's letter to, i. 13
Buonaparte, Charles, marriage of, i. 3; Napoleon's letters to, i. 5, 9; substitutes Napoleon for Joseph at Brienne, i. 4; appointed one of committee to govern Corsica, i. 4; goes to France, i. 4; death of, i. 12; Napoleon's letter on, i. 13; brilliant destinies of his family, i. 30
Buonaparte, Charlotte, Lucien's daughter, ii. 348, 349, 354
Buonaparte, Eliza, Grand Duchess of Tuscany, Napoleon's letters to, ii. 127, 143, 219, 232, 446; iii. 287; leaves school of St. Louis, i. 28; Grand Duchess of Tuscany, ii. 127, 177; enriched at the expense of the Queen of Etruria, ii. 228; flatters Napoleon, ii. 343
Buonaparte, Jerome, King of Westphalia, Napoleon's letters to, ii. 347, 358, 362, 396, 403, 411, 440, 457; iii. 12, 81, 127, 143, 156, 230; his return to Europe, ii. 125, 126, 130; joins the army, ii. 309; his first marriage with Miss Patterson, ii. 3, 76, 83, 129, 131, 201 *n*; his marriage with the Princess of Wirtemberg, ii. 193, 255, 256, 327, 328; his dissatisfaction with Napoleon, iii. 231; his wife returns to Paris, iii. 233; Napoleon's advice to him on a constitution, ii. 346; his account of Waterloo, iii. 400, 401
Buonaparte, Joseph, King of Spain, Napoleon's notes and letters to, i. 27, 45, 46—52, 58, 186, 207, 209, 215, 304, 350, 360, 383; ii. 152, 164, 165, 181, 188, 192, 193, 203, 205, 215, 219—221 *n*, 227, 234, 235; 241, 242, 244, 247, 251, 252, 254—

INDEX. 439

256, 265, 288, 290, 298, 306, 309, 348, 372, 373, 380, 382, 392, 397, 401—404, 407, 412, 416, 418, 433—436, 438, 444; iii. 14, 295, 302, 304—306, 308, 310—315, 319, 320, 325—327, 330, 333, 335—340, 386, 389, 401; his letters to Napoleon, ii. 402, 443, 470, 471; iii. 333 *n*; his letters to Berthier, iii. 103, 104; his letter to General Clarke, iii. 257; Napoleon's letter on his profession, i. 7; enters Brienne, i. 9; made war comissary, i. 31; settles in Genoa, i. 46; his marriage, i. 52; French minister in Rome, i. 193; his indignation at the rupture of the treaty of Amiens, ii. 13, 73; Napoleon's letter on murder of the Duc d'Enghien, ii. 49; made colonel, ii. 71; receives false commissions, ii. 72, 73; proclaimed King of Italy, ii. 111; King of Naples, ii. 198, 207, 225; declines throne of Italy, ii. 200, 207; projected marriage of his infant daughter, ii. 193; in Naples, ii. 219; made King of Spain, ii. 354, 387; his distress at Napoleon's conduct in Spain, ii. 419 *n*; his troubles in Spain, iii. 103, 107; forced to leave Madrid, ii. 404; leaves Spain, takes refuge in France, iii. 103, 204; is badly treated on his return from Spain, iii. 295; takes Marie-Louise to Tours, iii. 343 *n*; letter from Baron Fain to, iii. 388

Buonaparte, Laetitia, Madame Mère, Napoleon's letters to, i. 12, 18; ii. 365, 366; iii. 25, 51; settles at Marseilles, i. 31; in Paris, ii. 366; joins Napoleon at Elba, iii. 353

Buonaparte, Louis, King of Holland, Napoleon's letters to, ii. 242, 243, 245, 247, 251, 254, 277, 282, 295, 305, 376, 378, 385, 416, 443, 445, 462, 481; leaves Ajaccio with Napoleon, i. 21; at Chalons, i. 48; made King of Holland, ii. 199, 222, 236; in command of an army corps, ii. 222; Napoleon's advice on his government, ii. 277; finances of his kingdom, 1806, ii. 243; throne of Spain offered to, and declined, ii. 354, 376, 383; his quarrels with his wife, ii. 306; birth of his sons, ii. 103, 383; death and burial of his eldest son, ii. 311, 312, 316; asks for a divorce, iii. 33; quarrels with Napoleon, iii. 36—38, 40; abdicates, i. 22; iii. 46

Buonaparte, Lucien, Napoleon's letters to, i. 290, 293, 297, 315, 316, 323, 326; store-keeper at St. Maximin, i. 31; aids Napoleon at a critical time, i. 272, 274; ii. 75; minister of the interior, i. 290; death of his first wife, i. 303; ambassador at Madrid, i. 338; asks for Napoleon's portrait for Prince of the Peace, i. 349; recalled from Spain, i. 358; his marriage, ii. 76, 349; exiled, ii. 67; leaves Rome, iii. 46; quotations from his *Memoirs*, i. 54; iii. 427

Buonaparte, Pauline, Napoleon's letters to, ii. 70; iii. 280; Napoleon's criticism of, ii. 71; in St. Domingo, i. 407; marries Prince Borghese, i. 407; expected at Elba, iii. 354

Buttafuoco, M. de, Napoleon's letter to, i. 19

Burgos, sack of, ii. 418, 419

Busaco, battle of, iii. 61

Byng, Admiral, at Etaples, 1708, ii. 28

Buonaparte, Napoleon, birth of, uncertain identity, i. 3, 4; reasons for suppressing early correspondence, i. 2; at Autun, i. 4; at Brienne, i. 4; his prospects at father's death, i. 14; literary efforts, i. 10, 16, 23, 31, 53; at Douai, i. 14; in Corsica, i. 24, 25, 28, 30; at Auxonne, i. 16, 22; at Marseilles, i. 36; at Nice, i. 37, 39, 64; in Italy, i. 37, 67—143, 158—193, 305—315; ii. 126—136; in Malta, i. 210; in Egypt, i. 212—247, 258—264; in Syria, i. 248—257; in Switzerland, i. 300, 305; in Austria, i. 144—155, 194; ii. 154—170, 179—204, 448—479; in Germany, ii. 91; in Prussia, ii. 256—272, 314—325; in Poland, ii. 273—314; iii. 160, 193; in Russia, iii. 165—192; in Elba, iii. 350—361; obtains command of artillery at Toulon, i. 31; military reports by, i. 32, 38, 105, 152; becomes intimate with Barras, Freron, Salicetti, i. 32; attached to topographical department, i. 50, 54; in difficulties with Republican government, i. 39, 57; appointed to the army of the interior, i. 57; arrested, i. 6, 40; rapid promotions, i. 59; first commission of, i. 2; made first lieutenant, i. 24; lieut.-colonel Corsican volunteers, i. 25; captain of artillery, i. 28; brigadier-general, i. 36;

general of division, i. 58; defeats General O'Hara, i. 35; his desire to go to India, i. 54, 55, 58; summary of his success in 1796, i. 60; descends Alps at Montenotte, i. 62; marriage with Josephine, i. 63; ii. 231; iii. 5—7; with the Arch-Duchess Marie-Louise, iii. 1, 4, 9, 25—28, 31; takes command of army in Italy, i. 64; defeats the Austrians at Montenotte and Mellesimo, i. 69, 70; Mondovi, i. 72; his discipline in the army, i. 72, 73; signs armistice with Sardinia, i. 74; fines Genoa, i. 75; crosses the Po, i. 77; gains battle of Lodi, i. 81; his success alarms the Directory, i. 83; treasure levied in the wars, 1796—97, i. 87, 88, 97, 99, 163, 182; enters Venetian territory, i. 91; concludes armistice with Naples, i. 95; enters the Tyrol, i. 96; concludes armistice with the Pope, i. 99; siege of Mantua, i. 102; attacks Tuscany, i. 109; defeats Wurmser, i. 106, 108; negotiates for peace with Germany, i. 112; deposes Duke of Modena, i. 113; complains of army contractors, i. 113, 133; orders the occupation of Elba, i. 117; wins battle of Arcola, i. 119, 120; his critical position at close of 1796, i. 123; sends General Clarke to offer conditions of peace to Austria, i. 123, 124; wins battle of Rivoli, i. 125, 130; concludes treaties of Tolentino and Campo Formio, i. 125, 141, 142, 163, 190; destroys Venetian Republic, i. 126; threatens Papal territory, i. 134; defeats army, i. 136; resumes hostilities with Austria, i. 143; crosses Isonzo, i. 144; his criticism of the Archduke Charles, i. 145; concludes treaty with Sardinia, i. 147; consents to armistice with Austria, i. 147; sends instructions to General Kilmaine in Italy, i. 148; his perfidy to Lombardy, i. 149; complains of Moreau, i. 145, 150, 155; at Leoben, i. 150; signs preliminaries of peace, i. 152; his remarks on the negotiations with Austria, i. 152—154; raises money in Goritz and Trieste, i. 154; renews hostilities with Venice and Italian cities, i. 156; complains of embezzlement in Corsica, i. 157; concludes treaty with Venice, i. 126, 158; establishes himself at Montebello, i. 159; despatches General Gentili to the Ionian Isles, i. 162; authorises sales of Abbeys, i. 161, 166; Dumolard brings motion against, i. 167; tenders resignation, i. 168, 184; sends Lavallette to Paris to arrange with Barras, i. 172; sends Augereau to Paris, i. 172, 173; urges the dissolution of the Royalist clubs, i. 173; corresponds with Greece, i. 175; sends friendly overtures to Tuscany, i. 176; his designs upon Egypt, i. 178, 181; his contempt for Austrian negotiators, i. 179; his negotiations with Naples, i. 180; proposes seizure of Malta, i. 181; requires reinforcements, i. 183, 185; conscriptions levied by, ii. 425, 434, 437; complains of bad health, i. 187; his requirements for invading England, i. 191, 200; goes to Rastadt, i. 193; received and eulogised by the directors in Paris, i. 194, 195; elected member of the institute, i. 195, 207; coalition of powers against him, i. 196; threatens Naples, i. 198; sends Berthier to Rome, i. 198; prepares to invade Egypt, i. 201—203; publishes decrees against the English in the East, i. 203; appeals to Austrians to maintain treaty of Campo Formio, i. 206; sails for Malta, i. 208; takes Malta, i. 209; his organisation of Malta, i. 210, 211; reaches Alexandria, i. 212; his success in Egypt, i. 215; levies money in Alexandria, i. 216; his cruelty in Egypt, i. 217, 218, 227, 233, 237; creates institute at Cairo, i. 220; his conversation in the Grand Pyramid, i. 221—225; his idea of becoming a Mussulman, i. 225 n; is unpopular in Egypt, i. 231; wins battle of Sediman, i. 232; anxious for European news, i. 219, 235; his invasion of Syria, i. 235, 240, 242, 248; reassures the Sultan respecting Egypt, i. 237; wins battle of Aboukir, i. 242, 259; dissatisfaction of his army in Egypt, i. 237, 327; his discipline in Egypt, i. 243, 248, 249; his alliance with Tippoo Sáhib, i. 244; appeals to authorities in Syria, i. 249; wins battle of Gaza, i. 250; takes Jaffa, i. 250; lays siege to St. Jean d'Acre, i. 251, 255; his return to Egypt, i. 254; celebrates fête of the Prophet, i. 260; tries to close the war in Egypt, i. 261; leaves Egypt, i. 263; nominates General Kléber to command of army in the East, i. 264, 274; orders him to hold Egypt, i. 313; learns French reverses in Egypt, i. 360; restores Egypt to the Porte, i. 360; sends an agent to Egypt, iii. 67; his return to France, i. 263, 264, 270, 271; makes terms with Sieyes, i. 270; disperses the chambers, i. 271; Lucien's assistance to, i. 271, 272; elected consul, i. 272; his attention to details, i. 274, 377; ii. 137; abolishes the law of hostages, i. 277; the British Government refuse to treat with, i. 279; his government of France in 1800, i. 284, 285; requires money from the Dutch, i. 288, 289; his measures for suppressing the insurrection in La Vendée, i. 285, 287, 289; his duplicity towards the Count de Frotté, i. 292; resides in the Tuileries, i. 291; takes command of the Army of Reserve, i. 285; crosses the Alps, i. 286, 303, 304; his success in Italy, i. 286, 306; wins battle of Marengo, i. 286, 310; signs preliminaries of peace, i. 286, 315; leaves Italy, i. 314; offers a pension to Louis XVIII., i. 323; renews hostilities with Austria, i. 324; offers maritime truce to England, i. 324, 325; attempts made to assassinate him, i. 325, 326, 331, 332; his accusations against England, i. 295, 311, 312, 314, 337, 351; ii. 59, 78, 79; his projected expeditions against England, ii. 1, 32—34, 39, 69, 81, 83, 85, 96, 106, 145, 148; exchanges prisoners with England, i. 295, 296; his attempts to hinder English and colonial commerce, ii. 272, 335; iii. 57, 64—66, 68, 69, 72, 113, 114; offers terms to England, i. 361, 362; ii. 15, 197, 198; friendly overtures to Grand Duke of Tuscany, i. 176; orders General Brune to disarm Tuscany, i. 326; gives Tuscany to kingdom of Etruria, i. 356; requires funds from Tuscany, i. 348; quarters troops in Tuscany, i. 368; offended by Queen of Portugal, i. 226, 227; exacts money from Portugal, i. 288, 289, 342, 343; suggests seizure of Portugal by Spain, i. 328; orders Junot to march upon Portugal, ii. 336, 338; establishes his authority in the Batavian, Helvetian, and Cisalpine Republics, and becomes President of the latter, i. 384; his overtures to Spain, i. 299, 320, 328, 342; his arrogance to the King and Queen of Spain, i. 378—381; ii. 7; threatens war with Spain, ii. 26—29; endeavours to marry his niece to the Prince of Asturias, ii. 349, 353; his intrigue with the Prince of Asturias, ii. 336, 352, 353, 375; sends troops into Spain, ii. 354; his instructions to Soult in Naples, i. 348; his complaints of the Queen of Naples, ii. 198, 199, 209; French troops overrun Naples, ii. 199, 215; his schemes for the disposal of Naples, ii. 205, 207; makes Joseph King of Naples, ii. 206, 207; refuses to ratify the treaty of Badajoz, i. 357, 358; arranges the Concordat, i. 360; imposes it upon France, i. 393, 394; his intentions, had the Moscow expedition been victorious, i. 395; seizes Beneventum and Ponte Corvo, i. 395; demands an equal number of cardinals for France as Austria possessed, i. 396; his views on the political situation of France in 1802, i. 397; his message to Algiers, i. 397—399; refuses Vestris permission to leave France, i. 401; his protection to Christians in the East, i. 401; gives two ships to the Pope, i. 401, 402; obtains possession of Elba, i. 348, 403; threatens Helvetian Republic, i. 403; at Rouen, i. 404; orders demolition of cathedral at Alessandria, i. 406; his satisfaction with Paulette, i. 407; appeals for Pope's help in temporal designs, i. 408; despatches an expedition to St. Domingo, i. 372, 374, 377; despatches an expedition to the Cape of Good Hope, i. 337; makes peace with America, i. 286; considers treaty of Amiens, ii. 366, 373; his interference with the theatres, i. 297; iii. 23, 27; establishes horse-racing in France, ii. 147; proposes annual exhibition of inventions and manufactures, i. 345; his encouragement of art in France, i. 323; ii. 139, 140; his views on Trinidad, i. 378, 391; his ecclesiastical nominations, i. 289, 293, 400; his projected invasion of India, i. 334, 362; ii. 3, 115; his charities and pensions, i. 318; ii. 4; iii. 58, 59, 102; his scurrilous

442 INDEX.

articles against George III., ii. 14; he rules the press, ii. 17, 44, 45, 59, 134, 204, 374, 386, 437; iii. 76, 178; invades Hanover, ii. 18, 19; objects to ministers chosen by foreign states, ii. 22, 25, 78; conspires with United Irishmen, ii. 25; his designs upon Ireland, ii. 25, 26; iii. 111; orders erection of statue to Charlemagne, ii. 10, 11, 31; his arbitrary conduct towards individuals, ii. 41, 51, 56, 197; to women, ii. 32, 63, 74, 86; his treatment of the clergy, ii. 77; iii. 34—36, 90, 91 n, 106, 107; causes murder of the Duc d'Enghien, ii. 47—51, 66, 68—70; causes Moreau's banishment, ii. 51—53; is suspected of causing Pichegru's death, ii. 53—55; his coronation by the Pope, ii. 55, 84, 93; exasperates the foreign states, ii. 55; his attention to the internal welfare of France, ii. 59, 60; his duplicity, ii. 61, 63, 64, 112, 120; aspires to the purple, ii. 71 n, 72; makes Joseph a colonel, ii. 71—73; his ingratitude, ii. 75; becomes Emperor, ii. 75, 77; issues titles to form a court, ii. 77; complains of Russia, ii. 84, 87; delays passport to Russian ambassador, ii. 128; crowned King of Italy, ii. 105, 109, 132; proclaims Joseph King of Italy, ii. 111; appoints Eugene de Beauharnais Viceroy of Italy, ii. 121, 134; his schemes, Sept. 1804, ii. 97; commences hostilities against Austria, ii. 109, 141, 146; orders his generals to join their corps, ii. 116: his movements in spring of 1805, ii. 125, 127; unites Genoa to France, ii. 133, 136; mistakes Nelson's movements, ii. 136; his note on the naval action between Villeneuve and Sir R. Calder, ii. 140 —142; his frontiers in 1805, ii. 144; joins army in Austria, ii. 149; his successful operations, ii. 151, 155—161, 166, 181, 185; at Palace of Shœnbrunn, ii. 168; wins battle of Austerlitz, ii. 109, 181, 183, 185, 186; refuses to make peace with Austria, ii. 184; his overtures to Prussia, ii. 187, 188; re-establishes peace, ii. 190—192; his matrimonial arrangements for his family, ii. 193; hears of Trafalgar, ii. 170; suspected of causing Villeneuve's death, ii. 178, 179; his position during 1806, ii. 194 —200; his position with Prussia, ii. 194—197, 208; at Munich, ii. 200—204; his treatment of Ouvrard, ii. 212—214; orders rejoicings to celebrate return of the army to Paris, ii. 218; his territorial arrangements in Europe, ii. 221, 222, 255; makes Louis King of Holland, ii. 222, 236, 237; makes Berthier Prince of Neuchâtel, ii. 223; orders erection of the Arc de Triomphe, ii. 229; urges Joseph to capture Sicily, ii. 232; concludes Concordat with the Jews, ii. 233, 234; organises seminaries and introduces catechism into France, ii. 246, 247; his knowledge of his generals' capacity, ii. 237, 238; his alliance with Turkey, ii. 239, 274, 282, 289; iii. 50; prepares for war with Prussia, ii. 253; duplicity towards the King of Prussia, ii. 255; joins the army at Mayence, ii. 256; his overtures to Austria, ii. 257, 275, 300; his complaints against Prussia, ii. 259; commences war, ii. 258; his forces on the field, ii. 260; wins battle of Jena, ii. 261; refuses armistice to Prussia, ii. 263: takes possession of Hesse-Cassel, ii. 264; at Potsdam, ii. 265; enters Berlin, ii. 267; signs decree of Berlin, ii. 272; his troops enter Warsaw, ii. 273; at Warsaw, ii. 277; orders construction of the Madeleine, ii. 275; summary of his wars during 1807, ii. 279; his campaign in Poland, ii. 279; makes Jerome King of Westphalia, ii. 279; his activity, ii. 281, 295, 352; his immorality, i. 238; ii. 283, 306, 339; wins battle of Eylau, ii. 290 (see Eylau); his instructions to Bertrand in Prussia, ii. 292, 293; levies fresh conscriptions in France, ii. 295, 300; offers peace to Prussia and Russia, ii. 296, 308; his employment of foreign soldiers and prisoners, ii. 302; wins battle of Friedland, ii. 315; signs armistice with Russia, ii. 316: his alliance at Tilsit with the Czar, 318, 319, 347; his fears of poison, ii. 320; meets the Queen of Prussia, ii. 321: commences Peninsular War, ii. 336, 343, 344, 354; sends troops to Pampeluna and Madrid, ii. 369—371; issues two decrees of Milan, ii. 347—349; prepares for his divorce from Josephine, ii. 340, 341; his matrimonial proposals refused by Russia, ii. 342 ; iii. 1, 3, 4, 134; goes to Bayonne, ii. 354 ; his conversation with Escoiquiz, ii. 354—356 ; gives throne of Spain to Joseph, ii. 354, 387, 391, 392, 397 ; offers it to Louis, ii. 376 ; his desire for peace, ii. 357 ; his instructions respecting the invasion of the Papal States, ii. 359, 367, 371, 373 ; his naval resources, ii. 377, 378 ; concludes treaty of Erfurth, ii. 413, 415 ; threatens Lisbon, ii 417 ; enters Burgos, ii. 418 ; orders erection of temple of Janus, ii. 420 ; enters Madrid, ii. 421 ; attempts to create discord between England and Spain, ii. 422—424 ; orders fountain of the Bastille, ii. 425 ; his movements in 1809, ii. 428 —431 ; his reverses in 1809, ii. 432 ; leaves Spain, ii. 434 ; quarrels with Talleyrand, ii. 434 ; advises Joseph to use harshness in Spain, ii. 435—437 ; requires German assistance against Austria, ii. 439 ; joins army in Austria, ii. 447 ; strength of his army, ii. 448 ; his success in Austria, ii. 449 ; at Vienna, ii. 451 ; his battles at Essling and Aspern, ii. 454, 455 ; his victories at Enzersdorf and Wagram, ii. 459, 460 ; complains of Joseph's inactivity, ii. 456 ; agrees to suspension of arms, ii. 460; is excommunicated, ii. 461 ; makes peace with Austria, ii. 464, 479 ; his anxiety about Spain, ii. 467—469 ; foments an insurrection in Galicia, ii. 471 ; institutes a new order, Three Golden Fleeces, ii. 476 *n*; his note on title of Augustus, ii. 477, 478 ; annexes Papal States, ii. 430, 431 ; iii. 24, 25, 83; his peaceful assurances to the Czar, ii. 482, 483 : his questions to the bishops, iii. 13; his policy in Sweden, iii. 10, 11, 86, 87; cedes Hanover to Jerome, iii. 12 ; disputes with Russia about Poland, iii. 16, 17; his treaty with Holland, iii. 27; threatens Heligoland,' iii. 32 ; goes to Antwerp, iii. 34; quarrels with King of Holland, iii. 36—38, 40, 46 ; orders Oudinot to march upon Amsterdam, iii. 45, 46 ; annexes Holland, iii. 9, 47, 48; deprives Fouché of his portfolio, iii. 42, 43, 47 ; endeavours to cultivate cotton in Rome, iii. 51, 52 ; orders foreign archives to be sent to Paris, iii. 55 ; he occupies himself with the affairs of the Church, iii. 78 —82 ; his suspicions of Russia, iii. 73 ; annexes the Valais, iii. 72, 74 ; prepares for war with Russia, iii. 78, 85, 88, 101 ; appropriates Oldenburg, iii. 85; his overtures to Austria, ii. 87, 88; his son's birth, iii. 93, 94; threatens Mecklenburg and Prussia, iii. 95 ; objects to Russian establishment in Servia, iii. 95, 96, 98; reinforces his army from foreign states, iii. 97 ; his excuses for war with Russia, iii. 99 ; his overtures to the Pope, iii. 101 ; his message to General Belliard, iii. 107 ; complaints of smuggling in Germany, iii. 101 ; his speech at the opening of Parliament, iii. 108, 109 ; complains of Murat, iii. 111 ; his reply to a deputation of merchants, iii. 113, 114 ; his sale of licences for trade, iii. 112, 113 ; receives a deputation from the Ionian Isles, iii. 117 ; list of his clothes, iii. 117, 118 ; threatens war with Prussia, iii. 122, 127 ; visits Holland, iii. 123, 124 ; sets a spy on the Pope, iii. 125 ; threatens war with Sweden, iii. 126 ; rewards English prisoners, iii. 128 ; his dissatisfaction with the generals in Spain, iii. 131 ; organises secret police in case of war, iii. 131 ; his bickerings with Russia, iii. 134, 135 ; his reproaches to Prince Kourakine, iii. 135 ; Russia, Sweden, and Turkey unite against him, iii. 136 ; goes to Dresden, meets German princes, iii. 136, 158 ; strength of his army, iii. 136, 137 ; his disasters in Russia, iii. 138 ; reverses of his army in Spain, iii. 139 ; his note upon the continental blockage and sugar manufacture, iii. 141, 142 ; explains the situation to Jerome, iii. 143—145 ; complains of Colonel Czernitchef, iii. 151; sends instructions to Marmont in Spain, iii. 147—149, 152; his note on commerce in Corsica, iii. 156 ; dictates letter to Lord Castlereagh, iii. 156, 157 ; transfers the Pope to Fontainebleau, iii. 158 ; declares war against Russia, iii. 160, 161 ; his speech to the Polish deputies, iii. 164 ; forbids the exportation of corn from France, iii. 165 ; endeavours to induce Turkey to join him, iii. 165, 166 ; takes Smolensko, iii. 168 ; sufferings of his troops in Russia, iii. 170, 174 ; his views on

Salamanca, iii. 171; defeats the Russians at Borodino, iii. 172; in Moscow, iii. 174, 211; enormous losses amongst his troops, iii. 176; raises new conscriptions in France and Italy, iii. 176; becomes aware of his dangerous position, iii. 177, 178; attempts to negotiate with Russia, iii. 179, 195; leaves Moscow, iii. 181; orders Marshal Mortier to burn public buildings in Moscow, iii. 181; obliged to change line of retreat, iii. 181; resolves to take up a position half-way between St. Petersburg and Wilna, iii. 183; his reference to the damage done to Moscow, iii. 183, 184; sufferings and losses of the army during the retreat from Moscow, iii. 184, 185, 189, 190—192; crosses the Beresina, iii. 186, 187, 190; anxious for news from Paris, iii. 188; leaves the army, iii. 189 n, 192; reaches Paris, iii. 197; receives news from Spain, iii. 191; his army destroyed by the Russians, iii. 197; prepares to continue the war, iii. 198; his reply to the Senate on the war, iii. 198, 199; his anxiety to make peace with the Pope, iii. 199; his losses in the army during the Russian campaign, iii. 200; in 1813 coalition formed against him, iii. 201; new plan of campaign against him, iii. 202, 203; list of the defeats of his lieutenants, iii. 203; his instructions to Joseph in Spain, iii. 205, 221, 222; examines a new musket, iii. 206; orders Dantzic to be armed and provisioned, iii. 207; his description of the Russian campaign to the King of Denmark, iii. 207; guarantees Norway to Denmark, iii. 208; breaks up camp of Boulogne, iii. 208; his preparations for war, iii. 209; relates his Russian campaign to Jerome, iii. 210—212; complains of General York, iii. 209, 213; his glowing account of the state of affairs, iii. 212; appoints Prince Eugène to the command of the Grand Army, iii. 214, 215; makes an arrangement with the Pope, iii. 215, 216—219; changes his ambassador at Vienna, iii. 216; hopes of an alliance with Austria, iii. 217; his speech at the opening of the legislative body, iii. 223—226; reduces his equipment for the campaign, iii. 226; forces the King of Holland and the Czar to seize American ships, iii. 225 n; instructs Prince Eugène to hold Berlin, iii. 227; offers a home to the King of Saxony, iii. 227; orders General Clarke to watch the defences of the coast, iii. 228; his instructions to Prince Eugène, iii. 228, 229; intends to mislead the enemy and to march on Dantzic, iii. 229; complains of Jerome, iii. 230; Russia and Prussia unite against him, iii. 232; orders money to be sent to Spain, iii. 233; dismisses the representatives of Prussia in France, iii. 233; his refusal to grant Prussia any pecuniary relief causes the war, iii. 234; his faith in Austria, iii. 234, 237; at Mayenne, iii. 235; orders the formation of an army of Italy, iii. 237; doubts Murat's fidelity, iii. 238; becomes suspicious of Austria, iii. 238; dissatisfied with the minister of foreign affairs, iii. 239; wins battle of Lutzen, iii. 240; at Dresden, iii. 242; threatens the King of Saxony, iii. 242; the Czar refuses to treat secretly with him, iii. 202, 246; fights battle of Bautzen, iii. 246; at death of Duroc, iii. 246, 247; grants an armistice, iii. 202, 24, 249; complains of Austria, iii. 248, 249; writes for comedians to be sent to Dresden, iii. 251; dissatisfied with the minister of police, who wishes for peace, iii. 251; hears of Murat's intrigues, iii. 252; his interview with Metternich, iii. 253—255; sends Soult back to Spain, iii. 256; battle of Vittoria induces him to Austrian proposals, iii. 256; praises the Bishop of Nantes, iii. 257; makes Fouché governor of Illyria, iii. 258; concludes a treaty with Denmark, iii. 258; orders his troops to march towards Berlin, iii. 259; Austria declares war against him, iii. 202, 260; his views on the Congress of Prague, iii. 262; his note on the fête of the Empress, iii. 264; his instructions to Vandamme, iii. 265; wins battle of Dresden, iii. 202, 266; his views on the situation of affairs, iii. 267; forces opposed to him, iii. 267, 268; tries to escape the responsibility of Vandamme's defeat, iii. 270; reverses of his generals, iii. 203, 271, 272; dictates

INDEX. 445

the report to be published on the war, iii. 273; prepares for a battle, iii. 274; crosses Blucher and Bernadotte, iii. 275; nearly cuts off Sacken's corps, iii. 276; uncertain as to his movements, iii. 276; forced back upon Leipsic, iii. 277; anxious to carry the war into Prussian territory, iii. 277; issues orders to his generals to assemble at Leipsic, iii. 277; the Bavarian troops desert him, iii. 278; his precarious position, iii. 278; captures General Meerfelt, iii. 278; endeavours to make terms with the Emperor of Austria, iii. 279; his description of Leipsic, iii. 279; retreats to Erfurth, iii. 279; falls back to Gotha, iii. 280; takes 1,200,000*l.* from his private funds for the public service, iii. 280; is bent on raising a new conscription, iii. 280; orders the reconstruction of the fortifications of Geneva, iii. 282; returns to St. Cloud, iii. 282; orders the Swiss frontier to be armed, iii. 282; sends Fouché to Naples, iii. 283; doubts Murat's fidelity, iii. 283; the King of Bavaria endeavours to induce Prince Eugène to desert Napoleon, iii. 283; conditions of peace offered by the allies to him, iii. 284; temporises in order to gain time, iii. 285; orders all the troops of the Confederation to be disarmed, iii. 285; sends Admiral Allemand to Flushing, iii. 285; orders employment to be found for workpeople in Paris, iii. 286; his speech at the opening of Parliament, iii. 286; commands Eliza to refuse arms to the Neapolitans, iii. 287; enters into negotiations with the Prince of Asturias, iii. 287; concludes a treaty with the Prince, iii. 288; assures the Senate of his efforts to secure peace, and his disinterested love for France, iii. 288; his losses in the campaign, iii. 289; takes the field against the allies in France, iii. 291; his brilliant genius displayed, iii. 291; deserted by Marmont, iii. 291; orders a *levée en masse* in the departments, iii. 293; doubts the good faith of the allies, iii. 293; is willing to accept the terms offered at Frankfort, but not the later ideas of the allies, iii. 293, 294; his instructions to Caulaincourt, iii. 294; his treatment of Joseph on his return from Spain, iii. 295; orders to his generals, iii. 295, 296; his estimate of the forces opposed to him, iii. 296; the real relative strength of the opposing forces, iii. 297; makes overtures to Austria, iii. 297—299; complains of his generals, iii. 299; Murat deserts him, iii. 291, 299; appoints Marie-Louise regent and Joseph his lieut.-general, iii. 300; defeats Blucher at Brienne, iii. 292, 301; disapproves Barras's return to France, iii. 302; realises the horrors of war, iii. 302; his account of the battle of La Rothière, iii. 303; sends orders to Joseph to have all valuable furniture, &c., removed to Fontainebleau, iii. 305; charges Joseph with the safety of his wife and child, iii. 306—308, 339; his doubts of Eugène's fidelity, iii. 308; wins battle of Champaubert, iii. 291, 310; wins battle of Montmirail, iii. 291, 311, 312; his fears for Fontainebleau, iii. 313; his indignation against Murat and his wife, iii. 313; wins battle of Vauchamps, iii. 314; the allies, to gain time, offer to agree to terms of peace, iii. 315, 316; his reasons for being willing to treat before Champaubert, iii. 316; his indignation at the terms offered, iii. 317; orders the vice-reine of Italy to go to Paris iii. 318; his indignation at the excesses committed by the troops, iii. 320, 321; complains to Augereau of delay in taking the field, iii. 321; his letter to the Emperor of Austria on the political situation, and on the terms of peace offered, iii. 322—324; is aware of the state of public opinion in France, iii. 325; accepts an armistice from Austria, iii. 325; negotiations opened at Lusigny, his instructions to General Flahault, iii. 326; at Troyes, iii. 326; his anxiety for Soult to take the offensive, iii. 327, 329; his satisfaction with the navy, iii. 329; complains of the inactivity of his generals, iii. 330; evacuation of Bar-sur-Aube, iii. 331; wins the battle of Craonne, iii. 333—335; allows the Pope to return to Italy, iii. 334; Joseph intreats him to make peace, iii. 333 *n*, 334 *n*; reconnoitres the enemy's position at Laon, iii. 335; returns to Soissons, iii. 335; deprecates Joseph's idea that he will derive personal benefit from his alliance with an Austrian princess, iii. 336; the desperate position of the French, iii. 337; orders the fortification of Paris, iii. 337; retakes Rheims from the Russians, iii. 337, 338; sends Joseph instructions for Soult and Suchet, iii. 339; takes Méry, iii. 340; sends note to the *Moniteur*, iii. 341; finds himself confronted by the grand army of the allies, iii. 341; marches on St. Dizier, iii. 342; returns to Fontainebleau, finds that Paris has capitulated, iii. 343; tries to reopen negotiations, iii. 343; his speech to the Old Guard, iii. 344; assembles his generals, iii. 344; abdicates, iii. 344, 347; his proclamation to the army, iii. 345; complains of the Senate, iii. 346; endeavoured to poison himself, iii. 348, 350 *n*; his farewell to the Guard, iii. 348, 349; goes to Elba, iii. 347, 349; arranges the household at Elba, iii. 350, 351; his arrangements for some balls, iii. 352, 360; expects the empress, iii. 352; joined by his mother, iii. 353; his letters to the empress, iii. 354, 355; complains of Pauline, iii. 355; his anxiety for news of his wife and child, iii. 355; carries on negotiations for returning to France, iii. 356; his economies at Elba, iii. 360; leaves Elba, iii. 357, 361; his welcome in France, iii. 358, 364; his appeals to the people and army, iii. 361, 362; chooses his ministers, iii. 365; the European powers unite against him, iii. 357, 361; organises his army, iii. 358, 366, 375; writes to his old generals, iii. 366; orders a list of the treaties concluded during his reign, iii. 367; orders articles for the *Moniteur*, iii. 367; finds the finances of the country in good condition, iii. 369; his efforts to regain the society of his wife and child, iii. 359, 369, 377, 378; orders General Caulaincourt to assure the foreign powers of his good intentions towards them, iii. 370; his circular to the sovereigns, iii. 370; is accepted by the provinces, iii. 372; orders the payment of pensions to his family and others, iii. 372; maks inquiries respecting King of Naples, iii. 373;

finds employment for naval officers ashore, iii. 375; re-elected by the people, iii. 378; his speech to the electors, iii. 378; takes the oath to the people, iii. 380; his relations return to Paris, iii. 380; his speech to parliament, iii. 382, 383; goes to Laon, iii. 384; Ney rejoins him, iii. 384; orders Polish infantry to be sent to him, iii. 384; position of his army on the 14th June, iii. 385; writes a series of instructions for his war minister, iii. 386; addresses his soldiers, iii. 387; forces the passage of the Sambre, iii. 388; sends arrangements for the campaign to Marshal Ney, iii. 389; the battle of Ligny, iii. 390; orders Grouchy to march upon Sombreffe, iii. 391; his miscalculations, iii. 391; order of the day for the 18th June, iii. 391; his account of Ligny and Waterloo, iii. 392—400; passes the Sambre at Charleroi, iii. 400; his error respecting the movements of the Prussian army, iii. 403; at Laon, iii. 406; returns to Paris, iii. 406, 407; his message to the Chamber of Representatives, iii. 407; forms committee to treat with the allies of Waterloo, iii. 407; his declaration to the French people, iii. 411; proposes to abdicate and proclaims his son Napoleon II., iii. 411; asks for works on America, iii. 412; his farewell address to the army, iii. 413; deserted by his old companions, iii. 414; places himself under English protection, iii. 414; instructions to the captains of the two frigates provided for his safety, iii. 415; on board the *Bellerophon*, iii. 415; his protestation against England, iii. 416; his observations on the campaign of 1815, published at St. Helena, iii. 417—419, 425; his will, iii. 426—429; his death, iii. 429, 430; Talleyrand's opinion of him, iii. 430; his immense correspondence, iii. 431

C.

Cacault, citizen, Napoleon's letters to, i. 116, 117, 133
Cadiz blockaded by Saumarez, i. 340
Cairo, Napoleon at, i. 216—246;

quells revolt at, i. 233; orders of the day dated at, i. 217, 221, 230, 237, 239
Cairo, divan of, Napoleon's letter to, i. 258
Calais, Napoleon at, ii. 19
Calendar, Republican, ceases, ii. 192
Calder, Sir Robert, naval conflict with Villeneuve, ii. 107, 108.
Cambacérès, Prince, Napoleon's letters and notes to, i. 404; ii. 19, 24, 36, 37, 89, 98, 129, 132, 133, 165, 167, 200, 205, 273, 285, 290, 291, 302, 307, 309, 315, 316, 413, 420, 451, 464, 465, 467; iii. 115, 123, 126, 132, 192, 235, 239, 243, 247, 250, 251, 260, 261, 263, 275, 280, 281, 305; elected consul, i. 272; arch-chancellor, iii. 263
Campo Formio, treaty of, i. 125, 191, 194, 197
Canope, battle of, i. 354, 391
Canova, Napoleon's letter to, i. 176
Cantillon, sub-officer, receives a legacy from Napoleon, iii. 428, 429
Cape of Good Hope, Napoleon's projected expeditions to, i. 337; restored by the English to the Dutch, i. 182, 332; in English possession, i. 203, 204
Capefigue, historian, quotations from, iii. 401, 406, 411, 412, 414
Caprara, Cardinal, Napoleon's allocution to, i. 389
Caraman, Captain, Napoleon's instructions to, iii. 272
Carnot, Director, Napoleon's letters to, i. 70, 77, 82, 107, 116, 133, 145, 313, 319, 324; ii. 375; in difficulties, ii. 458; made war minister, i. 287; made one of committee to treat with allies after Waterloo, iii. 407
Castiglione, Napoleon's success at, i. 105
Castlereagh, Lord, letter dictated by Napoleon to, iii. 156
Catechism introduced into France by Napoleon, ii. 246
Caulaincourt, General, Napoleon's letters and notes to, ii. 398; iii. 235, 242, 249, 282, 293, 302, 317, 328, 339, 343, 365, 367; in Russia, ii. 367, 368; recalled from Russia, iii. 85, 98; his conduct in Spain, ii. 402; sent back to Russia, iii. 202; his titles, iii. 343; wishes to refuse the Foreign Office, iii. 365; his anger at the murder of the Duc d'Enghein, ii. 50; Napoleon's speech to, after Waterloo, iii. 406
Celerier, M., ii. 242
Ceracchi-Arena conspiracy, i. 325, 326, 331, 332
Chaboulon, M. Fleury de, quotations from *Memoirs* of, iii. 390, 406
Champagny, M. de, Duc de Cadouc, foreign minister, Napoleon's letters and notes to, ii. 120, 229, 284, 320, 332, 335, 360, 366—368, 394, 398, 407, 433, 444, 451, 453, 464, 468, 469, 471, 475; iii. 12, 15, 16, 20, 21, 23, 27, 29, 30, 33, 35, 38, 39, 44, 45, 50, 52, 57, 62, 66, 67, 69, 72, 74, 85, 86, 92, 95, 96, 98, 132
Chamberlain, Grand, Napoleon's note to, iii. 86; ordered to give a present to the Pope's servants, iii. 215
Champcentz, Madame, ordered to leave France, i. 386
Champaubert, battle of, iii. 291, 310
Champ de Mai, iii. 378
Chappe, citizen, inventor of telegraphy, death of, i. 325
Chaptal, citizen, Napoleon's letters and notes to, i. 330, 355, 363, 369
Charlemagne, Napoleon orders a statue to be erected of, ii. 10, 11, 31
Charras, M., quotations from, iii. 423 *n*
Charucca, Spanish admiral; *see* Trafalgar
Chateaubriand, M. de, on Napoleon's death, iii. 429
Chatillon, congress of, iii. 292, 328
Chaumon, treaty of, iii. 328, 357
Chayle, Rear-Admiral du, calumniated by Napoleon, i. 227; his real courage, i. 228
Christophe; *see* Toussaint Louverture
Cintra, Convention of, ii. 414, 415, 417, 422
Circular to the sovereigns by Napoleon on his return from Elba, iii. 370
Cisalpine Republic, Napoleon's conduct towards, i. 384; Napoleon becomes president of, i. 384
Clarke, General, war minister, Napoleon's notes and letters to, i. 63, 129, 174, 175; ii. 15, 263, 313, 336, 406, 409, 414, 445, 454, 456, 458, 460, 466—469, 471, 472, 477, 479, 480; iii. 11, 23, 28, 32, 41, 44, 49, 53, 55, 56, 62, 63, 68, 84, 92, 111, 118, 121, 126, 128, 143, 171, 205, 208, 221, 222, 231, 237, 248, 260, 282, 285, 301, 304, 309, 324, 327, 329, 332, 333, 340, 342; letter from Joseph

448 INDEX.

Buonaparte to, iii. 257; commissioned to conclude peace with Austria, i. 123; recalled, i. 185; praised by Napoleon, i. 185, 193; enters French Embassy in London, i. 193; becomes Duc de Feltre, i. 193; French ambassador in Florence, ii. 15; war minister at Berlin, ii. 298; leaves Paris with the Bourbons, iii. 365

Clary, Désirée, Crown Princess of Sweden, Princess of Ponte Corvo, i. 46, 52, 59; her marriage with Bernadotte, i. 52; ordered to leave Paris, iii. 126

Clermont, Bishop of, threatened by Napoleon, i. 403

Coalitions formed against Napoleon, i. 197; ii. 105, 199; iii. 201

Colbert, Brigadier, Napoleon's letter to, ii. 6; his mission to Russia, ii. 6

Colli, General; *see* Hermann

Cologne, Napoleon at, ii. 93

Commercial chambers created in France, i. 383

Committee for publishing correspondence, i. 1; letter of, to Napoleon, iii. 1; incorrect assertion of, i. 2

Committee of Arts, Napoleon's letter to, i. 161

Concordat, i. 360, 364, 393, 394; ii. 4, 57, 75; with the Jews, ii. 233, 234

Confederation of the Rhine arranged, ii. 110; armies required from the sovereigns forming the, iii. 97

Confederation of the Rhine, Prince Primate of, Napoleon's letter to, ii. 256, 257

Consalvi, Cardinal, quotations from *Memoirs* of, i. 394; opposes Napoleon's second marriage, iii. 6, 9

Conservatory, inspectors of the, Napoleon's letter to, ii. 171

Consuls of the Republic, Napoleon's letters and notes to, i. 301, 303, 304, 309, 385; decrees by, i. 276, 282; Napoleon elected First Consul, i. 272

Constitution of the Republican Year III. destroyed, i. 271

Contat, Mademoiselle, ii. 229

Contributions levied in Holland and Germany, ii. 221

Copenhagen, bombardment of, ii. 330

Corbineau, General, Napoleon's letter to, iii. 347

Corfu, General Gentili sent to, i. 162, 164; occupation of, i. 176; value Napoleon placed upon, i. 178; taken by Russians and Turks, i. 242;

Napoleon's change of opinion respecting its value, ii. 84

Cornwallis, Lord, in France, i. 372, 386

Coronation of Napoleon as King of Italy, ii. 105, 109, 133; as Emperor of France, ii. 132

Correspondence of Napoleon, immense, iii. 431

Corsica, notice of, i. 2, 3; Napoleon's history of, i. 10; disturbances in, i. 19, 24; in English hands, i. 42; generals sent to expel the English, i. 142; public works in, iii. 339

Corvisart, Baron, Napoleon's letter to, iii. 350

Council of State, Napoleon's address in, i. 390; proposes to invest him with the purple, ii. 71 *n*

Coucy, M. de, ex-Bishop of Rochelle, arrested, ii. 42

Craonne, battle of, iii. 333—335, 337

Cretet, M., minister of the interior, Napoleon's letter to, ii. 348, 425; in Corsica, ii. 339

Cuidad Rodrigo taken by Massena, iii. 53; by Wellington, iii. 139, 147

D.

Dalberg, arch-chancellor, ii. 230 *n*

Dalesme, M., commandant of Elba, Napoleon's letter to, iii. 349

Damas, Madame de, ordered to leave France, i. 386

Dantzic, capitulation of, ii. 313; declared a free town, ii. 318; claimed by Napoleon, iii. 70; invested by the Russians, iii. 222

Daru, Count, Napoleon's letters to, ii. 139; iii. 150, 151; Napoleon's instructions to, iii. 274

Daure, Commissionaire, Napoleon's letters to, iii. 309, 310

Davoust, General, Napoleon's letters to, ii. 30, 187, 336, 377, 465; iii. 58, 62, 81, 94, 100, 116, 121, 128, 129, 146, 163, 258, 259, 262, 366, 374—377, 381; against the Prussians, ii. 262; pillage by his men, iii. 163; at Dresden, iii. 234; war minister, iii. 365; his desertion of Napoleon, iii. 414

Decree by Napoleon to the soldiers, 1815, iii. 366

Decree of Milan, ii. 347—349

Decrès, Admiral, Napoleon's letters

INDEX.   449

and notes to, i. 392, 395: ii. 3, 24, 25, 34, 91, 94, 143, 146, 170, 225, 300, 329, 348, 363, 377, 378, 392, 397, 398, 439; iii. 49, 84, 91, 108, 116, 117, 119, 129, 146, 159, 215, 221, 255, 259, 329, 372; Villeneuve's letter to, ii. 171; minister of marine places two frigates at Napoleon's disposal after Waterloo, iii. 359

Dejean, General, Napoleon's letters to, ii. 301, 302, 418

Delmas, General, Napoleon's letter to, i. 154; exiled, i. 394

Demerara; *see* Tobago

Denmark, King of, Napoleon's letters to, ii. 462; iii. 207, 252; Napoleon's policy towards, ii. 326; declares war against England, ii. 330

Dennewitz, battle of, iii. 203, 271

Deputations to Napoleon from Finisterre, his answer to, iii. 91; from the Ionian Islands, iii. 117; from the Jews, ii. 233; from the merchants, iii. 113

Desaix, General, Napoleon's letters to, i. 248, 259, 300; at Marengo, i. 310, 311; signs treaty of El Arish, i. 337; death of, i. 310; Napoleon's disposal of his body, i. 312; Napoleon orders a monument to his memory, i. 322; Napoleon pensions his mother, i. 318

Despinoy, General, Napoleon's letter to, i. 89

Dessolles, General, in Hanover, ii. 65, 66 *n*

Director of Customs, Napoleon's letter to, iii. 54

Directory, Napoleon's letters to, i. 65, 67, 69, 72—74, 76, 81, 88, 91, 97, 110—116, 119, 122, 128, 130, 132, 135—141, 147, 149—152, 154, 158, 160, 162, 163, 165, 167—169, 171—177, 181, 183, 185, 191—193, 210, 215, 219, 226, 231, 233, 236, 246, 250, 253, 255, 257, 269; letter from —to Napoleon, i. 184; refuses to ratify the treaty with Sardinia, i. 147; wishes to recommence war with Austria, i. 184; decree by, relative to the invasion of Egypt, i. 203, 204; power passes from, to three Consuls, i. 272; overthrown, i. 284; President of, Napoleon's letter to, i. 204

Dissertation sur l'Autorité royale, by Napoleon, i. 17

Dolgorouki, Prince, Napoleon's interview with, ii. 183, 184

Don, General, exchange of, for Napper Tandy, i. 295

VOL. III.

Drake, Captain, British chargé d'affaires, ii. 35; Napoleon's designs against, ii. 36; intercepted correspondence of, ii. 60, 61

Dresden, battle of, iii. 266, 268; bridge of, blown up by Davoust, iii. 234

Droust, Comte, Napoleon's notes to, iii. 260, 351; sent to Elba, iii. 349

Dugommier, General, Napoleon's kindly remembrance of, i. 325

Duguesclin, pension given to descendants of, ii. 226, 227

Dumanoir, Admiral, at Trafalgar, ii. 175, 474

Dumas, General, ii. 203, 212

Dumberion, General, successfully commands army of Italy, i. 37

Dumesnil, M., commandant at Vincennes, iii. 83, 84

Dumolard, citizen, brings motion before Assembly against Napoleon, i. 167

Dundas, M., MS. quotation from speech by, i. 297

Duncan, Admiral, defeats the Dutch, i. 195

Dupin, M., minister, Napoleon's letters to, i. 33, 35

Duphot, General, killed in Rome, i. 197, 198; marriage arranged, i. 199

Dupont, General, defeated in Spain, ii. 404; defence of, ii. 404—406; capitulation of, iii. 108

Duroc, General, Duc de Frioul, Napoleon's letters and notes to, i. 353; ii. 146—148, 161, 298, 333; iii. 117, 228; sent to Russia, i. 367; death of, iii. 246, 247, 250

Duruy, M., historian, note by, ii. 36 *n*; quotation from, on decree of Berlin, ii. 272

Djezzar, nominated Pasha of Acre, i. 231; Napoleon's letter to, i. 249

E.

Egypt, Napoleon in, i. 212—247, 258—264; reaches, i. 212; his success in, i. 215; money levied in, i. 217; his cruelty in, 217, 218; operations in, i. 247; Napoleon leaves for Syria, i. 242; returns to, i. 242, 257; General Kléber instructed to hold, i. 313; evacuation of, by the French, i. 262, 334, 372; restored to the Porte, i. 360

Egypt, Pasha of, Napoleon's letters to the, i. 213, 214

G G

El Arish, treaty of, i. 337; Napoleon's note on, i. 298; British Government refuse to ratify, i. 301

Elba, occupied by the French, i. 117, 355; ceded by Naples, i. 180; Napoleon endeavours to obtain possession of, i. 348; Napoleon's treatment of, in 1802, i. 397; government organised by Napoleon, i. 403; requisitions from, ii. 133; Napoleon's life at, iii. 349, 350—356; his escape from, iii. 357, 361

Empire, French, founded, ii. 75—78

d'Enghien, Duc, arrest and assassination of, ii. 47—50, 66, 68, 70

England, King of, Napoleon's letters to, i. 278, 378; ii. 357

England, Prince Regent of, Napoleon's letter to, iii. 414

England, unsuccessful negotiations of, i. 182; without allies, i. 182; coalition formed by, i. 197; concludes peace with Russia and France, i. 333; strong feeling against in France, ii. 12; blockades the mouths of the Elbe and Weser, ii. 21, 23; Napoleon prepares to invade, ii. 32, 33, 148; Napoleon's suspicions of English arrested in France, ii. 16; ill-treatment of English vessels, ii. 14; navy in 1808, ii. 364; ministers in 1806, ii. 211; in Spain, ii. 426, 427; Napoleon's note for English ambassador, ii. 11

Enzersdorf, battle of, ii. 459, 460

Erfurth, treaty of, ii. 413, 415; iii. 134; Napoleon retreats to, iii. 279

d'Erlon, Comte, iii. 390, 392, 396

Escoiquiz, Juan, ii. 351, 352; his conversation with Napoleon, ii. 354—356

Essling, battle of, ii. 429, 454, 455

États des services furnished by Napoleon, i. 35, 36

Etruria, Count of Leghorn, becomes King of, i. 356; received in Paris, i. 356; Napoleon commands the Pope to recognise the, i. 358; Napoleon's note to, on the evacuation of Tuscany, i. 371; died, ii. 2

Etruria, Queen of, forced into war with England, ii. 81; robbed for Eliza Buonaparte, ii. 228; Napoleon's interference with Etruria, ii. 333, 334; ill-treated by Napoleon, iii. 120

Eylau, battle of, ii. 279, 290, 291, 293, 294, 295, 297, 298

F.

Faenza, town of, taken by the French, i. 136

Fain, Baron, quotation from, iii. 303, 304

Farewell, Napoleon's, to the guard before Elba, iii. 348, 349

Faypoult, citizen, Napoleon's letters to, i. 65, 76

Ferrara, Napoleon at, i. 115

Fersen, Baron de, Swedish ambassador, i. 194

Fesch, Cardinal, Napoleon's letters to, i. 7, 16, 21, 24; ii. 58, 70, 71, 94, 138, 202, 208, 214, 217, 230; storekeeper to the army of the Alps, i. 31; nominated to the embassy at Rome, ii. 10; promoted to be coadjutor of the elector arch-chancellor, ii. 236; his position with regard to Napoleon's marriage, iii. 7, 8

Flahault, General, represents France at Lusigny, iii. 326

Flanders, Napoleon enters, iii. 359

Finance minister, Napoleon's letters to, i. 87, 178

Finkenstein, Napoleon's letters from, ii. 304—313

Fontainebleau, treaty of, with Spain, ii. 338; the Pope at, iii. 158; Napoleon abdicates at, iii. 344, 347

Foreign affairs, minister of, Napoleon's letters to, i. 178, 180, 194; ii. 40, 210, 448, 451; iii. 12, 21, 45, 131, 165, 174, 186, 377; installed at Wilna, iii. 165

Forfait, M., Napoleon's letters to, i. 347, 359

Forli, Napoleon at, i. 136

Fort Carré, Napoleon committed to, i. 40

Fouché, M., Duc d'Otrante, minister of police, Napoleon's letters and notes to, i. 306, 356, 374, 385, 386; ii. 92, 96—100, 127, 129, 131, 133, 134, 162, 189, 204, 211, 243, 266, 286, 295, 296, 299, 301, 303, 307, 309, 312, 313, 315, 320, 322, 340, 367, 374, 386, 437, 440, 456, 459, 462, 463, 465, 472, 474; iii. 11, 34, 42, 44, 243, 283, 313, 364; appointed Governor of Rome, iii. 43, 47; deprived of his portfolio, iii. 42, 43; in disgrace, iii. 11, 243; ordered to Dresden, iii. 243; appointed governor of the Illyrian provinces, iii. 258; sent to Naples, iii. 283;

INDEX.   451

narrow escape of, iii. 364 n, 365 n; appointed one of committee to treat with allies after Waterloo, iii. 407; his desertion of Napoleon, iii. 414
Fouré, citizen, i. 238
Fox, Mr., on peace of Amiens, i. 383; procures the release of his countrymen in France, ii. 241; refuses to agree to Napoleon's plans, 1806, ii. 198; death of, ii. 198, 256
Foy, Marshal, in Spain, iii. 257
France, position of, in 1800, i. 284; invaded by the allies, 1813, iii. 290
Frankfort occupied by the French, ii. 205, 206; treaty of peace offered to Napoleon by the allies, iii. 293, 294
Friedland, battle of, ii. 279, 315; Napoleon's plans after, ii. 281
Frotté, Count Louis, pursued by General Brune, i. 292; assassinated, i. 292; Napoleon's duplicity towards him, i. 292, 294
Fulton, steamship inventor, i. 329, 347; ii. 38
Functionaries, public, Napoleon's letter to the, i. 324

G.

Gabrielli, Cardinal, ii. 400, 401
Gallo, Marquis de, meets Napoleon at Leoben, i. 151; visits Napoleon at Montebello, i. 159; ambassador in Paris, ii. 68, 69
Gardane, General, his mission to Persia, ii. 310, 311
Gaudin, M., minister of finance, Napoleon's letters and notes to, ii. 274, 328, 369; iii. 47, 121
Ganteaume, Admiral, Napoleon's letters to, i. 218, 329, 346; ii. 39, 91; Napoleon's instructions to, i. 344; sails from Brest for Egypt, i. 329, 339, 340
Gaza, Napoleon's letter from, i. 248; battle of, i. 250
Genoa offends France, i. 39; heavily fined, i. 65, 75; capitulates to Austria, i. 308, 309; annexed by France, ii. 105, 109, 110; Napoleon's letter to Archbishop of, i. 180
Gentili, General, sent to Corfu, i. 162; at Corfu, i. 164
Georges, Cadoudal, in La Vendée, i. 290, 292—294; his arrest ordered, i. 306, 351; sends emissaries to France, i. 352; his relations arrested, ii. 17; arrest, death of, ii. 51, 55, 62—64, 66
Germain, Count, Napoleon's letter to, iii. 236
Germany, Emperor of, Napoleon's letters to, i. 112, 311; Napoleon in, 1805, ii. 151—205
Gilot, Napoleon's orders respecting, i. 335
Gneisenau, General, on battle of Ligny, iii. 394 n; report on Waterloo, iii. 422 n, 423 n
Gobain, Grenadier, Napoleon's note on suicide of, i. 392
Godoi, Manuel, Prince of the Peace, i. 372; Napoleon refuses his portrait to, i. 349; pretensions of, i. 359; Napoleon threatens, ii. 28, 29; Napoleon's note to, ii. 209; concludes treaty of Bale, ii. 299, 350; unpopular in Spain, ii. 350, 351, 375; imprisoned, ii. 376, 384
Goritz, Napoleon at, i. 144, 145
Gorodina, Napoleon at, iii. 190 n
Gourdand, General, quotation from, iii. 423 n, 424 n
Grassini, Mademoiselle, ordered to sing before Napoleon, i. 313; promoted by him, i. 313; ii. 339
Gravina, Admiral, ordered to assist Admiral Brieux, i. 294, 393; at Trafalgar, 176, 178
Grenier d'Abondance, iii. 165 n
Grey, Lord, on Napoleon, i. 279
Gross-Beeren, battle of, iii. 203, 271
Grouchy, General, i. 295, 296; made chief of the staff at Waterloo, iii. 398, 402—405; Soult to Grouchy, iii. 404
Grouchy, Marquis de, defence of Marshal Grouchy, iii. 402
Guibert, citizen, Napoleon's letter to, i. 234

H.

Haller, citizen, Napoleon's letters to, i. 161, 166, 188
Hamburg, Napoleon's letter to Senate of, i. 282
Hamuda Pasha, Bey of Tunis, Napoleon's letters to, i. 379, 380; Nelson's letter to, i. 380

Hanau, battle of, iii. 281
Hanover invaded by Napoleon, ii. 18; offered to Prussia, ii. 144, 195; offered to England at the same time, ii. 197; ceded to England, ii. 249
Hardenberg signs treaty of Kalisch, iii. 232
Hatzfeld, Prince of, Napoleon's clemency to, ii. 269, 270; iii. 35
Haugwitz, M. de, ii. 180, 182, 187, 195
Hauterive, citizen, Napoleon's letters to, i. 380; ii. 480
Hawkesbury, Lord, his defence of British actions, 1803, ii. 36; his views in 1804, ii. 79; note to, i. 361; Napoleon refutes his insinuations, i. 356
Hédouville, General, Napoleon's letters to, i. 287; commander-in-chief of the army of England, i. 287; superseded in La Vendée, i. 289
Heliopolis, battle of, i. 286
Helvetian Republic threatened by Napoleon, i. 384, 403
Hermann, General, exchanged for Gene-Colli, i. 295, 296
Hesse Cassel taken possession of by Napoleon, ii. 264
Hill, Lord, iii. 140
d'Hilliers, General Baraguey, takes possession of Venice, i. 160
Hoche, General, acquiring fame, i. 30; sent to La Vendée, i. 51; imprisoned, i. 64; applied to by the Republican Government to prevent a Bourbon restoration, i. 172, 173; death of, i. 190
Hohenlinden, battle of, i. 287, 336
Hohenzollern, Prince, intercepted letter from, i. 306
Holland, Lord, *Reminiscences* by, quotations from, ii. 421 *n*; iii. 328, 329 *n*, 426
Holland forced into war, ii. 245, 246; annexed by France, iii. 47, 48; king of; *see* Buonaparte, Louis
Hompesch, General, Napoleon's interest in, i. 369
Hood, Admiral, capitulation with, i. 101
Hortense, Queen of Holland, Napoleon's letters to, iii. 15, 33, 48, 166; her reluctance to go to Holland, ii. 237; loses her son, ii. 261, 311; her delight at leaving Holland, iii. 49
Hullin, General, ii. 50
Hulote, General, report on the passage of the Sambre, iii. 388 *n*

I

India, Napoleon's desire to go to, i. 54, 58; Napoleon's designs upon, i. 362; ii. 68, 115, 394, 395
Imola, General Victor marches on, i. 135
Interior, minister of the, Napoleon's letters to, i. 165, 201, 326; ii. 218, 419; iii. 17
Ireland, Napoleon's designs upon, ii. 25, 26; orders an expedition to, ii. 96
Isabey, artist, iii. 378
Italian Republic placed under French protection, i. 396
Italy, Napoleon in, i. 37, 67—143, 158—193, 306—315; ii. 126—136; closed for English commerce, ii. 218; contributions levied in, ii. 218
Ivrée taken by Napoleon, i. 304

J.

Jacobins punished for Ceracchi-Arena conspiracy, i. 332
Jaffa, Napoleon's orders from, i. 248; proclamation from, i. 249; siege of, i. 250
James, historian, quotations from, iii. 146, 147, 159, 330
Jantzon, François, notice of, i. 149
Jarvis, battle of, i. 144
Java becomes a French colony, iii. 59
Jena, battle of, ii. 198, 261, 262
Jervis, Admiral Sir John, Nelson's letter to, i. 90, 117 *n*
Jesuits, Napoleon's grudge against the, ii. 116
Jews, convocation of the, in France, ii. 233, 234
Jomini, military historian, ii. 337; note by, on Marengo, i. 311; joins the allies, iii. 263; on Blucher's vigilance, iii. 385 *n*; Grouchy at Waterloo, iii. 405
Josephine, Empress, marriage to Beauharnais, i. 4; marriage to Napoleon, i. 63, ii. 231; iii. 5, 6; joins him in Italy, i. 79; Napoleon's letters and notes to, i. 79, 80; ii. 82, 88, 98, 154, 160, 261, 269, 271, 272, 276—278, 283—287, 291—293, 297, 303, 304, 308, 310, 311, 315, 317, 321, 323, 383, 415, 426, 427, 450, 455, 459, 476, 479, 480; iii. 15, 33, 42, 50, 59, 94; at Milan, i. 79; narrowly escapes capture in

INDEX.

Italy, i. 107; accompanies Napoleon to Toulon, goes to Aix, i. 206; immorality, i. 238; intercession for Duc d'Enghien, ii. 50, 51; in Strasburg, ii. 153; her jealousy, ii. 278, 283; accompanies Napoleon to Austria, ii. 447; is divorced from Napoleon, ii. 340—342; uses her influence for the Austrian marriage, iii. 5; her pension, iii. 342
Josephine, manuscript of, sent to Paris, i. 165, 166
Joubert, General, Napoleon's letters to, i. 165, 175
Jouberthon, Madame, ii. 348, 349
Jourdan, Marshal, Napoleon's letters to, i. 275, 307; ii. 401, 468; defeated by the Archduke Charles at Feldkirch, i. 241, 259; praised by Napoleon, ii. 234; proposed title for, ii. 399
Junot, Marshal, Duc d'Abrantes, ii. 414; Napoleon's notes and letters to, i. 40; ii. 229, 337, 343, 344, 370, 391; life in 1795, i. 48; takes Italian trophies to Paris, i. 73; conveys Napoleon's letter to Venice, i. 148; defeated at Vimeiro, 357; his rapacity in Portugal, ii. 415; Napoleon's instructions to him in Madrid, ii. 118, 119; concludes convention of Cintra, ii. 414, 415, 417
Jung, Colonel, quotation from his history, ii. 54
Justice, minister of, Napoleon's note to, ii. 41

K.

Kalisch, treaty of, iii. 232, 234
Kalitcheff, M. de, Russian ambassador in France, i. 340
Keith, Lord, at Genoa, i. 309; his treatment of Massena, i. 312
Kellerman, General, Napoleon's letters to, i. 133; iii. 55, 266; sent to Italy, i. 51; at Marengo, i. 311
Kilmaine, General, receives command of Lombardy, i. 127; receives Napoleon's instructions, i. 148
Kléber, General, Napoleon's letters to, i. 216, 220, 227, 262, 263; his division mutinies in the desert, i. 248; appointed chief of the Army in the East, i. 263, 264, 274, 277; authorised to make terms with Turkey, i. 262; receives orders from Napoleon to hold Egypt, i. 313, 316; wins battle of Heliopolis, i. 286; his death, i. 286; Napoleon orders a monument to be erected to his memory, i. 322
Kœnigsberg, Napoleon at, ii. 322
Kolli, M., iii. 84, 85
Kourakine, Prince, Russian ambassador in France, iii. 151
Kray, General, driven back upon Ulm, i. 316
Krasnoi, fighting at, iii. 185
Kremlin, the, occupied by the French, iii. 176, 180
Krusemark, M. de, Prussian ambassador, iii. 233
Kutusoff, General, Napoleon's letter to, iii. 179; appointed to command the Russian army, iii. 172; signs treaty of Kalisch, iii. 232

L.

Lacepede, General, Napoleon's letters to, ii. 211, 228, 313, 314, 339, 475, 476
Lacrosse driven from Guadaloupe, i. 383
Lacuée, General, Napoleon's letters to, i. 326; ii. 87, 417; iii. 143, 153
Lady of Loretto, Our, i. 140, 395
Laforest, M., Napoleon's letters to, iii. 70, 71
Laharpe, M., ordered to leave Paris, i. 385
Laine, report by, on the wars of Napoleon, iii. 289
Lake, Lord, ii. 129, 130
Lamiston, Count, ambassador in Russia, iii. 98, 99
Lance, Chevalier de, Napoleon's letter to, i. 19, 20
Lanfrey, quotations from *Memoirs* by, i. 251 *n*; ii. 20, 45, 52, 55, 61, 158; on Captain Wright's murder, ii. 164; on Villeneuve's death, ii. 172; 246, 294, 405, 429, 434, 455, 470 *n*; iii. 135
Lannes, General, at Vienna, ii. 451; death of, 455
Laon in the hands of the allies, iii. 335, 336; Napoleon at, iii. 359, 384
Lapi, General, Napoleon's letter to, iii. 361
Laplace, citizen, Napoleon's letters to, i. 272, 407; iii. 167
Lardner, historian, quotation from, iii. 137
La Rochefoucauld, M., ii. 25

La Rochefoucauld, Madame, Napoleon's letters to, ii. 410
La Rothière, battle of, iii. 291, 303
Latour, Foissac, disgraced for surrendering Mantua, i. 319, 320
Laugier, Captain, gives Napoleon an excuse for fresh hostilities against Venice, i. 155
Lauriston, Comte, Napoleon's instructions to, iii. 110; note to, iii. 226
Lavalette and Napoleon, iii. 428
Lebrun, General, ii. 205; Napoleon's letters to, ii. 206, 289; iii. 47, 59, 63; elected consul i. 272; Governor of Antwerp, iii. 285
Leclerc, General, Napoleon's letters and note to, i. 387, 397, 398, 407; at St. Domingo, i. 375, 376; death of, i. 407
Lefebvre, Marshal, Duke of Dantsic, Napoleon's letters to, ii. 300, 463; appointed to command the Old Guard, iii. 156
Le Gallois, Abbé, iii. 106, 107
Leghorn held by the French, i. 377; in a state of siege, ii. 63
Leichenstein, Prince, ii. 479
Leipsic, battle of, iii. 278, 279
Lemarois, General, ii. 231
Leoben, Napoleon at, i. 149, 150
Léon, private soldier, Napoleon's letter to, i. 289, 290
Lesegno, Napoleon at, i. 71
Letort, General, death of, iii. 388, 389
Le Tourneur, citizen, Napoleon's letter to, i. 63
Licences for trade, Napoleon's sale of, iii. 112, 113
Ligny, battle of, iii. 359, 390, 392—394
Lille, negotiations of, broken off, i. 182
Linois, Admiral, defeated by the English, ii. 94
List of masters at Brienne, i. 5; comrades at Brienne, i. 6; officers in the army of Italy, i. 67; Napoleon's generals in Italy, i. 69; treasures seized in Italy, i. 163; successes in 1797, i. 195; armies in 1799, i. 242; statues for the Tuileries, i. 290; Napoleon's clothes, 1811, iii. 117, 118
Locker, William, Nelson's letter to, i. 102
Lodi, battle of, i. 81; Napoleon's letters from, i. 82
Louis XVI., flight of, i. 23

Louis XVIII. returns to Paris, iii. 415
Lombardy, Napoleon's proclamation to the people of, i. 85, 88; contributions levied in, i. 85; general administration of, Napoleon's letter to, i. 149
Lonato, Napoleon at, i. 104—106
Londonderry, Lord, quotations from *Memoirs* of, on Peninsular War, ii. 344, 405 n, 406 n; iii. 140, 203, 204, 257; on Waterloo, iii. 420 n
Louisiana ceded to the United States, ii. 10, 60 n
Lucchesini, M. de, ii. 250
Luneville, treaty of, i. 333, 341
Lutzen, battle of, iii. 239—242
Luxembourg, Duc de, standards captured by, ii. 187
Lyndoch, Lord, Duke of Wellington's letter to, iii. 385 n
Lyons, Napoleon at, i. 315
Lyons, Archbishop of, Napoleon's letter to, i. 404

M.

Macaulay on Frederic the Great, iii. 290, 291
Macdonald, Marshal, Napoleon's letters to, iii. 295; Napoleon sends instructions to, iii. 163
Mack, General, captured, ii. 157; trial of, ii. 157, 158; exchanged, i. 295, 296
Madeleine, construction of the, ii. 275, 276, 420
Madrid, the French in, ii. 369—373; Napoleon enters, ii. 421; capitulation of, ii. 422
Maida, battle of, ii. 245
Maillard, Colonel, report on Napoleon, i. 26
Maitland, captain of the *Bellerophon*, Napoleon surrenders to, iii. 415, 416
Malmesbury, Lord, unsuccessful negotiations, i. 120, 182
Malta, Emperor of Russia negotiates for purchase of, i. 138, 192; knights of, expelled, i. 210, 213; French take possession of, i. 209; despatches for administration of the island, i. 210; sacrifices of the garrison, i. 317, 318; nomination of Grand Master, i. 261, 369, 400, 408;

INDEX. 455

Napoleon's note on, i. 388; evacuation of, by England refused, ii. 13; proposed exchange of Malta for Ireland, ii. 25, 26; Malta an excuse for war with England, 1804, ii. 59

Malta, Bishop of, Napoleon's letter to, i. 209

Manheim becomes French, i. 194.

Mansourah, Napoleon's letter from, i. 243

Mantua besieged by Napoleon, i. 102; taken, i. 125, 142; surrendered by the French, i. 319

Mamelukes, destruction of the, i. 214

Marbeuf, Comte de, friend of Charles Buonaparte, i. 3; Napoleon's letter to, i. 6; governor of Corsica, i. 3; gives Napoleon admission to Brienne, i. 4

Marengo, battle of, i. 286, 309, 310

Maret, General, Napoleon's letters and notes to, iii. 101, 102, 110, 112, 120, 127, 131, 147, 151, 154, 166—168, 170, 173, 176, 177, 180, 184, 186, 187, 188, 191, 194, 222, 223, 233, 239, 248, 263, 271, 272, 276, 371; made Duc de Bassano, iii. 239

Marie-Louise, Empress, Napoleon's letters to, iii. 26, 28, 250, 281, 347, 348; her marriage, iii. 9, 22, 25; appointed Regent, iii. 243, 247, 292, 300; celebration of her fête, iii. 264; her anxiety, iii. 305

Marine, minister of, Napoleon's letter and notes to, ii. 148, 474; iii. 39, 40, 56

Markoff, M. de, Russian ambassador, i. 385; Napoleon endeavours to procure his recall by the Czar, ii. 23, 24; offends Napoleon, ii. 86, 90

Marmont, General, Napoleon's letters and notes to, i. 219, 225, 232, 242, 250, 252; ii. 67, 73, 124; iii. 147, 148, 149, 338; at Mayence, i. 48; left at Alexandria, i. 240; replaces Massena in Spain, iii. 78, 153; at Salamanca, iii. 170; defeated by the allies in a nocturnal attack, iii. 335, 336; deserts Napoleon and joins the allies, iii. 291, 345, 362; is chosen as instructor by Duc de Reichstadt, iii. 427 *n*

Martinique, birthplace of Josephine, i. 362

Marseilles surrenders to Napoleon, 1815, iii. 372, 374

Marshal of the Palace, Grand, Napoleon's note to, iii. 226

Massena, Marshal, Napoleon's letters and notes to, i. 318, 321; ii. 449; iii. 374; Napoleon's note on, ii. 221 *n*; instructions to, in Spain, iii. 40, 41, 60, 61; in Napoleon's army, i. 67; success at Rivoli, i. 131; success in Switzerland, i. 242; embezzlements by, i. 281; ii. 203, 207; shut up in Genoa, i. 300; capitulates at Genoa to Melas, i. 286, 308, 309; treatment of by Lord Keith, i. 312; superseded by Brune in Italy, i. 321, 322; in charge of the army in Italy, ii. 14; present to, ii. 149, 150; with the army, 1806, ii. 202; his love of money, ii. 235; his character and talents, ii. 238; in Spain, iii. 11; takes Ciudad Rodrigo, iii. 53; repulsed at Busaco, iii. 61, 76; at Torres Vedras, iii. 68, 75; removed from command in Spain, iii. 78; Michaud's note on, iii. 105 *n*; Napoleon's note on, published at St. Helena, i. 308

Mattei, Cardinal, Napoleon's letters to, i. 110, 115, 132, 139

Maury, Cardinal, agent for Louis XVIII. at papal court, i. 347, 348

Mayence becomes French, i. 194

Meaux, Bishop of, Napoleon's answer to note from, i. 400

Meerfelt, General, at Leoben, i. 150; taken prisoner by the French, iii. 278, 279

Melas, General, opposed to Moreau, i. 285; at Marengo, i. 286; after Marengo, ii. 157; ignorant of Napoleon's movements in Italy, i. 306

Melito, Count Miot de, sent to Rome, i. 99; Napoleon's letter to, 160; his opinion on war with Austria, 1800, i. 324; sent to Corsica, i. 329; opinions on Corsica, i. 368; quotations from *Memoirs* by, ii. 13, 26, 72, 73, 112, 113, 207, 319, 406, 418, 419, 470; iii. 60 *n*, 113, 114, 206, 300 *n*, 358

Melpomène, frigate, iii. 381

Melzi, General, Duc de Lodi, iii. 287; Napoleon's letters to, i. 388; iii. 216, 251, 287

Menou, General, Napoleon's letters to, i. 218, 226, 327, 338, 379; Napoleon's criticism of, i. 267; governor of Piedmont and Venice, i. 267, 307 *n*; of Italian provinces, i. 379; Napoleon's allocution to, i. 391; Napoleon attacks his reputation at

456 INDEX.

St. Helena, i. 391; complains of ecclesiastics, ii. 239, 240
Méry retaken by Napoleon, iii. 340
Metternich, Prince, *Memoirs* of, quotation from, ii. 243, 244, 250, 281, 340, 356, 357, 412*n*, 413, 418, 429, 447; iii. 4, 6, 10, 297, 368 *n*; letter from, on Napoleon's divorce, ii. 340, 341; to Stadion, ii. 447; despatch from, ii. 352; a prisoner, ii. 429, 451; Napoleon's interview with, iii. 253—255; Napoleon's early opinion of, i. 207
Michaud, biographer, on Massena in Spain, iii. 105 *n*, 106 *n*
Milan, Napoleon at, i. 84, 110, 157, 171, 173—178, 286; ii. 128—134; allocution by Napoleon to clergy at, i. 307; Napoleon orders a *Te Deum* to be sung in the cathedral of, i. 307; crowned King of Italy at, ii. 105, 109, 132; decrees of, ii. 347
Millesimo, battle of, i. 70
Military Correspondence by Napoleon, i. 391
Mirabeau, notice of, ii. 312, 313
Modena, Duke of, deposed, i. 113; levies made on, i. 161
Modena, Napoleon's letter from, i. 114
Mohilef, battle of, iii. 166
Mollien, General, Napoleon's letters to, ii. 390; iii. 91, 120, 372
Moncey, Marshal, sent to coast of Brest, i. 51; Napoleon's order to, in Spain, ii. 358
Mondovi, battle of, i. 71
Monge, citizen, Napoleon's letter to, i. 202
Monnet, General, assumes command at Flushing, ii. 9; in Walcheren, ii. 466; trial of, ii. 473
Montalivet, Comte de, iii. 100; minister of the interior, iii. 102; Napoleon's letter to, iii. 51, 178, 286, 325
Montebello, Napoleon establishes himself at, i. 159
Montenotte, battle of, i. 69
Montesquieu, Count de, grand chamberlain, Napoleon's letter to, iii. 264; sent to Paris, iii. 188 *n*, 189 *n*
Montesquieou, Countess de, Napoleon's letters to, iii. 123, 158, 169, 179, 250
Montezemoto captured, i. 70
Montmirail, battle of, iii. 291, 310, 311

Moore, Sir John, hasty retreat of, ii. 428, 439 *n*
Moreau, General, Napoleon's letters to, i. 296, 300, 316, 335; Napoleon's jealousy of, i. 155; criticism of, by Napoleon, i. 336; Napoleon's instructions to, i. 277; his success in Austria, i. 285, 316; wins battle of Hohenlinden, i. 287; commander-in-chief of army in Germany, i. 296; receives handsome present from Napoleon, i. 326; arrested, ii. 63—65; transported, ii. 51, 53; joins the allies, ii. 86; in Berlin, iii. 263; joins the Russians, iii. 263; letter to his wife, iii. 266; his death, iii. 202, 263, 266; Napoleon's note on Moreau, published at St. Helena, i. 336
Moreau, J. B., commander at Soissons, tried and sentenced to death, iii. 332
Morla, General, Napoleon reproaches him with violation of treaty of Baylen, ii. 422 *n*
Morpeth, Lord, ii. 264, 267
Mortier, General, ii. 24; Napoleon's letters and notes to, ii. 21; iii. 295, 314; his conduct in Hanover, ii. 18, 19; instructed to burn Moscow, iii. 181; ordered to secure the safety of wounded soldiers, iii. 182.
Moscati, citizen, arrested, i. 201; Napoleon's letter on, i. 201
Moscow, Napoleon at, iii. 174, 181; burning of, iii. 175, 183; the French retreat from, iii. 181—191
Mourad Bey becomes friend of France, i. 268
Mulgrave, Lord, his answer to Napoleon, 1805, ii. 112
Munich, Napoleon at, ii. 200; captured by Bernadotte, ii. 156
Murat, General, Napoleon's letters and notes to, i. 363; ii. 64, 68, 131, 251, 369, 370, 373, 375, 377—379, 383, 387, 388, 391, 393—395, 397, 418, 445; iii. 197, 199, 269, 272, 274, 275, 367; accused of cowardice, i. 78; conducts Josephine to Italy, i. 79; lord high admiral, ii. 24 *n*; enters Brünn, ii. 179; receives Duchies of Berg and Cleves, ii. 197; Governor of Warsaw, ii. 275; sent to Naples, ii. 409; King of the two Sicilies, ii. 409, 418; his evil influence over Napoleon, ii. 53; King of Naples, ii. 425; Napoleon compliments him on his navy, iii 39; de-

feated at Winkowo, iii. 179; urges Napoleon to close the war in 1813, iii. 205; meditates treachery to Napoleon, iii. 252; Napoleon begins to doubt him, iii. 283, joins the allies, 205, 292, 299; takes arms against Austria and loses his throne, iii. 368 *n*; Napoleon inquires about him, iii. 373, 374

Muscat, Imaun of, Napoleon's letter to, i. 244

N.

Napier, quotations from *History of the Peninsular War* by, ii. 439 *n*, 440 *n*

Naples, Napoleon concludes an armistice with, i. 95; negotiations with, i. 180; the King of, menaced, i. 340; Napoleon's perfidy to, i. 354; forbidden to interfere with the Papal States, i. 395; occupied by the French, ii. 205; Joseph Buonaparte made King of, ii. 215, 219; Murat made King of, ii. 425

Naples, Joseph, King of; *see* Joseph Buonaparte

Naples, Murat, King of, Napoleon's letters to; *see* Murat

Naples, Queen of, Napoleon's letters to, ii. 22, 114, 118; her aid to Nelson rouses Napoleon's anger, ii. 199; his vengeance, ii. 192, 198, 199; her unpopularity in Naples, ii. 248, 251

Napoleon III., birth of, ii. 383

Napoleon, Louis, son of Louis, birth of, ii. 103; created Grand Duke of Berg, ii. 443

Narbonne, General Comte de, Napoleon's order to, iii. 193

Nassau and Frankfort regiments desert Napoleon, iii. 285 *n*

Naudin, commissary, Napoleon's letter to, i. 23

Naval Chronicle on Captain Wright, ii. 163

Nelson, Lord, letters to his wife, i. 43, 96, 212 *n*; to Captain Locker, i. 102; to George Baldwin, Esq., i. 245; to Earl Spencer, i. 220 *n*; ii. 96 *n*; to Hon. H. Wyndham, i. 251 *n*; to the Pope, i. 314; to Hon. H. Addington, ii. 8, 126; to Sir J. Acton, ii. 14; to Lady Hamilton, ii. 15; to Mr. Drummond, ii. 25; to Sir A. Ball, ii. 39 *n*; to French prisoners of war, ii. 65 *n*; note by, on the invasion of England, ii. 106; bombards Bastia, i. 42; misses Napoleon at Malta, i. 212

Neuchâtel, Prince of; *see* Berthier

Neutral League, dissolution of, i. 332; reconstituted, i. 332, 342

Ney, Marshal, Napoleon's letters to, iii. 243, 277, 389; notes to, iii. 259; accused of plundering in Spain, iii. 60; in Russia; iii. 162; repulsed by the Russians at Valtelina, iii. 169; at Krasnoi, iii. 185, 186, 211, 212; defeated at Dennewitz, iii. 203, 271; succeeds Oudinot in command of a corps at Wurzburg, iii. 233; successful at Dessau, iii. 276; in command of Army of the North, iii. 271; rejoins Napoleon, iii. 366, 384; at Ligny, iii. 390—392; at Quatre Bras, iii. 390, 394; in the Chamber of Peers after Waterloo, iii. 412

Nice, Napoleon in, i. 37, 39, 64

Nile, battle of the, i. 198, 218, 227, 228

Novi, battle of, i. 241

Normandy, Duke of, birth of, i. 13

Norway guaranteed to Denmark, iii. 208; to Sweden, iii. 208 *n*

Novosiltzoff, M. de, Russian ambassador in France, ii. 105

O.

O'Hara, General, defeated, i. 35

Oldenburg, Duke of, iii. 85, 86; duchy of, appropriated by Napoleon, iii. 85

Orange, Prince of, Napoleon's letter to, ii. 271; returns to Holland, iii. 285

Orchat, the French reach, iii. 185

Orient, Napoleon's letters on board the, i. 209

Orleans, Bishop of, ii 17; Napoleon's note to, ii. 42

Orleans, Duchess of, receives a pension from Napoleon, ii. 4; iii. 372, 373 *n*

Osterode, Napoleon at, ii. 295—304

Ostralenka, battle of, ii. 279, 295

Otto, citizen, French commissioner in London, ordered to exchange prisoners with England, i. 295; Napoleon's message to, i. 356; instructions to, i. 386; letters to, ii. 81

Ottoman Empire in danger, i. 306

Oudinot, General, ordered to march upon Amsterdam, iii. 45, 46; in

458　INDEX.

disgrace, iii. 270; defeated at Gross-Beeren, iii. 203, 270, 271; defeated at Bar-sur-Aube, iii. 331
Ouvrard, swindle by, ii. 212—214

P.

Pacca, Cardinal, ii. 461, 463, 465, 466
Palafox, General, ii. 444
Palm, trial and execution of, ii. 197, 249
Paoli, Corsican patriot, i. 3; Napoleon's letters to, i. 17; elected President of Corsican Assembly, i. 21; arrested by order of Convention, i. 29; buried in Westminster Abbey, i. 101
Pappacini, Bruni and Cinni, ii. 56
Papal States invaded, i. 135; retained by the Pope, but Ancona occupied by the French, i. 378; annexed to France, ii. 430, 482
Paradisi, citizen, arrested, Napoleon's note on, i. 201
Paris, Napoleon first goes to, i. 44; crowned Emperor in, ii. 55, 93; capitulates to the allies, iii. 291; the allies enter, iii. 343, 345 n
Paris, Archbishop of, Napoleon's letter to, ii. 186, 187
Parma, its destination, i. 349; in French possession, i. 404; death of Duke of, i. 406
Passariano, Napoleon at, i. 180, 190
Paterson, Miss; see Jerome's marriage
Paulz, inventor of a musket, iii. 206
Pavia, Napoleon at, i. 89; Alvinzi at, i. 118; university destroyed, i. 307
Peninsular War, ii. 338, 344, 345, 369—374—431
Perignon, General, exchanged for General Don, i. 295; afterwards Marshal, i 296
Perron, General, ii. 129, 130
Perregaux, citizen, Napoleon's letter to, ii. 40
Persia, Shah of, Napoleon's letters to, ii. 117, 123, 124, 286, 362
Pesaro, Napoleon at, i. 137
Peschiera, Beaulieu at, i. 93, 94; Austrians raised siege of, i. 106
Placentia, Napoleon at, i. 77
Pleiswitz, armistice of, iii. 202
Piedmont annexed to France, i. 377; ii. 5
Pichegru, General, General-in-Chief of army of the South, i. 30; prepares to cross the Rhine, i. 47; Napoleon's intentions respecting, i. 314; conspiracy by, ii. 47, 53; death of, ii. 51, 54, 55, 64
Pichon, citizen, Napoleon's speech to, on Jerome's marriage, ii. 74
Picot, false evidence against Duc d'Enghien, ii. 48; refuses evidence against Moreau, ii. 52
Pillau captured by the Russians, iii. 222
Pistoja, Napoleon at, i. 100
Pitt, Mr., death of, ii. 109
Po, Napoleon crosses the, i. 77
Polignac, Arnaud de, pardoned, ii. 80
Polish Confederation, Napoleon's reply to the deputies of, iii. 164
Pont de Briques, Napoleon at, ii. 82
Ponte Corvo, i. 395; ii. 235, 237; Princess of; see Clary, Desirée
Pope, Pius VI., Napoleon's letters to, i. 141, 174; concludes an armistice with France, i. 99, 100; signs treaty of Tolentino, i. 125; refuses to execute articles of armistice, i. 134; deserted by the Catholic powers, i. 140; attack of apoplexy, i. 167; restoration of body to Rome, i. 282, 283
Pope, Pius VII., Napoleon's letters to, i. 363, 370, 393, 400, 408; ii. 56, 61, 75, 93, 130, 201, 215—217; Napoleon's messages to, ii. 325, 326; iii. 17—20, 199; Nelson's letter to, i. 314 n, 315 n; receives two ships from Napoleon, i. 401, 402; crowns Napoleon, ii. 55, -93; ill-treated by Napoleon, ii. 132, 133; refuses to recognise the King of Naples, ii. 241; note on, ii. 453; excommunicates Napoleon, ii. 461; arrest of, ii. 462, 464—466; disposed to treat with Napoleon, iii. 74, 75; a prisoner at Savona, iii. 79; fisherman's ring demanded from, iii. 15; a spy placed with the, iii. 125; transferred to Fontainebleau, iii. 139, 158; Napoleon makes an arrangement with, iii. 215; his position in 1813, iii. 217—219; sent back to Italy, iii. 334, 334 n
Popes, notes by two, on democracy, i. 157
Porta, Dr., iii. 125
Portalis, citizen, Napoleon's letters and notes to, i. 402; ii. 44, 61, 150, 246
Potsdam, Napoleon at, ii. 265
Portugal, Queen of, offends Napoleon, i. 226, 227; war between Spain and Portugal, i. 358; left to England, i. 378; entered by the French, ii. 336,

345; paid for remaining neutral, ii. 336 n; Napoleon's designs upon, ii. 333, 338; the royal family go to Rio Janeiro, ii. 349; Napoleon requires a list of crown jewellery of, ii. 391
Portugal, Prince Regent of, Napoleon's letter to, ii. 16, 117
Poussielgue, citizen, Napoleon's letter to, i. 232
Pradt, Abbé de, ii. 194, 195, 472
Prague, congress of, iii. 256, 259, 262
Presburg, treaty of, ii. 111, 198, 227
President of Government of Amsterdam, Napoleon's letter to, iii. 48
Press, Napoleon's interference with the, ii. 45, 145, 204, 367, 374, 444
Proclamations, Napoleon's, to the army, i. 64, 74, 86, 134, 142, 170, 192, 208, 212, 213, 229, 248, 254, 273, 276, 280, 343; ii. 153, 156, 158, 159, 181, 257, 266, 316, 412, 413, 424, 448—450, 452; iii. 160, 172, 240, 345, 362, 363, 371; to the people of Lombardy, i. 85, 88; to the Milanese, i. 89; to the Venetian republic, i. 90; to the inhabitants of the Tyrol, i. 96; to the people of Goritz, i. 144; to the sailors of Admiral Brueys' squadron, i. 182; to the inhabitants of Cairo, i. 239; to sheiks, ulemas, and commandant of Jerusalem, i. 249; to the council of elders and national guard of Paris, i. 273; to the inhabitants of St. Domingo, i. 374, 375; to the Hungarians, ii. 452; to the French people on his return from Elba, iii. 361; on the eve of Waterloo, iii. 387
Promotions, Napoleon's rapid, i. 59
Protestants, persecution of, after the fall of the empire, i. 364
Protestation, Napoleon's, on board the *Bellerophon*, iii. 415, 416
Provence, Comte de, Napoleon's letter to, i. 323
Provera, General, to be expelled from Rome, i. 186; Napoleon's opinion of him, i. 187
Provisional Government, June, 1815, Napoleon's letter to, iii. 413
Prussia, Napoleon's letters to the King of, ii. 23, 91, 101, 187, 255, 259, 260, 292, 296, 411; Napoleon's letter to the Queen of, ii. 412; Napoleon's note to the Princess Ferdinand of, ii. 269; Napoleon's deference to the King of, i. 321; the King of, his alliance with the Czar, 1805,
ii. 179; the King of, his flight to Memel, ii. 285; Napoleon's rudeness to the Queen of, ii. 259, 265, 267; Napoleon meets the Queen of, at Tilsit, ii. 321; neutral in 1805, ii. 150; at war with France in 1806, ii. 259; position of, at beginning of 1806, ii. 195, 196; courage of, in 1807, ii. 280; her war indemnity to France, iii. 22, 38
Public worship, minister of, Napoleon's orders to, ii. 461; iii. 34, 35, 57, 101, 116
Pyramids, battle of the, i. 215; Napoleon's conversation in Grand, i. 221—225

Q.

Quatre-Bras, battle of, iii. 390, 394
Quell, Don José, Spanish author on Trafalgar, ii. 174—177

R.

Rapp, General, Napoleon's letter to, iii. 207
Rastadt, Napoleon at, i. 193, 194; congress of, i. 126
Ratisbonne, Archbishop of, Napoleon's letter to the, ii. 231
Raynal, Abbé, Napoleon's letter to, i. 10
Real, citizen, Napoleon's letter to, ii. 67, 68
Regent diamond, used for Napoleon's sabre, i. 369, 370
Regnier, General, Napoleon's letters and notes to, ii. 31, 32, 41, 60; defeated, ii. 199; with the army, 1806, ii. 203; defeated at Maida, ii. 245
Reinhard, citizen, Napoleon's note on, ii. 46
Rémusat, Comte de, Napoleon's letter to, iii. 22, 27, 28
Rémusat, Madame de, quotations from *Memoirs* of, i. 225, 226; ii. 48, 50, 53, 167, 168, 189, 195, 237, 246, 270, 272; iii. 5
Rennes, Bishop of, threatened by Napoleon, i. 402
Report by Napoleon on position of the armies of Piedmont in Spain, i. 38
Rissault, M., Napoleon's letter to, ii. 284
Revolution in France, 1791, i. 23

Rheims retaken by Napoleon, iii. 337, 338
Rhine, Confederation of the, formed by Napoleon, ii. 110
Richelieu, Duc de, enters the Russian service, ii. 9
Richpance, General, tranquillises Guadaloupe, i. 384
Rimini occupied and looted, i. 137
Rivoli, battle of, i. 125, 130
Robespierre, A. B. J., despatches by, i. 37 ; assists Napoleon, i. 31
Rohan, Comte de, iii. 23, 24
Rohan, Princess Charlotte de, ii. 47, 51
Romana, General, ii. 408, 440 n, 445 ; joins Wellington, iii. 63
Rome, King of, birth of the, iii. 93, 94 ; baptism of, iii. 100
Rome, Napoleon endeavours to cultivate cotton in, iii. 51, 52
Rouen, Napoleon at, i. 404
Roverbella, Napoleon's letters from, i. 79, 101, 130
Roverdo, battle of, i. 108
Rumbold, Sir George, arrested by Napoleon's orders, ii. 100
Rusca, General, Napoleon's letter to, i. 128
Russia, Emperor Paul of, Napoleon's letters to, i. 344 ; becomes Grand Master of Knights of Malta, i. 261, 369 ; joins France against England, i. 285 ; assassinated, i. 350 ; ii. 332, 334 n
Russia, Emperor Alexander of, Napoleon's letters to, i. 371, 385 ; ii. 23, 180, 323, 347, 364, 396, 399, 410, 416, 440, 460, 478, 483 ; iii. 38, 45, 58, 68, 88, 90, 99, 150, 157, 161, 174 ; coronation of, ii. 334 n ; refuses Napoleon's matrimonial overtures, ii. 342, 413 n ; concludes secret treaty of Tilsit, ii. 317, 318 ; his energy in France, iii. 341
Russia, Napoleon's conditions of peace with, i. 338, 339 ; Colbert's message to, ii. 6 ; doubts Napoleon's faith, ii. 27 ; orders mourning for the Duc d'Enghien, ii. 80 ; Napoleon takes measures against, ii. 91, 97, 98 ; enters into an alliance with England, ii. 131 ; at war with Napoleon, ii. 166 ; Napoleon's accusations against, ii. 169 ; cruelty of Russian soldiers, ii. 169, 186 ; armistice signed between, and France, ii. 316 ; declares war against Sweden, ii. 373, 374 ; conduct in 1809, ii. 430 ; French invade, iii. 165 ; the Russians devastate the country in front of the French, and retreat upon Moscow, iii. 170 ; the policy of, towards the French, iii. 173 n ; Napoleon in, iii. 165—192 ; Russian attitude in 1813, iii. 202 ; the Russians enter Berlin, iii. 227

S.

Sacken, General, in France, iii. 310 ; at Meaux, iii. 317
Salamanca taken by the Spaniards, i. 481 ; battle of, iii. 139, 171
Salicetti, citizen, Napoleon's letters to, i. 104 ; assists Napoleon, i. 31
Salo and Corona, i. 103
San Marino, Napoleon's imperious message to the Regent of, i. 137.
Saragossa, siege of, ii. 404 ; fall of, ii. 443, 444
Sardinia, French make an unsuccessful attack upon, i. 29 ; war with France, i. 62
Sardinia, King of, cedes Nice and Savoy to France, i. 62 ; sues for peace, i. 71, 73 ; signs armistice, i. 74 ; signs a treaty with France, i. 142
Sassy, Collier de, minister of commerce, Napoleon's letter to, iii. 164
Savary, General, minister of police, Napoleon's letters to, ii. 317, 330, 334, 337, 339, 342, 399, 400, ; iii. 64, 70, 123, 127, 239, 251, 260, 274, 312, 317, 320 ; at murder of Duc d'Enghien, ii. 43 ; went as messenger to the Czar, ii. 180 ; sent as ambassador to Russia, ii. 323 ; his reception in Russia, ii. 367
Saxe, Marshal, quotation from, on provisioning an army, iii. 140, 141
Saxony, King of, Napoleon's letters to the, ii. 288, 441, 449 ; iii. 34, 54, 65, 101, 214, 227, 234, 236, 243, 247 ; his loyalty to Napoleon, iii. 237 ; his people dissatisfied with his alliance with France, iii. 237 ; enters into a convention with Austria, iii. 239
Say, M. J. B., Napoleon's letter to, i. 202
Schœnbrunn, treaty of, ii. 198 ; Napoleon at, ii. 168
Schwartzenberg, Prince, iii. 169, 173, 188, 266 ; in France, iii. 297 ; defeats Macdonald, iii. 331

INDEX. 461

Sebastiani, General, i. 401, 402; ii. 238, 239, 282, 322, 360, 361; iii. 180, 182
Sediman, battle of, i. 232
Segur, M. de, grand master of the ceremonies under the empire, ii. 84; Napoleon's instructions to, ii. 332
Seid Mohamed el-Koraïm, accused of treason to Napoleon, i. 217
Senate, Napoleon's messages to the, i. 341; ii. 72, 73, 151, 289, 409; iii. 73; Napoleon's letter to the, i. 317
Serurier, General, i. 66; Napoleon's letter to, i. 71
Schèrer, General, report on Napoleon by, i. 44; goes to Italy, i. 51, 65; Napoleon succeeds him in Italy, i. 65; defeated by Kray, i. 241; superseded by Moreau, i. 241
Schill, ii. 301, 457
Sheridan on Napoleon, ii. 13
Siborne, historian, quotation from, iii. 385, 419
Sicily a cause of war in 1806, ii. 198
Sidney Smith, Sir, Napoleon's letter to, i. 251; aids in defence of St. Jean d'Acre, i. 6, 253; Napoleon's irritation against, i. 253, 256
Sieyes, i. 270, 284
Sismondi, historian, on Waterloo, iii. 408—410
Smolensko taken by the French, iii. 168
Soissons, capitulation of, iii. 291, 331, 332; evacuated by the allies, iii. 335
Souham, General, ii. 63
Soult, Marshal, Duc de Dalmatia, Napoleon's letters to, ii. 62, 64, 71, 79, 410, 476; iii. 256, 381; in Naples, i. 348; in command of the army in Spain, ii. 477; iii. 204, 206, 256; Napoleon complains of his inactivity, iii. 329; under Louis XVIII., iii. 376 n; his salaries, iii. 376; on Grouchy at Waterloo, iii. 404
Southey on the Peninsular War, ii. 345
Spain, Charles IV., King of, Napoleon's letters to, i. 328, 406; ii. 7, 28, 29, 80, 331, 336, 359, 369, 385, 441; signs treaty of Badajoz, i. 334; gives Napoleon six cordons of the Golden Fleece, ii. 138; disputes with his son, ii. 352—354; dethroned, ii. 354; his abdication, ii. 376, 381, 386; goes to Rome, iii. 123
Spain, Joseph, King of; *see* Joseph Buonaparte

Spain, Julie, Queen of, Napoleon's letter to, iii. 25
Spain, Louisa, Queen of, Napoleon's letters to, ii. 441; iii. 30; dresses sent to her by Napoleon, i. 306, 307
Spain enters into alliance with France, i. 320; threatened by Napoleon, ii. 62; summary of events in, 1795—1808, ii. 350; Napoleon's request for ships from, ii. 363; Spanish troops return to their country, ii. 408; Spanish troops defeated, ii. 418; crown jewels of, ii. 463; divided into military provinces, iii. 16 n
Speeches by Napoleon, iii. 108, 198, 199, 223, 282, 286, 288, 377, 382, 383
Staël, Madame de, ii. 32, 307
Statues sent to the Tuileries by Napoleon, i. 290
St. Aignan, M. de, prisoner of the Prussians, iii. 284
St. André, Jean Bon, in Corsica, i. 42
St. Cloud, Napoleon's instructions for furnishing, i. 371
St. Cyr, Marshal, Napoleon's notes to, iii. 264, 270; ambassador at Madrid, i. 379
St. Domingo, Napoleon sends an expedition to, i. 373—377; to be governed by special laws, i. 281; end of civil war in, i. 328; French expedition to, i. 373; difficult position of the French in, ii. 3; archbishop of, Napoleon questions the nomination of, i. 400
Stein, Baron, ii. 411; appointed minister of state in Russia, iii. 213
St. Helena, Napoleon at, iii. 426; quotations from his *Memoirs* and observations written there, ii. 263, 265, 308, 336, 395; ii. 51, 99, 220, 356 n; iii. 368 n, 417—425
St. Jean d'Acre, Napoleon's letter from, i. 251; order at, i. 252; defended by Sir Sidney Smith, i. 6; attacked, i. 251; siege raised, i. 242, 254; horrors of the retreat from, i. 255
St. Jean de Luz in English hands, iii. 283 n
St. Julien, Comte de, sent as ambassador to Paris, i. 311
St. Priest, General, ii. 299, 300; iii. 337, 338
Strasburg, Napoleon at, ii. 152, 153
St. Simon, Sire, ii. 437, 438
Stuart, Sir J., victory at Maida, ii. 199
St. Vincent, Lord, defeats the Spanish

462 INDEX.

fleet, i. 195, 196; at the Tagus, ii. 200
St. Vitry refuses to surrender to Napoleon, iii. 342
Suchet, General, iii. 339, 386; Napoleon's letter to, i. 319
Suchet, Madame, iii. 130 n
Sucy, commissary, Napoleon's letter to, i. 50
Suez Canal, Napoleon proposes to cut the, i. 204, 344, 345
Sugar industry, ii. 368; iii. 141
Sussy, Comte de, iii. 283
Suwarrow, General, his terms on the surrender of Mantua, i. 320; death of, i. 242
Sweden, King of, Napoleon's letters to, iii. 59; declares war against Napoleon, ii. 323; deposed, ii. 447
Sweden, Prince of, Bernadotte elected, iii. 10; his overtures to Napoleon, iii. 86; his wife ordered to leave Paris, iii. 126
Syria, Napoleon's campaign in, i. 248—257

T

Tagliamento, Napoleon's victory at, i. 143
Talavera, battle of, ii. 468—470
Talbot, Captain, iii. 152
Talleyrand, M. de, Napoleon's letters to, i. 179, 185, 186, 190, 268, 288, 294, 295, 298, 305, 320, 330, 338, 339, 342, 345, 347, 349, 351, 353 n, 356—359, 365, 367, 369, 372—375, 387, 388, 395, 397, 403, 405; ii. 10, 11, 18, 26—28, 30, 33, 35, 37, 38, 40, 42, 44, 46, 62, 78, 82, 83, 86, 88, 90, 99, 102, 103, 124, 134, 139, 141, 143, 145, 150, 165, 180, 181, 183, 191, 221, 222, 228, 232, 238, 240, 248—250, 263, 275, 290, 296, 297, 300, 317, 322, 324, 384, 385, 389, 391, 395, 397; iii. 57; Bishop of Autun, i. 51; his marriage, i. 395; succeeds Delacroix at the Foreign office, i. 174; secularised by the Pope, i. 395, 399; Napoleon's questions to him about Egypt, i. 315; endeavours to induce Napoleon to make peace with Austria, ii. 184; receives Beneventum, ii. 235; at Erfurth, ii. 413, 414; in disgrace, ii. 434; his opinion of Napoleon, i. 190; iii. 430; quotation from his *Memoirs*, ii. 312; Napoleon's opinion of him, iii 321
Talleyrand, Count Auguste de, Napoleon's letter to, iii. 132
Tallien, letter to his wife, i. 228; arrested for leaving Egypt without a passport, i. 335
Tarentum, evacuation of, ii. 12, 13
Tascher, citizen, Napoleon's letter to, ii. 56
Theatres, Napoleon's interference with the, ii. 266; iii. 22, 27
Thebes, fighting at, i. 256
Theodore, last King of Corsica, i. 101
Thielman, General, iii. 242, 243, 247
Thiers, M., quotations from history by, ii. 110, 390; iii. 5, 135
Thomé, Thomas, i. 274
Thorn invested by the Russians, iii. 222
Three Golden Fleeces, new order proposed by Napoleon, ii. 475, 476 n
Thurreau, General, in La Vendée, ii. 390
Tilly, citizen, Napoleon's letter to, i. 41
Tippoo Sahib, Napoleon's letter to, i. 244; overtures to France from, i. 244, 245
Tilsit, treaty of, ii. 279, 280, 318, 319, 347, 361; iii. 70, 87; Napoleon at, ii. 316—322; neutralisation of, ii. 317
Tobago taken by the English, ii. 3; restored to France, ii. 5
Tolentino, treaty of, i. 125, 142; Napoleon's letters from, i. 141
Tortona, Napoleon at, i. 76, 96
Toulon, siege of, i. 31, 32; Napoleon detained at, i. 208; blockaded, i. 260
Toulouse, Archbishop of, endeavours to remove Protestant disabilities, i. 364
Tourville, Admiral, ii. 173, 220
Toussaint Louverture, Napoleon's letters to, i. 375, 376; appointed captain general of French part of St. Domingo, i. 337; capture and ill-treatment of, i. 398, 399; fate of, ii. 3, 5
Trafalgar, battle of, ii. 108, 170, 171 n, 173—178, 474; Napoleon's reference to, in the Senate, ii. 219, 220; at St. Helena, ii. 220
Treasure levied by Napoleon in his wars, i. 75, 78, 84, 85, 87, 88, 95, 97, 99, 100, 118, 138, 140, 141, 153, 154, 158, 161, 163, 182; ii. 180
Treasurer of the Crown, Napoleon's orders to, iii. 342
Trebia, battle of, i 241
Trenta Coste, i. 21

INDEX. 463

Trinidad ceded to England, i. 334, 362, 378; Napoleon's views on cession by Spain of, i. 391
Tuileries, palace of, decorations for the, i. 290; Napoleon takes possession of the, i. 291
Tuleda, battle of, ii. 421
Turin, Archbishop of, ordered to Paris, i. 403
Turkey, Sultan of, Napoleon's letters to, ii. 116, 274, 281, 282, 305; Napoleon's wish to preserve his friendship, i. 371; incited to war with Russia, ii. 116; fate of, ii. 322
Turkey, Napoleon's note on, i. 55; Napoleon's letter to the Grand Vizier of, i. 261; declares war against France, i. 198; French negotiations with, i. 264; Empire of Turkey threatened, i. 327; position of, in 1806, ii. 239; Napoleon's promises to, ii. 361
Tuscany, Grand Duke of, Napoleon's letter to the, i. 176; iii. 355; dispossessed, i. 406 n; duchy of, attacked by Napoleon, i. 109; General Brune in, i. 326, 327; becomes kingdom of Etruria, i. 334; exchanged for Louisiana, i. 320, 368; claimed by Napoleon, ii. 343; given to Eliza Buonaparte, ii. 127
Tweedale, Marquis of, imprisonment and death of, ii. 89, 90
Tyrol, disturbance in the, ii. 463

U.

Ulm, capitulation of, ii. 157
Urquijo, i. 349; notice of, by Lord Holland, i. 349, 350

V.

Valais, Republic of, i. 396; annexed by Napoleon, iii. 72, 74
Vandamme, General, Napoleon's letter to, iii. 265; Napoleon's instructions to, iii. 265; attacks Prince of Wirtemberg, iii. 267, 268; defeated by the Austrians, iii. 269, 270
Vaubois, General, defeated, i. 119
Vauchamps, battle of, iii. 314
Vedel, General, in command at Willis, iii. 161; at Baylen, ii. 409
Venice, Doge of, Napoleon's letter to, i. 148; Napoleon's reassurance to municipality of, i. 164; Massena in, ii. 207; closed to English goods, ii. 218
Venetian Republic, Napoleon violates the neutrality of, i. 90, 91; Napoleon's letter to the Provéditeur-General of, i. 121; destroyed by Napoleon, i. 126; concludes treaty of peace with Napoleon, i. 158
Venus de Medicis, sent to France, i. 326
Verdier, General, Napoleon's letter to, i. 243
Ver Huell, Admiral, ii. 40, 41
Verona, Napoleon at, i. 92, 116—121; resists the French, i. 148; Napoleon's terms to, i. 156; occupied by the French, i. 92
Versailles used as a hospital for wounded soldiers, i. 275; note on the completion of, iii. 112
Vernégues, arrest of, ii. 58
Victor, Marshal, Napoleon's note to, iii. 274; instructions sent to, iii. 185
Victor Hugo on Waterloo, iii. 407, 408; his father, ii. 259
Vienna, congress of, iii. 357, 361
Villach, Napoleon's letter from, reassuring the Burgomaster of Lienz, i. 146
Villeneuve, Admiral, at Tarentum, i. 355; unsuccessful against the English, ii. 107, 108; Napoleon's views of his action, ii. 140, 141; in disgrace, ii. 147; removed from command of the squadron, ii. 149; at Trafalgar, ii. 170—173; his death, ii. 171, 178, 179; his conduct vindicated by his nephew the Marquis de Villeneuve, ii. 172, 177, 178; Napoleon's estimate of his character, ii. 144
Visconti, Madame, ii. 223, 224
Vittoria, battle of, iii. 204, 256, 257; Lord Londonderry on, iii. 257
Volney, report on civil condition of Corsica, 1791, i. 24
Voltaire, quotations from, ii. 113, 425

W.

Wagram, battle of, ii. 430
Walcheren, French defence of, ii. 9, 30; expedition, ii. 432, 466, 471, 474
Walewska, Count, ii. 283
War, Minister of, Napoleon's notes and letters to, i. 169, 200, 203, 352, 396;

ii. 469; iii. 84, 111, 342, 384; instructions to, before Waterloo, iii. 386
War waggons, i. 348
Warsaw, Napoleon at, ii. 281—290; entered by the Russians, iii. 222
Washington, Napoleon orders funeral honours to be paid to, i. 291
Waterloo, battle of, iii. 359; orders for the day, iii. 391, 392; Napoleon's account of, iii. 395—400; Jerome's account of, iii. 400, 401 : Marquis de Grouchy's account of, iii. 402, 403; quotations from other writers on, iii. 404, 405, 407; Victor Hugo on, iii. 407, 408; Sismondi on, iii. 408—410; *Drame de Waterloo*, iii. 417, 421 *n*; criticism on French inaction before, iii. 418
Weiss, quotation from, ii. 268
Wellesley; *see* Wellington
Wellington, Duke of, his letter to Lord Lyndoch, iii. 385 *n*; lands in Spain, ii. 431; at Talavera, ii. 470; repulses the French at Busaco, iii. 61; joined by Romana, iii. 63; at Torres Vedras, iii. 68, 75, 76; successes in Spain, iii. 139; at Waterloo, iii. 419—421

Westphalia, King of; *see* Jerome Buonaparte
Will, Napoleon's, iii. 426—429
William the Conqueror, statue erected to, ii. 230
Wilson, Sir R., ii. 299
Wirtemberg, Elector of, Napoleon's letter to, ii. 168, 184
Wirtemberg, King of, Napoleon's letter to, iii. 97, 98, 227, 238, 262, 268
Wirtemberg, Princess of, her marriage, ii. 193
Wrede, Marshal, defeated at Hanau by Napoleon, iii. 281
Wright, Captain, English officer captured by the French, ii. 88, 162—164
Wurmser, General, Napoleon's letter to, i. 114; saves Mantua, i. 103, 108; driven back, i. 105, 108; surrenders Mantua, i. 125

Y.

Yarmouth, Lord, ii. 197, 241
York, General, iii. 209, 210, 213

THE END.

LONDON : R. CLAY, SONS, AND TAYLOR, PRINTERS.

www.ingramcontent.com/pod-product-compliance
Lightning Source LLC
Chambersburg PA
CBHW022101300426
44117CB00007B/546